# Uncle John's BATHROOM READER

# HISTORY'S LISTS

## by the BATHROOM READERS' INSTITUTE

## The Bathroom Readers' Institute
Ashland, Oregon, and San Diego, California

# OUR REGULAR READERS RAVE!

"Comment heard from friends, 'How do you know so much stuff about any topic?' I learned it all from my Uncle John."
—Shane A.

"Before the BRI came along, I had a small library of just books. After the BRI, I now have a great library filled with incredible books."
—Green S.

"I just happened to see one of these sitting on the back of a friend's toilet one time eight years ago. Instead of reading the shampoo bottle, I picked this up. I have been hooked every since."
—Angela D.

"I love these books! I read them on my commute bus in the morning, and during my lunch hour. They are definitely not just for the bathroom."
—Alison G.

"Huge fan for years! I'm just now introducing my students to the kids' versions. They love them. I can't keep the books on the shelves."
—Margo F.

"Been a fan for many years. My friend and I test each other on UJBR trivia all the time."
—Lisa E.

"Hi from Germany. Can't go without BRI!"
—Norbert M.

"Brought *Uncle John's Unsinkable Bathroom Reader* to [a construction work site] and forgot it there. When I went back, they had put it in their boss' office because he loves them so much. He starts every meeting by reading out of one."

—Ce Ce R.

"I always blame my 4.0s on you guys!"

—Corbin C.

"My hubby was on a couple of game shows, and I know we can thank his love of the *Bathroom Reader* books for the winnings."

—Donna E.

"I love your books so much that in school, I'm doing a speech on the history of Uncle John's Bathroom Reader."

—Michelle M.

"I have them all, and cherish every one! My 20th anniversary edition sadly fell into the (clean) toilet. I managed to dry it out sufficiently enough to continue reading."

—Butch H.

"My friend in school was reading *Bathroom Readers*, so then I bought a couple, and now my mom says I'm just threatening her with my intelligence."

—Chase O.

"I've been a fan since the first edition 22 years ago! You might say this is why I'm flush with useless tirivia!"

—Joe C.

"Love the books so much, I keep track when I lend them out. Won't part with any of them! Thanks for the humorous and terrific reading."

—Susan B.

# UNCLE JOHN'S BATHROOM READER
# HISTORY'S LISTS

For information, write...
The Bathroom Readers' Institute
P.O. Box 1117, Ashland, OR 97520
www.bathroomreader.com
e-mail: mail@bathroomreader.com

ISBN 13: 978-1-60710-180-2

Library of Congress Cataloging-in-Publication Data

Uncle John's bathroom reader history's lists.
p. cm.
ISBN 978-1-60710-180-2 (pbk.)
1. American wit and humor. 2. History--Miscellanea. 3. Curiosi-
ties and wonders. I. Bathroom Readers' Institute (Ashland, Or.)
PN6165.U524 2010
081.02'07--dc22
2010013072

Printed in the United States of America

1 2 3 4 5    14 13 12 11 10

# THANK YOU!

*The Bathroom Readers' Institute thanks the following people whose hard work, advice, and assistance made this book possible.*

Gordon Javna
JoAnn Padgett
Melinda Allman
Dan Mansfield
Stephanie Spadaccini
Jay Newman
Amy Miller
Michael Brunsfeld
J. Carroll
Amy Ly
Jeff Altemus
Lilian Nordland
Ginger Winters
Jennifer Frederick
Angie Kern
Monica Maestas
Annie Lam
Sydney Stanley
David Cully
Cynthia Francisco
David Calder
Karen Malchow
Susan Volkman
Kim Schrader
Ken and Kelly Padgett

\*     \*     \*

"History is merely a list of surprises. It can only prepare us to be surprised yet again."

—**Kurt Vonnegut**

# CONTRIBUTORS

*We couldn't do it without you!*

Melinda Allman
Christine Ammer
Erin Barrett
Myles Callum
Erica Caridio
Jenness Crawford
Leslie Elman
Derek Fairbridge
Ian Fitzgerald
Kathryn Grogman
Chet Hearn
Vickey Kalambakal
Heidi Krumenauer
Carl Lavo
Dan Mansfield
Lea Markson
Scott McKibbin
Jack Mingo
Ryan Murphy
JoAnn Padgett
John Michael Scalzi, II
Terri Schlichenmeyer
Stephanie Spadaccini
Susan Steiner
Katie Terrazas
Diana Moes VandeHoef

\*     \*     \*

"Why can't somebody give us a list of things that everybody thinks and nobody says, and another list of things that everybody says and nobody thinks."

—Oliver Wendell Holmes

# CONTENTS

# INTRODUCTION

**YE OLDE BATHROOME RÆDERE**

Welcome friends, Romans, and other assorted country folk to our third book dedicated to the subject of history. At the Bathroom Readers' Institute, we've long been interested in how— and why—things got to be the way they are today. But as you no doubt remember from school, reading about history can be daunting…and mind-numbingly boring. So our goal in this book, as always, was to make learning about history accessible *and* fun. To that end, we decided to try something we've never done before: an entire book full of lists.

But to make for a truly entertaining read, a list has got to be more than just a series of facts and figures. Each and every item within a list has its own tale to tell. That's the mission we gave to the writers of *History's Lists*: bring the past to life, one entry at a time, by telling great stories. And that's exactly what you'll find in here—accounts of incredible achievements, heartbreaking disasters, bizarre rulers, and hilarious (a word we don't use lightly) blunders. And it wouldn't be a *Bathroom Reader* without a healthy supply of obscure details that we've unswept from under the rug.

So strap on your time-vortex goggles and fasten your seat belt, because you're about to take a ride through the centuries in Uncle John's patented wayback machine! Along your quest, you'll discover many of the ties that bring the past together, such as…

• The sporting world's biggest winners and losers of all time.

• All creatures great and small…that have orbited Earth.

• Bygone careers and the worst jobs in a medieval castle.

• Wall Street panics that might make you feel better about what's happening today.

• Mysterious mummies, lost Azetc gold, and fires that changed history.

• A stockpile of ancient weapons, including the trusty flamethrower. (Believe it or not, it's nearly 2,000 years old.)

- One-armed men who deserve a round of applause.

- The Great Decapitator: Henry VIII, and a list of the most notable heads he ordered removed from the bodies they once belonged to.

That is but a smidgen of what awaits you on the pages to follow. But before I go, I'd like to thank JoAnn and her dedicated staff of writers, editors, and researchers for sorting through mountains of dusty old texts and putting only the most entertaining, absorbing tidbits of days gone by in this book.

And finally, thank you, dedicated history-loving reader. No matter how many books we do, no matter how many facts we unearth, you always want more. That incredible thirst for knowledge should shore up our places on some future list of history's greatest curiosity seekers. Now, turn the page and let the past come alive.

*And as always, Go With the Flow!*

—**Uncle John and the BRI Staff**

# FRONT PAGE SHOES

*You probably think of shoes as fashion items or necessities for walking around, but they've also proven to be useful tools for getting into the news. Here are few examples.*

## 1. BEST FOOT FORWARD

In 1960, Soviet premier Nikita Khrushchev made an emphatic show of footwear during a meeting of the United Nations' General Assembly. Taking exception to the remarks of a delegate from the Philippines who charged that the USSR had "swallowed up" Eastern Europe, Khrushchev brandished his right shoe at his Filipino counterpart, then thumped it on the desk to express his discontent. Why this break with the traditional techniques of diplomacy? Why the shoe? According to the premier's granddaughter Nina—who took it upon herself to set the record straight 40 years later—Khrushchev first banged his fist on the desk, and did so until his watchband broke. He bent to the floor to retrieve the watch and saw his shoes, which he'd removed earlier because they were uncomfortable. In a show of Soviet ingenuity, he used one of the shoes as an effective gavel. This gesture became the signature move of his long career as a statesman.

## 2. A FOOTWEAR FETISH

Corruption reigned during Ferdinand Marcos's tenure as president of the Philippines from 1965 to 1986. In a country mired in poverty, Marcos's wealth was estimated at $35 billion. Marcos's wife, Imelda, a former beauty queen who was legendary for her ostentatious style and multimillion-dollar shopping sprees, became the symbol of a presidency defined by extravagance. But perhaps what she'll be most remembered for is what was found in her closet when the Marcoses were ousted in 1986 and forced into Hawaiian exile: Imelda had owned 1,060 pairs of shoes! One pair even featured battery-powered lights.

In 1991, the widowed Imelda returned to the Philippines. She showed no signs of remorse and even ran for president, placing fifth out of seven candidates. She remains active in politics and continues to claim that her husband's wealth was legitimately

---

**Elvis Presley bought his first guitar at Tupelo Hardware in Mississippi.**

earned during his days as a gold trader. As for her shoes, she says she's rebuilding her collection. She claimed, "Everywhere I go, the people give me shoes. I'll end up having more than what they stole from me. I am such an optimist. I believe I am in heaven."

## 3. HOT FOOT

Just over three months after the attacks of September 11, 2001, a London-born man named Richard C. Reid boarded a trans-Atlantic flight in Paris, bound for Miami. While the plane was in the air, a flight attendant, alarmed by the smell of lit matches, discovered Reid attempting to ignite the tongue of one of his shoes, which was rigged with explosives. Passengers and crew members were able to restrain him while two doctors onboard sedated him with Valium. The plane was rerouted to Boston, where authorities waited. A petty criminal who became a satellite member of the al-Qaeda terrorist network, Reid was sentenced to three consecutive life terms in a maximum-security federal prison. Authorities determined that his explosive shoes failed to detonate because the perspiration from his feet had ruined the mechanism.

## 4. KICKED OUT OF OFFICE

In December 2008, just over a month before the end of his presidency, George W. Bush held a press conference at the Iraqi prime minister's palace in Baghdad. It seemed like another run-of-the-mill media event until Muntadhar al-Zaidi, a young Iraqi journalist, took off both his shoes and flung them at Bush, yelling, "This is for the widows and orphans and all those killed in Iraq." Showing quick reflexes, Bush ducked and wasn't harmed. Al-Zaidi was subdued and carried off by Iraqi police and the U.S. Secret Service. Not only is throwing a shoe a gesture of contempt in Arab culture, the act was deemed illegal. Al-Zaidi was sentenced to three years in prison for assaulting a foreign leader, although he was released for good behavior after serving one year.

Soon after the press conference, a Turkish cobbler who claimed the shoes were one of his models (called the Ducati 271), saw this footwear-flinging as a business opportunity. He renamed the model the "Bush Shoe." Subsequently, in the Iraqi town of Tikrit, a monument was installed in honor of al-Zaidi's gesture: a couch-sized statue of a shoe, although it was quickly taken down by the police.

---

1894: World's largest silver nugget (1,840 pounds) is found near Aspen, Colorado.

# GUESS WHO'S GOING TO BE DINNER?

*Be careful about dinner invitations from people you don't know well—you might find yourself on the menu.*

## 1. BEANES AT EVERY MEAL

Some people believe that brawling, scrapping Alexander "Sawney" Beane was just a fictional legend, but many more contend that the Scottish character was a real guy. The story goes like this: Beane grew up in the town of East Lothian, in eastern Scotland, in the 15th century. Villagers considered him lazy and a liar, so they ran him (and his wife, who's described as having similar character traits) out of town. Taking shelter in a deep cave along the Scottish shore, the Beanes turned to a life of crime, attacking travelers or anyone who got close to their home.

But pretty soon, everybody had heard stories about Sawney and the missus, so as time went on, it got harder to hide the evidence of their crimes. Plus, times were tough, and famine was a common problem. That's when the Beanes started to eat their victims (or smoke their flesh to be preserved for later). Over the years, the couple prospered and had at least 14 children, who, in turn, grew up to have more children. Eventually, they were all caught by King James's men, but legend says that before that happened, the Beane family killed and ate about 1,000 people.

## 2. YOU GOTTA HAVE HEART

When Spanish conquistadors first marched across Mexico in the 16th century, they were surprised to find the Aztecs, but they were even more shocked by what the Aztec people were doing. For years, the Aztec nation had been sacrificing humans as part of its religious ceremonies. Much has been written about Aztec sacrifices: soldiers, slaves, and captors stoically went to grisly and bloody deaths in which their hearts were removed as offerings to the gods. What's not always mentioned is that other parts of the victims were passed out to high-ranking citizens to be eaten.

---

In England, Woolworth's 5¢ and 10¢ stores were called "Three-and-Sixpence" stores.

Historians estimate that in one year alone (1486–87), more than 20,000 people were sacrificed and consumed.

## 3. BUTTERFLIES IN YOUR STOMACH

While on a mission to collect butterflies for the Harvard Museum of Natural History in 1900, German butterfly collector Carl von Hagen was captured in Papua New Guinea. While the exquisite specimens are still on display in the museum, von Hagen didn't make it home. It seems he was captured and eaten by cannibals.

## 4. JOIN THE PARTY

In April 1846, a group of 31 pioneers left Springfield, Illinois. Their destination: Sutter's Fort in California, more than 2,500 miles away. As they traveled, the group grew to include 87 people, among them a pair of brothers—George and Jacob Donner—and their wives and children. They were led by George and a business-man named James Reed, who had read about a new way through the Sierra Nevadas that could save 300 or 400 miles. Despite the fact that Reed had been warned about how rugged and untamed the passage was, he and the group decided to head that way any-way. Bad decision.

In October, the group separated—the Donner family fell behind, and the Reeds continued on with most of the party. But then came the snow, which wasn't expected until mid-November. As blizzard after blizzard thwarted the groups, people were stranded in different places in the high mountains. The Reed group built shelters, but the Donners had nothing but a makeshift camp of blankets, firs, and wagon coverings. First, they used up their food rations and then started to eat their oxen. When that ran out, the freezing travelers began to starve. When some of them died, the survivors broached the idea of cannibalism. They dismissed it... at first.

Unable to stand the hunger, several members of the Donner group began to eat the people who'd perished. (The Reeds proba-bly also cannibalized their fallen brethren, though they always denied it.) But even that proved to be of little help as the weeks turned into months and they remained stuck in the snow.

Rescue finally arrived in February 1847, but the initial rescue party was just a few men who were able to carry little food. So even as they started leading people out of the mountains, those who remained continued to starve. Finally, in April, the last of the stranded travelers was rescued. Of the original 87 people, a surprising 46 of them survived.

## 5. PACKING IT IN

Alfred Packer could tell a tall tale better than anyone, so it's no surprise that he was able to convince 20 men that he knew the hills around Breckenridge, Colorado, well (he may or may not have). The group left for the Colorado Territory in early November 1873 on a search for gold.

By late January, the group was bedraggled, hungry, and stumbling through heavy snow when the chief of the Ute took pity on them and told the would-be miners that they could stay with his people until the snow melted. Five of the miners were determined to strike it rich, though, and waved some money at Packer, who set off with them to Breckenridge in early February, carrying a 10-day supply of food.

Two months later, Alfred Packer arrived at the Los Pinos Indian Reservation in Colorado and told a story of being abandoned by his companions. He said they had left him, one by one, and he had spent the waning winter alone, hungry, and frightened. But the men who had remained with the Ute were suspicious of Packer's obviously nourished physique and reported him to authorities. In May 1874, Packer admitted that he'd actually been with the five men until their end—after being stranded in the snowy wilderness, they'd all died one by one of disease, starvation, accidents, and in one case, self-defense. And as they did, he'd eaten pieces of the miners and had even carried some of their flesh around for weeks to stave off starvation. No one knew what to make of the story.

Then, in August 1874, the bodies of the five miners were found...laid out together at a campsite in the mountains. It appeared that they'd all been killed (one even showed defensive wounds as though he'd fought back). Packer was eventually convicted of murder and sent to prison.

## 6. A LITTLE MAC(QUARIE) AND CHEESE

Irish pickpocket Alexander Pearce should have just left well

...called *Chasing Rainbows* (1930). It opened two months after the stock market crash.

enough alone. After receiving 150 lashes for various infractions—including drunk and disorderly conduct, and theft—he went back to a life of crime and, in 1822, was sent to Macquarie Harbor, a harsh penal colony in Tasmania.

Within months, Pearce and a few of his fellow prisoners escaped. Tasmania was mostly uninhabited, though, so the men had nowhere to go—they hid in the mountains until starvation forced them to prey on one another. Pearce didn't commit the first murder, but he didn't refuse to partake of the grisly meal, either. And he had no aversion to killing the next victim for the table.

Later, after being caught for stealing sheep, Pearce was sent to Macquarie Harbor again. Soon, he escaped again with another fellow inmate…whom he subsequently killed and ate. Finally, in 1824, Pearce was hanged for his cumulative crimes.

## 7. NEED A TOOTHPICK?

In late October 1765, the sloop *Peggy* was in trouble. Rough weather and heavy seas had battered the little ship and its sails were badly ripped. Discouraged, hungry, and frightened, the crew seized the cargo (brandy and wine) and proceeded to get drunk. The situation got worse when the captain of another ship stopped to check on the *Peggy*'s crew, promised them a few crusts of bread, but then sailed away before actually giving them any food.

After the crew had eaten everything they could—including leather, candles, two birds, buttons, and a cat—they were desperate. They killed and consumed a slave, and then the men drew straws but were unable to sacrifice the friend who lost the draw, apparently because he was well liked. Fortunately, the morning after the aborted kill, the crew was saved by a passing ship but the man who'd narrowly missed being dinner had already gone mad from the torturous anticipation of becoming a meal. Bon appétit!

\*    \*    \*

### YUK, YUK

As the psychiatrist said to the cannibal at the end of a session, "Your problem is easy, you're just fed up with people."

---

**New York was the last state to add photographs to drivers' licenses, in 1984.**

# A FAMILY AFFAIR

*More than 350 sets of brothers have made it to the big leagues since the dawn of professional baseball in 1876. Some got by on pedigree alone, but others enjoyed long and prosperous careers. Here's a countdown of the top five sets of siblings in baseball history.*

### 5. PAUL AND LLOYD WANER

"Big Poison" (Paul) and "Little Poison" (Lloyd), as the Waner brothers were affectionately known, may not have crushed the hide off the ball, but they were pesky slap hitters with the kind of speed and base-running instincts that simply can't be taught. That's why these perennial all-stars and professional "hit" men (5,611 career hits combined, a record for brothers) are the only siblings in the Baseball Hall of Fame.

### 4. ROBERTO AND SANDY ALOMAR JR.

The sons of all-star infielder Sandy Alomar Sr., Roberto and Sandy Jr. redefined the game in the early 1990s with their consistent hitting and slick fielding. Although the Hall of Fame has yet to call their names, this genetically gifted pair can still hold their heads high knowing they combined for 18 All-Star Game appearances, 11 Gold Gloves, and two All-Star Game MVP awards during their prestigious careers.

### 3. PHIL AND JOE NIEKRO

It takes more than just a live arm to make it to the Major Leagues. In the case of Phil and Joe Niekro, it also took several gallons of spit. Masters of the spitball and knuckleball respectively, the Niekro brothers combined for an eye-popping 539 wins during their storied careers, the most of any sibling combo. They were also named to six All-Star Games before hanging up their gloves well into their 40s. Curiously, on May 29, 1976, Joe hit the only home run of his prolific 22-year career off of his brother Phil.

### 2. JESUS, MATTY, AND FELIPE ALOU

The Alous may not have been superstars, but it's impossible to flip through the annals of baseball history without seeing their names

---

**In 2003, the remains of a hobbit-sized human was discovered on an island in Indonesia.**

pop up repeatedly. Felipe was a three-time all-star and later the 1994 National League Manager of the Year. Matty was a two-time all-star and the 1966 NL batting champ. And Jesus was one of the finest outfielders of his day. In all, the Alou brothers combined for 5,094 hits in 5,129 games. They are also the only three brothers to have ever batted consecutively in a game, which they did one memorable afternoon on September 10, 1963, as members of the San Francisco Giants.

## 1. VINCE, DOM, AND JOE DiMAGGIO

Although "Joltin' Joe" may have made the DiMaggio name famous with his three MVP Awards and nine World Series titles, his brothers were also all-star talents who proved that skill ran in the family. Vince DiMaggio enjoyed two trips to the All-Star Game during a fruitful 10-year career, while Dom made the American League all-star squad seven times in 11 years with the Boston Red Sox. Overall, the DiMaggio boys were selected to 22 All-Star Games, more than any other set of siblings in Major League history.

## HONORABLE MENTION

Ed, Frank, Jim, Joe, and Tom Delahanty: The first family of baseball, Ma and Pa Delahanty sent five of their sons to the big leagues between 1888 and 1915. The most successful of the group was Ed, a hard-hitting outfielder who racked up a league-leading 19 home runs and 146 runs batted in for the Philadelphia Phillies in 1893. Ed played for 16 seasons, during which time he earned a reputation for being one of the game's finest batsmen. "When you pitch to [Ed] Delahanty, you just want to shut your eyes, say a prayer, and chuck the ball," pitcher Frederick "Crazy" Schmit once observed. "The Lord only knows what'll happen after that." In all, the Delahantys appeared in an estimated 3,599 combined games between 1888 and 1915.

\*　　\*　　\*

"If anyone wants to know why three kids in one family made it to the big leagues they just had to know how we helped each other and how much we practiced back then. We did it every minute we could. "

—Joe DiMaggio

Honeybees are only a small fraction of about 20,000 known species of bees.

# STAGECOACH RULES

*In the 1800s, stage travel was common. Up to nine passengers shared the coach. Second-class passengers rode on top with the luggage. To keep things friendly, Wells Fargo posted rules of etiquette in each of their coaches.*

**1.** Abstinence from liquor is requested, but if you must drink, share the bottle. To do otherwise makes you appear selfish and unneighborly.

**2.** If ladies are present, gentlemen are urged to forego smoking cigars and pipes as the odor of same is repugnant to the Gentle Sex. Chewing tobacco is permitted but spit WITH the wind, not against it.

**3.** Gentlemen must refrain from the use of rough language in the presence of ladies and children.

**4.** Buffalo robes are provided for your comfort during cold weather. Hogging robes will not be tolerated and the offender will be made to ride with the driver.

**5.** Don't snore loudly while sleeping or use your fellow passenger's shoulder for a pillow; he or she may not understand and friction may result.

**6.** Firearms may be kept on your person for use in emergencies. Do not fire them for pleasure or shoot at wild animals as the sound riles the horses.

**7.** In the event of runaway horses, remain calm. Leaping from the coach in panic will leave you injured, at the mercy of the elements, hostile Indians, and hungry coyotes.

**8.** Forbidden topics of discussion are stagecoach robberies and Indian uprisings.

**9.** Gents guilty of unchivalrous behavior toward lady passengers will be put off the stage. It's a long walk back. A word to the wise is sufficient.

---

A: Gwen Stefani. Q: Whose first job was mopping floors at a Dairy Queen?

# WHO'S DA BOSS?

*They arrived in the early 1900s among thousands of honest Italians immigrating to America and took the opportunity—in "the land of opportunity"—to build an empire that's still going strong.*

These five bosses—known to their underlings as *capos*—were instrumental in building their gangs into the national crime syndicate known as La Cosa Nostra, a.k.a. the Mob.

## 1. AL "SCARFACE" CAPONE

**The Rise:** Al Capone's parents emigrated from Naples to Brooklyn, where the gangster-to-be was born in 1899. Al was a B student until he quit school in sixth grade. He grew up in a rough neighborhood and joined two kid's gangs: the Brooklyn Rippers and the Forty Thieves. He had jobs as a candy store clerk, a cutter in a book bindery, and a pinboy in a bowling alley, but soon found he could make better money working for gangsters. He went to work for gangster Frankie Yale at his Brooklyn Inn, where he insulted a patron. Her companion attacked Capone with either a knife or razor, which is how Capone got the wounds that gave him the nickname "Scarface." By 1918, Capone had killed two men, and he fled to Chicago, where he started working for mobster Johnny Torrio.

**The Reign:** One of Capone's first jobs was to kill Torrio's boss. He was careful to arrange an alibi for the murder, a precaution he kept to during his career. He quickly became Torrio's second in command, and Torrio, as the new boss, assigned Capone to manage bootlegging, prostitution, and gambling operations in Chicago and its suburbs. In 1925, a rival tried to assassinate Torrio, who left Chicago for Italy, leaving the "business" to Capone.

Capone lived large and made headlines like a movie star. He controlled Chicago's politicians and police and was said to rule the city. He also launched ruthless wars on rival bootleggers, and on February 14, 1929, at a garage at 2122 North Clark Street, Capone's men and their machine guns mowed down seven rival gangsters in what came to be known as the St. Valentine's Day Massacre.

---

Smart cookies: During World War II, with shortages of sugar, butter, and flour...

**The Fall:** The massacre brought Capone to national attention as "Public Enemy Number One," but the authorities had trouble pinning a crime on the man who always had an alibi (and who owned the Chicago police force). Finally, an IRS investigator accidentally found incriminating receipts that sent Capone to the Atlanta federal prison in 1932 for tax evasion.

Capone ran his organization from prison until 1934, when he was transferred to Alcatraz to cut him off from his gang and the outside world. By 1938, he was serving his sentence in the prison hospital suffering from dementia brought on by syphilis. After his release in 1939, he retired to his estate in Palm Island, Florida. He died of natural causes in 1947.

## 2. CHARLES "LUCKY" LUCIANO

**The Rise:** Born in 1897, Lucky Luciano moved to New York from Sicily when he was nine. His Sicilian heritage put him in good stead with "Joe the Boss" Masseria, head of one of the most powerful gangs in New York.

In 1929, Masseria was at war with Salvatore Moranzano, the leader of a rival gang. Each man wanted to be *capo di tutti capi*, or the "boss of all bosses." Since Luciano worked for Masseria, Moranzano's men attacked him and left him for dead. But instead of taking revenge, Luciano cut a deal with them: he arranged Masseria's execution in 1931, took over for Masseria, and let Moranzano become the boss of all bosses—for about six months. Then Luciano had Moranzano killed, too.

**The Reign:** With both old bosses gone, Luciano revamped what became known as La Cosa Nostra (known to the FBI as LCN). Officially doing away with the "boss of all bosses" position, Luciano allowed New York's five bosses to run their own crime families. They and major crime bosses from across the country each held a place on the "Commission," which had the power to settle disputes for LCN, which was now a national crime syndicate.

Under Luciano, LCN concentrated on making money from gambling, extortion, loan sharking, arson, and labor racketeering, and even started investing in legitimate businesses.

**The Fall:** Lucky's luck ran out in 1935, when the authorities convicted (some say framed) him for running a prostitution ring. Luciano controlled his crime family from prison until he was deported to Italy in 1946. He died of a heart attack in Naples in 1962.

## 3. MEYER "LITTLE MAN" LANSKY

**The Rise:** Born Maier Suchowljansky in 1902 in Grodno, Russia, Meyer Lansky came to New York with his family when he was nine. The studious Meyer was known as "a good Jewish boy" until he teamed up with Bugsy Siegel to form the Jewish "Bugs Meyer Gang," which specialized in auto theft, gambling, and racketeering.

The small-statured Lansky provided the planning and financial know-how, while Siegel and friends provided the muscle. In 1920, Prohibition was the law of the land, so Lansky and Siegel joined forces with their old friend Lucky Luciano. Together they made a fortune selling liquor to speakeasies. In 1931, Lansky helped Luciano rise to power and create LCN.

**The Reign:** La Cosa Nostra grew so powerful that Lansky later described it as "bigger than U.S. Steel." The Mob was pulling in millions, and the bosses were coming to Lansky for financial advice. Some historians believe that Lansky, nicknamed the "Mob Accountant," actually ran the Mafia through Luciano. In any case, Lansky stayed under law enforcement's radar.

After Prohibition ended, Lansky opened illegal gambling casinos in New York, New Orleans, and Florida. They were so profitable that, when Lansky wanted to open some offshore casinos in the 1950s, Cuban dictator Fulgencio Batista welcomed him into Havana. Bugsy Siegel's hotel-casino in Vegas had lost so much money that the Commission had him killed in 1947 (Lansky ordered the execution), but Lansky stayed alive and in power because he made crime pay.

**The Fall:** Even Lansky couldn't win forever, though. In 1959, he lost $7 million in Mob money when Fidel Castro overthrew Batista and nationalized Cuba's casinos. In the 1970s, the feds went after him, so he fled to Israel. Two years later, he was deported back to the United States.

On his return in 1973, Lansky faced income-tax evasion charges but was acquitted. He never spent a day in jail, but the FBI claimed that he had millions socked away when he died of lung cancer in 1983. *Forbes* magazine believed it, too, listing him among their 400 wealthiest people in America in 1982.

Lincoln Logs were invented in 1916 by John Lloyd Wright, architect Frank Lloyd Wright's son.

## 4. FRANK "THE PRIME MINISTER" COSTELLO

**The Rise:** Francesco Castiglia was born in Cosenza, in southern Italy, in 1891 and arrived in New York's East Harlem with his family when he was four. By age 24, he was serving 10 months in prison for carrying a gun. As an ex-con, Costello vowed he would reform—he'd commit crimes but let other people carry the guns.

Costello became close friends with Lucky Luciano in 1920. In 1937, when Luciano was in jail and underboss Vito Genovese—who'd been the boss in Luciano's absence—was hiding out in Italy to avoid a murder charge, Costello became the acting boss of the powerful Luciano crime family.

**The Reign:** Costello was known as the "Prime Minister" because he expanded his power not with violence but by using negotiation and bribes. He was always expensively dressed, with a carefully cultivated front of respectability; he was rarely around when rough stuff went down.

The Luciano crime family made huge profits in gambling, bookmaking, loan sharking, and labor racketeering under Costello, who used part of the profits to buy cops, politicians, and judges. Because J. Edgar Hoover refused to admit that the Mafia was alive and well in America, some even said that Hoover was in Costello's pocket.

**The Fall:** Costello was making about $1 million a year, but life at the top wasn't easy. In 1946, Vito Genovese returned to New York when the Italian authorities sent him back to face his murder charge. Then, in 1950, the U.S. Senate set up the Kefauver Committee to investigate organized crime, with Costello as its main target. The combination—plus a desire to become a respected member of high society—drove an anxiety-ridden Costello to a psychiatrist, who advised him to start associating with a better class of people.

After he was shot in 1957 by a hit man that Genovese had hired, Costello retired and let Genovese take over. But he got his revenge. Working in secret, Costello set Genovese up on drug charges that sent him to prison (where Genovese died). The Prime Minister took revenge his way—without using a gun. Cotello died of a heart attack in Manhattan in 1973.

---

During the Vietnam War, radio operators used Slinky toys as antennas.

## 5. ALBERT "LORD HIGH EXECUTIONER" ANASTASIA

**The Rise:** Born in 1902 in Tropea, Italy, Anastasia was a seaman who jumped ship and entered the United States illegally when he was about 17. He worked as a longshoreman, where his need for anger management became apparent when he quarreled with a fellow workman and killed him. Anastasia served only 18 months for the crime because the witnesses who could have kept him in prison "disappeared."

Anastasia often worked alongside Lucky Luciano, and when Luciano made his bid for power, it was rumored that Anastasia worked for him as an executioner. When the Commission was set up, Anastasia helped head up its "enforcement" arm: Murder, Inc.

**The Reign:** Working out of a Brooklyn candy store until the 1940s, Murder, Inc. is said to have killed hundreds of people in the service of La Cosa Nostra. Anastasia was never prosecuted for any killings because witnesses against him still had a way of disappearing.

In 1951, Anastasia became boss of what is now known as the Gambino crime family, one of the largest in New York. He managed it by killing the family's former boss and by staying in the good graces of Costello, who probably allied himself with Anastasia because the guy was so wild and violent that no one would touch his friends.

**The Fall:** Anastasia's ties with the longshoreman's union helped him grow rich and powerful, but he got too murderous, even for the Mob. (Once, he ordered a hit on a stranger he saw on television because the person had testified against a bank robber, and Anastasia hated squealers.) His enemies whispered that he was too crazy to be a boss. In addition, Vito Genovese wanted to become the boss of all bosses, and in order to gain the position, Anastasia and Costello needed to be killed. In 1957, Anastasia was shot and killed while he sat in a barber's chair at the Park Sheraton Hotel. Newspapers proclaimed at the time that the Mob's worst murderer finally "got the chair."

\*　　\*　　\*

"Organized crime in America takes in over forty billion dollars a year and spends very little on office supplies."
　　　　　　　　　　　　　　　　　　　　　　　　—Woody Allen

The average CD can hold 74 minutes' worth of music.

# FAST-FOOD FIRSTS

*From hot dogs to drive-throughs to obesity*
*lawsuits, somebody had to do it first.*

Fast food. It's the food you hate to love, and it's been brought to you by the perpetrators mentioned on these pages.

**1. First Fast-Food Restaurant:** White Castle is considered the first fast-food restaurant. J. Walter Anderson and Edgar Waldo "Billy" Ingram started their business in 1921 in Wichita, Kansas. They wisely focused on hamburgers, which had been sold as sandwiches by street vendors since the 1890s.

**2. First Automat:** Joe Horn and Frank Hardart opened the first automat—a cafeteria where food is obtained from vending machines—in Philadelphia on June 9, 1902.

**3. First Drive-ins:** Two fast-food chains claim the honor of being the first drive-in. A&W Root Beer launched theirs in California in 1919; the Pig Stand opened in 1921 in Texas. Both featured curbside service courtesy of "tray boys" and "car hops," respectively.

**4. First Drive-through:** Esther Snyder laid claim to the first drive-through restaurant with the use of speakers to order food when she and her husband, Harry, founded the burgers-and-fries joint In-N-Out in Southern California in 1948.

**5. First McDonald's:** In 1948, Richard and Maurice McDonald opened the first McDonald's restaurant in San Bernardino, California, and called it the McDonald Brothers Burger Bar Drive-In. In 1954, Ray Kroc, who sold milk-shake mixers, came across their establishment and sold the brothers several of his machines. Kroc suggested they expand their business and offered to be their agent. In 1955, Kroc opened his first McDonald's in Des Plaines, Illinois, and founded the McDonald's Corporation. Six years later, he bought out the McDonald brothers.

**6. First Mascots:** Among the first fast-food mascots was Big Boy, a plump boy wearing red-and-white-checkered overalls with the

---

words "Big Boy" spread across his chest. (The first McDonald's mascot was Speedee, a little chef with a hamburger hat. He was replaced by Ronald McDonald in 1963.)

**7. First Restaurant Founded in a Broom Closet:** The Papa John's franchise was founded in 1984 when "Papa" John Schnatter knocked out a broom closet in the back of his father's tavern and used the space to sell pizzas. By 2005, he had opened more than 3,000 restaurants in the United States and 20 international locations, which, by the way, were in buildings much bigger than broom closets.

**8. First Happy Meal:** The Circus Wagon Happy Meal, which debuted in 1979, was the first McDonald's meal for kids, featuring either a regular hamburger or cheeseburger, fries, a McDonaldland Cookies sampler, a soft drink, and either a McDoodler stencil, a puzzle toy, a McWrist wallet, an ID bracelet, or McDonaldland character erasers. All for $1.

**9. First Value Menu:** In 1989, Wendy's was the first burger joint to offer a value menu for $1. They followed it up with a price reduction to 99 cents, which set the stage for their competitors to offer their discount menu items for $1.

**10. First Trans Fat–Free Chain:** Domino's Pizza became the first fast-food chain to ban trans fats from its products in February 2007. Trans fats, used in cooking oils, have been linked to infertility and heart disease.

**11. First Public Fast-Food Diet:** Jared Fogle became known as the "Subway Guy" after he lost 245 pounds in a year by skipping breakfast and eating two subs a day (a small turkey and a large veggie), baked potato chips, and a diet soda at Subway. The company hired Fogle to appear in its ads in 2000, and he became an official spokesman four years later.

**12. First Hot Dog Stand:** German butcher Charles Feltman opened the first in Brooklyn, New York, in 1867. He started out delivering pies in a "pie wagon" to inns and saloons, but his customers wanted hot sandwiches, so he came up with the idea of serving a hot sausage on a roll. With a few modifications to his pie

---

**In 1816, Thomas Jefferson wrote that banks are "more dangerous than standing armies."**

wagon, Feltman's contraption would boil the sausages and keep the buns warm. He sold 3,684 sausages in a roll during his first year in business.

**13. First "Obesity" Lawsuit:** A lawsuit claiming that McDonald's was responsible for making people obese was dismissed by U.S. District Judge Robert Sweet in February 2003. The suit, filed by the parents of two teenage girls who suffered from obesity and multiple other health issues, claimed that McDonald's advertising was luring children into eating unhealthy food. Sweet allowed the plaintiffs to revise their suit, but dismissed the revised suit in September of the same year.

**14. First Fast Food for the Poor:** In 1882, a Swiss flour manufacturer produced the first commercially made bouillon cubes (compressed cubes of dehydrated and concentrated meat or vegetable stock). He wanted to give the poor people living in the slums a nutritious soup that was also inexpensive.

\* \* \*

## HISTORY'S FOOD NETWORK STARS

Before the Food Network made a celebrity out of every chef, these cooks, chefs, and restaurateurs made a name for themselves the old-fashioned way—through hard work and innovation.

| | |
|---|---|
| Apicius | M. F. K. Fischer |
| James Beard | Pierre Franey |
| Louis Bechamel | Mrs. Hannah Glasse |
| Mrs. Beeton | Pierre de La Varenne |
| Paul Bocus | Dione Lucas |
| Anthelme Brillat-Savarin | Posper Montagne |
| Alex Cardini | Oscar of the Waldorf (Tschirky) |
| Antoine Careme | Jacques Pepin |
| Julia Child | Cesar Ritz |
| Adelle Davis | Irma Rombauer |
| Lorenzo Delmonica | Edward Sacher |
| Andrew Dornenburg | Vincent |
| George Auguste Escoffier | Sardi |
| Fanny Farmer | Toots Shor |

*Uatchitodon,* the earliest known venomous reptile, lived about 200 million years ago.

# LET THE GOOD SWINES ROLL

*When you find yourself in times of trouble, call on a pig to help you out.*

### 1. KING NEPTUNE
In 1942, an Illinois farmer donated a piglet to the U.S. Navy's annual roast. Recruiter Don Lingle, however, saw a great opportunity. World War II was raging, and the country needed money for a new battleship. So Lingle saved the pig from slaughter, named him King Neptune, and turned him into an American icon. Lingle dressed up the pig in a navy blue blanket and silver earrings and took him to war bond fund-raisers, where the pig's "parts" were auctioned to raise money for the battleship. (King Neptune's squeal once went for $25.) No one ever actually kept any of the parts they bought; instead, the buyers always donated the pig back to the navy so he could live to raise another dollar. In 1946, after helping to bring in more than $19 million in war bonds, King Neptune retired to a farm in Illinois. He died in 1950.

### 2. MAX
Actor George Clooney was living in Los Angeles in 1994 when the city was rocked by the Northridge earthquake. The disaster killed more than 60 people and caused $20 billion in damage, but Clooney escaped unscathed. He credits his potbellied pig, Max, who woke him up just before the temblor. Without Max, the world may have been a bleaker place, without movie gems such as *Up in the Air*, *O Brother, Where Art Thou?*, and *Good Night, and Good Luck*.

### 3. PIGASUS
Abbie Hoffman and Jerry Rubin, leaders of the 1960s Youth International Party (Yippies), wanted someone from their party to run for president. Who better to "support" than a 150-pound gray hog? In 1968, during one of the most contentious elections in U.S. history, Hoffman and Rubin announced Pigasus's "candidacy" outside the Democratic National Convention. (He didn't win.)

---

The oldest continually operating roller coaster is in Melbourne, Australia...

# FIRST JOBS OF WORLD LEADERS

*Everyone's got to start somewhere. While many world leaders had their futures handed to them or were involved in politics from their school days on, there were also those who actually went out and did honest work beforehand.*

**1. Joseph Stalin** was a seminary student.

**2. Adolf Hitler** sold paintings to Viennese tourists. (He copied the scenes from postcards.)

**3. Mahatma Gandhi** was a lawyer who, after unsuccessfully trying to establish a law practice, made a modest living drafting legal documents.

**4. Nelson Mandela** served briefly as a guard at a mine in South Africa.

**5. Tony Blair** idolized Mick Jagger and tried to achieve fame as a rock music promoter and musician in a band called Ugly Rumours.

**6. Lech Walesa,** president of Poland from 1990 to 1995, spent most of his life before politics as a ship worker and electrician.

**7. Harry Truman,** the only 20th-century president without a college degree, worked as a mail boy for the *Kansas City Star*, a timekeeper on the Santa Fe Railroad, and a sales clerk in his own men's clothing store.

**8. Leonid Brezhnev** was hired as a metallurgical engineer.

**9. Mao Zedong** spent his childhood on the family farm before he left home and became a school librarian.

**10. Yasser Arafat** worked as a civil engineer and schoolteacher.

---

...The Luna Park amusement park's Scenic Railway was built in 1912.

**11. Helmut Kohl** was assistant to the directory of a foundry.

**12. Nikita Khrushchev** was a herder, brick maker, and metal-worker.

**13. Ho Chi Minh** came to the United States as a cook's helper on a ship. Living in Harlem and Boston, he worked as a baker at the Parker House Hotel. He later moved to London and Paris, and worked as a pastry chef and waiter before eventually returning to his home country to lead the nationalist movement.

**14. Golda Meir** helped run the family store in Milwaukee, Wisconsin.

**15. Benito Mussolini** was a blacksmith and stonemason.

**16. Kim Jong-Il** apprenticed as a builder of roads and television towers.

**17. Idi Amin** served as a cook in the British Colonial Army. He was also Uganda's light heavyweight boxing champion from 1951 to 1960.

**18. Boris Yeltsin** worked as a construction foreman and a civil engineer specializing in plumbing and sewage.

**19. Vladimir Putin** worked for the KGB, monitoring the activities of foreigners in Leningrad.

**20. Andrew Johnson** apprenticed to a tailor, and made his own clothes even while he was president.

\* \* \*

"A lot of fellows nowadays have a BA, MD, or Ph D. Unfortunately, they don't have a J-O-B."
—**Fats Domino**

The names of 72 scientists and other notables are engraved on the Eiffel Tower.

# BYGONE CAREERS

*Study this list to prepare yourself for the next time
Grandpa talks about the good old days.*

## 1. LECTOR

Churches everywhere use *lectors*, or readers, to read aloud biblical
text (apart from the Gospels) at services today, but the lector as a
profession outside the church is one that goes back to the early
19th century, and was especially rooted in the cigar industry of
Cuba. The lector sat above the factory workers, reading the day's
news, keeping everyone abreast of events in the outside world.
Lectors sometimes read works by authors such as Charles Dickens,
Miguel de Cervantes, and Harriet Beecher Stowe (effectively turning cigar factory workers into some of the most highly educated
men in Cuba), but their main source of reading material was the
daily newspaper. The lector was chosen and paid by the workers
themselves, not by management. Thus, when labor unions grew in
prominence in the 1930s, Cuban cigar factory owners became suspicious of lectors as a source of the unrest, believing that they
were responsible for spreading radical political ideas among the
workers. In 1932, the owners collectively put an end to the practice of having a lector on the floor, replacing them with state-
approved radio broadcasts.

## 2. ELEVATOR OPERATOR

Pushing a button in an elevator is simple enough these days, but
in the early 20th century, when the elevator was still a curiosity,
skilled elevator operators relieved their passengers' fears about
being carried hundreds of feet into the air by a mechanical contraption. Before the advent of automatic elevators in the 1950s,
elevators were worked by an operator who not only got the passengers where they needed to go but also served as a sort of
security guard. Elevator operators were often on a first-name basis
with all of a building's occupants, and were aware of all the comings and goings. A lever would be turned to the right or left to
control a motor and was then "jogged" by the operator to bring
the elevator even with the landing before the doors were opened.
Although only a few buildings employ manual elevator operators

today, those buildings' occupants often report that they feel more secure, not only inside the elevator but elsewhere in the building as well, with the knowledge that a pair of human eyes is watching out for their well-being.

## 3. MILKMAN

Refrigerators and large dairy corporations have all but made the milkman's job obsolete. Milkmen were often independent retailers who bought their products from local dairies and then transported said products in trucks cooled with ice. Milkmen were often treated as a member of the extended family and were a fixture in many communities. Besides advanced refrigerators, supermarkets can be blamed for the milkman's downfall, as they offered a wider range of cheaper dairy products that could be obtained at the customer's convenience. Milkmen can still be found on today's streets, though, delivering to rural communities and even to some suburban areas where customers appreciate the personalized service.

## 4. TEA LADY

The tradition of afternoon tea as a social meal goes back to Anna, the Duchess of Bedford, who introduced the practice around 1840, but the tea lady has been serving British workers since 1666. It was that year that the wife of an officer in the East India Company decided to serve tea at a committee meeting; little did the polite woman know that she was hatching a tradition that would survive for more than 300 years. By the 20th century, the tea lady was a fixture at offices in England, pushing a cart loaded with tea and afternoon snacks up and down the halls of the building, serving employees at their desks.

The tea lady dispensed not only caffeine but often gossip as well, bringing a dose of social excitement during the doldrums of the workday. In the 1980s and 1990s, the tradition began to die out as companies invested in vending machines, break rooms, and automatic tea and coffee dispensers. Today, just 2 percent of British companies report having a tea lady in their employ, but a survey of workers indicated that the tea lady is the one tradition they would like to see reintroduced more than any other.

---

Animal with the biggest eyes? It's the colossal squid, with an eye diameter of about...

## 5. TYPESETTER

From the time Johannes Gutenberg invented the printing press in the mid-15th century, printers have sought more efficient methods for putting words to paper. The earliest printing presses required that an operator manually set individual blocks of letters, numbers, and other figures—known as movable type—into rows on the press, ink the raised surfaces with rollers, and then press or roll paper over the type to produce a printed page. Typesetters who worked at newspapers had drawers with huge collections of movable type in different sizes, so they could print large or small headlines according to their needs.

Typesetting techniques evolved steadily and typesetters' jobs became easier—fewer typesetters were needed to produce more books and newspapers than before—but it was not until digital printing came on the scene in the 1960s that typesetters saw the writing on the wall. Today, most large newspapers and book publishers use computers for nearly every stage of the process. But typesetting has seen a recent revival among hobbyists who produce elaborate printed souvenirs, as well as among small publishers of high-end books.

## 6. BOBBIN BOY

In the 19th century, at the height of the Industrial Revolution, textile manufacturing got a boost when people started using water power, and then steam power, to drive the looms. Textiles could now be made much more efficiently, but thread still needed to be replaced on the looms to keep the manufacturing process continuous. Enter the bobbin boy, who had the dangerous task of replacing the spindles of thread, or *bobbins*, on the machines while they remained in operation. Small, quick hands were a must, so young boys were often given this assignment: crushed fingers were routine. Andrew Carnegie's first job was as a bobbin boy at a textile mill in Pennsylvania at age 13. He worked 12 hours a day, six days a week, and earned a grand total of $1.20 per week. Not exactly a promising start, but Carnegie got out in time, switched his career path to the steel industry, and became one of the richest men in the world.

## 7. PINSETTER

Bowling has existed in various forms since as early as 3200 BC in Egypt, and players were largely responsible for setting up their own pins until the game became popular in the United States in the late 19th century. Any establishment that hoped to keep its customers satisfied employed young boys as pinsetters. The boys worked quickly to clear away and set up the pins, roll balls back to the bowlers, and then hop up onto shelves to get their legs out of the way before the next ball was launched. Injuries such as bruised feet and shins were common, but a skilled pinsetter could get up onto the shelf quickly and was always on the lookout for incoming balls. A battle in the 1940s between the large bowling companies—AMF Bowling and Brunswick—to attract more customers to their establishments with more efficient semiautomatic pinsetters (which allowed for more lanes, as well as faster matches) led to the first fully automatic pinsetters being introduced in 1956.

## 8. SODA JERK

It's the quintessential all-American scene: Teenagers gathered around a counter in a fountain drugstore, drinking sodas and milk shakes while music plays from a jukebox. And in the background, serving everyone's needs, a white-clad soda jerk, always happy to whip up a frothy concoction and slide it down the counter. Today, this scene is played out in just a few throwback diners, and the players are more likely to be senior citizens hoping for a taste of the past than they are to be teenagers living on the edge. Soda jerks—the term came from the jerking motion used to pull on the soda fountain handle—hit their heyday in the 1940s and '50s, when most drugstores were independent neighborhood businesses rather than a counter tucked away inside a supermarket. When fast-food restaurants became popular in the mid-20th century and soda fountains were replaced by automated dispensers, soda jerks became expendable—and the art of blending a milk shake with that perfect consistency was all but lost.

## 9. LAMPLIGHTER

Before the early 19th century, some cities required that private citizens whose homes faced a public street hang a lamp at night to ensure that nighttime travelers did not stumble around in the

President Calvin Coolidge refused to use the telephone while in office.

dark. In 1807, London's Pall Mall became the first public street to be illuminated by gaslights, and other cities across the world soon adopted the system. Lamplighters were responsible for lighting all the gas lamps along their routes one hour before dark; they would climb a ladder (which they carried along their route) to reach the lamp, turn a handle to get the gas flowing, and then ignite the gas with a match. At dawn, each lamp was extinguished in turn by shutting off the flow of gas. Some lamplighters could light as many as 300 lamps an hour, but when the use of electrical grids spread in the early 20th century, thousands of streetlights could be turned on and off with the flick of a switch—and the duties of a lamplighter became a small part of a maintenance worker's job description. Although some cities still use gaslights for historical ambience, the lights are controlled by electrical switches.

\*     \*     \*

## OTHER CANDIDATES FOR THE DUSTBIN:

Copy boy
Switchboard operator
Typist in typing pool
Telegraph operator
Museum taxidermist
River driver
Iceman
Cobbler
Draftsman
Miner
Film processor
Animation cel painter
Grocery store cashier
Construction worker
CD store manager
Fighter pilot
Bank teller
Union organizer
Call center representative
Encyclopedia writer
Oil wildcatter

---

**Almonds and pistachios are the only nuts mentioned in the Bible.**

# WRITTEN IN THE PEN

*Jawaharlal Nehru (India's first prime minister) once said, "All my major works have been written in prison. I would recommend prison not only to aspiring writers but to aspiring politicians too." Here are some other notable jailhouse jotters who seem to agree with that advice.*

## 1. SIR THOMAS MALORY (1405–71)
## LE MORTE D'ARTHUR

The English legends of King Arthur, Sir Lancelot, Guinevere, and the Knights of the Round Table have been around for centuries, and no one knows for sure who actually invented the tales. But we do know that Sir Thomas Malory wrote the legends down, added some of his own flair, and published them in a collection that is today's best-known telling of the Arthurian legend. Malory was a soldier and Member of Parliament, but went on to a life of crime and was in and out of prison. Ironically, many scholars believe that Malory wrote the tales of knights and chivalry while awaiting trial for theft, extortion, home invasion, banditry, and rape.

## 2. NICCOLÒ MACHIAVELLI (1469–1527)
## THE PRINCE

Niccolò Machiavelli lived during a time of great plotting and political upheaval in Italy. Initially, he aligned himself with a government that expelled the ruthless and powerful Medici family, which had ruled Florence for 60 years. But when that government fell apart and the Medicis came back with a vengeance, Machiavelli was tossed into prison and tortured. Behind bars, he wrote *The Prince*, a philosophical treatise on politics that said leaders should rule by force instead of by law. In *The Prince*, Machiavelli wrote, "Anyone compelled to choose will find greater security in being feared than in being loved." It was from this book that the term "Machiavellian" came into use to describe a ruthless, deceitful, and cunning leader. Reportedly, Soviet dictator Joseph Stalin was a fan of *The Prince* and kept a copy next to his bed.

## 3. SIR WALTER RALEIGH (1552–1618)
## HISTORY OF THE WORLD

Sir Walter Raleigh was a favorite of Queen Elizabeth I and made

---

Home-schooled and famous: Agatha Christie, Thomas Edison, Alexander Graham Bell.

two trips to the New World to try to colonize Virginia. Although those settlements failed, they paved the way for future colonies. He alienated the queen, though, by secretly marrying one of her ladies-in-waiting, and in 1591 Elizabeth had Raleigh imprisoned in the Tower of London for about a year.

After Elizabeth died in 1603, her successor, King James, tried Raleigh for treason and sent him back to the Tower of London for 13 years. It was there that he wrote the first volume of his *History of the World*, which recounted the histories of ancient Greece and Rome. In 1616, James granted Raleigh a release from prison in order to search for El Dorado, the legendary city of gold, in Venezuela. Instead, Raleigh looted a Spanish settlement there. To keep the peace with Spain, James had the explorer beheaded. Ever the writer, Raleigh left the world with a quotable quip—after inspecting the executioner's axe, he remarked, "This is a sharp Medicine, but it is a Physician for all diseases and miseries."

## 4. DANIEL DEFOE (1660–1731)
## "A HYMN TO THE PILLORY"

Daniel Defoe, most famous for the book *Robinson Crusoe*, wrote perhaps the most immediately useful piece of prison writing while incarcerated. In 1703, he was sentenced to the pillory for three days for satirizing church intolerance. With his head, arms, and legs locked in the wooden frame and then set up in the market-place, Defoe typically would have been mocked, assaulted, and pelted with garbage by passersby. (The goal of the pillory was to shame criminals back to the straight and narrow.) But while in prison awaiting transfer, Defoe quickly wrote "A Hymn to the Pillory," a poem that satirized the punishment he was about to receive. Friends sold copies in front of his pillory, and according to legend, the crowds pelted him with flowers instead of garbage.

## 5. THE MARQUIS DE SADE (1740–1814)
## *JUSTINE*

Because of his wicked, wicked ways, the man who gave his name to the word "sadism" spent 32 years of his adult life inside French mental institutions and prisons, including 10 years in the infamous Bastille, where he wrote many of his sexually explicit books. *Justine* (published in 1791) tells the story of a young woman's "search for virtue" from the ages of 12 to 26. Considering that this is a Marquis de Sade book, it's not surprising that she doesn't find much of it. Instead, Justine (also called Therese in the novel) is mistreated, abused, and conned into participating in dirty deeds for many years, until she finally meets a woman who wants to help her. (The woman turns out to be Justine's long-lost sister.) In the end, though, the virtuous life just depresses Justine, and she ends up dying after being struck by a bolt of lightning.

## 6. OSCAR WILDE (1854–1900)
### DE PROFUNDIS

*De Profundis* is sometimes confused with "The Ballad of Reading Gaol"—the first was written while Irish writer Oscar Wilde was in prison; the second was a poem about his time in prison, but was written after he was released. In 1895, Wilde was sentenced to two years of hard labor after being convicted of "gross indecency" (i.e., homosexuality). *De Profundis* ("From the Depths") was a dark and angry 50,000-word letter to his former lover, Lord Alfred Douglas, who had abandoned Wilde when he was convicted.

## 7. EZRA POUND (1885–1972)
### PISAN CANTOS

At the beginning of World War II, American Ezra Pound lived in Italy and made propaganda radio broadcasts in which he voiced his support of Fascist leader Benito Mussolini and criticized the American government, the British government, and the Jews. After the war, he was charged with treason and imprisoned by the U.S. Army near the city of Pisa, where wrote 10 of his best cantos for an epic poem. (A canto is like a stanza, but longer.) Pound also had a nervous breakdown in prison and spent more than a decade in a series of mental institutions until 1958, when he was labeled incurably insane, but not a danger to others, and released.

## 8. ADOLF HITLER (1889–1945)
### MEIN KAMPF

After the Nazi Party tried and failed to overthrow the German government in 1923, Adolf Hitler spent nine months in prison working on his memoir and political diatribe. Hitler's publisher convinced him to shorten his title to *Mein Kampf* ("My Struggle").

The book was originally called *Viereinhalb Jahre (des Kampfes) Gegen Lüge, Dummheit und Feigheit* ("Four and a Half Years [of Struggle] Against Lies, Stupidity and Cowardice").

## 9. MARTIN LUTHER KING JR. (1929–1968) "LETTER FROM BIRMINGHAM JAIL"

In the spring of 1963, the Southern Christian Leadership Conference, led by Martin Luther King Jr., waged a nonviolent campaign in Birmingham, Alabama, to protest racial discrimination and segregation. The protesters participated in sit-ins at segregated restaurants, marches for voter registration, and kneel-ins at white churches. These activities were illegal at the time, and King (among others) was arrested and held at the city's jail. While he was there, a group of white clergymen wrote a letter urging African Americans to use the courts instead of protests to further their cause. King drafted "Letter from Birmingham Jail" as a response and argued that civil disobedience was justified when the laws it protested were unjust. The letter—which included famous statements like "injustice anywhere is a threat to justice everywhere"—appeared in national magazines and newspapers and helped bring even more attention to the growing call for civil rights in America.

## 10. HONORABLE MENTIONS—STARTED IN PRISON

Two great writers are widely reported to have written works in prison. Miguel de Cervantes began his masterpiece, *Don Quixote*, while in debtor's prison. Reportedly it is the second most popular book among prisoners at Guantanamo Bay.

O. Henry, wrongly imprisoned for embezzlement, began many of his short stories inside and then continued them after his release.

\* \* \*

### MORE 20TH CENTURY PRISON WRITERS
**Nelson Algren:** *The Man with the Golden Arm*
**Jeffrey Archer:** *A Prison Diary*
**John Bunyan:** *The Pilgrim's Progress*
**Eldridge Cleaver:** *A Soul on Ice*
**Charles Colson:** *Life Sentences*
**Malcolm X:** *The Autobiography of Malcolm X*

# 1929

*The most famous event of 1929 was the October stock market*
*crash that plunged the world into the Great Depression.*
*But a lot more history happened that year.*

**FEBRUARY 14: The St. Valentine's Day Massacre.** On the
order of Al Capone, four men sneaked into a Chicago garage and
gunned down seven members of "Bugs" Moran's rival gang. It was
the bloodiest Mob murder in Chicago's history at the time and
marked the end of Capone's run as the city's Mob boss. The federal government stepped up its efforts to incarcerate Capone after
the attack and, within two years, had tracked him down. Ultimately, he was convicted of tax evasion and sent to prison on
Alcatraz Island in San Francisco Bay.

**FEBRUARY 26: Grand Teton became a national park.** The
Wyoming park, part of the Rocky Mountain Teton range, is
best known for its huge rock spires, called the Tetons, but
there's still some controversy over the park's name. Some people
claim the term means "big teat" in French, maybe the result of
French Canadians exploring the area. But others say the range
and the spires were named for the Teton Indians who once lived
in the area.

**MARCH 4: Herbert Hoover was inaugurated as the 31st U.S.**
**president.** Hoover won the 1928 election by a landslide, with
58 percent of the vote. But the October 1929 stock market crash
and his unwillingness to allow any government help (Hoover believed in limited government interference) made him a one-term
president. He was defeated in 1932 by Franklin Delano Roosevelt.

**JUNE 7: Vatican City became a sovereign state.** Italian prime
minister Benito Mussolini signed the Lateran Treaty to give the
110-acre city autonomy. Before that, it was part of Rome.

**NOVEMBER 7: New York's Museum of Modern Art opened.** It
was the first American museum to exhibit works from European
Postimpressionists. Some of the first painters to have their works
exhibited: Vincent van Gogh, Paul Cézanne, and Paul Gauguin.

---

A 2004 poll found that 29% of Americans have had sex on the first date.

# ASSASSINS

*Among our list of the top 10 assassins, you'll find cold-blooded killers, hotheaded radicals, and just plain cuckoos, all of whom thought they had good reasons to dispose of the VIPs of their time.*

## 1. BRUTUS

Marcus Junius Brutus was the classic Roman big cheese. Born into a well-connected family, Brutus was raised to believe in the traditional virtues of the Roman republic. This meant rule by an elite group of senators and wealthy citizens—men like himself. So when a rabble-rousing populist politician named Julius Caesar came along, the bigwigs decided he had to be stopped...in the name of the republic, of course. Caesar, they said, wanted to make himself dictator. They may have been right, but we'll never know, because on March 15 (the ides of March on the Roman calendar) in 44 BC, Brutus and some 60 of his senatorial colleagues stabbed Caesar 23 times on the floor of the senate building.

**This Means War!** Displaying staggering political naïveté, Brutus and his coconspirators assumed the Roman people and army would support their preemptive strike against Caesar. But while some welcomed Caesar's death, most didn't. The assassination unleashed a fierce civil war: on one side, Brutus and the defenders of the republic; on the other, Caesar's supporters, led by his general Mark Antony and Caesar's 18-year-old adopted son, Octavian. Within two years of Caesar's assassination, Brutus was dead. He committed suicide after losing the Battle of Philippi in Greece.

**Death and Rebirth.** Octavian had the backing of Caesar's supporters, and the senate considered Antony the greater threat. So Octavian went after Antony. Like Brutus, Mark Antony committed suicide—along with his lover, Cleopatra—following their defeat by Octavian at the Battle of Actium. Octavian, having defeated all his rivals, assumed total control. The Roman republic, after 700 years of history, was at an end. Octavian renamed himself Augustus Caesar and inaugurated the Roman Empire—and another 500 years of death, debauchery, and conquest.

---

**In 1942, the first nuclear reactor generated only enough power to light a flashlight.**

## 2. CHARLOTTE CORDAY

The French Revolution of 1789 produced plenty of revolting characters. One of the worst was Jean-Paul Marat, the uncompromising journalist for whom any aristocratic head still attached to its shoulders was one head too many. But it wasn't his royalist enemies who killed him in July 1793. It was a fellow revolutionary—and a woman to boot!—Charlotte Corday.

**Whose Side Are You On?** Marat and Corday personified the two wings of the French Revolution. Marat, born in Switzerland in 1743, was a member of the Jacobins, the shock troops of the revolution. Their leader was Maximilien Robespierre, who instituted the Reign of Terror in mid-1793, a vicious onslaught on those deemed to be enemies of the people. Marat was Robespierre's most enthusiastic cheerleader, using his newspaper *L'Ami du peuple* (*Friend of the People*) to denounce, terrorize, ridicule, and persecute enemies.

**And in the Other Corner...** The Jacobins' fellow revolutionaries the Girondins were also their main enemies. Girondin leader Georges Danton was a boozing, brawling, much-loved idealist whose followers included Charlotte Corday, a young woman drawn in by the romance of revolution. Disgusted by the extremism of Robespierre and Marat, she visited Marat at his Paris home on July 13, 1793, claiming knowledge of a Girondist plot. Marat, who suffered from an unsightly and painful skin disease, received Corday while lying in one of his medicinal baths. With her enemy defenseless, Corday wasted no time in stabbing him to death.

**Off with Her Head!** Robespierre was quick to avenge his sidekick. Corday was guillotined within a week—to be followed by countless other Girondists over the next few months as the Jacobins ratcheted up the Terror. By April 1794, Danton himself had been executed; three months later, the same fate befell Robespierre as the revolution devoured its own children—and the Reign of Terror that Corday so detested finally came to an end.

## 3. JOHN WILKES BOOTH

If you think politics is a divisive issue today, consider the state of the nation during the Civil War—the country was polarized into two factions, each believing their cause was just, and sometimes even pitting brother against brother. And at no time was the war more divisive than near its end. The nation was shocked when President Lincoln was shot by John Wilkes Booth at Ford's Theatre in Washington, D.C., on April 14, 1865, but even today, the reasons—and the perpetrators—behind Booth's actions are hotly debated.

**A Superstar Goes South.** History remembers Booth as a mad-eyed assassin, but to some he's still a champion of the Confederacy's right to seek its own destiny—a soldier cut down at the age of 26, just 12 days after his "heroic" shooting of the tyrant Lincoln. He certainly didn't do it for the money. Once dubbed "the handsomest man in America," Booth was a successful stage actor who commanded huge fees and played to packed houses filled with swooning female fans. When the Civil War broke out, the Maryland-born Booth became a passionate believer in the Southern cause. By the end of the war in 1865, he had made the decision to throw away his brilliant acting career in favor of the role of rebel.

**He's Number One!** By cold-bloodedly murdering the president of the United States, Booth became the archetypal young idealist prepared to sacrifice everything in the name of a principle—however misguided. He's probably the most infamous assassin. To prove our point, ask the next person you come across to name an assassin and see if he or she doesn't blurt out Booth's name.

## 4. CHARLES GUITEAU

Of all the presidential assassins, Charles Guiteau is the least known. (Just a reminder: he's the one who killed Garfield.) Elected 20th president of the United States in 1880, James A. Garfield was the low-key chief executive that the country needed following the tumultuous presidencies that preceded him. Guiteau, on the other hand, was far from low-key. By 1881, the 40-year-old Guiteau had tried his hand as a teacher, newspaper proprietor, lawyer, revivalist preacher, and businessman—and had failed at them all. He was such a loser that although he joined the notorious free-love, partner-swapping Oneida Community religious cult in 1861,

---

In 1915, football (soccer) was suspended in Europe because of World War I.

and was a member on and off for seven years, he still managed to leave it in 1868 with his virtue intact.

**A Legend in His Own Mind.** With his record of failure, self-delusion, and insane self-belief, Guiteau had just one option left to him—he entered politics. A staunch Garfield man, he wrote a number of supportive speeches (which no one ever heard) and pamphlets (which no one ever read). When Garfield won the presidency, Guiteau believed it was all due to his own masterly writings, so he wrote to Garfield requesting he be made ambassador to Vienna in return. When Garfield failed to reply, Guiteau bought a pistol and, on July 2, 1881, shot the president as he strolled through the old Baltimore and Potomac Railroad Station at the corner of Constitution and Sixth Street in Washington, D.C.

**Hang Him High.** Even as an assassin, Guiteau failed; his bullet only wounded Garfield. It was left to the doctors to finish Garfield off with their botched treatment. The president died two months later of blood poisoning. Guiteau's trial for murder was a true media circus, with the deranged assassin claiming from the dock that he was innocent because: a) God told him to do it; and b) it was the doctors who "killed" Garfield anyway. The court—and public opinion—disagreed. Charles Guiteau was hanged on June 30, 1882.

## 5. GAVRILO PRINCIP

Not many men could claim they single-handedly started a global conflict, but Gavrilo Princip did. We can all thank him for World War I. Born in 1894 in the melting pot of ethnic, religious, and political conflict that was the Balkans, Princip's life was dedicated to freeing his native Bosnia and Herzegovina from foreign rule. At the time, all of the Balkans—Serbia, Croatia, Bosnia, and Albania—were part of the Austro-Hungarian Empire. There were countless freedom-fighting terrorist groups dedicated to kicking out the Austrians, including Young Bosnia and the Black Hand. Princip's particular faction was called the Union or Death.

**Little Big Man.** The undistinguished son of a postman, Princip was small of stature and unassuming. He'd floated around the fringes of various terrorist groups without impressing the hard-headed Serbs who dominated most of these factions. But when it was announced that the heir to the Austro-Hungarian throne, Archduke Franz Ferdinand, was paying a visit to the Bosnian capital of Sarajevo in 1914, Princip saw his chance.

**A Very Warm Welcome.** When Franz Ferdinand arrived in Sarajevo on June 28, 1914, with his wife Sophie, their motorcade was attacked by bomb-wielding freedom fighters. Several people were injured, but the archduke escaped unhurt. Later that day, he decided to pay an unscheduled visit to a hospital and his car took a wrong turn. He literally bumped into Gavrilo Princip, who was sitting in an outdoor café. Seizing the opportunity, Princip opened fire and killed both the archduke and his wife.

**Give Me Liberty or Give Me Jail!** In the dueling parlance of the day, Austria demanded "satisfaction" from Serbia. Backed up by their fellow Slavs in Russia, Serbia refused, and the next thing you know...World War I. As for the 19-year-old Princip, he was sentenced to 20 years, the maximum penalty for someone his age. When he was 22 he underwent surgery to amputate an arm because of bone tuberculosis and died shortly thereafter on April 28, 1918.

*For Part II, See page 225.*

\*   \*   \*

### LADIES LAST

These women paid the ultimate price for their crimes:

• Poor Phoebe Harrius's claim to fame is being the last person burned at the stake...for making counterfeit currency in England—a crime that was considered high treason. She was incinerated at a stake in front of Newgate Prison in 1786.

• Ruth Ellis was the last woman hanged in England. Capital punishment was abolished shortly after her 1955 execution.

• The last women hanged for witchcraft in the American colonies were Mary Eastey, Martha Corey, Ann Pudeator, Mary Parker, Alice Parker, Wilmot Redd, and Margaret Scott on September 22, 1692, in Salem, Massachusetts.

# GOING OFF TRACK

*Steam engines first started transporting passengers and cargo
in the early 1800s, and it wasn't long before thieves
figured out how to exploit them for ill-gotten gains.*

## 1. THERE'S GOLD IN THAT THAR TRAIN!

When you think of train robberies, you probably think of the Old
West. But the most lucrative train robbery of the 19th century
took place in England, and it didn't involve horses or blazing six-
guns. Instead, the robbery was the culmination of great planning
and execution. Edward Agar and William Pierce masterminded
the plot, recruiting a couple of railroad employees and others as
needed. They knew that, on May 15, 1855, three boxes of gold
would be traveling by train across England. For the robbery, they
boarded the train and, with keys made from wax impressions, were
able to open the railroad safes, remove 200 pounds of gold from
sealed boxes, fill the boxes with lead shot as a decoy and seal them
up again, and then saunter off the train at the Dover station, making their escape. For a year they remained uncaught and may have
gotten away with the crime, except for one problem: Agar had
been arrested for writing bad checks and sentenced to serve time
in an Australian penal colony. He instructed Pierce to pay the
mother of his child £7,000 (almost $750,000 in today's dollars);
when she didn't get the money, the woman went to the railroad
managers and told them what she knew about the robbery. Agar
corroborated her story and turned state's evidence, resulting in
long sentences for his co-conspirators. Authorities were able to
recover only £2,000 worth of gold. The rest is still missing.

## 2. JESSE JAMES: THE FIRST ROBBERY

As Confederate guerrillas, brothers Frank and Jesse James engaged
in looting, killing Union soldiers and civilians, and destroying
property during the Civil War. After the war ended, they formed a
gang and turned to bank robbery, sometimes killing bystanders in
the process. (In letters sent to sympathetic newspaper editors, they
claimed that they were avenging the South's defeat.) In 1873, the
gang turned to robbing trains, and their first heist took place near

First city in Europe to pave its streets: Florence, Italy, in 1339.

Adair, Iowa. Wearing Ku Klux Klan costumes, they derailed a train, which killed the engineer, and then they terrorized the dazed and wounded passengers into giving up their valuables. Between that and the train's safe, the gang netted $2,337, which was more than enough to inspire them to try again. Despite cultivating an image as modern-day Robin Hoods, the James brothers kept most of their ill-gotten gains for themselves.

### 3. WANT A LITTLE MONEY WITH YOUR DYNAMITE?

Butch Cassidy and the Sundance Kid have been a part of American folklore for more than a century. The first movie to tell of their exploits was released in 1903, but it was the 1969 movie starring Robert Redford and Paul Newman that immortalized the pair. The real Butch (Robert Leroy Parker) and Sundance (Harry Longabaugh) headed a gang called the Wild Bunch, who robbed banks and trains mostly in Wyoming. They started out in 1896 as small-time hoods, often wearing cloth napkins pilfered from local restaurants. When they discovered the magic of dynamite, they began to use it with increasing regularity to open safes, create shock and awe among train crews, derail trains, and destroy cars and engines. On June 2, 1899, they got a little too explosion-happy after commandeering a Union Pacific train. When mail clerks refused to open the door, the gang blew it open, leaving the clerks too deafened and dazed to remember the combination to the train's safe. So the impatient gang decided to blow open the safe. Unfortunately, they also blew up the walls and ceiling of the train car, launching $20,000 skyward and damaging many of the remaining bills in the $30,000 that they escaped with.

### 4. "SOMEONE HAS STOLEN OUR TRAIN!"

On April 12, 1862, conductor William Fuller and his crew had just sat down for breakfast at a stop called Big Shanty outside Atlanta, Georgia, when he saw his train rolling out of the station. Fuller couldn't send a telegram ahead to stop the train—the little outpost didn't have a telegraph station. It wouldn't have mattered anyway. The thieves were 22 Union army spies led by James Andrews, a Kentucky smuggler who also did espionage work for the North. The men, posing as passengers, had boarded the train in small groups. Their mission was to cut telegraph wires, dyna-

---

You're so vain: Rembrandt painted more than 80 self-portraits.

mite bridges, and sabotage tracks to keep the Confederate army from sending reinforcements and supplies as the Union army marched toward Chattanooga, Tennessee.

For more than 80 miles, Andrews and his men did what they could to throw off the chase, but Fuller and his crew switched trains to get around obstacles and followed on foot. Near the end, they barreled along the tracks full speed in a train going in reverse. Andrews and his men ran out of fuel a few miles from Chattanooga, and they scattered into the woods, hoping for escape. Eventually, they were all caught (as were two conspirators who missed the train because they'd overslept). Andrews and seven others were hanged and buried in an unmarked grave, six were traded to the North as prisoners of war, and eight escaped from their prison camp to safety. Secretary of War Edwin M. Stanton awarded Medals of Honor to six of Andrews's men—some of the first such medals ever given out in U.S. history.

## 5. BEZDANY RAID

"I haven't got money and I must have it for the ends I pursue." So wrote Józef Piłsudski in a letter to a friend on September 26, 1908...right before his team of Polish revolutionaries embarked on a daring train robbery. Their target? A mail train carrying tax money from Warsaw to St. Petersburg, Russia. (Russia, Prussia, and Austria had conquered and divided up Poland in the late 1700s, and Piłsudski was leading a charge to free his people.) That evening, the 16 men and four women boarded the train in two waves. Then at the tiny station in Bezdany, Lithuania, they sprang into action—one group captured the station and cut telecommunications wires; the other assaulted the train with guns and bombs. Using dynamite, they ripped open the fortified mail car and stuffed the money into cloth bags. Then they escaped in different directions and all got away. The haul was a spectacular 200,812 rubles, more than $4 million in today's dollars—a fortune in impoverished Eastern Europe. It kept Piłsudski's paramilitary organization in good stead for many years. In 1918, Poland became one country again, and Piłsudski was its first leader.

## 6. ENGLAND'S GREAT TRAIN ROBBERY

At about 3:00 a.m. on August 9, 1963, engineer Jack Mills saw a

---

Sandalwood thimbles were once kept in fabric stores to keep moths away.

red signal light at a crossing near Buckinghamshire, England, and slowed his mail train to a stop. The signal was phony—the green light had been covered up and replaced with a battery-powered red one. So began one of England's greatest train heists, in which 15 thieves led by an ex-con named Bruce Reynolds made off with £2.6 million (about $61.5 million in modern American dollars). After neutralizing the crew, the men transferred 124 sacks of currency from the train to a waiting truck and escaped into the night.

They weren't on the run for long. One by one, the conspirators were picked up, victims of their own carelessness. One attracted suspicion when he paid his rent three months in advance. Others hadn't bothered wearing gloves, leaving behind a wealth of fingerprint clues. Twelve of the bandits were quickly picked up and sentenced to up to 30 years. One—Ronnie Biggs—escaped from prison and went to Paris, Australia, and Brazil, where he lived for years before returning to England, where he as rearrested in 2001.

\*　　\*　　\*

### WANTED MORE DEAD THAN ALIVE

Elmer McCurdy wasn't a nice guy, and had few friends—mostly thieves like himself. In 1911, he robbed $46 from a train and died in an Oklahoma barn after a shootout with a posse. When no one claimed him, the mortician embalmed McCurdy with an arsenic-based preservative and charged people a nickel (dropped into McCurdy's gaping mouth) to see the body of "the Bandit Who Wouldn't Give Up." After seeing the profit potential, McCurdy's brothers showed up to claim the corpse for "proper burial." One "brother" was a con man who took the body and exhibited it in the West. Over the next 60 years, McCurdy's body—now coated in wax—was sold and resold to a succession of wax museums and carnivals. In 1976, The Six Million Dollar Man came to the Long Beach Nu-Pike Amusement Park to film a scene in the "Laff in the Dark" fun house. Asked to move what appeared to be a wax dummy hanging from a noose, a technician accidentally broke off an arm, revealing mummified skin and an arm bone. After six decades of amusing adults and scaring kids, Elmer McCurdy was laid to rest in Guthrie, Oklahoma.

Albert Einstein is the only scientist to have a ticker-tape parade in New York City (1921).

# RENAMED

*22 countries whose names have changed over the years.*

| NOW | THEN |
|---|---|
| **1.** Bangladesh | **1.** East Pakistan |
| **2.** Zimbabwe | **2.** Southern Rhodesia |
| **3.** Myanmar | **3.** Burma |
| **4.** Suriname | **4.** Dutch Guiana |
| **5.** Benin | **5.** Dahomey |
| **6.** Thailand | **6.** Siam |
| **7.** Central African Republic | **7.** Ubangi-Shari |
| **8.** Zambia | **8.** Northern Rhodesia |
| **9.** Vanuatu | **9.** New Hebrides |
| **10.** Botswana | **10.** Bechuanaland |
| **11.** Malawi | **11.** Nyasaland |
| **12.** Lesotho | **12.** Basutoland |
| **13.** Indonesia | **13.** Dutch East Indies |
| **14.** Sri Lanka | **14.** Ceylon |
| **15.** Iran | **15.** Persia |
| **16.** Ghana | **16.** The Gold Coast |
| **17.** Colombia | **17.** New Granada |
| **18.** Cambodia | **18.** Kampuchea |
| **19.** Belarus | **19.** Belorussia |
| **20.** Belize | **20.** British Honduras |
| **21.** Burkina Faso | **21.** Upper Volta |
| **22.** Mali | **22.** French Sudan |

# LAST CALL BEFORE THE REVOLUTION

*In which we ask, "Which came first—the whiskey or the rebellion?"*

For centuries, local watering holes—normally places of good cheer and fraternity—have played an important role in holding together the social fabric of communities. There have been a few that, instead, served as breeding grounds for revolt.

## 1. CONKEY'S TAVERN, PELHAM, MASSACHUSETTS (1786)

**The Uprising:** In the years after the American Revolution, western Massachusetts was in an economic depression. The region's farmers, in particular, were feeling the pinch due to high taxes, debt collections, and land seizures. Led by Daniel Shays, a veteran of the Revolution, a group of farmers—regulars at William Conkey's local tavern—launched an uprising against the state government. Calling themselves the "Regulators," Shays and company headed first to the state supreme court in Springfield to try to halt foreclosures, then tried to seize control of a nearby federal armory.

A team of militiamen organized by the Massachusetts governor eventually quelled what came to be known as "Shays' Rebellion," but the uprising had a lasting effect on governmental reform and became a turning point in the creation of the U.S. Constitution. And it all started among a bunch of farmers out for a beer.

**Open for Business?** No. The original Conkey's was torn down in 1880. A reproduction of the old building, along with a few surviving artifacts, can be found in—of all places—the American Museum in Bath, England.

## 2. MONTGOMERY'S TAVERN, TORONTO, CANADA (1837)

**The Uprising:** The causes of Canada's Rebellions of 1837 are many and complicated. A general atmosphere of political upheaval

---

A nautical mile is 796 feet longer than a land mile.

in the British colonies of Upper Canada (present-day southern Ontario) and Lower Canada (present-day southern Quebec and Labrador) created issues ranging from ethnic tensions and regional disharmony to economic reform and political representation.

Confusing as it all was, one thing is for certain: the most turbulent flashpoint in the Upper Canada Rebellion was centered in this otherwise unassuming tavern on Yonge Street in downtown Toronto. It was here that an armed group of rebels—estimated at 500 strong—organized a march to seize the arms and ammunition stored at Toronto's city hall with the intent of overthrowing the ruling power in favor of responsible government. An army of British troops and Loyalist volunteers, more than twice the size of the rebel army, easily overpowered the disorganized forces. Though the uprising failed, it did eventually lead to greater autonomy in the Canadian colonies.

**Open for Business?** No. At the end of the rebellion, British soldiers burned Montgomery's Tavern to the ground. Though the original building no longer exists, the location was designated as a National Historic Site in 1925. Today, the spot is occupied by Postal Station K, and displays a memorial plaque commemorating the uprising.

### 3. MUSEUM TAVERN, LONDON, ENGLAND (1850s)

**The Uprising:** Standing just opposite the British Museum in the Bloomsbury section of London, this tavern is a kind of museum itself. Technically, the only uprising fomented in this tavern was in the mind of expatriate German political philosopher Karl Marx. During the 1850s, he used it and the nearby British Library to formulate and write down his ideas for a mass proletariat revolt against the capitalist ruling class. After hours of reading on the subject of political economy at the library, Marx would slake his thirst at the tavern, where he compiled the notes that formed the basis of the "ism" that would bear his name.

**Open for Business?** Yes. The classic Victorian pub is a popular spot for tourists visiting the British Museum and for locals in search of a good English ale. The Museum Tavern was also the haunt of other notable British writers such as J. B. Priestley and Sir Arthur Conan Doyle, but none as revolutionary as Mr. Marx.

## 4. BÜRGERBRÄUKELLER, MUNICH, GERMANY (1923 and 1939)

**The Uprising:** This German beer parlor was the site of two separate events inextricably linked in history. The first took place in November 1923 when a young Adolf Hitler, in an attempt to restore German pride after the humiliating defeat and diplomatic concessions of World War I, led a group of upstart Nazis in an attempted coup d'etat called the "Munich Beer Hall Putsch." The revolt was quelled and Hitler was thrown in jail. During his time behind bars, he completed his book *Mien Kampf* (*My Struggle*), which essentially defined the Nazi Party's philosophy. Ten years later, Hitler would take control of Germany.

While in power, Hitler continued to acknowledge the importance of the *putsch,* or coup, by holding annual gatherings at the Bürgerbräukeller. At the 1939 get-together, a German woodworker and opponent of Nazism, Johann Georg Elser, tried to assassinate Hitler by planting a bomb in the beer hall. But Mother Nature intervened: bad weather forced Hitler to take the train back to Berlin earlier than scheduled, 13 minutes before the bomb detonated, killing eight and wounding 60. Elser was captured and sent to the Dachau concentration camp, where he was eventually killed.

**Open for Business?** No. Elser's bomb destroyed the Bürgerbräukeller's main gallery. What remained of the building was demolished after World War II.

\*     \*     \*

## COUNTDOWN: THE OLDEST BARS IN THE U.S.

**10.** Bell in Hand, 1795, Boston, MA

**9.** Warren Tavern, 1780, Charlestown, MA

**8.** The Tavern, 1779, Abingdon, VA

**7.** Griswold Inn Taproom, 1776, Essex, CT

**6.** The Horse You Came In On Saloon, 1775, Baltimore, MD

**5.** Jean Lafitte's Blacksmith Shop, 1772, New Orleans, LA

**4.** Fraunces Tavern, 1762, New York, NY

**3.** The Pirate's House, 1753, Savannah, GA

**2.** Middleton's Tavern, 1750, Annapolis, MD

**1.** The White Horse Tavern, 1673, Newport, RI

# KABOOM!

*Four stories of explosive materials that should have
been handled with caution—but weren't.*

They may have been minor disasters in the grand scheme of
history, but they might easily have been prevented if the
deadly combination of volatile chemicals hadn't been
mixed with bad management, bad judgment, or just plain bad
luck.

## 1. THE TEXAS CITY DISASTER (1947)

The Germans started making ammonium nitrate, one of the components of TNT, during World War II. It was found to be an excellent fertilizer, too, and in 1945, American factories started making
their own—and treating it with no more care than garden soil.

More than 2,000 tons of the stuff was being unloaded from
the cargo ship *Grandcamp* at the port of Texas City on April 16,
1947, when a small fire started in the hold. Rather than douse it
with water, the captain ordered his men to "steam the hold," a
common shipboard firefighting technique where the hold was
sealed and steam from the ship's boiler pumped in to smother the
fire. Working with most cargo, this would be perfectly safe, but on
the *Grandcamp* the steam first melted the fertilizer, then started a
runaway chain reaction.

**In Hot Water.** As the hold heated up, the water around the ship
started to boil. Billows of nitrous oxide gas—the same gas given
off by nitroglycerine when it's about to explode—attracted a large
crowd on the pier. At 9:00 a.m., the ship exploded, shattering
windows in Houston, some 40 miles away. The sound was heard
more than 160 miles away.

**Collateral Damage.** Bits of the ship were later found more than
two and a half miles away, buried six feet into the ground. The
blast incapacitated Texas City's fire department, leaving no one
to fight the fires it started, one of them in a neighboring chemical
plant. It knocked two neighboring ships into each other, fusing
them together. One of the ships was also loaded with fertilizer,

which caught fire, and though workers tried to cut the ship free and tow it away from the port, it exploded.

**Casualty List.** The blasts and fires destroyed a third of Texas City. As many as 600 people were killed and 4,000 injured. To give some perspective on the size of the explosion, two tourist planes that were circling the scene a half mile above the *Grandcamp* were completely destroyed in the blast. The Texas City disaster was the worst industrial accident in American history.

## 2. THE PEPCON DISASTER

The Pacific Engineering Production Company, or PEPCON, had its plant on eight acres of desert outside the Las Vegas, Nevada, suburb of Henderson. Their sole product was ammonium perchlorate, the fuel in solid rocket boosters used on missiles and the space shuttle. By 1988, they'd been in business for 30 years without any incidents. As a result, ammonium perchlorate wasn't considered particularly dangerous. But on May 4 of that year, the plant had an unusually large amount stored—8.5 million pounds—because the *Challenger* disaster had temporarily halted space shuttle flights. A welding torch in a drying shed ignited the shed's fiberglass structure, and despite attempts to put it out, the fire quickly spread.

**Big Bang #1.** The first explosion happened 10 to 20 minutes later, when 55-gallon plastic drums of ammonium perchlorate stored next to the shed caught fire. After that first explosion, the plant's 75 employees gave up fighting the fire and ran out into the desert. The employees of the Kidd & Company marshmallow factory 500 feet away also evacuated when they heard the explosion. Only two PEPCON employees didn't make it out. One was in a wheelchair, and the other stopped to call the fire department. The call was unnecessary: the chief of the Henderson Fire Department had seen a column of smoke—which would eventually reach several thousand feet and be visible for more than a hundred miles—and immediately ordered all his units to the plant.

**Great Ball of Fire.** As the fire department approached, the fire in the plant became a massive hundred-foot-wide fireball, spreading to the main area where the ammonium perchlorate was stored.

Crocodile-dung suppositories were used as contraceptives in ancient Egypt.

The plant exploded, shattering the windshield of the fire chief's car. Warned by one of the fleeing plant workers that there was imminent danger of further explosions, the chief ordered his department to pull back, even though most of them had already turned around.

**Big Bang #2.** Four minutes later, there was a second major explosion. Witnesses saw a visible shock wave come toward them across the ground. The blast blew in the rest of the fire department's car windows, injuring several firefighters with flying glass. There were a total of seven explosions that day; the two big ones registered 3.0 and 3.5 on the Richter scale. They destroyed cars, knocked buildings off their foundations, downed power lines, blew doors off their hinges, shattered hundreds of windows in a 10-mile radius—and left a 200-foot-long, 15-foot-deep crater. The neighboring marshmallow factory was completely destroyed. The explosions also ruptured a natural-gas pipeline under the plant, spewing a jet of flame into the air.

**Duh!** In FEMA's report about the accident, they concluded, "Although not previously considered to be explosive, this incident obviously gives testimony to the fact that ammonium perchlorate can explode." A settlement involving dozens of insurance companies and over 50 law firms was arrived at in the end: $71 million was divided among the victims and their families. The company never rebuilt the Henderson site. PEPCON changed its name to Western Electrochemical Company and built a new ammonium perchlorate plant in Cedar City, Utah, where there's been only one deadly explosion to date.

### 3. THE UFA TRAIN DISASTER

A major natural-gas pipeline runs through the Ural Mountains in Russia. So does the Trans-Siberian Railroad. These two interacted in the worst way imaginable on the evening of June 4, 1989, when engineers on the pipeline noticed a sudden drop in pressure. Rather than investigating, they increased the flow of gas to bring the pressure back up to its previous level. The dip had been caused by a burst pipe, so when the flow of gas was increased, liquefied propane and butane poured out of the pipe and rolled toward the train tracks a half mile away. The railway ran through a valley in the mountains, and the fuel gathered there, forming a dense—and highly flammable—lake of gas.

**It's a Blast.** At 1:15 in the morning, three hours after the pipe burst, two trains, going in opposite directions, passed each other in the valley. No one knows what ignited the cloud—it could have been a cigarette or sparks from the tracks—but the fuel exploded with the force of a 10-kiloton bomb, just slightly less than the power of the bomb that was dropped on Hiroshima. The fireball destroyed 37 train cars, reducing seven to ash, and killed more than half of the 1,200 people on those trains. The official death count was 645, but some estimates are as high as 780; many bodies were incinerated by the fireball. Given the intensity of the fire, few bodies were found, making a final count impossible. Hundreds of survivors required hospitalization. Many of the dead were children who were on their way to summer camps near the Black Sea.

**Aftermath.** It was the worst train disaster in Soviet history. President Mikhail Gorbachev, speaking shortly after the accident, blamed it on "mismanagement, irresponsibility, disorganization." Coming as it did on the heels of Chernobyl, this second disaster caused widespread speculation about the imminent demise of the Soviet Union.

## 4. THE ENSCHEDE FIREWORKS DISASTER

Fireworks are dangerous to manufacture, but they're almost as dangerous to store. In the small Dutch city of Enschede, SE Fireworks had a warehouse in a densely populated working-class neighborhood. Most townspeople, including the mayor, were unaware of the warehouse's existence; when it had been built in 1977, it was well outside city limits, but urban sprawl had encroached and surrounded it in the years since. On May 13, 2000, the warehouse would make itself known—and cease to exist at the same time.

**Disturbing the Peace.** It was a Saturday, so most residents of the neighborhood were relaxing at home while a fire started outside the warehouse. Some residents reported hearing the sound of fireworks going off—one even called the police to complain about the noise. Firefighters responded to the blaze and were attempting to put it out when the 177 tons of fireworks inside exploded,

---

...21 missions, four presidios (forts), and three pueblos (civilian settlements).

killing four firefighters and 19 other people, and injuring 947 more. It flattened most of the neighborhood, destroying 400 apartments and damaging 1,000 more. The blast was felt nearly 20 miles away.

**Justice Department.** The warehouse had passed a safety inspection only the previous Wednesday, but an inquiry into the explosion found the warehouse's two owners guilty of violating safety regulations in their methods of storing the fireworks; they were sentenced to 15 months' imprisonment. A local man was convicted of setting the fire and sentenced to 15 years in jail, but his conviction was overturned in 2003. The exact cause of the fire is still unknown.

\* \* \*

## WATCH OUT

The following volcanoes have a history of large and destructive eruptions, recent geological activity, and are located near heavily populated areas—from tens to hundreds of thousands of people. Known as decade volcanoes, they have been identified for study by the United Nations–sponsored International Decade for Natural Disaster Reduction. The organization seeks to educate the public about the dangers presented by the volcanoes and hopes to reduce the severity of any potential future natural disaster.

1. Avachinsky-Koryaksky, Kamchatka
2. Colima Volcano, Mexico
3. Mount Etna, Italy
4. Galeras Volcano, Colombia
5. Mauna Loa, Hawaii
6. Merapi Volcano, Indonesia
7. Niragongo Volcano, Democratic Republic of the Congo
8. Mount Rainier, Washington
9. Sakurajima Volcano, Japan
10. Santa Maria/Santiaguito Volcano, Guatemala
11. Santorini Volcano, Greece
12. Taal Volcano, Philippines
13. Teide Volcano, Spain
14. Ulawun Volcano, Papua New Guinea
15. Unzen Volcano, Japan
16. Vesuvius Volcano, Italy

# ALL ABOUT EVA

*Eve made her mark by being the first woman ever,*
*but as this story shows, Evas can change the world too.*

## 1. EVA BRAUN

In 1929, Eva Braun was a respectable 17-year-old Catholic girl when she met Adolf Hitler. Two years later, she had become his long-term mistress. Even during the privations of World War II, Braun lived a sheltered and privileged existence, watching TV and reading romance novels, surrounded by furnishings confiscated from Jewish and European royal families. Historians still argue about how much Braun knew about Hitler's atrocities and whether she shared his murderous prejudices, politics, and tactics.

The Führer kept his relationship with Braun a secret from the German people because, he reasoned, German women wouldn't support him as passionately if they thought he was already taken. The couple did eventually marry in 1945 but, with the Russian army closing in, they committed suicide just 40 hours after exchanging vows.

## 2. EVA "EVITA" PERÓN

A champion of labor, women, and the poor, Eva Perón gave her husband Juan Perón's Argentine dictatorship a friendly and charismatic face. Juan Perón admired Adolf Hitler and Benito Mussolini, established friendly relations with Francisco Franco's fascist regime in Spain, and after World War II knowingly provided a safe haven for a huge colony of Nazi war criminals. While "Evita" ("Little Eva" in Spanish) charmed the country with acts of charity and speeches about justice and freedom, her husband fired professors, closed universities, arrested dissidents, and closed down hundreds of publications.

When Eva died of cancer in 1952, she was so beloved by the public that Juan had her body embalmed and put on permanent public display...until a coup ran him out of the country in 1955 and he had to leave Eva's body behind. Trying to wipe out all traces of Perónism, the new leaders secretly shipped Eva's body to Milan, Italy, and had it buried under the name "Maria Maggi." It was dug up 16 years later and flown to Juan Perón's home in

---

July 7, 1977: Hanako, a scarlet koi fish, died at the age of 226.

Spanish exile, where he and his third wife cohabitated with the corpse for two years until he regained the Argentine presidency. Then Eva Perón was laid to rest yet again, this time for good in Buenos Aries.

## GOOD VS. EVA

Despite the examples of the two most famous Evas, not all of them went bad:

• **Eva Ekeblad**, an 18th-century Swedish noble and scientist, discovered how to make flour, booze, and face powder out of potatoes, saving scarce grain for food and her fellow Swedes from starvation.

• In March 1921, **Eva Beatrice Dykes** became the first African American woman to complete all the requirements to earn a PhD. She was awarded her degree a couple of months later.

• During her short career (just 10 years before a brain tumor took her life), artist **Eva Hesse** made a name for herself in the 1960s by injecting feminine themes into the traditionally masculine minimalist genre. Hesse was one of the few sculptors who managed to make the tricky transition from minimalism to post-minimalism. According to Hesse, "The best way to beat discrimination in art is by art."

• **Eva Narcissus Boyd** became the singer Little Eva—she taught 1960s teens how to do a dance called the Loco-Motion with a song of the same name.

• Also in the 1960s, **Eva Gabor** entertained America with her multiple marriages and a role as a city-loving rural transplant on the TV show *Green Acres*.

• In 1986, **Eva Burrows** from Australia became the 13th person to hold the post of general of the international Salvation Army.

\*     \*     \*

"When the rich think about the poor, they have poor ideas."

—Evita Perón

# STREAKERS!

*If winning is everything, then these six sports personalities are at the top of their respective classes. Each took winning to new lengths with the longest streaks of victory ever seen.*

## 1. HORSE RACING: KINCSEM

The fastest horse of her time—and maybe in all of history—was Kincsem (1874–87). Her name means "my treasure" in Hungarian. Her coat was brown and she wasn't much to look at, so she didn't attract much attention—at least at first. Foaled in Hungary, Kincsem belonged to Ernst von Blaskovich, who first raced the filly as a two-year-old in 1876. Surprisingly, she won, and kept on winning.

During the 1876 season, Kincsem raced in Hungary, Austria, and Germany. She competed against both colts and fillies and won every contest she entered. As a three-year-old, the filly began to attract large crowds when her unbeaten streak extended to 17 victories over the best horses in Europe. Remaining unbeaten in her fourth and fifth years of racing, Kincsem became a celebrity in Europe, especially after she captured big trophies in England and France.

Royalty, including the Austrian emperor Franz Joseph, were among her fans. Newspapers described Kincsem as having the temperament of a demanding movie star—she wouldn't travel without her favorite cat, or drink any water that didn't come from a well at her home stables. By the time Kincsem retired from racing, her streak had extended to 54 wins in 54 starts. Her record for consecutive wins stood until 1955 when the colt Camarero won 56 races in a row in Puerto Rico. But many historians contend that Camarero isn't comparable, since he never ran against the top horses of his day as Kincsem did.

## 2. BOXING: JIMMY WILDE

Jimmy Wilde (1892–1969) was a Welsh kid working in the mines when he got his start as a "booth fighter" at the age of 16, entering competitions in boxing booths put up on vacant lots or at fairgrounds. It's estimated that he participated in as many as 500 exhibition fights before he began professional boxing. Wilde was

---

Goulash, a beef stew, was invented by ninth-century Hungarian cowboys.

only 5' 2", and usually weighed in at little more than 100 pounds. The contrast between his skinny, sickly appearance and his explosive and accurate punching skills amazed spectators, and earned him nicknames like "the Mighty Atom" and "the Ghost with a Hammer in His Hand."

Wilde fought professionally for the first time on December 26, 1910, a fight that ended in a draw. He won his next fight six days later, and stayed undefeated until 1915, even though he often took on much heavier opponents. Wilde's unbeaten streak lasted for 103 fights, a record that's never come close to being met. And after his streak ended, he went right back to winning, becoming the World Flyweight Champion in 1916; he did not lose another fight until 1918.

When the Mighty Atom retired, he'd recorded 137 wins, 99 of them by knockout. He lost only five fights in his professional career. Pound for pound, Jimmy Wilde has been hailed by many as the greatest boxer of all time.

## 3. BASEBALL: JOE DiMAGGIO

If Joe DiMaggio (1914–99) had become a crab fisherman like his father wanted, baseball would have missed out on one of its biggest heroes. But the smell of dead crabs made Joe nauseous, so he quit fishing to play shortstop for the Pacific Coast League's San Francisco Seals. From May through July of 1933, the 19-year-old DiMaggio set a minor league record with a 61-game hitting streak, recording at least one base hit per game. In 1934, the New York Yankees bought his contract from the Seals, and even his father agreed that baseball was Joe's calling.

In 1936, DiMaggio debuted at center field for the Yankees and became known as "Joltin' Joe" (for his batting prowess) and "the Yankee Clipper" (comparing his speed to fast sailing ships). By the end of 1940, he'd won two batting titles and the Most Valuable Player Award. In 1941, DiMaggio put together a hitting streak that's never been matched: 56 straight games. On May 15, batting against the Chicago White Sox, DiMaggio drove in a run with a base hit. He continued to get a hit in every game he played well into July.

America took notice. During the streak, headlines and special radio bulletins told the country whether or not Joe got a hit that day. Members of Congress appointed a special page boy to keep them informed on DiMaggio's hitting status, and the popular Les Brown band recorded the song "Joltin' Joe DiMaggio," which became a nationwide hit. The Cleveland Indians finally kept DiMaggio hitless on July 17. But he immediately had another 16-game hitting streak and led the Yankees to the World Series title. After he retired in 1951, DiMaggio stayed in the headlines with his marriage to Marilyn Monroe, but when they wed in 1954, baseball's hitting hero was, by far, the bigger star.

## 4. GOLF: BYRON NELSON

John Byron Nelson Jr. (1912–2006) began his golf career in Fort Worth, Texas, as a caddie at the Glen Garden Country Club. When the 12-year-old took the job, caddies weren't allowed to play at the club, so Nelson snuck onto the course at night. He'd place a white handkerchief over the golf hole so he could find it in the dark.

In 1932, Nelson began touring as a golf pro and won a couple of small tournaments, but it wasn't until 1937 that he won a major tournament at the Masters in Augusta, Georgia. It's said that his wife, Louise, encouraged Nelson to continue playing golf until he could afford to buy the ranch that he dreamed of. Her encouragement paid off when Nelson followed up his 1937 Masters victory with wins at the 1939 U.S. Open and the 1940 PGA Championship.

In 1941, World War II sent some pro golfers overseas, but Nelson remained a civilian because of a blood clotting problem and, during that time, he kept improving his game. By 1945, he'd developed such a consistently powerful swing that he was often compared to a machine. That year, the 33-year-old Nelson was unstoppable, taking victories in 11 consecutive tournaments—a record that's never been matched. He won 18 tournaments in all, and compiled an average score per round of 68.33—a record that held up until Tiger Woods broke it in 2000 with an average score of 68.17. Nelson's winning streak made 1945 the greatest year for any male pro golfer, and, in 1946, with all of his winnings, he was able to retire to his dream ranch.

## 5. TENNIS: MARTINA NAVRATILOVA

The greatest winning streak in professional tennis belongs to women, thanks to Martina Navratilova. Born in Prague, Czechoslovakia, in 1956, Navratilova won the Czech national championship when she was just 15 years old. At 17, she won her first professional singles title in Orlando, Florida—and that was also when she fell in love with the United States. She defected from her communist homeland in 1975 and became a U.S. citizen.

At first, Navratilova was more famous for her addiction to American fast food than for winning tournaments. Few thought she'd ever win a major tournament—something many top tennis players have accomplished as teenagers. But after being mocked as "the Great Wide Hope," Navratilova embarked on a tough fitness routine that gave her the power to launch an aggressive barrage against her opponents, as well as the endurance to keep it up.

In 1978, at age 21, Navratilova finally won a major tournament with a victory at Wimbledon, but it was in the 1980s that her career really took off. In 1983, she won again at Wimbledon and then went on to victories at six straight major tournaments. In 1984, she won her first Grand Slam, claiming the doubles titles (with partner Pam Shriver) at all four major tournaments held that year. She also strung together the longest match winning streak in modern tennis history, a stunning 74 matches in a row. To get some idea of Navratilova's achievement, the longest match winning streak in men's tennis is 46, held by Guillermo Vilas of Argentina.

## 6. SQUASH: JAHANGIR KHAN

Back in the 1830s, British schoolboys developed the sport of squash, which is played with a racket and a soft (squashy) ball on an enclosed court similar to a racquetball court. In the 1980s, squash experienced a worldwide surge of popularity when a great Pakistani athlete dominated the game.

Born into a family of international squash stars, Jahangir (whose name means "world conqueror") Khan carried on the family tradition by winning the 1979 World Amateur title at just 15 years old. At 17, Khan became the youngest player to win the World Open.

Keeping himself extremely fit, Khan could exhaust his oppo-

---

Medieval lingo: those tall, narrow slits in castle walls were called "loopholes."

nents with long rallies before finishing them off with a devastating shot to the back of the court. His World Open win in 1981 launched an incredible run of 555 consecutive victories that lasted five years and eight months, the longest unbeaten streak in professional sports history. Khan finally lost the 1986 World Open in Toulouse, France, but after pointing out that "every winning streak will have to end sometime," he rallied by going unbeaten for another nine months. During his career (which ended in 1993), he also won ten straight British Opens—another record that has yet to be matched.

\* \* \*

## WINNING BUSINESS STREAKS

**1. Coney Island, New York.** In the early 1900s, Coney Island—a peninsula in Brooklyn, New York—and the beach attached to it were a haven for city residents sweltering in the summer heat. Just a train ride away was a refreshing seaside town that boasted rides, restaurants, and sideshows. So, thought Polish immigrant Nathan Handwerker in 1916, why not open up a hot dog stand and make a few dollars off the tourists? But it was New York, and hot dogs were a staple. He'd have to set himself apart. So Handwerker charged 5¢ for each weiner—half as much as his competitors—and hired people wearing white lab coats and stethoscopes (to make them look like distinguished doctors) to stand around eating his hot dogs and declaring them the best in the city. And thus, Nathan's Famous, *the* most famous hot dog chain in New York, was born.

**2. Key West, Florida.** In 1977, while lounging on the sand in Key West, Florida, Jimmy Buffett wrote a song that would change his life: "Margaritaville" is Buffett's best-selling single. It's also the name of a chain of restaurants and a satellite radio station. Despite his slacker image of "wastin' away again in Margaritaville," Buffett turned his laid-back lifestyle into a fortune any ambitious capitalist would be jealous of: he's worth more than $40 million, was named #97 on *Vanity Fair*'s 2009 list of the 100 Most Influential People in the World, and still sells out concerts. His philosophy: "If life gives you limes, make margaritas."

April 20, 1841: First detective story (Poe's "Murders in the Rue Morgue") is published.

# CAR TALK

*Automobile records and firsts.*

**1. FIRST POLICE CAR.** Officer Louis Mueller Sr. operated the first police car in Akron, Ohio, in 1899, when he was assigned to pick up an intoxicated man. Run by electricity, the vehicle could reach a speed of only 16 miles per hour and travel 30 miles before needing to recharge its battery. The car cost $2,400 and was equipped with electric lights, a stretcher, and gongs for a siren.

**2. FIRST SOLAR-POWERED CAR.** When William G. Cobb of General Motors showcased the first solar car at the Chicago Powerama convention in 1955, there was one small problem—at only 15 inches high, it was too small to drive. Seventeen years later, the International Rectifier Company unveiled something a little more realistic: a 1912 Baker electric car converted to run on solar power.

**3. FIRST LAND-SPEED RECORD.** French race-car driver Count Gaston de Chasseloup-Laubat (better known as the "Electric Count") set the world's first land-speed record when he raced his electric car down a deserted road near Paris, France, in 1898...at the "incredible" speed of 39.24 mph. The count was not satisfied with his feat, though, so tried again in January 1899, screeching down the road and breaking his own record with a new speed of 43.64 mph.

**4. FIRST GAS PUMP.** On September 5, 1885, Sylvanus Bowser of Fort Wayne, Indiana, delivered the first gasoline pump to a local gas station. Bowser had manufactured a pump tank that held one barrel of gasoline. Thirteen year later, pumps were manufactured that could draw fuel from an underground tank.

**5. FIRST SANCTIONED DRAG RACE.** On April 10, 1949, California street racers and hot-rodders gathered in the town of Goleta, north of Santa Barbara. Their race would take place on an airstrip that the military used to train pilots. Complete with a flagman at the starting line and another at the finish a quarter-mile away, the fastest local roadsters showed up to race each other side-by-side. Thousands of spectators also came and watched the 10-second race.

---

The earliest known bracelets, anklets, and rings date back to about 2500 BC.

# E.T. PLAYLIST

*What kind of music should a discerning space alien be listening to? Here's what the good folks at NASA suggested over 30 years ago.*

In 1977, NASA launched two unmanned *Voyager* spacecrafts to explore the outer reaches of the galaxy. Both ships carried a kind of interstellar audio greeting from earthlings to any alien life-form that might be encountered. On board each spacecraft was a gold-plated phonograph record containing songs selected by a NASA committee chaired by cosmologist and best-selling author Carl Sagan. These songs were chosen as the sounds that best represented the musical diversity of our planet. Here's hoping that the aliens can get their hands (tentacles?) on an old-fashioned turntable so they can actually play the thing. If they do, here's what they'd hear.

• Bach's Brandenburg Concerto No. 2 in F, First Movement, performed by the Munich Bach Orchestra; Karl Richter, conductor

• Javanese gamelan music

• Senegalese percussion

• Zaire pygmy girls' initiation song

• Australian aborigine songs "Morning Star" and "Devil Bird"

• Mexican song "El Cascabel," performed by Lorenzo Barcelata and the Mariachi México

• "Johnny B. Goode," performed by Chuck Berry

• New Guinean men's house song

• Japanese song "Tsuru No Sugomori" ("Crane's Nest"), performed by Goro Yamaguchi

• Bach's "Gavotte en rondeaux" from the Partita No. 3 in E-major for Violin, performed by Arthur Grumiaux

• Mozart, *The Magic Flute*, "Queen of the Night" Aria No. 14, performed by the Bavarian State Opera, Munich; Edda Moser, soprano; Wolfgang Sawallisch, conductor

• Georgian song "Tchakrulo"

• Peruvian panpipes and drum

---

First four words spoken by Lisa of *The Simpsons*: "Bart," "Mom," "David Hasselhoff."

- "Melancholy Blues," performed by Louis Armstrong and his Hot Seven
- Azerbaijani bagpipes
- Stravinsky's *Rite of Spring*, "Sacrificial Dance," performed by the Columbia Symphony Orchestra; Igor Stravinsky, conductor
- Bach's *The Well-Tempered Clavier*, Book 2, Prelude and Fugue in C, No. 1, performed by Glenn Gould, piano
- Beethoven's Fifth Symphony, First Movement, performed by the Philharmonia Orchestra, London; Otto Klemperer, conductor
- Bulgarian song "Izlel je Delyo Hagdutin," sung by Valya Balkanska
- Navajo chant
- Holborne, Paueans, Galliards, Almains, and Other Short Aeirs, "The Fairie Round," performed by David Munrow and the Early Music Consort of London
- Solomon Island panpipes
- Peruvian wedding song
- Chinese song "Flowing Streams," performed by Kuan P'ing-hu
- Indian raga "Jaat Kahan Ho," sung by Surshri Kesar Bai Kerkar
- "Dark Was the Night," performed by Blind Willie Johnson
- Beethoven's String Quartet No. 13 in B-flat, Opus 130, Cavatina, performed by the Budapest String Quartet

\*   \*   \*

## TRAVELING THROUGH TIME

Burying a time capsule for future generations to open is a time-honored tradition that dates back to the seventh century BC. One famous missing capsule is the one George Washington is supposed to have buried in the cornerstone of the U.S. Capitol building. No one is sure if he actually buried one or if it was lost due either to the War of 1812 or to various building renovations. Searches for the Washington cornerstone have come up empty-handed. It's fun to speculate on what George might have put inside.

In 1922, Walt Disney incorporated his first film company, Laugh-O-Gram Films...

# PAGE OF LISTS: STATE OF THE STATES

*Some information about these united states from the BRI's trivia files.*

## 5 LARGEST STATES BY AREA

1. Alaska
(586,412 square miles)
2. Texas
(268,820 square miles)
3. California
(163,696 square miles)
4. Montana
(147,165 square miles)
5. New Mexico
(121,593 square miles)

## 13 ORIGINAL COLONIES

1. Delaware (1787)
2. Pennsylvania (1787)
3. New Jersey (1787)
4. Georgia (1788)
5. Connecticut (1788)
6. Massachusetts (1788)
7. Maryland (1788)
8. South Carolina (1788)
9. New Hampshire (1788)
10. Virginia (1788)
11. New York (1788)
12. North Carolina (1789)
13. Rhode Island (1790)

## 5 SMALLEST BY AREA

1. Rhode Island
(1,214 square miles)
2. Delaware
(2,490 square miles)
3. Connecticut
(5,543 square miles)
4. New Jersey
(8,729 square miles)
5. Hawaii
(10,931 square miles)

## 4 STATES THAT TOUCH EACH OTHER (THE FOUR CORNERS)

1. Arizona
2. Colorado
3. New Mexico
4. Utah

## 8 STATES THAT BORDER THE GREAT LAKES

1. Minnesota
2. Wisconsin
3. Illinois
4. Michigan
5. Indiana
6. Ohio
7. Pennsylvania
8. New York

# LINES IN THE SAND

*Borders, fences, fortifications, demarcations—whatever*
*you call them, there are a lot of dividing lines in*
*history. Here are some of the most famous.*

## 1. HADRIAN'S WALL

In AD 122, the Roman Empire was near the height of its power, but in the far-flung imperial province of Britannia, the empire was having some trouble near its northern border. To control that line in the heath, Emperor Hadrian ordered the construction of what became the most heavily fortified border in the Western world at the time: a 73-mile wall of limestone and turf, with small forts roughly every Roman mile occupied by a few dozen troops. Additional, larger forts were also constructed. The Romans built the wall well enough that it survived the Roman Empire, and what remains of it became a World Heritage Site in 1987.

## 2. THE TORDESILLAS MERIDIAN

There's a reason that the citizens of Brazil speak Portuguese while nearly all the rest of South America speaks Spanish: that reason is the Tordesillas Meridian. In 1493, Pope Alexander VI offered a papal edict saying that Spain (Alexander VI's native country) would control any lands west of a meridian (a line stretching from pole to pole) that lay 100 leagues west of the Cape Verde islands, which were off the coast of Africa. This meant that the pope was giving the Americas to Spain, which did not sit well with the Portuguese, who thought they were entitled to it.

In 1494, the Spanish and Portuguese signed the Treaty of Tordesillas, which nudged that papal line farther west—giving Portugal the eastern "bump" of the South American continent that would become Brazil.

## 3. THE PALE

When is a line not just a line? When it is "the Pale"—an area on the eastern shore of Ireland that was directly under the control of the English crown during the Middle Ages. It derived its name

---

**In 1630, Massachusetts governor John Winthrop introduced the fork to America.**

from the Latin word *palus*, which literally meant a stake, but figuratively meant a fence or a line, the lands beyond which one does not have control (and indeed, the Pale had a border fence, or some say a line of dikes). This is what people are referring to when they use the expression "beyond the pale."

## 4. MASON-DIXON LINE

The Mason-Dixon Line is a shorthand term for noting the cultural division between the northern and southern states in the United States, but it's also an actual surveyed line...one that in truth falls across the borders of just four states: Pennsylvania, Delaware, Maryland, and West Virginia (which was once a part of Virginia). The line was charted out between 1763 and 1767 by Charles Mason and Jeremiah Dixon in order to settle a long-standing and sometimes violent border dispute between the then-colonies of Maryland and Pennsylvania. After 1780, the line became shorthand for the difference between the north and south when Pennsylvania outlawed slavery and the Mason-Dixon Line (along with the path of the Ohio River) became the effective border between states that allowed slavery and the ones that did not.

## 5. THE 49TH PARALLEL

The border between the United States and Canada is the longest undefended border in the world, and much of that border—from Washington State to Minnesota—runs almost entirely on a single line: the 49th parallel north. That long line was fixed as the border in two steps: the first in 1818, which secured the border from Minnesota's Lake of the Woods to the Rocky Mountains, and then in the 1846 Oregon Treaty, which extended the line from the Rockies to the Strait of Georgia (in Washington State).

## 6. THE PRIME MERIDIAN

Anyone who looks at a map can see that the 0° meridian runs through England, but the question is: *Why* does it run through England? Because the Greenwich observatory is there, and in 1851, Sir George Airy, the United Kingdom's royal astronomer, decided that's where the prime meridian should be placed. Several European countries (and the United States) adopted Britain's prime meridian for navigational purposes, and then in 1884, the

International Meridian Conference fixed it as the prime meridian for the entire world (although France, hoping to have the prime meridian run through Paris, abstained from voting on the treaty).

## 7. MAGINOT LINE

After the devastation of World War I, and facing the specter of a new, strong German state in the 1930s, the French decided that the best offense was a good defense. Under the direction of the minister of war Andre Maginot, from 1930 through 1940 the French built a line of defensive forts and obstacles that ran from the border with Switzerland to the border with Belgium. Unfortunately, it was through Belgium that the invading Germans were able to outflank the Maginot Line, paving the way for a successful invasion of France in May 1940. This line turned out not to be such a good defense after all.

## 8. THE IRON CURTAIN

In March 1946, Winston Churchill gave a then-unpopular speech about an "iron curtain" that had descended across Europe. The metaphorical curtain represented the political and economic control that the Soviet Union was exerting over the countries of Eastern Europe in the wake of World War II. Eventually, it became literal in the form of the Berlin Wall, which was built around what was then West Berlin by the Soviet-controlled government of East Germany. The Berlin Wall fell in 1989, and the Soviet Union followed in 1991.

## 9. DISTANT EARLY WARNING LINE

During the Cold War, the United States wanted to be ready for a war with the Soviet Union that could erupt at any moment. In the 1950s, along with Canada they devised the Distant Early Warning Line: a series of radar stations stretching from the Aleutians to Baffin Island, designed to spot and report on Soviet bombers coming over the North Pole toward the North American continent. Shortly after its completion in 1957, however, the system became outdated because radar couldn't track intercontinental missiles—the new preferred vehicle of nuclear annihilation. Outposts of the line continue their existence as the North Warning System today.

---

**Dr. Seuss's *Green Eggs and Ham* uses only 50 different words...**

# PIGS...IN...SPACE!

*Pigs haven't distinguished themselves high above the atmosphere, and probably won't until—well, until pigs fly. Still, other heroic animals have taken to the skies in the name of science. Here are our favorites.*

## A GAME OF CAT AND SQUIRREL

Almost 100 years before NASA was experimenting with spaceflight, 19th-century French science-fiction writer Jules Verne test-launched an unlikely pair of animals to the Moon in his novel *From the Earth to the Moon*. The book, published in 1865, featured soldiers who set out to launch a space capsule to the Moon from a cannon. Before they shot a man into space, they first launched a cat and a pet squirrel. The capsule traveled 1,000 feet into the air, arched, and then fell into the water off the Florida coast. When the men recovered the capsule to see how its occupants fared, the outcome was a bit distressing:

> "Hardly had the shell been opened when the cat leaped out, slightly bruised, but full of life, and exhibiting no signs whatever of having made an aerial expedition. No trace, however, of the squirrel could be discovered. The truth at last became apparent—the cat had eaten its fellow-traveler!"

Fortunately, that never happened in real life. Here are some animals that actually visited space.

## 1. A BAAA, A QUACK, AND A COCK-A-DOODLE-DOO

**Event:** First untethered hot-air balloon ride
**Animals:** A sheep, a duck, and a rooster

On September 19, 1783, French king Louis XVI and Marie Antoinette watched inventors Jacques and Joseph Montgolfier herd a sheep, a duck, and a rooster aboard their invention, a hot-air balloon.

Word got out about their experiments and the brothers were summoned to Paris to demonstrate. The king wanted, for military reasons, to see if people could fly and survive. There was a rationale behind the selection of these aeronautical pioneers; the brothers reasoned that if the sheep or the rooster died, it would indicate danger for a person because neither of these creatures were used to high altitudes, whereas the duck's death would be a sign that something other than high altitude was responsible, since it was accustomed to flying at high altitudes. After they settled the animals in the hot-air balloon's basket, the Montgolfiers inflated their balloon and let it go. It flew for eight minutes and came down more than two miles away—with all of its occupants safe and sound. Reassured, Jacques became the first human to lift off a month later.

## 2. ROGER! RAM JET

**Event:** First rocket ride
**Animal:** A sheep

By the early 1800s, hot-air balloons were no longer at the cutting edge of flight. Rockets were all the rage—mostly in the form of unguided but terrifying weapons raining down from above. However, inventor Claude Ruggieri had a better idea: a rocket for launching people into the air. Although his individual rockets were too small to support the weight of a human, Ruggieri devised a "rocket necklace"—clusters of rockets festooning a metal chamber that all went off at the same time. In 1806, Ruggieri launched a ram 600 feet into the air and landed it safely with a parachute. But when the French government caught wind of Ruggieri's next plan (to send up a small child), it immediately stopped his experiments.

## 3. TREATING PASSENGERS LIKE CATTLE

**Event:** First cow milked in an airplane
**Animal:** A cow named Elm Farm Ollie (a.k.a. "Nellie Jay" and "Sky Queen")

Mostly as a publicity stunt, but ostensibly to see how farm animals fared in flight, organizers of the 1930 International Air Exposition in St. Louis, Missouri, flew a cow named Elm Farm Ollie 72 miles in an airplane. During the flight, a Wisconsin dairy farmer milked the cow, producing 24 quarts of milk. The milk was packaged in paper cartons and dropped via parachutes to thirsty onlookers.

## 4. FRUIT FLIES LIKE A BANANA

**Event:** Very early space shot
**Animals:** Fruit flies

The first real space travelers weren't dogs, apes, or even monkeys, but plain old fruit flies. In 1947, at the start of the space race, the United States launched a V-2 rocket carrying corn seeds, fungal spores, and fruit flies from a base in White Sands, New Mexico. The rocket rose to a height of 60 miles before its payload returned to the ground. All the contents survived the journey.

## 6. SHOULDN'T HAPPEN TO A DOG

**Event:** *Sputnik II*
**Animal:** A dog named Laika (Russian for "Barker")

In addition to putting the first man in orbit—Yuri Gagarin on April 12, 1961—the Russians were also the first to put a mammal into orbit, which they did on November 3, 1957. Unlike the Americans' later monkey astronauts, the Russians used mostly stray dogs. The first of the bunch was a mutt named Laika, who was shot into space to see if a mammal could survive the launch and the weightlessness of space. She did—for a while. Unfortunately, the Russians didn't make any accommodations for bringing her back down. She didn't last long as her damaged capsule heated to over 100°F. Laika's corpse circled Earth 2,570 times before her capsule reentered the atmosphere and burned up on April 14, 1958. She was the first of at least 57 dogs to make spaceflights over the next two decades; many of the later dogs survived.

## 5. WHEN THE CHIMPS ARE DOWN

**Event:** First American animals to go into space and live
**Animals:** Monkeys named Able and Baker

On May 28, 1959, NASA made a big deal when two monkeys returned successfully from space; the unspoken message was that the brutal Russians might callously sacrifice animals in space, but the Americans would not. (Unmentioned were Gordo and Albert II, two monkeys that had died on earlier flights.)

Both monkeys survived the 1959 flight on a ballistic missile, but Able died four days later during an operation to remove an infected medical electrode that had tracked his vitals during space travel. Baker lived in retirement at the U.S. Space and Rocket Center until he died in 1984. Their flight paved the way for chimps Ham and Enos. They were launched in 1961, on two different missions, as a rehearsal for human spaceflight. Enos was the

---

first chimp to achieve an actual Earth orbit on November 29, 1961.

## 6. SPACE MENAGERIE
**Event:** Multiple launches by the United States, Soviet Union, China, and France
**Animals:** Too many to count
A series of successful launches unleashed a zoo's worth of space animals in the 1960s. Mice, frogs, guinea pigs, a tortoise, and more dogs were sent up by the Soviet Union. France launched monkeys, a cat, and rats (not at the same time, perhaps thanks to Jules Verne). China sent mice, rats, and dogs into space. The United States went through another insect phase with fruit flies, flour beetles, parasitic wasps, and also sent up frog eggs, plants, amoebas, and mushrooms. Once the space stations and space shuttles became commonplace, no creature was safe from space travel.

## 7. DISARMING NEWTS
**Event:** Russian launch of *Bion 7*
**Animals:** Iberian ribbed newts
In 1985, the Soviet Union added to its reputation for the inhumane treatment of animals when its scientists operated on 10 newts, amputating part of their front limbs to study whether their missing limbs would regenerate in zero gravity in the same way they do on Earth. *Bion 7* also carried 10 rats and two rhesus monkeys, none of which had limbs amputated prior to launch.

## POSTSCRIPT: ONLY THE SMALL SURVIVE
When the space shuttle *Columbia* disintegrated over Texas during its reentry on February 1, 2003, its seven crew members were not the only ones to meet a tragic end. The shuttle also carried silkworms, golden orb spiders, carpenter bees, Japanese killifish, and harvester ants in a gel-filled ant farm. The only known survivors were microscopic nematodes (roundworms) that were found intact in the debris.

\*     \*     \*

"The dinosaurs became extinct because they didn't have a space program. And if we become extinct because we don't have a space program, it'll serve us right!"
—**Larry Niven**

Hollywood actress Julie Newmar patented ultra-sheer, ultra-snug pantyhose.

# JUSTICES FOR ALL

*When U.S. citizens lose a court case, they often appeal the decision to a higher court—sometimes right up to the U.S. Supreme Court in Washington, D.C. That court usually hears fewer than 100 cases a year, but many of those have had a huge impact on our lives and history. Such as...*

## 1. MARBURY v. MADISON, 1803

**Background:** In 1801, just before he left office, President John Adams (a Federalist) appointed William Marbury to be the justice of the peace in Washington, D.C. Problem was, the incoming administration of Thomas Jefferson (a Republican) didn't want to give Marbury the job, and Jefferson's secretary of state, James Madison, refused to honor the appointment. Marbury sued, insisting that under the Judiciary Act of 1789 (which, among other things, gave the president the power to appoint judges and justices of the peace), he was entitled to the position.

**The Decision:** This one was incredibly tricky. In 1803, the Supreme Court declared that Marbury was indeed entitled to his position, but because of several other provisions in the Judiciary Act of 1789, the Supreme Court didn't have any power to enforce its ruling. The court also declared that any law that contradicted the U.S. Constitution would be voided; the Constitution always took precedence. According to the court, the 1789 law violated the Constitution because it monkeyed around with the Supreme Court's jurisdiction. That meant the entire law was unconstitutional, and thus, by default, Marbury had no right to the job. By declaring the Judiciary Act unconstitutional, the court gave itself "judicial review," which was basically "the right to declare laws unconstitutional"—and this is still the court's main role in government today.

**Whatever Happened to...** William Marbury remained an important man in the commercial world as a banker and corporate director. His home, the Forrest-Marbury House, is now the Ukrainian Embassy in Washington, D.C. Marbury's adversary, James Madison, became the fourth president of the United States.

---

**The "Little Ice Age" started circa AD 1250.**

## 2. DRED SCOTT v. SANDFORD, 1857

**Background:** Dred Scott was a slave. His owner, John Emerson, traveled a lot and, in the 1830s, took Scott to live in several northern states where slavery was prohibited. After Emerson died, Scott petitioned a court in St. Louis, Missouri, for his freedom from Emerson's widow. Since her brother, John Sanford, was managing her inheritance, Sanford's name is attached to the case. (Sanford's name was misspelled as Sandford on the court records.)

**The Decision:** The Supreme Court declared that no person of African ancestry could be a U.S. citizen and therefore had no rights, even in states or territories that banned slavery. The court also declared that African Americans—free or enslaved—had no legal rights anywhere in the United States. The *Dred Scott* decision just deepened the animosity between the North and South that eventually erupted in the Civil War.

**Whatever Happened to...** Dred Scott was sent back to the widow of his owner. She had remarried, and her new husband freed Scott. Sadly, Scott enjoyed only a few months of freedom before he died of tuberculosis. John Sanford was committed to an insane asylum before the case was settled, and died there.

## 3. PLESSY v. FERGUSON, 1896

**Background:** Slavery ended with the passage of the Thirteenth Amendment after the Civil War, but race was still an issue. Louisiana passed a law requiring that blacks and whites travel in separate railway cars. In 1892, Homer Plessy, who was of mixed race, was arrested when he sat in a coach reserved for whites. Lower courts convicted him, so Plessy appealed his case all the way to the Supreme Court.

**The Decision:** It was for this case that the justices devised the infamous phrase "separate but equal" to rationalize Louisiana's law. They declared that as long as African Americans had a coach to travel in (the "equal" part), they could be separated from white passengers. "Separate but equal" became the law of the land for more than 50 years. The separate facilities were never equal, but the Supreme Court had spoken.

**Whatever Happened to...** Homer Plessy became an insurance agent and died in 1925.

October 15, 1860: Grace Bedell, age 11, wrote to President Lincoln to suggest...

## 4. BROWN v. BOARD OF EDUCATION, 1954

**Background:** The father of Linda Brown, a little girl in Topeka, Kansas, wanted her to attend an all-white school. But Linda was black, so she was refused admission. Her father and other like-minded parents sued and lost…sued and lost…until they reached the Supreme Court.

**The Decision:** In 1954, Chief Justice Earl Warren delivered the court's unanimous decision: segregation (including "separate but equal" facilities) was damaging, unfair, and henceforth illegal.

**Whatever Happened to…** Linda Brown and her younger sister were only two of a dozen children in the lawsuit, but their names began with a B, so they were listed first. They still live in Topeka and run an educational consulting firm.

## 5. ENGEL v. VITALE, 1962, AND ABINGTON TOWNSHIP v. SCHEMPP, 1963

**Background:** In both of these cases, parents of children in public schools objected to the schools' reading of prayers or Bible verses as part of the school day.

**The Decision:** The court found that by forcing children to recite a prayer or read the Bible, the schools were violating the First Amendment of the Constitution, which forbids laws that establish a government-sponsored religion or prevent the free exercise of religion. People were horrified—and some are still horrified—at the decision to remove prayer from schools. However, the court did not actually ban prayer, only prayers mandated by the school authorities.

**Whatever Happened to…** Ellery Schempp, one of the children who rebelled against the Bible readings (he tried to read from the Koran instead, though he wasn't a Muslim), is now a noted physicist, speaker, and author.

## 6. MIRANDA v. ARIZONA, 1966

**Background:** In 1963, police in Phoenix, Arizona, arrested Ernesto Miranda for rape. They interrogated him, got him to confess, and demanded that he write out his confession—which ultimately got Miranda convicted. Miranda's attorney appealed, saying that his client never saw a lawyer and was never even told he could see a lawyer, until after he confessed. In effect, the police had denied him his constitutional right to legal counsel.

**The Decision:** The Supreme Court found that the police had violated Miranda's Fifth Amendment right to avoid incriminating himself. Today, people accused of crimes have to be told they have the right to an attorney's advice if they're going to be interrogated by the police. In fact, there's a whole list of rights, and if you've ever seen a cop show on TV, you know what they are: "You have the right to remain silent," etc. These are now known as the Miranda rights.

**Whatever Happened to...** Ernesto Miranda won a new trial, but a surprise witness turned up to testify against him and he was convicted again. In 1976, in a bit of irony, he got out of prison and was stabbed to death during a bar fight. The suspect was read his Miranda rights and chose to remain silent. He was released, and no one was ever charged with Miranda's murder.

## 7. ROE v. WADE, 1973

**Background:** Before 1973, many states had laws prohibiting abortion. Jane Roe (a pseudonym for a woman named Norma McCorvey) sued Henry Wade, a prosecuting attorney in Texas, when she was denied the right to terminate her pregnancy.

**The Decision:** The court decided that Jane Roe's choice to have an abortion was protected by her Fourteenth Amendment right to privacy, and state antiabortion laws were struck down. Still, the controversy never ceased, and cases retesting the legality of abortion are still being brought before the court.

**Whatever Happened to...** In 1984, Norma McCorvey revealed that she was Jane Roe. The child she'd had (because she'd been denied an abortion) was given up for adoption. In the 1990s, McCorvey began working for Operation Rescue, saying she no longer believed that abortions should be legal.

## 8. BUSH v. GORE, 2000

**Background:** Democrat Al Gore and Republican George W. Bush ran for president in 2000. The voting was close, and the votes of one state—Florida—determined the winner. Floridians cast six million votes, and in the end, Bush pulled ahead there by less than 1,800 votes. When some of Florida's counties retallied their ballots, Bush's lead shrunk to 300 votes. The Democrats pushed for a statewide recount, but the Republicans resisted. Their candidate had won, they said. Both political parties filed lawsuits, and the case quickly ended up in the hands of the Supreme Court.

**The Decision:** The court stopped the recount, ensuring victory for Bush. Technically, the justices were just deciding whether to allow a recount of the ballots in Florida, but in actuality, they were deciding who would be president, which ruffled some feathers of Americans who believed that wasn't the justices' job.

**Whatever Happened to...** George W. Bush served two terms as president. Al Gore didn't do too badly, either, even though he lost the election. He starred in the Academy Award–winning documentary *An Inconvenient Truth* in 2006, and won the Nobel Peace Prize in 2007.

*     *     *

## MEET THE JUSTICES

• Sandra Day O'Connor was the first woman to serve as a justice on the Supreme Court of the United States, though her appointment did not come until 1981.

• Oliver Wendell Holmes was the oldest justice to sit on the Supreme Court. At his retirement in 1932, he was almost 91 years old.

• The first African American Supreme Court justice was Thurgood Marshall, who was appointed in 1967. He was known for his work on civil rights cases such as *Brown vs. Board of Education*.

• William Howard Taft was the first president of the United States who was formerly a federal judge. After his presidency, he also became the only former president to serve on a federal court when he was appointed to the position of chief justice of the United States in 1921.

• The longest-serving Supreme Court justice was William O. Douglas, who was appointed in 1939 by Franklin D. Roosevelt and remained on the court until his death in 1980.

The Aztec emperor Montezuma reportedly drank 50 goblets of hot chocolate a day.

# IF THE SHOE FITS...

*These four types of footwear changed how we walked through history.*

## 1. PLIMSOLLS

The forerunner to modern sneakers, plimsolls are athletic shoes with a canvas upper and a rubber sole. (Think Keds.) They were first made in England in the 1830s and quickly became popular with people vacationing at the country's beaches—which is why they're sometimes called "sand shoes" in England. Eventually, kids started wearing them to gym class, and in 1924, athletes at the Paris Olympics sported the shoes. The name comes from a "plimsoll line," the waterline painted on the hull of a ship. If plimsoll wearers stepped in puddles higher than the rubber sole, their feet got wet, just as water coming over the plimsoll line soaked a ship.

## 2. FRYE BOOTS

Civil War soldiers, homesteaders, even Teddy Roosevelt and the Rough Riders all wore these knee-high, soft leather boots. John A. Frye opened his shoe company in New York in 1863 and immediately started selling boots to Union soldiers. Both sides were soon clamoring for his comfortable, rugged shoes. They are still around today, and the company remains in New York, making it the oldest continuously operating shoe manufacturer in the United States.

## 3. STILETTOS

These sultry shoes with the spiked heels first appeared on Paris runways in 1952 at a Christian Dior fashion show and have been ruining women's feet ever since. The shoe's name comes from the heel's resemblance to a stabbing weapon called a "stiletto dagger" that was first used during the Renaissance.

## 4. FLIP-FLOPS

Some say flip-flops were born in the 1940s, which is when rubber sandals were first mass-produced. But flip-flops have ancient roots: Egyptian art shows figures wearing something like flip-flops, and the Japanese have worn zoris (thonged straw sandals) for centuries. New Zealanders began to wear rubber sandals in the 1930s, and flip-flops (named for the sound they make when you walk) may have migrated to the U.S. via soldiers stationed in the Pacific in World War II.

At 151 feet (not counting the pedestal), the Statue of Liberty is the tallest U.S. statue.

# THE BIG TOP'S TOP 10

*They came in all shapes and sizes, and we gawked and gasped, just like we were supposed to do. Ladies and gentlemen and children of all ages: our list of the top ten attractions ever to grace the sawdust stage of circus big tops and sideshows!*

## 1. JUMBO

P. T. Barnum brought Jumbo the elephant to New York City on Easter Sunday 1882, just in time for the annual opening of "the Greatest Show on Earth" at Madison Square Garden. In the first six weeks, Jumbo helped the show gross $336,000. Twelve feet tall at the shoulders and weighing in at six and a half tons (in fact, the word "jumbo" as we use it comes from his name), he's considered the greatest circus attraction in American history. Jumbo traveled like royalty in a private railroad car called "Jumbo's palace car," a crimson-and-gold boxcar with huge double doors. Unfortunately, popularity and size were no match for a speeding freight train that took Jumbo's life on September 15, 1885, in St. Thomas, Ontario, as he was being loaded onto his palace.

## 2. EMMETT KELLY

Emmett Kelly's best known routine was trying to sweep a spotlight into a dustpan on the Ringling circus stage. From 1942 to 1956, he appeared as a classic tramp clown called "Weary Willie," his version of a Depression-era hobo. Kelly's style was different from his flashy peers: he wandered around the arena dressed in tattered clothing, using pantomime instead of words to connect with the crowd. He died, aged 80, of a heart attack in Sarasota, Florida—the longtime winter quarters of the Ringling Bros. and Barnum & Bailey Circus.

## 3. GENERAL TOM THUMB

In 1842, Barnum hired four-year-old dwarf Charles Stratton, who soon became world-famous as General Tom Thumb. Only 25 inches tall, Stratton started touring the United States with Barnum's circus, impersonating characters like Cupid and Napoleon Bonaparte. He also sang, danced, and participated in

---

You've probably been wondering when eunuchs won the right to vote in India: 1994.

skits. In 1844, Barnum took him on a European tour, where he appeared twice before Queen Victoria and became an international celebrity. But it was his wedding (by which time he'd grown to his adult height of 2'11') to 2'8' Lavinia Warren, in 1863 that drew the greatest public attention. Barnum charged $75 per ticket and 2,000 people—including congressional representatives, millionaires, and generals—attended. During their honeymoon, the little couple were wined and dined by President and Mrs. Lincoln at the White House.

## 4. ZIP THE PINHEAD

With all due respect, William Henry Johnson was an oddity. His body developed normally, but his head remained small and tapered at the tip. Van Emburgh's Circus in Somerville, New Jersey, paid Johnson's parents to display their son and billed him as a "wild negro boy" who had been caught in Africa and put on display in a cage. Johnson's popularity came to the notice of P. T. Barnum, who gave him a new look by putting him in a furry suit and shaping his Afro to a tiny point that accented his sloping brow; Barnum also renamed him "Zip the Pinhead." It's said that during his 67 years in show business, more than 100 million people visited Zip at the circus. His last words were "Well, we fooled 'em for a long time, didn't we?"

## 5. THE FLYING WALLENDAS

In 1922, Karl Wallenda formed a foursome called the Great Wallendas. They toured Europe, performing daredevil acts like forming a four-man pyramid and cycling across a tightrope high above the crowd. John Ringling was so impressed with a performance he saw in Cuba that he hired them to perform for the Ringling Bros. and Barnum & Bailey Circus. They debuted at Madison Square Garden in 1928 and performed without a net because it had been lost in transit. The act was a crowd pleaser, but it wasn't always failproof—or fall-proof. At an Akron, Ohio, performance, the group fell from the high wire to the ground, but they were unhurt. A reporter who witnessed the accident said, "The Wallendas fell so gracefully that it seemed as if they were flying"—and that's how the Great Wallendas became the Flying Wallendas. Forty-odd years later, on March 22, 1978, in San Juan, Puerto Rico, Wallenda fell to his death from the high wire at the age of 73.

Indonesia's most-visited attraction: Borobudur, a Buddhist monument in Java.

## 6. HARRY HOUDINI

One of the world's greatest magicians got his start with the Welsh Brothers Circus in Lancaster, Pennsylvania, in 1895. For 26 weeks, Harry Houdini and his wife, Beatrice, sang, danced, and performed a trick called "metamorphosis," in which they switched places in a locked trunk. Houdini continued to hone his voice and showmanship while becoming an expert at handcuff manipulation. The rest was history: his expertise in escapism launched him into international stardom far away from the circus world.

## 7. MARIO ZACCHINI

Wanted: "Man who wishes to be explosively propelled ninety miles an hour out of a cannon across a circus tent into a net." Mario Zacchini apparently thought that sounded like a good job because after committing to the feat, he and four of his brothers spent years being launched from a silver-painted cannon three times a day with the Ringling Bros. and Barnum & Bailey Circus. The Zacchinis have acknowledged that their shattering cannon blasts were purely sound effects achieved by igniting half a cup of black gunpowder, but Mario and his family never revealed the secret of the launching mechanism. Mario often said that "flying isn't the hard part; landing in the net is."

## 8. GARGANTUA

Billed as "the world's most terrifying living creature," the gorilla known as Gargantua the Great saved the Ringling brothers from bankruptcy when he joined the show in 1938. The circus claimed that the scar-faced, snarling gorilla, captured in Africa as a baby, hated humans—thus piquing the interest of a lot of humans. In his early years, Gargantua, known as "Buddy," was renamed by new owners after a giant in French literature, which, quite frankly, sounded a lot more frightening than "Buddy." Gargantua apparently had a circus mate named Mrs. Gargantua, but her title was in name only because he never showed any interest in her.

## 9. MABEL STARK

She may have been small in stature—standing just five feet tall— but the Marvelous Mabel Stark stood above the crowd as the greatest female tiger trainer in history. For a time, in the early

---

Only "Oscar" to win an Oscar (in fact, two of them): writer/producer Oscar Hammerstein II.

1920s, her act was the most popular of all six of Ringling's wild animal acts. In 1928, after she slipped in a muddy arena, two tigers knocked her to the ground and attacked her, clawing at her shoulders, arms, and chest, and tearing muscles in her back, thigh, and hip; her injuries required 378 stitches, but in just a few weeks, she was back in the steel cages, swathed in bandages and walking with a cane. In 1950, Mabel was attacked so brutally by one of her tigers that it took 175 stitches to save her right arm. The incidents didn't stop fearless Mabel, though; she spent 57 years in the limelight, and died of a self-administered drug overdose after being fired from her last job at a theme park called JungleLand.

## 10. THE MIDDLEBUSH GIANT

Billed as the world's tallest man, Arthur James Caley (a.k.a. the Middlebush Giant), was given the stage name of Colonel Routh Goshen by P. T. Barnum. Stories about him abounded: Barnum either discovered him while traveling abroad or first saw him on the streets of New York; he was either born on the Isle of Man in 1827 or in Jerusalem in 1837—Barnum made up so many stories about the big guy that he himself might not have remembered which one was true. At any rate, the circus billed the Middlebush Giant as standing 7'11" and weighing 620 pounds, but he most likely topped no more than 7'5", around the same height as today's tallest pro basketball players. "Colonel Routh Goshen" died in Middlebush, New Jersey, in 1889 and is buried there.

\*     \*     \*

"I remember, when I was a child, being taken to the celebrated Barnum's circus, which contained an exhibition of freaks and monstrosities, but the exhibit...which I most desired to see was the one described as 'the Boneless Wonder.'"
—**Winston Churchill**

# CHEERLEADERS:
# THE RAH! TRUTH

*We weren't shocked to discover that Paula Abdul, Cameron
Diaz, and even Steve Martin were once cheerleaders,
but we did have trouble imagining pom-poms
in the hands of Dwight D. Eisenhower.*

### 1. WE LIKE IKE!
**Who:** Dwight D. Eisenhower
**Team:** United States Military Academy at West Point, 1912–13
**Life After Cheerleading:** Five-star general, president of the United States
**The Rah:** After blowing out his knee playing football at West Point, Eisenhower went into a deep depression. He wrote to a friend that he was "never cheerful anymore. The fellows that used to call me 'Sunny Jim' call me 'gloomy face' now." If you're cheerless, he decided, why not join the group that has cheer in its name? He became a cheerleader, quickly moving up the ranks to the five-star position: head cheerleader.

### 2. BUSH 'EM BACK, WAAAY BACK!
**Who:** George W. Bush
**Team:** Phillips Academy, 1963–64
**Life After Cheerleading:** Businessman, baseball team owner, governor of Texas, president of the United States
**The Rah:** A "legacy" admission (George H. W. Bush also went to Phillips), George W. Bush did his best to not let his influential family connections get in the way of his fun. He kept spirits high with weekly pep rallies, skits, and stunts at Phillips Academy, then an all-boys prep school in Massachusetts. For example, he once dressed his cheer squad in drag to mock the female cheerleaders of competing schools. During his senior year, he diversified into creating an intramural stickball league that featured teams with tasteless but funny names. (For example, the Nads, which allowed lusty public shouts of "Go Nads!")

### 3. GO, HORNS, GO!

**Who:** Kay Bailey Hutchison

**Team:** University of Texas at Austin, 1961–64

**Life After Cheerleading:** First female newscaster in Texas, first female U.S. senator from Texas

**The Rah:** Kay Bailey was a cheerleader and sorority girl at the University of Texas, known for its famous "Hook 'Em Horns" hand gesture (index and pinky fingers extended like kids at a heavy metal concert). In 2005, the university hosted a special 50th anniversary Hook 'Em Horns celebration—Hutchison and the rest of her squad all attended.

### 4. HIP, HIP! RAH, RAH, RAH!

**Who:** Jimmy Stewart

**Team:** Princeton University, 1930–32

**Life After Cheerleading:** Actor

**The Rah:** The man who played the main characters in *Harvey*, *It's a Wonderful Life*, and *Mr. Smith Goes to Washington* once performed as head cheerleader at Princeton. In that position, Stewart helped carry on the legacy of the world's oldest known cheer, called the "Princeton Locomotive," first heard in the early 1880s at a football game. It starts slowly and speeds up, trying to duplicate the sound of a train engine starting up with these words:

> *Hip, hip!*
> *Rah, rah, rah!*
> *Tiger, tiger, tiger!*
> *Siss, siss, siss!*
> *Boom, boom, boom!*
> *Ahhhh! Princeton! Princeton! Princeton!*

### 5. GIMME AN "F," GIMME ME A "D," GIMME AN "R"!

**Who:** Franklin D. Roosevelt

**Team:** Harvard University, 1901–2

**Life After Cheerleading:** President of the United States

**The Rah:** Before he became paralyzed from the waist down by polio at age 39, FDR was active on and off the sports field. While

---

Obsidian scalpels are many times sharper than surgical scalpels made of steel.

at Harvard, he became one of three cheerleaders, but he wasn't necessarily proud of the gig. Biographers quote him as saying that he "felt like a fool" while cheering during a Harvard–Yale football game. This revelation mirrored the opinion of Harvard president A. Lawrence Lowell who, a decade later, called cheerleading "nearly the worst means of expressing emotion ever invented."

## 6. LEAN TO THE RIGHT! THE FAAAR RIGHT!

**Who:** Thad Cochran and Trent Lott
**Team:** University of Mississippi, 1955–59 and 1959–1963
**Life After Cheerleading:** United States senators
**The Rah:** Between 1989 and 2007, the state of Mississippi had the unique distinction of having former cheerleaders serving as both of its U.S. senators. Cochran cheered for the University of Mississippi in the late 1950s and, during his senior year, became head cheerleader. Lott was there during the early 1960s and experienced the school's tumultuous antisegregation riots of 1962, sparked by the enrollment of the college's first African American student, James Meredith. As a cheerleader, Lott started a tradition of carrying the Confederate battle flag onto the field—as president of Sigma Nu, he also pushed through a nationwide resolution barring nonwhites from joining the fraternity.

## 7. EX POST FACTO, LAW, LAW, LAW!

**Who:** Ruth Bader Ginsberg
**Team:** James Madison High School, 1950
**Life After Cheerleading:** Lawyer, Supreme Court justice
**The Rah:** Ruth Bader, nicknamed "Kiki" by her family, was very active at her New York high school. She played cello in the orchestra and served as editor of the school paper. Besides being a cheerleader, the future Justice Ginsberg was also a baton twirler.

\*　　\*　　\*

"Two farmers each claimed to own a certain cow. While one pulled on its head and the other pulled on its tail, the cow was milked by a lawyer."

—**Jewish parable**

By 1922, the British Empire held sway over a population of about 458 million people.

# THEY'VE GOT A SECRET

*We've been sworn to secrecy, but this much we can tell you...Freemasonry is a worldwide fraternal organization that's been around for centuries—its first Grand Lodge was founded in England in 1717. The largest secret society in the world, it claims quite a few celebs among its members. Here's our (far-from-complete) inventory of famous Masons.*

| | |
|---|---|
| Edwin "Buzz" Aldrin | Rudyard Kipling |
| Louis Armstrong | Charles Lindbergh |
| Gene Autry | Franz Liszt |
| Irving Berlin | Douglas MacArthur |
| Kit Carson | Thurgood Marshall |
| Marc Chagall | Harpo Marx |
| Winston Churchill | Wolfgang Amadeus Mozart |
| Ty Cobb | Brad Paisley |
| Nat King Cole | Arnold Palmer |
| Davy Crockett | Prince Philip of England |
| Cecil B. DeMille | Paul Revere |
| Jack Dempsey | Roy Rogers |
| Sir Arthur Conan Doyle | Will Rogers |
| John Elway | Franklin Delano Roosevelt |
| Benjamin Franklin | Peter Sellers |
| Clark Gable | Red Skelton |
| John Glenn | Joseph Smith |
| Warren G. Harding | John Philip Sousa |
| J. Edgar Hoover | Harry S. Truman |
| Harry Houdini | Mark Twain |
| Andrew Jackson | George Washington |
| Jesse Jackson | John Wayne |
| John Jay | Oscar Wilde |

**More than 400 species of mammals have been discovered since 1993.**

# SEALED WITH A KISS

*Kissing is fun…sometimes. Other times, it can be downright dangerous.*

## 1. THE KISS FELT 'ROUND THE WORLD

According to several passages from the Bible, it appears that Judas Iscariot betrayed Jesus with a kiss. The story goes that for a handful of change, Judas agreed to identify Jesus to the Roman soldiers who wanted to arrest him. The secret code: a kiss on the cheek. Some biblical scholars discount the story, saying that Jesus actually gave himself up. Either way, the phrase "the kiss of death" comes from this betrayal.

## 2. SAVED FROM THE GATES OF HELL

You've probably seen images of *The Kiss* (1886) by sculptor Auguste Rodin—carved in marble, two lovers sit intertwined, her hand around his head, his hand on her hip, their lips locked in a passionate kiss. Along with Rodin's equally famous *The Thinker*, the couple was supposed to be part of a monumental work of 180 figures that would decorate a massive set of 20-foot-tall doors called *The Gates of Hell*, based on Dante's *Inferno*. Rodin worked on the doors on and off for 37 years, but they remained unfinished at his death in 1917.

## 3. AN INFECTIOUS BIT OF BLARNEY

The tradition of kissing Ireland's Blarney Stone dates back to about 1800, but the stone itself has been around for ages. Some people say it's part of the legendary "Stone of Scone," on which the first king of Scotland sat during his coronation in the ninth century. Others claim the prophet Jeremiah brought it to Ireland or that it was given as a gift to the king of Munster who built Blarney Castle near Cork, Ireland, in the 14th century. Regardless of the stone's origin, it now sits at the top of Blarney Castle, and visitors who want to kiss it for good luck have to hang upside down over a wall high above the ground. These days, there are safety bars to hold on to, but there's still Blarney Stone danger to beware: with 200,000 people kissing the Blarney Stone every year, the *Daily Telegraph* has declared it "the World's Most Unhygienic Tourist Attraction."

San Francisco's cable cars are America's only mobile national monuments.

## 4. NO, NO, NANOOK

What do you call a "documentary" that just makes stuff up? Well, maybe you can't be too hard on Robert J. Flaherty. In 1913, he headed to Canada to record the traditional life of the Inuit, but his footage was destroyed in a fire, and he had to return in 1920. Filmmaking was young and there were no rules for documentaries. Flaherty's full-length silent movie *Nanook of the North* was a big hit with Americans when it came out in 1922. Flaherty captured amazing footage of the Inuits' traditional ways. However, he faked a lot of things. Some of them were dictated by necessity: for example, he built an igloo with an open side so that he'd have enough light to film. Some were dictated by commercial considerations: he renamed the main characters and gave the film's protagonist, an Inuit hunter named Nanook, a replacement wife who was more photogenic than his real one. Other falsities, though, were completely unnecessary and caused lasting misimpressions. One of the things Flaherty made up for no good reason was the "Eskimo kiss" of two people rubbing noses. He'd filmed a mother nuzzling her child and reported that the Inuit kissed that way all the time to keep from freezing their mouths together. It wasn't true.

\*      \*      \*

### 8 REAL (DUMB) HEADLINES

"Two Soviet ships collide—one dies"

"Nicaragua sets goal to wipe out literacy"

"Iraqi head seeks arms"

"Queen Mary having bottom scraped"

"Is there a ring of debris around Uranus?"

"Prostitutes appeal to Pope"

"War dims hope for peace"

"British Left Waffles on Falkan Islands"

---

Brierfield, the Mississippi plantation of Confederate president Jefferson Davis...

# THE MEANEST TOWNS IN THE WEST

*From the archives of the old West, we've culled a list of the most notorious places on the frontier. Here's our countdown of the baddest of the bad, meanest of the mean Wild West towns.*

Some historians say that the Wild West wasn't as dangerous as we've been led to believe by Hollywood, but there's no doubt that some frontier towns were beyond the immediate reach of the law—places where mischief, mayhem, and murder were everyday occurrences.

## 8. FORT GRIFFIN, TEXAS

One of the wildest places in the old West, Fort Griffin sprouted at the intersection of the West Fork of the Trinity River and the Clear Fork of the Brazos River in northern Texas. Built in the 1860s on a hill overlooking the Brazos, the fort itself was designed to protect the folks—mostly farmers and ranchers—who lived below in the settlement of Fort Griffin.

The town was soon invaded by outlaws and cowboys driving their cattle north to Dodge City. By the 1870s, skirmishes with the Kiowa and Comanche in the north diverted the soldiers from Fort Griffin and, as a result, law enforcement broke down, which attracted even more rough types to the town.

**Visiting Celebrities.** The motley collection of buffalo hunters, gamblers, gunfighters, and "painted ladies" brought with them a penchant for violence. Among them were a gambler and prostitute named Big Nose Kate and her pal, the legendary gambler Doc Holliday. Also passing through were Wyatt Earp (who met Holliday for the first time at the fort), lawman Pat Garrett, and John Wesley Hardin—by some accounts the most sadistic killer to ever come out of Texas. Dustups and gun violence became so frequent that the commander of the fort finally placed the town under martial law in 1874.

---

...was once sold to Benjamin T. Montgomery, a former slave on the estate.

## 7. RUBY, ARIZONA

From the days of the Spanish explorations, prospectors had searched for veins of gold, silver, copper, lead, and zinc near Montana Peak in southern Arizona close to the Mexican border. In 1891, high-grade gold was discovered. A local assayer judged it to be a bonanza, and the rush was on. The town of Ruby was born practically overnight.

**Here Comes Trouble.** Most of the miners lived in tents or rough adobe huts, and bought their meager supplies at George Cheney's Ruby Mercantile, the one and only general store. The men provided for themselves and their families by hunting and rustling cattle. But the primary source of trouble came from Mexican bandits who frequently terrorized the settlement. By the early 1900s, Ruby was so dangerous that Phillip and Gypsy Clarke, who owned a general store, kept weapons in every room of their house as well as at the store. When Phillip eventually sold the store to a pair of brothers, he warned them of the danger. They didn't heed Clarke's warning and were soon found shot to death. Today, Ruby is a well-preserved ghost town.

## 6. DELAMAR, NEVADA

Delamar got its reputation as a notorious Wild West town not from gun violence but from dangerous conditions in the mines. The 1889 discovery of gold in nearby Monkey Wrench Gulch unleashed a stampede of miners intent on digging for the peculiar form of gold, encased as it was in crystallized quartz. A former ship's captain named Joseph Raphael De Lamar bought most of the profitable mines in 1893 and built a mill to crack the quartz and refine the gold. Within a few years, the town had 1,500 citizens, a hospital, post office, opera house, school, several churches, and plenty of saloons. But then the deaths began to mount.

**Dust to Dust.** Operations at the mill exposed the miners—and the town—to clouds of silicon dust. The mill workers were at greatest risk of breathing in the dust, which slowly caused silicosis of the lungs and death. At one time, 400 widows lived in Delamar, giving the town its reputation as the "Widowmaker." Delamar began its decline in 1909 when Captain De Lamar tore down the mill. Operations started up in the mines two decades later, but eventually slowed to a halt. The last resident moved away in 1934.

During the ancient Roman festival of *Saturnalia*, masters served their slaves.

## 5. DODGE CITY, KANSAS

Fights and gunplay were all too familiar in Dodge City in the 1870s. In its first ten years, it became a well-known gathering hole for gunslingers—so well known that companies such as the Atchison, Topeka, and Santa Fe Railroad came to Dodge to hire fighting men when they needed to protect their business interests. Fearless buffalo hunters, cowboys, muleteers, and bullwhackers (wagon train drivers) populated the city. Characters with colorful nicknames arrived, among them Cherokee Bill, Prairie Dog Dave, Fat Jack, and Cockeyed Frank. Said one resident, "With a few drinks of red liquor under their belts, you could reckon there was something doing. They feared neither God, man, nor the devil, and so reckless they would pit themselves, like Ajax, against lightning, if they ran into it."

**The Upside to the Downside.** There were plenty of deaths and gunfights in the streets of "Wicked Dodge," as writers termed it, but it could have been worse. Because so many inhabitants were widely known as "sluggers, bruisers, and dead shots," most of them were wary of starting trouble with one another. Also happening on the scene were legendary lawmen such as Wyatt Earp, Bat Masterson, Charlie Bassett, and Bill Tilghman, who stood ready to step in and jail anyone who got out of hand.

## 4. ELDORADO CANYON, NEVADA

Spanish explorers in the late 18th century gave Eldorado Canyon its name, but it was American gold miners a century later who gave the mining camp at the canyon its reputation. The miners were drawn to a gorge on the Colorado River after prospectors discovered a vertical vein of gold there in 1861. They established the Techatticup Mine, which eventually fell into the hands of California senator George Hearst (father of publisher William Randolph Hearst). Eventually, dozens of mines in Eldorado Canyon became a magnet for prospectors, entrepreneurs, Civil War deserters, and "sporting women." Their only connection to the outside world was a steamboat that carried the gold, silver, copper, and lead down the Colorado to distant Yuma, Arizona.

**The Original Fight Club.** Political clashes among supporters of the North or South in the Civil War and greed, vigilante justice,

November 15, 1937: Al Capp introduced Sadie Hawkins Day in his *Li'l Abner* comic strip.

and disputes over claims made for frequent brawls, stabbings, and gunfights. Killings became so common they were nearly a daily event. And the canyon was so remote—300 miles from the closest civilized town—that lawmen simply refused to enter it. A military post was eventually established near the settlement in 1867 to protect the steamboats and bring a sense of civility to the neighborhood.

## 3. DEADWOOD, SOUTH DAKOTA

Like many other famous Wild West towns, Deadwood owes its reputation for violence to the discovery of gold. In 1874, U.S. Army general George A. Custer led an expedition into the Black Hills to confirm the existence of gold. The U.S. government tried to keep the gold a secret in honor of the 1868 Treaty of Fort Laramie, which recognized the Black Hills as belonging to the Lakota-Sioux. But in 1875, when a miner found gold in a narrow canyon lined with dead trees, news of the find in "Deadwood Gulch" spread like wildfire. Within a year, miners stormed into the area and established the rough-and-tumble mining camp of Deadwood.

**Deadwood Comes to Life.** The Black Hills gold rush was in full bloom by 1876. Deadwood swarmed with men determined to get rich by any means. Dozens of saloons, gambling parlors, dance halls, and brothels competed for their attention and dollars. Legendary characters Wild Bill Hickok and Calamity Jane were town fixtures. But danger lurked everywhere. Henry W. Smith, a Methodist minister, was murdered while walking to church, and Hickok was shot in the back of the head while playing poker in one of the saloons. By 1879, the rowdy nature of Deadwood began to ebb after a town government was established. Today, the well-preserved city is a gambling destination for tourists as well as a National Historic Landmark.

## 2. TOMBSTONE, ARIZONA

Many consider Tombstone the most dangerous of all the Wild West towns because of its lawlessness and frequent gunfights. The name seems appropriate enough, but it wasn't derived from the Boothill graveyard outside town—it came from a nearby mine named by prospector Ed Schieffelin, who filed the claim in 1877. He was told by a soldier that warring Apaches controlled the area.

"All you'll find in those hills is your tombstone," said the soldier. But Schieffelin was undeterred and named his mine the Tombstone. News of the strike brought other miners to the site, and the town of Tombstone soon came into being.

**Lovely Downtown Tombstone.** Consisting of 40 buildings, a post office, and 500 residents by 1878, Tombstone began to draw the usual collection of men and women from the fringes of society. Within a few years, the town boasted more gambling parlors and saloons than anywhere in the Southwest, as well as the largest red-light district. Wyatt Earp arrived at the end of 1879 with intentions of establishing a stage line but instead invested in a gaming parlor while riding shotgun for Wells Fargo stagecoaches. Four of his brothers followed: James opened a saloon, and Warrren, Virgil, and Morgan went into law enforcement. Wyatt's friend Doc Holliday arrived in 1880 with Big Nose Kate, who established a brothel in a tent. The Clanton gang and the McLaury brothers terrorized the countryside, running afoul of the Earps, which led to the showdown at the town's O.K. Corral, thus sealing Tombstone's legend. The city has survived into the 21st century, as has its newspaper, the *Tombstone Epitaph*, which memorializes Tombstone as the "Town Too Tough to Die."

## 1. CANYON DIABLO, ARIZONA

Nowhere in the Southwest was there a more violent place than the railroad town of Canyon Diablo, giving it the top spot on our list of the meanest Wild West towns. The settlement was born when workers laying tracks for a railroad came to the edge of the canyon, with no way to cross over until a bridge was built. Constructing the bridge took ten years, during which time the town that came into being took its name from the canyon. It was as despicable a place to live as there was in the West. With the closet U.S. marshal 100 miles away, Canyon Diablo quickly attracted drifters, gamblers, and outlaws. Fourteen saloons, ten gambling parlors, four brothels, two dance halls, a couple of cafés, a grocery, and a dry goods store did business 24 hours a day. The buildings faced each other across the aptly named Hell Street, the town's single rocky road just off the railroad right-of-way.

**They Shot the Sheriff.** Fights and gun duels were frequent among the town's 2,000 residents, filling dozens of graves at the town's cemetery. Bandits regularly held up the stage that ran between Flagstaff and Canyon Diablo. When mounting violence persuaded the townspeople to hire a police officer, the first one put on his badge at three o'clock in the afternoon and was dead by eight o'clock that evening. Five more who tried it lasted a month or less before being slain. But what the law couldn't do, completion of the bridge accomplished. The town died, and according to Western lore, completely disappeared by 1899 when its last resident, a trading post owner named Herman Wolfe, died peacefully.

\*     \*     \*

### FAMOUS BOY SCOUTS
David Attenborough, TV personality
David Bowie, musician
David Beckham, soccer player
Bill Clinton, Former U.S. president
Walter Cronkite, U.S. journalist
Jean-Louis Dumas-Hernes, head of Hermes fashion house
Harrison Ford, actor
Bill Gates, Microsoft founder
Jacques Chirac, French politician
David Hockney, artist
Bruce Jenner, U.S. athlete
James Lovell, astronaut
Willard Marriott, founder Marriott Corp
Paul McCartney, Beatle
Armandou M'Bou, director general UNESCO
Daniel Moi, president of Kenya
Julius Nyere, president of Tanzania
Jamie Oliver, chef
H. Ross Perot, self-made billionaire
Alberto Salazar, New York Marathon winner
Stephen Spielberg, film director
Mark Spitz, U.S. Olympic swimmer

Mass-market paperbacks were first published in the U.S. in 1939.

# THE CABINET

*Every four years, Americans elect a president, and then he gets to work choosing his cabinet. But who are those people?*

## THE LINE FORMS HERE

The cabinet is made up of 16 positions that are considered advisors to the president. Article II, Section 2 of the U.S. Constitution gives the president the power to appoint the members of his cabinet, so long as they're approved by Congress.

Without further ado, the cabinet positions (in order of succession to the presidency) are...

1. Vice President
2. Secretary of State
3. Secretary of the Treasury
4. Secretary of Defense
5. Attorney General
6. Secretary of the Interior
7. Secretary of Agriculture
8. Secretary of Commerce
9. Secretary of Labor
10. Secretary of Health and Human Services
11. Secretary of Housing and Urban Development
12. Secretary of Transportation
13. Secretary of Energy
14. Secretary of Education
15. Secretary of Veterans Affairs
16. Secretary of Homeland Security

## WHAT IF MARS ATTACKS?

These nine vice presidents have taken over for their bosses due to death or resignation. (The line of succession has never gone further than vice president.)

1. John Tyler (1841)
2. Millard Fillmore (1850)
3. Andrew Johnson (1865)
4. Chester Arthur (1881)
5. Theodore Roosevelt (1901)
6. Calvin Coolidge (1923)
7. Harry S. Truman (1945)
8. Lyndon B. Johnson (1963)
9. Gerald Ford (1974)

**By 2008, 32.5 million Americans had at least one foreign-born parent.**

# NAME'S THE SAME

*But the personalities couldn't be more different.*

**FRANCIS BACON**

**1.** The first Francis Bacon was a true Renaissance man, and not just because he was born in 1561. An exceptional philosopher, politician, scientist, lawyer, and author, his biggest fans (and he has plenty even though he's been dead for nearly 400 years) think so highly of him that some of them believe he—not Shakespeare—wrote the plays we think of as the Bard's.

**2.** The 20th-century Francis Bacon was a modern artist who former British prime minister Margaret Thatcher called "that man who paints those dreadful pictures." His fans would disagree with Thatcher's eye for art. Even though they're known for their "tortured imagery," Francis #2's paintings are considered brilliant by art cognoscenti.

(These two might actually be related: #2 was named for #1 by his father, who claimed to be descended from #1's half-brother.)

**CASSIUS CLAY**

**1.** The first Cassius Marcellus Clay was born in 1810 in Kentucky. His father was a wealthy landowner and slaveholder. Rather than following in his father's footsteps, Cassius #1 became a prominent abolitionist as a Kentucky state representative, an early member of the Republican Party, and unofficial adviser to President Lincoln.

**2.** The three-time world heavyweight champion, better known by his adopted Muslim name of Muhammad Ali (and who styled himself "the Greatest"), was christened Cassius Marcellus Clay Jr. in 1942. He and his father, the elder Cassius Marcellus Clay, were both named for the 19th-century abolitionist cited above. Clay Jr. changed his name when he joined the Nation of Islam in 1964.

**HARRISON FORD**

**1.** Our two Harrison Fords have more in common than anyone else on this list: both have stars on the Hollywood Walk of Fame and have been described as "handsome Hollywood leading men." The only difference is that you probably never heard of the one born in 1884, who starred in silent movies with the likes of Gloria Swanson and Clara Bow. His first film appearance was in 1915 and his last in 1932, when silent movies were replaced by talkies.

**2.** The other Harrison Ford—the one that you've undoubtedly heard of—was born in 1942 and has played strong, silent types, but all his movies have been talkies. He appeared in scads of TV shows and movies from 1966 on before making it big as Han Solo in the first three installments of *Star Wars*.

## GRAHAM GREENE
**1.** Mr. Greene #1, born Henry Graham Greene in 1904, was an English author, playwright, and literary critic. More than a few of his novels have been made into movies, including *The Third Man*, *Our Man in Havana*, *The End of the Affair*, and *A Gun for Sale*, on which the film noir classic *This Gun for Hire* was based.

**2.** Our second Graham Greene was born in 1952 on the Six Nations Reserve in Ontario, Canada. A familiar face in Hollywood films, Greene was nominated for a Best Supporting Actor Oscar for *Dances with Wolves*, and appeared in scads of movies (including *Thunderheart* and *The Green Mile*) and in TV adaptations of Tony Hillerman's mystery novels *A Thief of Time* and *Coyote Waits*.

## JESSE JAMES
**1.** The notorious outlaw was born in Missouri in 1847. A celebrity when he was alive, he was elevated to legendary status after his death at the hands of the "dirty rotten coward" Robert Ford, who shot him in the back when he was unarmed, in St. Joseph, Missouri, in April 1882.

**2.** The 20th-century Jesse, born in 1969, is CEO of West Coast Choppers, a manufacturer of custom-made motorcycles, and an American TV personality. The host of TV's *Motorcycle Mania* and the former Discovery Channel series *Monster Garage*, he became notorious in his own way in 2010 when it was revealed that he had had numerous affairs while married to actress Sandra Bullock.

## HOWARD JOHNSON
**1.** The Howard Johnson whose name was once plastered all over more than 1,000 restaurants (a.k.a. HoJos) was born in 1897. He

parlayed a small soda shop in Quincy, Massachusetts, into an empire: in 1935, with a partner, he created the first modern restaurant franchise.

**2.** Howard Johnson #2 (a.k.a. HoJo) was born in 1960 and played third base for four major league teams from 1982 to 1995: the Detroit Tigers, New York Mets, Colorado Rockies, and Chicago Cubs. The Mets got him back in 2007, when he was named the team's hitting coach.

## JOSEPH McCARTHY

**1.** The Joseph McCarthy born in 1885 was an American lyricist of the sentimental persuasion whose most famous songs include "You Made Me Love You," "Alice Blue Gown," and "I'm Always Chasing Rainbows" (based on part of Chopin's *Fantasie-Impromptu*).

**2.** There was nothing sentimental about Joseph McCarthy #2, the Republican senator from Wisconsin born in 1908. He staked his claim to fame on the post–World War II fear of Communist subversion, claiming that there were large numbers of Soviet spies and sympathizers inside the federal government, and also under your bed. Ultimately, his tactics—along with his inability to substantiate his accusations—led to his censure by the Senate.

## JANE SEYMOUR

**1.** Both Janes were born in England, but only one was married to King Henry VIII. The third of Henry's six wives, Jane #1, born in 1508, married him ten days after her cousin Anne Boleyn was beheaded for alleged adultery, incest, and treason in May 1536. Jane died the following year, soon after giving birth to Prince Edward—the male heir that King Henry coveted.

**2.** Actress Jane Seymour (*Dr. Quinn, Medicine Woman* and TV jewelry pitchwoman) was born Joyce Frankenberg in 1951; she changed her name at age 17. Her lineage isn't as inbred as the first Jane's (who was a fifth cousin to her husband). Jane #2's father's family was from Poland; her mother's family was from the Netherlands. Unlike Jane #1, who was married once and only for a year, Jane #2 has been married five times, putting her in position to challenge King Henry VIII's mark of six spouses.

---

October 17, 1933: Albert Einstein arrived in the U.S. as a refugee from Nazi Germany.

# THE WORST JOBS IN THE CASTLE

*If you think today's job market stinks, take a look at some of the job openings in Tudor England.*

**M**ost of us like to watch movies and TV shows about the lives and loves of the Tudors, the royal family who ruled England from 1485 to 1603. But what about the little people who made the Tudor lifestyle possible?

## 1. THE GROOM OF THE STOOL

Yes, that kind of stool. Just as his title implied, this man was in charge of every aspect of the king's defecation. His job description included making sure that "the house of easement be sweet and clear" because, since the monarch was considered divine, everything that came out of the king was therefore sacred. Royal poop was not like ordinary poop.

A cushy and prestigious job that could only be performed by someone of noble lineage and impeccable breeding, it paid well for the time, and came with special perks, not the least of which was complete access to the royal presence.

**In the Throne Room.** The royal potty was a magnificent piece of furniture: a wooden contraption covered in black velvet and stuffed with pounds of goose down to ensure His Majesty's comfort. The tools of the groom of the stool's trade were a pewter flagon (bottle), a pewter bowl, and a white cloth (called a "diaper") woven with a special diamond pattern. Given the royal diet of the day—Henry VIII's, for example, relied heavily on meats, fats, and sweets (vegetables were considered peasant food)—the groom of the stool was periodically called upon to give the king a royal enema.

**Losing His Head Over the Queen.** As desirable, and occasionally unpleasant, as the job was, it could be dangerous. One of Henry VIII's grooms of the stool, Sir Henry Norris, was accused of being intimate not only with the king's bottom but with the queen's as

---

In 1884, the cost of a roller-coaster ride at Coney Island, New York, was 5¢.

well. He was convicted on a trumped-up charge of adultery with Anne Boleyn and was beheaded.

**All the King's Men.** The groom of the stool was also in charge of all the king's precious possessions (including the royal jewels) and an army of royal attendants of the king's private domain. These included the following:

• 12 gentlemen of the privy chamber (the king's private apartment): six were on duty at all times.

• 4 esquires of the body: attendants who watched over the king day and night and helped him dress in clothes that had been carefully warmed by the fire.

• 2–4 gentlemen ushers: glorified doormen to the king's entryway.

• Yeomen of the chamber: lesser nobles whose jobs were to oversee the making of beds, keeping of fires, and general housekeeping. One of them had to roll around on the bed each night before the king retired, to make certain there were no daggers hidden among the bedclothes.

• 6–10 gentlemen waiters

• 3 cup bearers

• 3 carvers (of meat and/or wood)

• 3 sewers (i.e., tailors)

• 2–6 physicians and surgeons

• 1 barber

• Assorted secretaries and gofers (not an official title)

## 2. THE GONG FARMER

The Tudor castle was home to a lot of people: the king and his family, their households and servants, visiting dignitaries, assorted nobles, hangers-on, and workers. All of them needed to relieve themselves, and all that waste needed to go somewhere. That's where the gong farmer came in. "Gong" was the Tudor euphemism for dung, "farming" meant "shoveling," and that's what the gong farmer did. His workplace consisted of the castle's privies and cesspits. His job was to shovel all that excrement into buckets and take it outside the city gates.

The first national horseshoe-throwing championship was held in Bronson, Kansas, in 1909.

**A Nine-to-Five Job.** The gong farmer lived in designated areas, among other gong farmers, and was allowed to work only at night—between the hours of 9:00 p.m. and 5:00 a.m., when he was unlikely to run into anyone. Part of his pay was usually in brandy (possibly in an attempt to keep him happy in his work). Not only was the profession socially undesirable, it was dangerous too. Many gong farmers succumbed to noxious fumes while working, and the methane gas that built up in those enclosed spaces had a way of exploding. It's unlikely that any gong farmer eventually climbed the ladder of success—even if he could find it amid all that excrement.

## 3. THE EXECUTIONER

The Tudors kept their in-house executioner busy. What with religious unrest, courtly intrigues, and a monarch who liked to rid himself of inconvenient wives, being a noble in Tudor England could be pretty dangerous. In those days, only the well-born lost their heads; the rabble were usually hanged.

The headsman—the executioner in charge of beheadings—was an unpopular fellow, and the mask he wore did little to hide his identity: some executioners even were recruited from among those about to lose their own heads. There was no training for the job, and the tools were crude. All of the headsman's work was done in public, as executions were entertainment and attracted large, rowdy crowds.

**Heads Will Roll.** Beheading usually took several blows of the axe and the headsman often had to finish the job with a knife or dagger. However he managed to do it, blood gushed everywhere, and he alone was responsible for cleaning up the mess. The head would roll around on the floor, and what some considered the best part of the entertainment came after the deed was done. The headsman would hold up the severed head by the hair and proclaim, "This is the fate that befalls traitors," or words to that effect. And the crowds would cheer.

There was one more step in the process. After the severed head was boiled in a mixture of salt and cumin seed (too keep the birds from feasting on it), it was usually stuck on a pike and displayed in a prominent place, ostensibly as a warning to other potential miscreants.

**Au Revoir to Anne.** The headsman's victims often tipped him quite handsomely to ensure a quick, clean end, but there were no money-back guarantees. Henry VIII's second wife, Anne Boleyn, imported a French executioner, who used a sword rather than the English axe and managed to detach her head from her body with just one blow.

## 4. THE SPIT BOY

As Tudor jobs went, this one doesn't sound so bad...at first. The Tudors loved to eat and spent many hours of the day at the table. Meals were made up of a prodigious number of courses, each more magnificent than the next, and mostly consisting of various meats roasted on a rotisserie that had to be cranked by hand: this was the job of the spit boys.

**Is It Hot in Here or Is It Just Me?** Six or so at a time stood at the huge enclosed fire pit, turning the iron spit hour after tedious hour. Each spit could hold hundreds of pounds of animal carcasses, leaving no need for upper-body workouts at ye olde Tudor gym. The spit boys stood pretty close to where the meat itself was roasting, and were likely to be partly roasted themselves. Nevertheless, castle decorum being what it was, they were obliged to remain fully dressed at all times.

## WHAT COULD BE WORSE?

As crummy as these jobs were, they were still better than unemployment. In Tudor England, the unemployed were labeled "vagabonds." They could be apprehended, branded with the letter "V" on their chests, and forced to wear a metal collar and do any kind of menial work for whoever reported them—at no pay other than bread and water—for a period of two years. Today's job market hardly seems bad by comparison.

\*　　\*　　\*

"No man goes before his time—unless the boss leaves early."

—Groucho Marx

People in medieval England ate a lot of pottage. Ever wonder what that is?...

# CATATONIC

*Some people love cats. Some people
don't. Some things never change.*

## 1. LOVER: ERNEST HEMINGWAY

The writer of such classics as *A Farewell to Arms* and *The Old
Man and the Sea* so loved cats that his former home in Key
West, Florida, is today a haven for the descendants of one feline
Hemingway received as a gift in the 1930s. That cat, Snowball,
was a unique creature—it was polydactyl (had six toes). But
Snowball wasn't the only cat the author loved. During his lifetime, Hemingway owned about 30 cats, and as he mentioned in
his memoir *A Moveable Feast*, the one he called F. Puss—short
for Feather Puss—was occasionally left to "babysit" for his infant
son. Hemingway also immortalized his cat Crazy Christian in a
poetic eulogy written after the cat's death.

## 2. HATER: IVAN THE TERRIBLE

Sixteenth-century Russian czar Ivan IV Vasilyevich was known for
rage-filled outbursts, including one in which he killed his eldest
son. In childhood, the story goes, he also liked to toss cats off of
high balconies and out windows, simply for sport.

## 3. LOVER: WINSTON CHURCHILL

This jowly statesman was an avid pet lover—especially of cats.
Among his favorites were Nelson (a gray cat to whom Churchill
sneaked bits of salmon from the dinner table) and an orange mar-
malade given to him for his 88th birthday. Churchill named the
cat Jock. After the former prime minister died, his home was given
to the National Trust, and his family asked that an orange cat
named Jock always be in residence. Jock IV lives there today.

## 4. HATER: AMBROSE BIERCE

American writer Ambrose Bierce didn't pull any punches. In his
satirical book *The Devil's Dictionary*, published in 1911, he defined
"cat" as "a soft indestructible automaton provided by nature to be
kicked when things go wrong in the domestic circle."

## 5. LOVER: MARK TWAIN

Mark Twain grew up in a house with 19 cats, and as an adult he continued the tradition, filling his homes with cats of various shapes and sizes...and unusual names. Among them: Apollonis, Blatherskite, Buffalo Bill, Sour Mash, Zoroaster, Beelzebub, and Sin. In 1905, when Twain was living in New York City, his cat Bambino disappeared. Twain was so distressed that he ran an ad in the newspaper offering a $5 reward for Bambino's safe return. Twain's secretary found the cat and brought him home.

## 6. HATER: DWIGHT D. EISENHOWER

History remembers Dwight D. Eisenhower as a military master-mind who helped plan the Allied invasion of France during World War II. Then he became the president who integrated America's public schools and built the interstate highway system. He also hated cats. In fact, it's been said that Eisenhower hated cats so much that he ordered any cat found wandering onto his farm in Gettysburg to be shot on the spot.

## 7. LOVER: CARDINAL RICHELIEU

Armand-Jean du Plessis Cardinal-Duc de Richelieu—the chief adviser to France's King Louis XIII—didn't always love his fellow man, but he did love his cats. He owned 14 of them when he died in 1642, and he made provision for their care in his will. One of Richelieu's favorites was Ludovic le Cruel, so named for his excellent mice-catching and killing skills.

## 8. HATER: NOAH WEBSTER

American lexicographer (and dictionary-maker) Noah Webster was a closet cat hater. No stories exist of him shooting any felines or tossing them from balconies, but an entry in his first dictionary belies a deep-seated kitty mistrust. He defined "cat" in this way: "The domestic cat is a deceitful animal and when enraged extremely spiteful."

\*     \*     \*

"Curiosity killed the cat, but for a while I was the suspect."
—Stephen Wright

In a single feeding, a Bengal tiger can eat up to 70 pounds of meat.

# GOT JACK?

*In 1888, a serial murderer terrorized London. But who was he?*

**M**URDER IN THE EAST END
The story of Jack the Ripper is one of history's most famous unsolved crimes. Between August and November 1888, five prostitutes in London's Whitechapel neighborhood—a poor area in the city's East End—were violently murdered. They were strangled, their throats cut, and their bodies mutilated. Some of them were even missing internal organs.

The neighborhood was terrified, and the city's police dumbfounded. Despite the participation of both London's city police and the famous Scotland Yard, interviews with more than 1,500 witnesses, and the investigation of hundreds of possible suspects, the case was closed in 1892, unsolved.

### THE PROFILE

Attempts to figure out who Jack the Ripper was, though, continued. Everyone from Queen Victoria's personal doctor to the city's midwives (police theorized that the murders may have been abortions gone wrong) came under suspicion. Over the years, new names were attached to the case—author Lewis Carroll was even considered a suspect, though no one took the accusation seriously.

In 1988, the FBI took on the case and came up with a criminal profile of Jack the Ripper. Supposedly, he was...
- A resident of Whitechapel.
- The product of a broken home.
- Someone with training in medicine, as a butcher, or as a mortician's assistant.
- Single—since he could stay out all night stalking women without anyone missing him.
- Someone with a regular job—since he killed on the weekends or in the early morning hours, as though he had to be somewhere during the day.
- Between the ages of 28 and 36.
- Neat, orderly, shy, a loner, and a man who hated women.

---

**July 1965: Little Richard fired Jimi Hendrix from his band for missing the bus.**

## A DIP IN THE SUSPECT POOL

Based on those criteria and more than 120 years of speculation, the BBC came up with five main suspects in 2008:

**1. Montague John Druitt.** Considered the prime suspect at the time, Druitt also has very little evidence against him. He was a teacher, lived in the town of Blackheath, and did not match most descriptions of the killer. However, he was the son of a doctor, had a history of mental problems, and played in cricket tournaments near Whitechapel around the time of several of the murders. Then, in December 1888, just weeks after the last victim was found, Druitt drowned himself in the Thames River. Investigators believed his suicide was the reason the murders stopped and, according to lead inspector Melville Macnaghten, "From private information, I have little doubt that his own family suspected this man of being the Whitechapel murderer."

**2. Prince Albert Victor Christian Edward ("Prince Eddy").** The grandson of Queen Victoria, Prince Eddy didn't really become a suspect until 1970, when an English surgeon named Thomas Stowell published a magazine article that implicated him in the crimes. According to Stowell, the prince was driven crazy by syphilis and committed the murders while consumed by madness. The author also claimed that the royal family knew the prince was Jack the Ripper and covered it up. It's a good theory, but unlikely. None of the papers Stowell cited can be corroborated, and according to logs kept by the royal family, Prince Eddy had alibis for most of the murders. Of course, that could've been part of the cover-up.

**3. Michael Ostrog.** Another unlikely suspect, Ostrog was a con man who'd been in and out of prison for years, mostly for robbery. None of his previous crimes were violent or targeted women. Plus, he was in his 50s or 60s in 1888, too old according to descriptions given by witnesses to be the man last seen with the victims. However, Ostrog had always expressed an interest in medicine—he even claimed to be a surgeon, though he had no training in the field—and had shown signs of insanity during previous trials. So Inspector Macnaghten considered him a suspect and even called Ostrog "a mad Russian doctor and a convict and unquestionably a homicidal maniac," despite the fact that there's no historical evidence of this.

**4. Nathan Kaminsky ("David Cohen").** In December 1888, just a few weeks after the last Whitechapel murder, police in the East End discovered a man wandering the streets and muttering to himself in Yiddish. He was taken to a lunatic asylum, named "David Cohen" (what Jewish John Does were called in London back then), and eventually proved to be a violent patient. He attacked a guard with a lead pipe, spat out food, and kicked people who walked by him. Eventually, Cohen was confined to his bed and died in the asylum.

It turned out that "David Cohen" was probably a man named Nathan Kaminsky, a cobbler and tailor who had syphilis and was treated in early 1888 at the Whitechapel Workhouse Infirmary... right in the center of the murderer's domain. According to the hospital's records, Kaminsky was "cured" in May 1888 and released. The Ripper murders began in August, so many modern researchers theorize that Kaminsky was the killer. And their evidence is pretty good: He was released into the East End population at the right time and fit witness descriptions. The infirmary treated prostitutes, among other lower-income people, so Kaminsky may have met some of the victims there. And he was incarcerated at the lunatic asylum as David Cohen right around the time the murders stopped, making him—in many people's minds—the most logical suspect.

**5. Walter Sickert.** In 2002, crime novelist Patricia Cornwell (who'd also once worked at Virginia's Office of the Chief Medical Examiner) wrote a book that claimed she'd solved the Jack the Ripper mystery once and for all. According to her, a British painter named Walter Sickert did it. Cornwell focused on letters sent to the police and newspapers at the time of the murders that claimed to be from Jack the Ripper. The letters taunted investigators and made fun of them for not being able to solve the crimes. Cornwell had the stamps of several letters tested for mitocondrial DNA, and she claimed to have found a match to Walter Sickert. It's an imaginative theory, but most people consider the Ripper letters to be hoaxes written by many different people. The handwriting varies from letter to letter, and sending Ripper letters became a popular prank in late 19th-century London. (And beyond—Scotland Yard says it received Ripper letters as late as the 1960s.) And what of the DNA? That theory has holes too.

---

In 1935, inventor Israel Pilot coined the name "Wonder-Bra."

Mitochondrial DNA isn't unique. It just shows similar patterns, and the ones that matched Sickert could also have matched hundreds of thousands of people living in London in the 1880s. (The kind of DNA used in modern forensic science is called "nuclear DNA.")

It appears that still, even after more than 120 years, no one knows. Jack the Ripper wasn't the world's first serial killer, but he has become one of the most famous. He also has the distinction of being one of the most elusive criminals in history.

*     *     *

## JACK HANGS TEN

By 1907, Jack London had published his most famous works, *The Call of the Wild* (1903) and *White Fang* (1906). On a well-earned vacation in Oahu he watched a group of Hawaiians use wooden boards to ride the waves at Waikiki Beach. Intrigued, London decided then and there to learn to surf.

On his first try, London never made it past the breakers. But he persisted the next day...and the next. Soon, London had caught a wave and ridden it on his stomach all the way to the shore. After just a few days of "surf-riding," London wrote a short piece in which he described the beach, the sport of surfing...and his first Hawaiian sunburn: "Sunburn at first is merely warm; after that it grows intense and the blisters come out...That is why I spent the next day in bed. I couldn't walk. And that is why, today, I am writing this in bed...But tomorrow, ah, tomorrow, I shall be out in that wonderful water, and I shall come in standing up."

"A Royal Sport: Surfing in Waikiki" was published in a magazine called *The Ladies Home Companion* in October 1907 and then republished in 1911 as part of *The Cruise of the Snark*, a collection of nonfiction articles detailing London's time sailing around the South Pacific. It was the first time most people in the Western world had ever heard of surfing.

# ART HISTORY 101

*This may be an unscholarly look at art through the ages, but Uncle John thinks these are works you should be familiar with.*

## 1. UNLUCKY NUMBER

*The Last Supper*

**Artist:** Leonardo da Vinci

**Where:** Santa Maria delle Grazie, a church and convent in Milan, Italy

**Medium:** Tempera on stone

**Appearance:** If you've never seen the real thing, the mural's size is surprising—15 feet high by 29 feet wide. Jesus sits at a long, food-laden table with his apostles, who are reacting to his announcement that one of them will betray him. Most look surprised; Judas, fourth from left, clutches a small bag—filled with 30 pieces of silver, no doubt.

**Details of Interest:**

• His patrons, the duke and duchess of Milan, commissioned the work in 1495. Da Vinci painted *The Last Supper* on a drywall (sealed with gesso, pitch, and mastic) rather than on wet plaster (which would have made it a "fresco" as opposed to a mural). Leonardo chose the drywall method because—unlike a fresco—it can be modified as the artist works.

• The mural began to deteriorate a few years after da Vinci finished it in 1498, and it has been restored multiple times. Santa Maria delle Grazie was bombed by British and American planes in August 1943. The mural's wall had been sandbagged for protection, so it wasn't hit by bomb splinters, but it's thought to have been damaged by the vibrations. A cleaning and stabilizing restoration from 1951 to 1954 fixed that damage. The most recent restoration took more than 20 years, from 1978 to 1999.

• Dan Brown's novel *The Da Vinci Code* suggested that the person seated on Jesus's left (from the observer's point of view) isn't one of the apostles, but we're not saying who, in case you haven't read the book.

---

**The electric toaster was successfully marketed (1909) before sliced bread (1930).**

## 2. A NICE JEWISH BOY

*David*

**Artist:** Michelangelo

**Where:** *David* has always lived in Florence, Italy. After spending a few centuries outdoors, mostly in the Piazza della Signoria, the statue was moved indoors to the Accademia di Belle Arti in 1873.

**Medium:** Marble sculpture

**Description:** He's big—17 feet tall—he's naked, and he's anatomically correct. The gorgeous statue is of the biblical King David contemplating his battle with Goliath, as proven by the slingshot he carries casually over his shoulder. Michelangelo began carving the sculpture from a huge slab of white Carrara marble when he was in his mid-20s and finished it four years later in 1504.

### Details of Interest:

• *David* isn't circumcised. Historians note that, while this is at odds with Judaic practice, it is consistent with the conventions of Renaissance art.

• There's a full-size cast copy of the sculpture in London's Victoria and Albert Museum, with a detachable plaster fig leaf displayed nearby. At one time, the fig leaf was placed temporarily over *David*'s private parts when Queen Victoria and other important ladies visited the museum. If you can't make it to Italy or London, there's an exact replica overlooking the Scajaquada Expressway in Delaware Park, Buffalo, New York. *David* has also been spotted at Forest Lawn Cemetery in Glendale, California, and—where else?—at Caesar's Palace in Las Vegas.

## 3. WHAT'S SO FUNNY?

*Mona Lisa*

**Artist:** Leonardo da Vinci

**Where:** At the Louvre in Paris. Like any superstar, she needs protection from the masses: she sits behind bulletproof glass and visitors (about 8 million annually) have to stand behind a rope barrier to catch a glimpse of her.

**Medium:** Oil on poplar wood

**Appearance:** This is probably the world's most famous painting. The *Mona Lisa* is a half-length portrait of a seated woman who

---

Benjamin Robbins Curtis (1851) was the first U.S. Supreme Court justice to have a law degree...

has been identified as Lisa Gherardini, the wife of wealthy silk merchant Francesco del Giocondo (hence the painting's other name: *La Gioconda*). Dressed in a simple gown, she sits on a balcony that overlooks a bucolic Renaissance background and looks at you with that famous enigmatic smile. The piece of wood she's painted on measures 30 inches high by 21 inches wide.

## Details of Interest:

• It was probably da Vinci's favorite painting; he took it with him when King Francis I invited him to France in 1516. After da Vinci's death in 1519, the king bought the painting from the artist's heirs. King Louis XIV inherited it and hung it in the palace at Versailles. After the French Revolution, it was moved to the Louvre. When Napoléon came to power, he hung it in his bedroom for a while, but it was later returned to the Louvre.

• The painting was stolen on August 21, 1911, by an Italian who kept it in his apartment for two years before trying to sell it. When he was caught, the painting was returned to the Louvre.

• Two crazies attacked the painting in 1956: The first threw acid, damaging the lower part of the painting. The second threw a rock at it, removing a speck of pigment near the *Mona Lisa*'s left elbow, which was repaired.

• In 1919, artist Marcel Duchamp added a moustache and goatee to a cheap reproduction and added the inscription "L.H.O.O.Q.," which when read out loud in French sounds like "Elle a chaud au cul" (literally: "she has a hot ass"; in slang: "she's horny"). In 1954, Salvador Dalí superimposed his own mustachioed face on a copy of the painting and called it *Self Portrait as Mona Lisa*. Andy Warhol created serigraph prints of multiple *Mona Lisas* called *Thirty Are Better than One*. Lesser-known artists have had their fun, too, adding an eye patch, blue hair curlers, sunglasses, a Santa hat, and even a slice of pizza for her to hold.

## 4. HI, MOM!

*Whistler's Mother* (officially known as *Arrangement in Grey and Black No. 1: The Artist's Mother*)
**Artist:** James McNeill Whistler
**Where:** The Musée d'Orsay, Paris, France

**Medium:** Oil on canvas

**Appearance:** You've seen it—a sweet-looking old lady in a long black dress and a white lace cap veil sits in profile on a straight-backed chair, her hands folded demurely in her lap. The surprise is that the painting is bigger than you'd expect, around 4 feet 8 inches high by 5 feet 4 inches wide.

**Details of Interest:**

• Whistler called it *Arrangement in Grey and Black* because he wanted his audience to know that it was less a portrait of his mother (who had in fact posed for the painting in 1871) than a piece of art. But old sentimental Victorian England wouldn't stand for it—Whistler had to add the colon and *The Artist's Mother* to the title. His uptight British audience gave it its final nickname: *Whistler's Mother.*

• The picture on the wall behind Mrs. Whistler is an etching of her son's called *Black Lion Wharf.*

• Whistler eventually pawned the painting for money to buy paints, but after his mother died in 1881, he borrowed some money to redeem it.

• When the French government bought the painting in 1891 and hung it in the Musée du Luxembourg in Paris, Whistler finally felt that the work was appreciated for its artistry.

• The unsentimental artist died long before he could see the 1934 postage stamp engraved with a stylized image of *Whistler's Mother*, accompanied by the slogan "In Memory and in Honor of the Mothers of America."

*Art History 101 continues on page 384.*

\*       \*       \*

"All art is subversive."

—**Pablo Picasso**

"You know it's not a good wax museum when there are wicks coming out of people's heads."

—**Rick Reynolds**

**Egads! The purl stitch was unknown before the 16th century.**

# ORDEAL OR NO DEAL

*No DNA. No fingerprints. No jury. For judges in medieval Europe, every trial was he said, she said, so they sometimes looked for divine intervention to determine guilt or innocence. If you were accused of a crime, you might be asked to prove your innocence through one of these ordeals.*

## 1. GLOWING IRON

An iron rod was heated until it was red-hot and, after an elaborate series of prayers and blessings, the accused carried it a distance of nine feet. His hands were then wrapped and inspected three days later. The logic was that God would protect the innocent and his hands would be healing. If his hands were festering, he was guilty.

## 2. BOILING WATER

The accused would be asked to plunge his hand into a cauldron of boiling water (that had been blessed by a priest) and pull out a pebble or other object. As with the glowing iron, the accused's hand would be bound and inspected three days later. If it was healing, he was found innocent; if it wasn't, the verdict was guilty.

## 3. COLD WATER

The accused's hands and feet were bound and he was tossed into a river or pond. In the early Middle Ages, it was believed that God protected the innocent, so he would float, following the logic of other ordeals. But by the end of the Middle Ages, the reasoning was inverted. The new idea was that, since the water was blessed and thus served as a baptism for the accused, it would reject the guilty, making them float. This left the innocent to sink and hope for a quick rescue.

## 4. THE CROSS

This ordeal was used to settle disputes. Both parties faced the cross and extended their arms to the sides, imitating the shape of the cross. Whoever was the first to tire and put his arms down was in the wrong, since God would give strength to the righteous.

## 5. THE BLESSED MORSEL

The accused was given communion in a church before the altar. If he could swallow the blessed bread without choking, he was found innocent.

---

**In 1937, Pan Am made the first commercial flight across the Pacific.**

# IF THE NAME FITS...

*Uncle John didn't need a last name to make his
mark on the world, but some people do.*

C ertain historical figures did a fine job of living up to (or in
some cases, living down) the meaning behind their sur-
names. Here are a few of our favorites.

### CHÁVEZ
**Where It Came From:** Derived from the Spanish *llaves*, "keys"; a
name given to a key maker.
**Made Famous By:** César Chávez (1927–93), cofounder of the
United Farm Workers. Chávez was a key (ahem!) figure in secur-
ing fair labor practices to benefit agriculture workers in the United
States. In 2003, he was honored on a 37-cent stamp by the U.S.
Postal Service.

### FREUD
**Where It Came From:** In Middle High German, *vreude* means
"joy."
**Made Famous By:** Sigmund Freud (1856–1939), the founder of
psychoanalysis. Freud was a regular user of cocaine, which he also
recommended to patients and friends as an antidepressant. After
one of Freud's good friends developed "cocaine psychosis," the
good doctor lost confidence in the drug's ability to elicit joy and
stopped endorsing it (though it's speculated that he continued to
use it himself).

### GEIGER
**Where It Came From:** A German name meaning "fiddler."
**Made Famous By:** German physicist Hans Geiger (1882–1945).
Fiddling around in his lab, Geiger produced the first version of his
Geiger counter in 1908. Modern radiation-detecting devices work
on different principles but are still called Geiger counters. In 1939,
Geiger became part of Nazi Germany's project to build a nuclear
bomb, which—happily for the rest of the world—ended in failure.

---

Blind and impoverished in 1667, John Milton sold the rights to *Paradise Lost* for £10.

## KELLOGG

**Where It Came From:** An English name that originated in the Middle Ages, meaning "killer of hogs" (in other words, a butcher).
**Made Famous By:** W. K. Kellogg (1860–1951), founder of the Kellogg Company. Despite his name, Kellogg was a vegetarian, and he made his fortune by promoting cereal products over traditional breakfast foods like bacon and eggs. His cereals were among the first food products to include nutrition information on the labels.

## KENNEDY

**Where It Came From:** The Gaelic *ceann*, "head," and *éidigh*, "ugly" ("ugly head").
**Made Famous By:** John F. Kennedy (1917–63), the 35th president of the United States. Despite his name, Kennedy is considered one of the best-looking presidents in U.S. history. In 1960, he used his good looks and calm demeanor to trump Richard M. Nixon and his five o'clock shadow in the first televised debates between presidential candidates. A majority of radio listeners felt that Nixon had won the debates, but Kennedy won the election by about 112,000 votes.

## O'LEARY

**Where It Came From:** The Irish Gaelic *ó*, "descendant of," and *laoghaire*, "keeper of cattle."
**Made Famous By:** Catherine O'Leary (1827–95), whose cow was said to have started the 1871 Great Chicago Fire by kicking over a lantern in her barn. Mrs. O'Leary was exonerated two years later when a *Chicago Tribune* reporter admitted to fabricating the story. Despite the reporter's confession, popular culture continues to revel in the tale of Mrs. O'Leary and her careless cow.

## SPINOZA

**Where It Came From:** The Spanish *espinoso*, "thorny."
**Made Famous By:** Dutch philosopher Baruch de Spinoza (1632–77). Spinoza was a thorn in the side of the Roman Catholic Church, which placed every one of his works on its list of prohibited books—a list that wasn't abolished until 1966. In fact, Spinoza's opinions made pretty much everyone uncomfortable: raised a

In 1961, Pampers disposable introduced diapers.

Jew, he was banned from the Jewish community at age 23 because of his controversial ideas.

## WASHINGTON

**Where It Came From:** A town in England of the same name, likely derived from a landowner named *Hwœsa*, meaning "wheat sheaf"; thus, "Hwœsa's town."

**Made Famous By:** America's first president, George Washington (1732–99). Before Washington became commander in chief, he was a successful wheat farmer in Virginia. After his presidency, Washington returned to the farm and set up the largest whiskey distillery in the United States.

## XAVIER

**Where It Came From:** The Basque *exaberri*, "new house."

**Made Famous By:** Saint Francis Xavier (1506–52), one of the founders of the Jesuit order. Xavier spent much of his life on missions in Asia, traveling under the flag of the Portuguese empire. His body was enshrined at Goa, India, but in 1614 his right forearm was detached and given a new home in an altar at a Roman church.

\*     \*     \*

## 11 THINGS THAT CHANGED EVERYDAY LIFE
You decide if they were for better or for worse.

1. Matches, 1827
2. Flashlights, 1890
3. Safety glass, 1903
4. Cellophane, 1908
5. Stainless steel, 1913
6. Kleenex, 1924
7. Teflon, 1938
8. Superglue, 1942
9. Velcro, 1949
10. Bubble wrap, 1957
11. Internet, 1989

---

June 18, 1873: Susan B. Anthony was fined $100 for attempting to vote for the president.

# ALL'S FAIR IN WAR

*The best-known war gambit, albeit a legendary one, was the Greeks' "gift" of a giant wooden horse to the army Odysseus had failed to defeat after a 10-year siege of Troy. Here are some real war tricks.*

"All war involves deception. Even though you are competent, appear to be incompetent. Though effective, appear to be ineffective." —Sun Tzu, *The Art of War*

## 1. SHOFAR SO GOOD

**Who:** Gideon and the Israelites
**When:** c. 1190 BC
**Gambit:** "We've got you surrounded!"

Making your army look bigger is the oldest trick in the book. We mean that literally, as some biblical scholars believe Gideon's victory over 135,000 Midianites and Amalekites happened around 1190 BC and the accounts of the battle were written 600 years later.

The story has it that the Israelite army was outnumbered four to one, so Gideon decided on a desperate psychological gambit. He selected 300 men from his force of 32,000 for a daring mind game on the invading armies. In the dark of night, he armed each of the 300 with a *shofar* (a bugle made from a ram's horn) and a torch somehow kept burning out of sight within an earthenware pitcher.

After traveling quietly through the darkness, the men spread out in a circle that completely surrounded the enemy camp. On signal, the men revealed their lights, blew their horns, and began shouting at the tops of their lungs. The enemy soldiers, composed of two rival tribes, leaped out of their beds in confusion. Believing that the lights and trumpets were backed up by a massive army and perhaps also suspecting that the other tribe was engaged in some treachery, the soldiers panicked, lashing out at anything that moved in the darkness.

Unfortunately, that happened to be their equally disoriented fellows and allies. The sound of actual battle in the dark within their own camp added to the confusion and frenzy. The result was a self-inflicted bloodbath that allowed the Israelites to drive off the survivors with few casualties of their own.

## 2. NOTHING IS BETTER FOR THEE THAN ME

**Who:** Colonel William Washington

**When:** December 4, 1780

**Gambit:** "Trust me. This is a real gun!"

Colonel William Washington (George's cousin, twice removed) had been skirmishing with British loyalists throughout the South Carolina backcountry. Although both sides had managed to kill a lot of each other's soldiers, neither side was strong enough to chase the other out of the area. In December, though, Washington got a break. He got word that local loyalist Colonel Rowland Rugeley had briefly returned to his own farm in Camden, South Carolina, along with 125 men. Surrounding Rugeley's house and barn, Washington and his men were kept out of shooting range by a constant volley of bullets from the well-protected defenders.

After a long standoff, someone came up with a crazy idea that just might work. Washington ordered some of his men deep into the forest to fell a tall, straight pine, cut and carve it to the shape of a cannon, and blacken it using whatever they could find: paint, pitch, or bootblack. When the soldiers poked it out of the woods and aimed it at the farmhouse, threatening lethal bombardment, it looked real enough that Rugeley and his men surrendered without firing another shot. After that, both sides used these fake "Quaker guns" (so called because Quakers—the Religious Society of Friends—hold a religious opposition to waging war).

During the American Civil War, the Confederacy especially made them an art form, sometimes mounting them on real gun carriages, to compensate for having less artillery than the Union. By doing so, they could impede Union movements and assaults. One use deserves special mention, as the following story will tell.

## 3. GONE WITH THE WIND

**Who:** Confederate General G. T. Beauregard

**When:** May, 1862

**Gambit:** "Now you see us, now you don't"

In the Battle of Shiloh, General P. G. T. Beauregard became over-confident. He had the forces of Union general Ulysses S. Grant with their backs to the Tennessee River, but decided not to deliver the coup de grâce and to call off the battle for the night. However,

Union reinforcements arrived before morning, and suddenly Beauregard was on the defensive.

Retreating from the superior Union army, the rebels holed up in the railroad hub of Corinth, Mississippi, and waited while the army led by cautious Major General Henry W. Halleck approached, dug trenches in anticipation for battle, and began shelling the outer fortifications of the city. Beauregard knew his situation was bad, so he tried a gambit. He distributed three days of rations to soldiers and ordered them to prepare for an attack, knowing that word would get back to the Union army. Without reinforcements to be had, he arranged to have empty trains run in and out of town. When they stopped, he had his men whoop and holler as if reinforcements of men and matériel had arrived.

Meanwhile, he put his men to work building Quaker guns out of logs and switching his real armaments with the phony ones. On May 29, he began loading his real artillery and wounded soldiers into trains and evacuated most of his men, leaving just a skeleton crew of buglers and drummers to play into the night and keep campfires burning. By daylight, the skeleton crew had also slipped away to a meeting place in Tupelo, leaving the fires and phony armaments in place. By the time Union patrols approached the town, there was nobody left to fight.

## 4. CLOSE BY NO CIGARS

**Who:** Fidel Castro
**When:** February 17, 1957
**Gambit:** "Our army is so big!"

Fidel Castro knew the power the American press had in molding public opinion both in America and Cuba. After a bad defeat and being reported as dead by Fulgencio Batista's Mafia-supported Cuban government, Castro invited *New York Times* reporter Herbert Matthews to meet him in Cuba's Sierra Maestra mountains. Castro wanted to make an overwhelming impression, but there was one problem: the underwhelming appearance of his ragtag revolutionary army, only 18 members strong. To disguise his weakness, Castro met Matthews in a small clearing. His 18 guerrillas created a bustle of comings and goings by entering the clearing in ones and twos from all directions, then changing clothes and hats

---

...For example, their drinking cups included built-in straws.

and appearing as different characters a few minutes later. To further the illusion, a man rushed in midway through the interview with a report from a completely fictitious Army #2.

Matthews came away convinced that Castro was leading a huge army, and he wrote a long article with the conclusion that "General Batista cannot hope to suppress Castro's revolt." The effect was immediate; the story became a self-fulfilling prophecy as Castro supporters in the United States mailed copies of the story to influential people in Cuba. Finally, on January 1, 1959, Batista fled the country with a reported $300 million, and the 32-year-old Castro became the head of Cuba.

## 5. INFLATIONARY PRESSURES

**Who:** The Allied forces

**When:** February 17, 1944

**Gambit:** "The real attack is coming somewhere else"

Inflatable tanks and plywood artillery, phantom armies led by famous generals, and a network of double-crossing German spies managed to hide the biggest secret the Allies had in 1944: where the Allies would land on D-Day. Operation Fortitude was the name of an elaborate campaign to convince the Germans that the invasion forces would be landing in Norway and the Pas de Calais instead of the real site in Normandy. To accomplish this, the Allies pulled out all stops to give the impression that there was a huge invasion force massing in parts of England where no armies actually existed. The Allies built dummy tanks, aircraft, and landing craft and set them out in large numbers so that German spy planes would see them. They planted photos in newspapers showing inspection tours of his "army" by General George Patton, nominally in charge of the Calais armies. It worked. Even after the Allies landed en masse in Normandy, Hitler held back the bulk of his armies, believing that the Normandy landing was just a diversionary feint. By the time he realized that Normandy was the real thing, it was too late. In April 1945, Berlin was captured, Germany surrendered, and Hitler committed suicide.

---

**Cleopatra used cucumber juice as a skin lotion.**

# LOST!

*Someday we may find the answer to these
mysteries…but for now they're lost.*

## 1. WHERE'S ZEUS?

One of the seven wonders of the ancient world is Phidias's statue
of the Greek God Zeus. Created in ivory and gold in fifth century
BC, the statue presided over the Olympic Games in Olympia.
From coins and engravings, we know that the statue was of the
seated Zeus, who held a statue of Nike in one hand and a scepter
in the other. Since the statue was 40 feet high, it would seem to
be hard to misplace. Although there are reports of the Romans
taking the statue from Olympia, there's no agreement on where it
went or how and when it might have been destroyed. All we
know for certain is that it's lost.

## 2. LOST AZTEC GOLD

In 1520, Spanish conquistador Hernando Cortés killed Aztec
emperor Montezuma and then looted the Aztec treasury, which
was filled with gold. Taking as much as they could carry, Cortés
and his army left, but angry Aztec soldiers attacked them at the
Battle of Tenochtitlan (known to the Spanish as La Noche Triste).
The Azetecs found Cortés and forced him and his men to flee.
Some histories say that most of the treasure was lost in Lake
Tenochtitlan during the battle, others that the Aztecs buried it
fearing the Spaniards' return. Adventurers follow many legends,
searching for that lost Aztec gold.

## 3. THE LOST LEGIONS OF ROME

In 53 BC, Roman legions, sent to conquer Parthia (now a region
of Iran) under Marcus Crassus, were defeated at the Battle of Carrhae. Most of Crassus's army was killed, but some Roman soldiers
were taken prisoner while others evaded the enemy and marched
east. When the two sides made peace and exchanged prisoners,
the whereabouts of the soldiers who'd survived Carrhae was
unknown. Historians believe that Liqian, China (where residents
have Roman features, light eyes, and blonde hair), was founded by
the lost legions of Rome.

---

**Norway consumes more Mexican food than any other European country.**

# BALLADS & BALLOTS

*Politicians aren't all just work and scandal. Some of them are music lovers too. Some are even musicians and songwriters.*

## 1. "YOU ARE MY SUNSHINE"

Jimmie Davis, a two-term governor from Louisiana, gets credit—along with Charles Mitchell—for penning this popular song with the well-known refrain "Please don't take my sunshine away." (Since several earlier versions of the song exist, though, Davis most likely just put his name on it after he bought the authorship rights from another country songwriter.) Davis recorded the song in 1939 and sang it at campaign stops both times he ran for governor of Louisiana. It must have worked, since he won—once in 1944 and again in 1960—and "You Are My Sunshine" became one of Louisiana's official songs. ("Give Me Louisiana" is the other.)

Davis enjoyed his days in the sun for a long time; he died in 2000 at the age of 101. But "You Are My Sunshine" lives on and has been recorded by the likes of Bing Crosby, Brian Wilson, Bob Dylan, Johnny Cash, and the Soggy Mountain Boys, who included it on the movie soundtrack for *O Brother, Where Art Thou?*

## 2. "EVERY MAN A KING"

Singer-songwriter Randy Newman rarely records other people's songs, but on his 1974 *Good Old Boys* album, Newman sings a rousing ditty written by former Louisiana governor and U.S. senator Huey "Kingfish" Long (1893–1935). The song talks about sharing the nation's wealth and includes the chorus "Every man a king / For you can be a millionaire…" Huey Long was a Democrat who intended to run for president on a platform that called for taxing corporations to relieve the Great Depression's crushing poverty. In 1935, Long recruited the band director of Louisiana State University to help him write this song. It may have been catchy, but it didn't do Long much good—later that same year, he was assassinated in the Louisiana state capitol building.

## 3. "ALOHA 'OE"

There is a bittersweet longing in "Aloha 'Oe" ("Farewell to

Thee") that resonates across various cultures, even when listeners have no knowledge of the Hawaiian language or culture. The song evokes even more melancholy if you know the story of its author, Queen Lili'uokalani, the last monarch of Hawaii. She wrote it in 1877 after witnessing a farewell embrace between an American colonel and his Hawaiian girlfriend. Sixteen years later, in 1893, Lili'uokalani was deposed by American pineapple and sugar magnates who were aided by the U.S. Navy. Her crime? She drafted a new constitution that would give more rights to native Hawaiians. That ended Hawaii's sovereignty—it became a republic, and later a territory, occupied by the United States. In 1959, Hawaii became the 50th state in the union.

The queen, who never abdicated her throne, was placed under house arrest for five years, during which time she wrote her autobiography and a songbook's worth of music.

## 4. "EIGHT DAYS OF HANUKKAH"

Republican Utah senator and Mormon Orrin Hatch may seem like an unlikely songwriter, especially for a tune about Hanukkah, but he's been writing songs and hymns for years. Formerly the manager of a folk music group, Hatch plays keyboards and violin, which might explain his unexpected friendship with activist and U2 front man Bono. (Bono reportedly advised Hatch to publish songs under a pen name "because it's you, man.") In Hatch's hybrid musical/political life, he has written "Heal Our Land" for George W. Bush's second inauguration, a posthumous tribute to his friend and fellow senator Ted Kennedy, and the bridge for a country song by liberal Democrat Al Franken. Go figure...politics makes for strange bedfellows.

## 5. "I GOT YOU BABE," "THE BEAT GOES ON," "BANG BANG," "YOU BETTER SIT DOWN, KIDS"

Before Salvadore Phillip "Sonny" Bono became the Republican mayor of Palm Springs, California, and a member of the United States House of Representatives, he was a songwriter, drummer, and singer. His musical career took off when he grew his hair long, donned a fur vest, and teamed up with his second wife, Cher. Yet despite the appearance that Bono was a member of the 1960s counterculture, he was always a conservative, appearing in

---

Circa 200 BC: Sri Lanka was the first country in the world to have a nature preserve.

antidrug films and naming his daughter Chastity in honor of his views on premarital sex. Elected to the House of Representatives in 1994, Bono served only three years before suffering a fatal collision with a tree while skiing.

## 5. "PEDRO NAVAJA"

If you're a fan of salsa music, you'll know the name Rubén Blades. The Panamanian singer's album *Siembra* (1978) is the most successful salsa recording in history—it sold 25 million copies. Blades has since recorded with Elvis Costello, Lou Reed, Little Steven, and Sting, but still had time to run for president of Panama in 1994. He didn't win, but in 2004, he was appointed Panama's minister of tourism and served for five years before resuming his music career full-time.

\*     \*     \*

## PRESIDENTIAL MEDAL OF FREEDOM

Although it grew out of an earlier medal honoring military service, the Presidential Medal of Freedom was created by executive order in 1963 by President John F. Kennedy. The first 31 winners (announced on July 4, 1963) received their medals from President Lyndon Johnson in the White House's State Dining Room on December 6 of that year, only two weeks after Kennedy's assassination. The honorees included the following:

• Marian Anderson, the African American contralto who sang at the Lincoln Memorial in 1939 after being turned away from another venue by the Daughters of the American Revolution.

• George Meany, labor leader and president of the AFL-CIO.

• Writers Thornton Wilder, Edmund Wilson, Mark S. Watson, and E. B. White, as well as musicians Pablo Cassals and Rudolf Serkin, architect Ludwig Mies van der Rohe, photographer Edward Steichen, and artist Andrew Wyeth.

Johnson also added two Medals of Freedom of his own, one for Pope John XXIII, who had died six months earlier, and one for the late president. Attorney General Robert F. Kennedy received the Medal for his brother, while Jacqueline Kennedy—moving out of the White House that day—watched from a nearby room.

In 1964, Jean-Paul Sartre was the first person to voluntarily decline a Nobel Prize.

# MONKEY SEE, MONKEY DANCE

*Here at the BRI, we're big supporters of going with the flow, but sometimes that gets out of hand. Consider these three examples of mass hysteria, a phenomenon in which entire groups of people believe they are suffering from the same mysterious (and often wacky) circumstance or affliction.*

## 1. THE DANCING PLAGUE

Life in Strasbourg, France, in 1518 was tough. A severe famine had swept across the region. Diseases like smallpox and syphilis spread among the weakened population, killing even more people. Strasbourgians were scared...and superstitious. An old Catholic myth said that if the martyr Saint Vitus got angry with humanity, he'd send down a plague of dancing. And so it began. First one woman, then another, then hundreds of men and women took to Strasbourg's streets and boogied like there was no tomorrow.

For many of them there wasn't. Ultimately, about 400 people joined in the hysteria. The "plague" lasted about a month, and during that time of nonstop dancing, many people died of heart attacks, dehydration, and exhaustion. Sixteenth-century authorities believed the dancing was caused by the Saint Vitus curse—today, most historians think it was simple mass hysteria. Once one person was afflicted, others thought they had it too.

## 2. *THE WAR OF THE WORLDS* RADIO BROADCAST

On October 30, 1938, a theater group headed by actor Orson Welles staged a radio play based on author H. G. Wells's science-fiction novel *The War of the Worlds*. Welles had written the play to seem like a real emergency news broadcast detailing an invasion from Mars, and people bought it. Police stations were flooded with calls asking how to escape the attack. Residents prowled their neighborhoods with guns, while others took refuge in their basements. Some went to hospitals, complaining of dizziness, nausea, and rapid heartbeats caused by the poisonous gas Martians had unleashed on the world. Others said they could actually see and hear bombs falling near their homes.

---

The eight traditional courses at a Chinese wedding dinner don't include dessert.

None of it was true. The broadcast was an elaborate hoax, set up by Welles and CBS. They created a radio program that so closely imitated news broadcasts of the day that it fooled people and made them feel scared and sick. Later reports estimated that only about 20 percent of the listening public (about 2 million people) believed the hoax, but the scope was large enough for Welles to regret the hysteria his radio play had caused. He said, "I don't think we will choose anything like this again."

## 3. THE MILK MIRACLE

What would you do if, suddenly, religious statues started to drink milk? In India in 1995, the reaction was amazement and wonder at one of the world's true miracles. On September 21, a temple-goer offered a spoonful of milk to a white stone statue of Lord Ganesh...and the statue "drank" the milk. At least, the liquid seemed to disappear. Word of the miracle spread quickly, and within hours, people all over India, and then around the world, flocked to temples—spoons and milk in hand—to test the miracle for themselves. Many discovered that it worked. In fact, so many people wanted to feed the statues that stores in New Delhi, India, sold out of milk.

Then the scientists got involved. They wanted to figure out just how the supposedly supernatural event was happening, so they filled a spoon with milk containing food coloring (so it would be a different color than the stone) and offered it to a statue. According to the scientists, the milk was pulled out of the spoon and then spilled down the front of the statue by means of a process called "capillary action"—where surface tension pulls liquid away from an object, and then gravity pushes it back down. The believers didn't want to hear it, however—most rejected the scientists' findings and simply maintained that the statues had indeed drunk the milk. To this day, the Hindu milk miracle is considered by many religious groups to be one of the miracles of the modern world.

\*     \*     \*

"After twelve years of therapy my psychiatrist said something that brought tears to my eyes. He said, '*No hablo ingles.*'"

—**Ronnie Shakes, standup comic**

The "Iceberg theory" refers to Ernest Hemingway's writing style, characterized...

# UNCIVIL WARS

*Not all state rivalries are about college football.*

## 1. PENNSYLVANIA VS. MARYLAND

When the colony of Pennsylvania was chartered in 1681, nearly five decades after Maryland, the king of England wanted to make sure he didn't accidentally give away the town of New Castle, which belonged to his brother, the Duke of York. So in Pennsylvania's charter, he specified that the border between Pennsylvania and Maryland would run along the 40th parallel, except for the area around New Castle. But New Castle is 25 miles below the 40th parallel, so the two never intersect. Predictably, Maryland decided the border was on the 40th parallel; Pennsylvania said it ran west from New Castle. Within the disputed land was the head of Chesapeake Bay and the city of Philadelphia.

**The Dispute Goes On.** In 1726, a staunch Marylander, Thomas Cresap, wrangled a grant for 500 acres in the disputed area from Lord Baltimore, much of it already settled by Pennsylvanians. He convinced these farmers to buy their own land back from him, then started collecting taxes. By 1734, he was evicting settlers from their homes—the ones they'd already bought back from him—and giving the land to his friends.

This did not go over well with Pennsylvania. Several attempts were made to arrest Cresap. During one attempt, Cresap shot a deputy through his front door, then refused to give the sheriff's men a candle so they could tend to the injury. The deputy died, and the governor of Pennsylvania demanded Cresap be arrested for murder. Instead, the governor of Maryland made him the captain of the militia. Cresap was eventually arrested in 1736, but wasn't held for long. He went on to fight in the French-Indian War, and died a wealthy and respected veteran.

**The Mason-Dixon Line to the Rescue.** Both colonies petitioned King George II of England to settle the dispute, and a border was finally set in 1767. It was surveyed by Charles Mason and Jeremiah Dixon, becoming the Mason-Dixon Line. The border today lies below the 40th parallel because the governor of Maryland provided a faulty map during the dispute, and Philadelphia remains in Pennsylvania.

## 2. OHIO VS. MICHIGAN

Toledo, Michigan? It very nearly happened. The ordinance that initially carved up what was then the Northwest Territory into the future states of Ohio, Michigan, Indiana, Illinois, and Wisconsin (and part of Minnesota) also set the border between Ohio and Michigan as running from the southernmost tip of Lake Michigan due east to Lake Erie. The problem was that Congress had no idea where Lake Michigan actually ended. At the time, most maps put it quite a bit farther north than it actually is.

The difference from where Congress thought the bottom of Lake Michigan was and where surveyors later found it to be is about eight miles. Between the two possible borders lies a strip of farmland that includes the city of Toledo. The Michigan Territory thought the "Toledo Strip," as the section was called, was theirs. Ohio, which was already a state, thought that Congress should stay with the northern border.

**The Toledo War.** In 1835, the Ohio legislature passed an act putting the Toledo Strip under their jurisdiction. Michigan retaliated by passing an act that made any support of Ohio in Toledo subject to a $1,000 fine. Michigan sent its militia to enforce the act. Ohio sent its militia to watch Michigan's. Throughout the summer of 1835, both militias engaged in raids on Toledo, arresting and fining citizens who claimed allegiance to the other side. During one of these raids, a Michigan sheriff was stabbed in the leg by an Ohioan. This was the so-called Toledo War's only casualty.

The war ended when Michigan ran out of money to keep its militia in Toledo. President Andrew Jackson, needing Ohio's swing vote in the upcoming election, gave them the Toledo Strip. In exchange, Michigan got most of the Upper Peninsula, then a part of Wisconsin. At the time, it was thought to be useless land, but was later discovered to have rich deposits of copper, meaning Wisconsin was the real loser in a war it didn't even fight. The border between Ohio and Michigan was not officially ratified until 1973. But that's another story.

## 3. MISSOURI VS. IOWA

Although John C. Sullivan is a name forgotten to history, some vague wording on his part caused the citizens of Missouri and Iowa to take up arms against each other. In 1816, Sullivan surveyed the boundary between Missouri and Iowa, stating that the line ran through "the rapids of the river Des Moines." But which rapids? Iowa thought this phrase referred to a section of rapids in the Mississippi River (which is probably what Sullivan meant). When Missouri became a state in 1821, they sent surveyors up the Des Moines River to look for rapids—and decided that Sullivan meant some small rapids nine miles farther north.

**The Taxing Honey War.** In 1839, Missouri tried to collect taxes from settlers in the disputed area. The Iowans chased them off, but one Missourian chopped down a few well-known honey trees in the area, which is why this scuffle is known as the Honey War. Shortly after the incident, a sheriff from Iowa arrested a sheriff from Missouri for trying to collect taxes. Militias from both Missouri and Iowa (which was still a territory) soon gathered at the border. Accounts of the standoff report over a thousand men were assembled, with whatever weapons they could find—blunderbusses, ancestral swords pulled off walls, and even a sausage stuffer wielded by one person.

The governor of Iowa had coincidentally been the governor of Ohio during its 1835 dispute with Michigan, and tried to head off the conflict by referring the matter to the U.S. Supreme Court. By the time the Iowan militia sent a peace delegation, they found that the Missourians had already gone home.

The Supreme Court decided that the rapids Missouri was using to mark the border weren't prominent enough to qualify, and that decided that the state line would be the familiar Sullivan line. This time, surveyors marked the border with iron pillars, which can still be seen today.

\* \* \*

"War is the unfolding of miscalculations."

—Barbara Tuchman

According to reports, Abraham Lincoln's voice was high-pitched and shrill.

# OFF WITH THEIR HEADS

*England's King Henry VIII managed to ensure his place in history as one of the most brutal kings who ever lived. The older he got, the more bloodthirsty Henry seemed to become, as he sent not only criminals to be beheaded but also some of his closest friends, councilors, and even two of his wives. Here are some of the unfortunate souls who met with Henry's wrath.*

- Edmund Dudley, speaker of the House of Commons, 1510
- Richard Empson, chancellor of the Duchy of Lancaster, 1510
- Duke of Suffolk, 1513
- Duke of Buckingham, 1521
- John Fisher, Roman Catholic bishop, cardinal, 1535
- Thomas More, friend and Lord High Chancellor of Great Britain, 1535
- George Boleyn, brother-in-law, 1536
- Mark Smeaton, court musician accused of committing adultery with Anne Boleyn, 1536
- Francis Weston, gentleman accused of adultery with Anne Boleyn, 1536
- Anne Boleyn, Queen of England, Henry's second wife, 1536
- Henry Courtenay, Earl of Devon, 1539
- Thomas Cromwell, first Earl of Essex and chief minister to Henry, 1540
- Margaret Pole, eighth Countess of Salisbury, 1541
- Francis Dereham, courtier, most famous for his affair with Catherine Howard, 1541
- Thomas Culpeper, courtier, affair with Catherine Howard, 1541
- Catherine Howard, fifth wife of Henry, 1542
- Jane Boleyn, sister-in-law to Anne Boleyn, lady-in-waiting to Catherine Howard, 1542
- Anne Askew, poet and heretic, 1546
- Henry Howard, third Earl of Surrey, 1547

**Humans and armadillos are the only animals that can get leprosy.**

# ROADS MOST TRAVELED

*All roads lead somewhere, but unlike the five on this list, not all of them led to legendary status. Part one looks at ancient byways; part two on page 432 looks at modern highways.*

## 1. THE APPIAN WAY

The ancient Romans called their Via Appia "the queen of roads." Begun in 312 BC by the censor Appius Claudius Caecus (hence the name), the Appian Way was the first paved Roman road in what was to become an extensive network of 50,000 miles of paved roads across the Roman Empire, built between the third century BC and the second century AD.

**Purpose:** The Appian Way was constructed to speed the movement of Roman legions in a war against the Samnites, a group of tribes that lived to the south and east of Rome. The Romans won that war and credited their success to the road's effectiveness in aiding the supply and movements of troops.

**Construction:** Caecus drained the Roman treasury for construction of the road's first 132 miles, which ran southeast from Rome to Capua. The road eventually crossed the Italian peninsula, connecting Rome with the port of Brindisi on the Adriatic coast. From Brindisi, ancient Romans boarded ships bound for Greece, Egypt, and the rest of the eastern Mediterranean.

**Specs:** Roman roads were so well built that they often went 100 years before repairs were needed. Built like an underground wall, the foundations were five feet thick and were crested in the center for drainage. Paved with large, flat stones that interlocked with one another, the road was wide enough for two carts to pass, and portions of it even had raised sidewalks for pedestrians. Causeways raised the road over swampy ground, and milestones along the route marked the distance to or from the Roman Forum.

**Factoids:**

• The first 38 miles south of Rome were perfectly straight and are, to this day, the longest stretch of paved road in Europe. Romans liked straight roads so much that they generally built them straight up and down hills rather than using a winding path.

- Caecus built the first Roman aqueduct, which was also named for him: the Aqua Appia.

- The Roman road system had way stations every 12 to 18 miles with inns for travelers and stables where wheelwrights and animal handlers could take their carts, chariots, and horses. Using this system to change horses and chariots, the emperor Tiberius traveled 400 miles in 24 hours to see his brother, who was dying of gangrene.

- The Appian Way was the scene of the crucifixion of the men who joined Spartacus in his slave rebellion. When Spartacus's slave army was defeated in 71 BC, 6,000 men were hung from crosses lining the Appian Way for 132 miles. The bodies were left to hang for months, sometimes years, as a warning to other slaves. (But contrary to the movie, Spartacus himself is believed to have died in battle.)

- Jesus Christ is said to have appeared to St. Peter along the Appian Way.

- Just outside Rome, the Appian Way is lined with elaborate aboveground tombs and the entrances to the tunnels of the city's catacombs. According to ancient laws, no one was permitted to be buried within the city of Rome.

- The fact that all the roads the Romans built went outward to the borders of the empire led to the saying "All roads lead to Rome."

## 2. THE INCAN HIGHWAY

Until it was conquered by a mere 200 Spaniards in the early 1500s, the Incan Empire encompassed what is now Peru, Ecuador, and parts of Bolivia, Argentina, and Chile. The empire's warrior-king, known as the "Inca," ruled this vast territory from Cuzco, Peru, high in the Andes. The Incas' far-flung empire was held together by a network ranging from 14,000 to 25,000 miles of road, depending on the source.

**Purpose:** The road system was used primarily for military movement, supply transport, and an ingenious system of relay runners carrying messages that had to be memorized because the Incan people had no written language.

**Construction:** The Incan Empire lasted less than 100 years, from

A seed from the previously extinct Judean date palm was coaxed to sprout after...

roughly 1438 to 1532. Prior dynasties may have built parts of the road system, but since the Incas had no written language, much of their history is lost. Also, like all Native peoples of the Americas, they didn't have the wheel, so the stones that paved the road had to be dragged, carried by hand, or packed in by llamas. The Incan people paid their taxes in the form of labor; many of them did their part by building and maintaining the road network.

**Specs:** The road system had two parallel tracks: a coast road that ran 3,000 miles and a mountain route that followed the spine of the Andes. The two major roads were connected by lateral routes, many of which were paved with markers that noted the distance to Cuzco. In the mountains, the road was so steep it was more like a series of stairways. In the deserts, rock piles marked the road.

**Factoids:**

• For the relay system, young men were stationed along the route every two miles. They were chosen for speed, endurance in the thin mountain air, and—of course—a good memory. Running at full speed, a runner would blow a conch shell to announce his approach. The next runner would fall into step beside him, hear and memorize the message, and then run at top speed to the next messenger.

• Using the relay system, news traveled at 150 miles per day.

• The runners didn't just carry messages; they were so fast that they could carry fresh fish from the Pacific to the Incan king high in the Andes without it spoiling.

• The road system had a series of rest houses, called tambos, every 15 to 30 miles with storehouses that held fresh supplies and food.

• The paved roads weren't particularly flat or smooth, but they didn't have to be since there was no wheeled transport. They were built for foot traffic and llamas.

• The Incas planted and irrigated fruit trees along some routes so that travelers could have fresh fruit on their journeys.

• Where the road crossed slow-moving rivers, the Incas built pontoon boats out of reeds and covered them with wooden walkways.

• To get across a swift-moving river, a traveler would get into a basket and be pulled across the river via a rope cable.

---

...nearly 2,000 years. It's the oldest human-assisted seed germination.

• Suspension bridges made of hand-braided grass were strong enough to carry the Spanish and their horses. Unfortunately for the Incas, it was the road system that led the Spanish conquistadors directly to the Incan capital, making it easy for them to conquer the empire.

• Today, hikers can take the Incan highway to Machu Picchu.

\*　　\*　　\*

## FOUR WEDDINGS AND A FUNERAL

**1. Wedding:** In ancient Rome, couples sacrificed an animal before their wedding ceremony, and a priest called a *haruspex* examined the entrails. If the haruspex determined that the entrails looked good (markings or discoloration on the right side of the liver), the ceremony went forward. But if the entrails looked bad (markings or discoloration on the left side), the Romans took it to mean the gods didn't support the union, and the wedding was canceled.

**2. Wedding:** In ancient Sparta, a "wedding" consisted of a bride being kidnapped by her husband and then having her head shaved. Next, the pair consummated their union with the bride wearing men's clothes and sandals. Afterward, she was taken back to her parents' house, and the marriage was considered legal and complete.

**3. Wedding:** During the Middle Ages, most wealthy European brides wore brightly colored gowns trimmed with fur. It wasn't until 1840—when Queen Victoria of England chose white for her wedding to Prince Albert—that white gowns became a trend.

**4. Wedding:** In 1907, the English Parliament passed a law called the Deceased Wife's Sister's Marriage Act, which said that a man could wed his wife's sister as long as the wife was dead. Before then, marriage between in-laws was considered incest and illegal.

**5. Funeral:** The ancient Koreans put hair and nail clippings from the deceased in the coffin with the body. And about 3,000 years ago, they started putting pieces of jade on the tongue and over the eyes of a corpse. They thought it protected bodies from decay. (It doesn't.)

June 13, 1920: The U.S. Post Office said children could no longer be sent via parcel post.

# GOOD FOR WHAT AILS YOU

*If you're thinking about joining a wagon train and heading west soon, you'd best read this right quick, just in case you or the young 'uns take sick or get injured.*

The Old West was a dangerous enough place, but with doctors so few and far between—and not a Walgreens in sight—settlers had to rely on hand-me-down folk remedies or, if they were lucky, a friendly medicine man or woman. Here are treatments for ailments pioneers encountered out on the lone prairie.

**1. Boils and Carbuncles:** Painful red bumps on the skin most commonly caused by staph bacteria, boils and carbuncles (clusters of boils) were treated with a mixture of two parts soap and one part sugar that was heated and then applied as a poultice; that is, spread on a cloth and placed on the affected area.

**2. Choking:** Dr. Henry Heimlich, inventor of the Heimlich maneuver, wasn't born until 1920, so the old-timers used a different method for dislodging something stuck in the throat: they would grab the choking person's wrists and jerk the arms upward. It worked especially well with children; if done fast enough, the child would scream and cough and the object would be dislodged—either up or down—immediately.

**3. Cuts and Minor Wounds:** To stop the flow of blood, a cobweb or a handful of soot was applied to the cut. Some Native American healers used mashed pumpkins as a poultice for cuts and scrapes.

**4. Ear Infection:** Nowadays a doctor will drain an ear abscess or prescribe antibiotics. Back then, the cure-all was about the handiest thing you could come up with: just a few drops of urine in the ear, and—voilà!

**5. Fever:** If you could have asked any Chinese railroad worker, he'd have told you the best thing for lowering a fever would be snake oil. The closest most settlers and cowboys could come to that was a dose of rattlesnake oil prepared by a Native American healer. Another treatment, also a specialty of Native American medicine, was the sweat lodge. Besides being considered a way to purify the soul and body, the sweat lodge was used in an attempt to "sweat out" a fever.

**6. General Aches and Pains:** Aspirin wasn't readily available until the turn of the 20th century (and then only with a prescription), so folks who suffered from regular recurring pains such as headaches, muscle soreness, or old injuries might depend on laudanum (a combination of opium, codeine, and morphine) or straight morphine, both of which were available without a prescription in the 19th century.

**7. Infected Wounds:** Good thing the average pioneer usually had some preserved meat hanging around. In the case of an infection, a piece of salted pork was applied to the wound until it healed.

**8. Rabies:** The sure cure for rabies during the 19th century was something called a "madstone," named for the delirious behavior that accompanies the disease. Madstone is a stony, calcified mass (like a hair ball) taken from the stomach of a deer. It's round or oval in shape, has a porous surface texture, and is very light in weight. Applied to a bite, the madstone would stick to it and draw out the poison.

**9. Rheumatism:** On *The Beverly Hillbillies*, Granny Moses used to cook up a batch of home-brewed "medicine" when her "rheumatiz" started acting up. It worked for her, but most pioneer types didn't take their cures internally; they relied on goose grease, bear oil (from rendered bear fat), or rattlesnake oil rubbed into the painful area.

**10. Snakebite:** It was a good idea to travel in groups in the Old West; that way, if you were bitten by a snake, one of your companions could open the wound with a knife and suck out the venom. If you were traveling alone and you were able to reach the area of the bite yourself, you could do the sucking. Better yet, if you were traveling prepared, a madstone would also work.

**11. Sprains and Bruises:** To relieve the pain and swelling of a sprain or bruise, the hardy pioneer boiled some comfrey leaves in water for a minute or two, drained the leaves, wrapped them in a rag, and applied them to the injured area like a compress. (This one is still a favorite of herbalists and is said to work like a charm.)

**12. Stomachache:** A sure cure for an upset tummy was peppermint oil or mustard oil stirred into hot water and sipped slowly.

**13. Sunstroke:** The best way to prevent sunstroke was to wear green leaves or a wet cloth inside the crown of your hat. In the event of actual sunstroke, the idea was to keep the head wet either by pouring warm—not cold—water on the head or to use rags dipped in water, changing them as needed before the water evaporated.

**14. Toothaches:** One remedy was whiskey—and lots of it. A whiskey-and-turpentine mixture held against the tooth was said to work, as was a mixture of pokeberries (caution: pokeberries are poisonous!) and whiskey. If all else failed, the tooth would be yanked—and not by a dentist in an antiseptic office with soft music playing in the background.

**15. Whooping Cough:** The old-timer's favorite cure was a rag soaked in a mixture of beeswax, coal oil, sheep tallow (fat), and turpentine slathered on the whooper's chest.

**16. Warts:** Far from life-threatening, but unsightly depending on its location, a wart could be removed thusly: After a small piece of beef had been soaking all day in vinegar, it would be applied to the wart and tied on with rags, then left on overnight. The beef could be removed during the day and reapplied at night. Two weeks later, the wart would die and fall off.

\* \* \*

"The best cure for hypochondria is to forget about your body and get interested in someone else's."
—Goodman Ace

...She developed a line of hair care and beauty products for black women.

# POLITICS IS THE THING

*Some people just can't get enough of fame, and the world offers no better stages than entertainment and politics. Here are some celebrities who became prominent political figures.*

**1. Clint Eastwood:** Actor with attitude turned mayor of Carmel, California, 1986–88

**2. Frederick L. Grandy:** Lovable *Love Boat* Gopher turned Iowa congressman, 1987–1994

**3. Ben Jones:** Greasy *Dukes of Hazzard* mechanic turned Georgia congressman, 1989–92

**4. Al Franken:** *Saturday Night Live* funnyman turned Minnesota senator, 2009–

**5. Jesse "the Body" Ventura:** Pro wrestler turned Minnesota governor, 1999–2003

**6. Sonny Bono:** Cher's hubby turned mayor of Palm Springs turned California congressman, 1995–98

**7. Alessandra Mussolini:** Fascist Italian dictator's granddaughter turned actress and model turned member of the European parliament, 1992

**8. Tina Keeper:** TV Mountie turned member of Canada's House of Commons, 2006–08

**9. Shirley Temple Black:** Precocious child star turned delegate to UN, 1969–70, turned U.S. ambassador to Ghana, 1974–76, and Czechoslovakia, 1989–92

**10. Arnold Schwarzenegger:** Bodybuilder who won Mr. Universe five times and Mr. Olympia six years in a row (1970–75) turned actor turned California governor, 2003–11

**11. Glenda Jackson:** British Academy Award winner turned member of Parliament in Labour Party, 1992–

**12. Ronald Reagan:** Actor turned California governor, 1967–75, turned 40th U.S. president, 1981–89

**Reversing the Order:** A politician who became a celebrity…

**13. Jerry Springer:** Cincinnati, Ohio, mayor, 1977–78, who after a failed bid for governor turned daytime talk show host

---

**"Speed dating" was invented by Rabbi Yaacov Deyo of Los Angeles in 1999.**

# FIRST CLASS

*Come along as we examine the first winners of major awards in the NBA, MLB, NFL, and NHL.*

## NBA

**1. Most Valuable Player: Bob Petit, St. Louis Hawks (1955–56).** Bob Petit was literally head and shoulders above his peers during the 1955–56 season. The 6' 9" power forward led the league in field goals, free throws, total points, and total rebounds while guiding the Hawks to the Western Division Finals. Petit won the award again in the 1958–59 season, a remarkable achievement for a player who was cut twice from his high school basketball team.

**2. Defensive Player of the Year: Sidney Moncrief, Milwaukee Bucks (1982–83).** A five-time all-star with the Bucks, Moncrief hauled in 437 rebounds and 113 steals during the 1982–83 season while also providing clampdown defense on the league's top perimeter scorers. "Sid the Squid" is one of only five guards to be named the NBA's top defender.

**3. Rookie of the Year: Monk Meineke, Fort Wayne Pistons (1952–53).** A graduate of the University of Dayton, the 6' 7" Meineke lasted only five seasons in the league before retiring. This lumbering forward holds the dubious record of being the only player to win the Rookie of the Year Award while also leading the league in personal fouls and disqualifications.

**4. Sixth Man of the Year: Bobby Jones, Philadelphia 76ers (1982–83).** A true sixth man in every sense of the word, Philadelphia forward Bobby Jones finished the 1982–83 season ranked sixth on the Sixers in minutes played, field goals made, assists, and turnovers.

**5. Coach of the Year: Harry Gallatin, St. Louis Hawks (1962–63).** A former seven-time NBA all-star, Gallatin was named the NBA's Coach of the Year in his first season on the bench. He went on to coach for an additional four years before being inducted into the Basketball Hall of Fame as a player in 1991.

---

The word "father" (from Old English *faeder*) was first used in the 1500s.

## MLB

**1. National League Most Valuable Player: Frank Schulte, Chicago Cubs (1911).** Frank Schulte did far more than just win the National League's inaugural MVP Award in 1911. He also became the first player in history to record at least 20 doubles, 20 triples, 20 home runs, and 20 stolen bases in a season. Only three other players have accomplished the feat since.

**2. American League Most Valuable Player: Ty Cobb, Detroit Tigers (1911).** One of the most dreaded competitors in major league history, Ty Cobb enjoyed a career season in 1911 when he led the league in 12 offensive categories. The "Georgia Peach" was later among the first five players inducted into the Baseball Hall of Fame in 1936.

**3. Cy Young: Don Newcombe, Brooklyn Dodgers (1956).** A former member of the Negro Leagues, Newcombe was the first African American pitcher to win 20 games in a single season at the major league level. This talented hurler is also the only player in history to have won the Rookie of the Year, Most Valuable Player, and Cy Young awards during his career.

**4. Rookie of the Year: Jackie Robinson, Brooklyn Dodgers (1947).** Jackie Robinson had quite the season in 1947. In addition to breaking baseball's color barrier, he also led the league in stolen bases and sacrifice hits and finished fifth in the MVP voting. The Cairo, Georgia, native was inducted into the Baseball Hall of Fame in 1962.

**5. National League Manager of the Year: Tom Lasorda, Los Angeles Dodgers (1983).** A member of the Baseball Hall of Fame, Lasorda managed the Dodgers to World Series championships in 1981 and 1988. He has served the organization now for six decades, making him the Dodgers' longest-tenured employee.

**6. American League Manager of the Year: Tony LaRussa, Chicago White Sox (1983).** One of the game's greatest tacticians, Tony LaRussa was the first man to have won Manager of the Year honors on four occasions. He also holds the distinction of being one of only two managers to have won the World Series with teams in both the American League and the National League. This Tampa, Florida, native is currently the manager of the St. Louis Cardinals.

## NFL

**1. Most Valuable Player: Mel Hein, New York Giants (1938).**
A towering player from Redding, California, Hein remains the only offensive lineman to ever win the NFL's top honor. This distinguished Pro Football Hall of Famer was also known for his exceptional durability, having never missed a single down during his stellar 15-year career.

**2. Rookie of the Year: Alan Ameche, Baltimore Colts (1955).**
A four-time Pro Bowl selection as a fullback, Ameche is best known for scoring the winning touchdown in the 1958 NFL Championship. Football historians labeled this hard-fought match between the Colts and Giants "the Greatest Game Ever Played."

**3. Offensive Player of the Year: Larry Brown, Washington Redskins (1972).** A four-time Pro Bowl selection, Washington running back Larry Brown led the league in yards per game and yards from scrimmage during the 1972 season while helping the Redskins finish first in the NFC East.

**4. Defensive Player of the Year: Alan Page, Minnesota Vikings (1971).** A member of Minnesota's famed "Purple People Eaters" defense, Page was inducted into the Pro Football Hall of Fame in 1988. He currently serves as an associate justice with the Minnesota Supreme Court.

**5. Coach of the Year: Joe Kuharich, Washington Redskins. (1955).** Kuharich discovered the hard way that winning the league's Coach of the Year Award doesn't necessarily ensure job security. After 1955, a string of losing seasons had this South Bend, Indiana, native coaching in the college ranks by 1959, though he returned to the league from 1964 to 1968.

## NHL

**1. Hart Memorial Trophy (Most Valuable Player): Frank Nighbor, Ottawa Senators (1923–24).** An 18-year veteran, Nighbor had his finest individual season in 1923–24, recording 17 points in 20 games. The "Pembroke Peach" was later inducted into the Hockey Hall of Fame in 1947.

**2. Vezina Trophy (Top Goalie): George Hainesworth, Montreal Canadiens (1926–27).** One of the top netminders of all time,

Hainesworth was awarded the Vezina Trophy on three occasions between 1926 and 1929. Ironically, he was signed by the Canadiens to replace Georges Vezina, who died of tuberculosis in 1926.

**3. Calder Memorial Trophy (Top Rookie): Syl Apps, Toronto Maple Leafs (1936–37).** An outstanding football player and Olympic pole-vaulter, Apps topped all other rookies in the league in 1936–37 by recording 45 points in 48 games. He went on to play an additional nine seasons with the Leafs, helping guide the team to four Stanley Cup titles in the process.

**4. Art Ross Trophy (Top Point Scorer): Elmer Lach, Montreal Canadiens (1947–48).** A member of Montreal's prolific "Punch Line" along with fellow Hall of Famers Maurice Richard and Toe Blake, Lach scored 61 points in 60 games during the 1947–48 season. This high-scoring center helped the Canadiens win three Stanley Cups before retiring in 1954.

**5. James Norris Memorial Trophy (Top Defenseman): Red Kelly, Detroit Red Wings (1953–54).** One of the game's most gentlemanly players, Kelly helped the Red Wings capture the Stanley Cup in 1954 after tallying 16 goals and 33 assists during the regular season. This popular playmaker entered Canadian politics following his retirement, serving as an elected Member of Parliament from 1962 to 1965.

\*     \*     \*

### FUN FACTS ABOUT GEORGE WASHINGTON

Uncle John's can't vouch for where George Washington actually slept. But these factoids are known:

• The first president was born on February 11, 1732. But in 1751 Great Britain decided to change their calendar, moving from the Julian to the Gregorian accounting, which added 11 days to the year. That forced George to celebrate his birthday on the 22nd. Because he had a single tooth and was bothered by the pain of wearing dentures, Washington delivered the shortest inaugural address on record on March 4, 1793. It lasted all of 90 seconds and contained 135 words.

• The country's first president is the only president to never live in the White House—or in the nation's capital!

---

The first version of the *Book of Common Prayer* was published in 1549.

# PANIC ON WALL STREET

*A look at some of the worst of the Street's nearly two dozen panics,
what caused them, and their impact on the country.*

In the 17th century, Dutch settlers built two walls on the southern tip of Manhattan Island—one on the East River and the other on the Hudson River to the west—to protect the island from attack by the English, who were at war with Holland at the time. Eventually, the path between the walls became known as Wall Street, where, 100 years later, 24 merchants founded the New York Stock Exchange. Ever since, the stock market's ups and downs have defined America's good and bad times. When stock values plunged precipitously, it was known as a "panic."

## 1. THE PANIC OF 1819

**Cause:** The first major run on the stock market brought an end to the economic expansion that had begun following the War of 1812 with the British. The U.S. government had borrowed heavily to finance the war and, in order to repay the debt, had suspended payment through specie—gold and silver—and issued paper currency backed by the promise of precious metals. New banks sprouted, issuing unsecured banknotes and spawning an economic boom. That boom burst in the Panic of 1819.

**Effect:** It brought on a wave of foreclosures, bank failures, massive unemployment, and declines in agricultural and manufacturing production. It took five years for the economy to recover. Many economists today believe this was Wall Street's first boom-to-bust cycle, characterized by deficit spending during times of war leading to a postwar expansion of the economy (the boom) followed by retraction a few years later (the bust).

## 2. THE PANIC OF 1837

**Cause:** President Andrew Jackson precipitated this panic in 1836 by refusing to renew the charter of the Second Bank of the United States (a central, national bank was still a new idea at the time) and by not allowing the U.S. Treasury to continue to accept state banknotes—only specie would be acceptable. To further complicate things, Congress ordered Jackson to return to the states the first federal surplus of specie, which helped to fuel an inflationary expansion of railroad and canal construction amid enormously overextended bank credits. When Jackson's successor, Martin Van Buren, implemented the specie policy, the value of state banknotes began to plummet, and on May 10, 1837, the bubble burst.

**Effect:** Every bank in New York City stopped payment in gold and silver, which devalued paper money. Within two months, 343 U.S. banks had failed. This caused a panic among stock market investors and helped to initiate a crash. As businesses cut back, high unemployment touched off food riots in some cities. It took five years for the nation to recover. Poor Van Buren was blamed for the entire mess. Things improved once Congress established "subtreasuries" around the United States to restore stability to the paper currency.

## 3. THE PANIC OF 1857

**Cause:** In the Mexican-American War of 1846, the United States seized a third of Mexico—the entire American Southwest. In the next decade, the country was awash in prosperity from rapid expansion and the discovery of gold in California. But in 1857, a reduction in agricultural exports to Europe caused grain prices to fall, and overspeculation in real estate and railroads spooked the economy. In September, the economy took another jolt when 30,000 pounds of gold being shipped to Eastern banks from the San Francisco mint were lost when the ship carrying it foundered in a storm and sank. Aggravating the situation was the failure of the embezzlement-wracked Ohio Life Insurance and Trust Company. For the first time in history, thanks to the development of the telegraph, news of the bankruptcy spread within hours to New York, where panic gripped the stock market.

**Effect:** Banks vainly tried to stop runs by depositors. The panic spread to Europe, South America, and the Far East. The effects of the resulting depression didn't dissipate in the United States until the Civil War. Unlike the industrialized North, the South wasn't seriously affected, which convinced a lot of Southerners that the economic system below the Mason-Dixon Line was superior to that of the North.

Care for some *zongzi*? It's a Chinese rice dumpling, also known as "Chinese tamales."

## 4. THE PANIC OF 1873

**Cause:** The failure of Philadelphia's respected Jay Cooke and Company banking firm in September combined with the collapse of the stock market in Vienna, Austria, ushered in the Panic of 1873. Both events came at the tail end of an economic expansion following the Civil War. A huge infusion of cash from speculators caused frenetic growth of the nation's rail system. When President Ulysses S. Grant tightened the money supply to slow the pace, businesses were unable to get credit. Cooke and Company, the prime investors in the Northern Pacific Railroad, was overextended, and declared bankruptcy to void its debt.

The announcement shook Wall Street. According to the *New York Times*, "The brokers stood perfectly thunderstruck for a moment. The brokers surged out of the Exchange, tumbling pell-mell over each other in the general confusion, and reached their respective offices in racehorse time."

**Effect:** In an attempt to calm the situation, the New York Stock Exchange closed for ten days. But the panic gained steam as nearly a quarter of the 364 railroads in the country went bankrupt. Over the next two years, some 18,000 smaller businesses closed, creating a 14 percent unemployment rate in what came to be known as "the Long Depression," which was characterized by violent clashes among workers, employers, and federal troops. The downturn finally ended in 1879.

## 5. THE PANIC OF 1893

**Cause:** A run on the nation's gold supply trip-wired the Panic of 1893, the worst economic crisis in U.S. history to that point. Before it ended five years later, one out of every five Americans was unemployed. It began with the vast quantities of silver that were being mined in the West. Speculators brought on the crisis by redeeming silver notes for gold in such quantity that the statutory limit for minimum gold reserves was soon reached. When rumors began to circulate that the government was in financial distress, depositors pulled out their savings and bankers called in their loans. Banks, especially in the West, began to fail—as did the Northern Pacific, Union Pacific, and Atchison, Topeka, and Santa Fe railroads. The crisis only got worse, taking down 15,000 companies and 500 banks.

---

May 1, 2010: Expo 2010, the largest World's Fair in history opened in Shanghai, China.

**Effect:** Hundreds of unemployed workers—called "Coxey's Army" after their organizer, Jacob Coxey—marched on Washington to demand relief. Violent strikes and a walkout by rail workers shut down much of the nation's rail system in 1894. The presidential election was fought over the gold vs. silver standard of the U.S. economy. Pro-gold Republican William McKinley defeated pro-silver candidate William Jennings Bryan and the economy rebounded, sending it into a ten-year growth spurt until the Panic of 1907.

## 6. THE PANIC OF 1907

**Cause:** The speculative practices of a few banks and trusts lay at the root of the panic that began in March 1907. At its center were F. Augustus Heinze and his bank, the Knickerbocker Trust Company. Heinze and his brother borrowed money from the trust and tried to corner the market on the stock of the United Copper Company. When the plan failed, the National Bank of Commerce stopped honoring Knickerbocker's checks, which in turn caused a run on the bank, sparking runs on all of the other trusts in New York.

**Effect:** Fearing a complete collapse of the national economy, the U.S. Treasury ended up contributing $35 million to stem the crisis. Banker J. P. Morgan led a rescue operation, putting together a team of bank and trust executives to hammer out a deal in which money was redistributed among the banks. The banks also bought shares of solvent corporations caught in the downturn. Within a year, the panic eased. A congressional investigation led to the Federal Reserve Act of 1913, which mandated the creation of a central banking system that could move in to put out the fire in any future panics.

## 7. THE PANIC OF 1929

**Cause:** After World War I, the U.S. economy took off. The Roaring Twenties created stock prices that far exceeded the worth of the companies that issued them. In fact, by 1929, values had ballooned to 400 percent of what they had been in 1924. Business insiders had convinced Americans they were on the cusp of unprecedented wealth by filling newspapers and magazines with investor rags-to-riches stories. A new wave of Americans began investing in the stock market, borrowing money to buy speculative stocks that weren't actually invested in legitimate businesses. Banks across the country became weighted down with government bonds, vastly overpriced real estate mortgages, and shaky securities. By 1929, savvy investors who pulled out in time had made fortunes, but the stock market was on the eve of destruction. In fact, economists had been warning people for months to protect themselves before the expected crash.

**Effect:** The bust came in a seven-day period culminating on October 29, 1929, with an unprecedented crash and loss of $30 billion in stock valuation. The gloom was so great on Wall Street that some investors and brokers leaped to their deaths from office buildings. In the years that followed, unemployment surged to 25 percent at its worst in 1933. Deflation took hold for nearly four years with the Dow Stock Market Index hitting a low of 41.22 in 1932. Congress passed the Glass-Steagell Act of 1933, which required a complete separation between commercial banks that accepted deposits and issued loans and investment banks that distributed stocks, bonds, and securities. Experts believed that the crash was caused by commercial banks that strayed into investment bank territory in a culture of fraud and conflicts of interest.

**Postscript.** The nation would not recover economically from the Great Depression until World War II. The Glass-Steagell Act remained in place for the next 66 years until it was overturned in 1999 by Congress after 12 years of intense lobbying by U.S. banks. Commercial banks once again were able to offer the speculative products of investment banks. The stage was set for what was to come nine years later—the "Great Recession" that began in 2008.

\*     \*     \*

### ADVICE FROM THE RICH AND FAMOUS

"The way to make money is to buy when blood is running in the streets."

—John D. Rockefeller

"Formula for success: rise early, work hard, strike oil."

—J. Paul Getty

# AN AGE-OLD QUESTION

*When it comes to sports, age is just a state of mind. Just ask these athletes, who represent the youngest and oldest players to ever suit up for a game in the NFL, NBA, NHL, and MLB.*

## NBA

**Youngest: Andrew Bynum.** One of the last players to enter the NBA directly from high school, Andrew Bynum was just 18 years and six days old on November 2, 2005, when he played his first regular-season game for the Los Angeles Lakers. The young center picked up two rebounds and two blocked shots in that match, and scored his first points on a rim-rattling dunk two weeks later. As a 21-year-old "veteran" in 2009, he helped the franchise win its 15th NBA championship.

**Oldest: Matthew "Nat" Hickey.** Nat Hickey is proof that age and wisdom don't always go together. A former guard with the Cleveland Rosenblums and Indianapolis Kautskys, Hickey was coaching the Providence Steamrollers during the 1947–48 season when he decided to insert himself into the lineup. Although player-coaches weren't uncommon at the time, Hickey's decision did raise eyebrows around the league, since he was just two days shy of his 46th birthday. Not surprisingly, the 5' 11" hoopster missed all six of the shots he attempted and wisely retired following the final whistle.

## MLB

**Youngest: Joe Nuxhall.** Desperate times call for desperate measures. That was the case in the summer of 1944 when many Major League teams found themselves scrambling for talent after their top players joined the war effort. The Cincinnati Reds responded by signing Joe Nuxhall, a junior high school pitcher with a decent fastball and little else. Needless to say, Nuxhall was completely overwhelmed and lasted only one game after giving up five hits and five runs in two-thirds of an inning against the St. Louis Cardinals. "I was pitching against seventh-, eighth-, and ninth-graders, kids thirteen and fourteen years old," he recalled later. "All of a sudden, I look up and there's Stan Musial and the likes. It was a very scary situation." The shell-shocked teen didn't return to the big leagues again until 1952, when he won one game and lost four as a 23-year-old starter for the Reds. He later went on to win 135 games over the course of a productive 16-year career and made it to the All-Star Game in 1955 and 1956.

**Oldest: Satchel Paige.** Age was just another statistic for Satchel Paige, a legendary Negro League pitcher who didn't make his Major League debut until his 41st birthday. The sinewy Hall of Famer acquitted himself well over the next five seasons, earning two invitations to the All-Star Game before hanging up his cleats in 1953 at the advanced age of 46. Baseball fans got one final glimpse of Paige on September 25, 1965, when Kansas City Athletics owner Charles O. Finley convinced him to take the mound against the Boston Red Sox. The 59-year-old happily complied and proceeded to strike out one batter over three scoreless innings before leaving the field to a thunderous ovation. Paige later shared his secrets to staying young in an issue of *Collier's*, warning readers to "avoid fried meats, which angry up the blood" and to never "look back—something might be gaining on you."

## NFL

**Youngest: Amobi Okoye.** Youth was served at the beginning of the 2007 season when Houston Texans defensive tackle Amobi Okoye became the youngest player ever picked in the first round of the NFL draft at the age of 20 years and 91 days. Okoye appeared in all 16 regular-season games for the Texans that year and was even named Defensive Rookie of the Month for September 2007 after leading the conference with four sacks.

**Oldest: George Blanda.** George Blanda demonstrated that football isn't strictly a young man's game on January 4, 1976, when he participated in the AFC Championship at the age of 48 years and 109 days. Although his team lost the contest, this ageless wonder provided fans with a pair of highlights by kicking an impressive 41-yard field goal and converting an extra point. Blanda was later inducted into the Pro Football Hall of Fame in 1981 and still holds numerous playoff and regular-season records.

## NHL

**Youngest: Armand "Bep" Guidolin.** Another beneficiary of

wartime shortages, Bep Guidolin made his debut for the Boston Bruins on November 12, 1942, at the age of 16 years and 11 months. His accomplishment is all the more impressive when you consider that this crafty left-winger didn't even begin skating until he was 13 years old. Guidolin remained in the league for an additional eight seasons before going on to coach the Bruins from 1972 to 1974.

**Oldest: Gordie Howe.** Gordie Howe took age discrimination to task during the 1979–80 season when he recorded 15 goals and 26 assists for the Hartford Whalers as a 52-year-old right-winger. His exceptional play earned the Whalers a berth in the playoffs and led to his 23rd and final All-Star Game selection, where he tallied an assist. "Mr. Hockey" went on to appear in one more professional game in 1997 at 69 years of age when he played a single shift with the Detroit Vipers of the International Hockey League. He is the only player to have played professional hockey in six different decades.

\*　　\*　　\*

## HEIGHTS OF FAMOUS SPORTS TROPHIES

America's Cup (Winner sailing regatta of same name): Originally 27" (68.5 cm), but the base has been extended twice

Stanley Cup (NHL Playoff champs): 35" (89.5 cm)

Vince Lombardi Trophy (SuperBowl winner): 22" (56 cm)

Ryder Cup (Prize for competition between American and British golfers): 17" (43 cm)

FIFA World Cup (Winner of world cup soccer): 14" (36 cm)

Liam McCarthy Cup (Winner All-Ireland Senior hurling championship): 10" (26 cm)

Webb Ellis Cup (Winner of Rugby world cup) 15" (38 cm)

Wimbledown (1 of 4 Grand Slam tennis events, considered the most prestigious): 18.5" ( 47 cm)

The *Titanic's* sister ship, *Britannic*, was originally intended to be named the *Gigantic*.

# PARTNERS IN CRIME

*When it comes to crime, two heads aren't always better than one.*

## 1. ALFRED AND ALBERT STRATTON

**Crime:** In 1905, in South East London, Chapman's Oil and Colour paint shop store manager Thomas Farrow lay dead from a beating, and his wife Anne, who was unconscious, would die a few days later. The shop and living space above the shop were ransacked, and police found an empty cash box with a greasy fingerprint lying on the floor.

**The Pair:** Suspicion fell on Alfred (22) and Albert (20) Stratton. Neither brother had an arrest record, but neither had a job either, and locals claimed they were petty thieves. A milkman thought he'd seen two men resembling the Strattons near Chapman's at the time of the murders, but he failed to identify them after their arrest. Authorities thought there was little chance of convicting the brothers of murder—until they took their fingerprints and discovered that Alfred's print matched the one on the cash box.

**The Trial:** In 1905, fingerprints were a new forensic tool and prosecutors weren't sure that a jury would accept a fingerprint as sufficient evidence, let alone evidence that could hang two men. The trial hinged on testimony from forensic expert Inspector Collins, who explained how Alfred's prints had been carefully matched to those on the cash box by tracing and comparing the ridges, and how the two impressions corresponded exactly.

**The Verdict:** Guilty

**Historic Consequences:** With fingerprints accepted as a method of identification in a murder case, this was the real beginning of using forensic science to establish guilt or innocence. And it was the end for Alfred and Albert who were hanged.

## 2. NICOLA SACCO AND BARTOLOMEO VANZETTI

**The Crime:** On April 15, 1920, in Braintree, Massachusetts, witnesses saw the paymaster and guard of the Slater & Morrill shoe factory gunned down by two men who stole $15,773 in cash.

**The Pair:** Nicola Sacco and Bartolomeo Vanzetti, two Italian

---

In 1991, a dress made of rotting meat was displayed as a work of art in an Ottawa gallery.

immigrants, were known anarchists. When cops stopped them on a streetcar, they were armed and evasive when questioned. When the cops learned that Sacco hadn't gone to work on the day of the shoe factory killings, they arrested both men for murder.

**The Trial:** At the 1921 trial, prosecution witnesses placed Sacco and Vanzetti at the scene of the crime, and the prosecution's gun experts said that the men owned the type of guns used in the Braintree murders. The defense countered with alibis—Sacco was seen in Boston getting a passport, and Vanzetti had been seen selling fish. As for the gun, experts for the defense contradicted the prosecution's gun experts and insisted that the defendants' guns hadn't been used in the murders.

The trial became internationally famous when the defense lawyers claimed that Sacco and Vanzetti were being railroaded to the electric chair because they were poor immigrants who held unpopular political views.

**The Verdict:** Sacco and Vanzetti were found guilty, and demonstrations raged in the United States, Europe, and South America. Some legal experts, claiming anti-immigrant prejudice on the part of the judge and prosecutor, fought for a new trial. In 1925, when a jailed bank robber confessed to the killings and exonerated Sacco and Vanzetti, the Massachusetts governor finally empowered a commission to go over the evidence. The commission upheld the guilty verdict; Sacco and Vanzetti were executed in 1927.

**Historic Consequences:** Over the years, researchers have continued to question the verdict. Lies and contradictions have been found in the evidence against Vanzetti, but modern ballistic tests reveal that a bullet from Sacco's gun did kill the Slater payroll guard. Today, many historians contend that Vanzetti was probably an innocent man who refused to turn in his guilty comrades, including Sacco.

### 3. NATHAN LEOPOLD AND RICHARD LOEB

**The Crime:** In 1924, the body of a boy was found nude and drowned in a culvert in Wolf Lake, Indiana. He'd been struck on the head and then suffocated. Police identified the victim as Bobby Franks, the son of a Chicago millionaire. Nearby, cops also found an expensive pair of glasses, which they eventually traced to 19-year-old Nathan Leopold.

Leopold had spent the day with Richard Loeb, a distant cousin of Bobby Franks. Under police questioning, both men broke down and confessed to killing Franks. Each blamed the other.

**The Suspects:** Leopold and Loeb were graduate students at the University of Chicago. Brilliant scholars who were pampered by their wealthy families, the teens came to believe that they were superior beings, or what the philosopher Fredrich Nietzsche called "supermen." To prove their status, they decided they would commit a perfect crime.

They picked up Franks in their car, struck him on the head with a chisel, and suffocated him. After throwing his clothes in the brush and pouring acid on his corpse to thwart identification, the pair notified the Franks that their son had been kidnapped and asked for a $10,000 ransom. But before the supermen could get their money, Bobby's body was found—and so were Leopold's glasses.

**The Trial:** Leopold and Loeb were represented by the famous American trial lawyer Clarence Darrow. Expected to argue that the pair was innocent by reason of insanity, Darrow instead stunned the country when he made them plead guilty—to avoid a vengeful jury and give sentencing power to a thoughtful judge. Darrow also brought in psychiatric experts who testified to the immaturity and emotionally "diseased" state of his teenage defendants. Darrow reminded the court that it was capable of mercy—unlike his deranged clients.

**The Verdict:** Life plus 99 years

**Historic Consequences:** Clarence Darrow's closing argument took 12 hours and is still referred to in anti–death penalty arguments. The men that he'd saved became model prisoners, running a school to educate prisoners. In 1936, Loeb was murdered by another inmate, and in 1958, Leopold was paroled. He moved to Puerto Rico, where he worked at a hospital and dreamed of making a great medical breakthrough so he'd be remembered as a hero instead of a killer—it didn't pan out, and he died in 1971.

## 4. JULIUS AND ETHEL ROSENBERG

**The Crime:** In 1950 the United States and the Soviet Union were facing off in the Cold War, and American communists were suspected of helping the enemy. In the midst of this, the FBI began arresting communists for stealing American atomic bomb

---

The highest rating a diamond can have is D-flawless. (The diamond is called a *paragon.*)

secrets and passing them to the Soviet Union. The accused were allowed to forgo the death sentence if they helped the government and named others.

**The Suspects:** Julius Rosenberg was an electrical engineer; his wife Ethel stayed home with their two young sons. They were an ordinary 1950s couple—except for their communist politics.

**The Trial:** Proclaiming their innocence, the Rosenbergs didn't cooperate with authorities and went to trial on March 6, 1951, facing the death penalty. U.S. Attorney Irving Saypol's case relied completely on accusations against the Rosenbergs from known spies. Defense attorney Emanuel Bloch pointed out that these witnesses needed leniency—they had to say whatever the government wanted. The Rosenbergs stated their innocence on the stand, and Bloch asked jurors to avoid anticommunist "hysteria."

**The Verdict:** Guilty

**Historic Consequences:** For the next two years, thousands of letters to President Eisenhower, including one from the pope, asked for mercy for the Rosenbergs. Even J. Edgar Hoover, head of the FBI, worried that execution looked bad because the evidence was thin and the Rosenberg children would become orphans. Still, in 1953, the Rosenbergs were executed.

After the Soviet Union collapsed in 1991, KGB agents admitted that Julius gave them secret information, but it wasn't about the bomb, and Ethel wasn't involved at all. In 2001, Ethel's main accuser (her own brother) admitted that he'd lied about her involvement because prosecutors asked him to—they wanted to use Ethel's possible execution to make Julius confess.

\*     \*     \*

## TOP FIVE GUNS USED MOST OFTEN IN CRIMES

**1.** Smith and Wesson .38 revolver

**2.** Ruger 9 mm semiautomatic

**3.** Lorcin Engineering .38 semiautomatic

**4.** Raven Arms .25 semiautomatic

**5.** Mossberg 12-gauge shotgun

(*Source: ATF study, as published in* Time *in 1993*)

# ROOM SERVICE

*Some hotels are famous for their architecture
or location. But others make headlines for
what happens inside their hallowed halls.*

## 1. THE CHURCHILL SUITE
### Mena House Oberoi Hotel, Cairo, Egypt

In November 1943, while World War II raged, U.S. president
Franklin Delano Roosevelt, Chinese president Chiang Kai-shek,
and British prime minister Winston Churchill met in Cairo, Egypt,
to try to figure out how to win the war against Japan. (Soviet premier Joseph Stalin was also invited, but chose not to attend—he
was boycotting Chiang's appearance, fearing that negotiating with
the Chinese leader would ignite a new war between the Soviet
Union and Japan.) While at the conference, Churchill stayed at a
suite in the Mena House Oberoi Hotel, where he could devise a
plan for winning the war while gazing out a large window at the
Great Pyramid of Giza.

## 2. ROOM 217
### The Stanley Hotel, Estes Park, Colorado

Stephen King's 1977 novel *The Shining* tells the story of Jack
Torrance, who takes a job as the winter caretaker of the Overlook
Hotel in Colorado and moves there with his wife and young son.
Over the course of several months, as snow piles up and ghosts materialize, Torrance goes crazy and eventually tries to kill his family.
King's inspiration for the story came a few years earlier when he
stayed at Colorado's Stanley Hotel, considered one of the most
haunted places in the United States. The hotel opened in 1909,
and ghosts have been around ever since. Supposedly, the original
owners (F. O. and Flora Stanley) still roam the halls, ghosts throw
parties in the ballroom, and pianos sometimes play by themselves.
That spooky feel inspired King—the author even stayed in the
Stanley's room 217, which appears in the book as a forbidden and
ominous place. For its part, the hotel takes its role in *The Shining*'s
history very seriously. The 1980 Stanley Kubrick movie adaptation
plays continuously on guests' TVs.

---

**The United States has 104 working nuclear reactors, more than any other country.**

## 3. BLOSSOM ROOM
**Roosevelt Hotel, Los Angeles, California**
Today, the Academy Awards are a decadent affair of designer dresses, an hours-long ceremony, and swanky after parties. But when the first awards were given out in May 1929 at the Roosevelt Hotel in Los Angeles, things were very different. The Academy of Motion Pictures Arts and Sciences had just been formed two years earlier, and its president (acclaimed actor Douglas Fairbanks Sr.) handed out the 15 original awards. The winners had been announced three months before the ceremony, so the 270 people who attended were likely more excited about their fancy dinner—filet of sole sautéed in butter, and half a broiled chicken on toast—than they were about who would win. One thing remains the same, though: the gold statuettes handed out that night are virtually identical to the ones winners get today.

## 4. ROOMS 510, 511, 610, AND 611
**Savoy Hotel, London, England**
Claude Monet was one of the founders of the 19th-century art movement known as French Impressionism, in which painters used techniques like visible brushstrokes and variations of light to show movement and the passage of time. Between 1899 and 1901, Monet visited London during the winter and stayed at the Savoy Hotel. (Why winter? Because he loved the fog. In the days before the clean-air legislation of the 1950s, wintry London was often covered in a thick, coal-saturated fog. Of it, Monet once said, "It is the fog that gives [London] its magnificent breadth.") He stayed in suites that overlooked the river Thames, and from an easel set up next to the windows, Monet painted more than 70 canvases, including some of his most famous works: *Waterloo Bridge*, *Gray Day*, and *The Houses of Parliament, Sunset*.

## 5. THE PRESIDENTIAL SUITE
**Hotel Adlon Kempinski, Berlin, Germany**
When pop star Michael Jackson visited Germany, he liked to stay at the Hotel Adlon. The building has hosted many famous guests over the years—everyone from Bill Clinton to Queen Elizabeth— and is known for luxurious accommodations at an outrageous price (the presidential suite runs about $8,000 a night). But in 2002,

The term "Impressionism" comes from a review by art critic Louis Leroy...

Jackson made it even more (in)famous when he dangled his baby son Prince Michael II (a.k.a. "Blanket") over his suite's balcony railing, showing the boy off to a cheering crowd below. The world was shocked that Jackson would be so careless with his child. Jackson seemed to agree, later calling the incident "a terrible mistake."

## 6. ROOMS 1738, 1740, AND 1742
### Queen Elizabeth Hotel, Montreal, Canada

All they needed was love...or so claimed Beatle John Lennon and his wife Yoko Ono in 1969. As a way of "championing peace," Lennon and Ono staged two bed-ins: the first in Amsterdam in March; the second, and most famous, in three rooms at Montreal's Queen Elizabeth Hotel in May. When the couple announced their bed-ins, the press expected they'd get some salacious photos— maybe Lennon and Ono would have sex in front of the cameras... or at least appear in the nude. Alas, the press was disappointed. Instead, the pair wore pajamas and tube socks, lay in bed, and spent eight days talking with reporters about world peace and recording a version of the song "Give Peace a Chance" with everyone there.

## 7. ROOM 8
### Joshua Tree Inn, Joshua Tree, California

Gram Parsons was a country singer who'd played with the Byrds and Emmylou Harris. He also had a drug problem and, in September 1973, died of an overdose in room 8 at California's Joshua Tree Inn. But what happened next is the *really* weird part: Parsons had always wanted to be cremated, his ashes sprinkled in the park. But his family wanted a traditional burial and made arrangements for a private ceremony...to which none of Parsons's druggie musician friends were invited. So while the coffin was awaiting transport at the Los Angeles International Airport, a few of those friends broke into the hangar, stole the body, and took it back to the desert. There, they lit a bonfire and tried to cremate it themselves. It didn't work. The huge fire attracted police and the "friends" ran off. They were eventually caught, but at the time, there was no law against stealing a body. So they were charged a fine of $750 (the cost of the coffin) and let go. Then Parsons's charred remains were buried near his family in Louisiana.

# REST IN PIECES

*Whatever comes to pass after you've breathed*
*your last, it probably won't be as fractionated*
*and unrestful as these burials—among*
*the most bizarre in history.*

## 1. ROSSETTI'S WIFE

When poet and painter Dante Gabriel Rossetti's wife, Elizabeth
Siddal, died of an overdose of laudanum following the birth of a
stillborn child in 1862, Rossetti was distraught with grief. Impul-
sively—and, without a doubt, dramatically—he threw most of
his poems into the coffin beside her before she was lowered into
her grave. Seven years later, after having second thoughts, Rossetti had Elizabeth disinterred so that he could recover his (by
then slightly icky) creative works.

## 2. GALILEO GIVES "THE FINGER" FOR ETERNITY

After he proved that the Earth wasn't the center of the galaxy,
Galileo was condemned by the Catholic Church as a heretic,
which meant that he wasn't given a religious burial when he
died in 1642. And that meant that his bones were merely placed
on a shelf in a church in Santa Croce, Italy, after he died, where
they sat for a long time.

Then, in nearly 100 years after the great scientist's bones
were prepared for entombment, one of his admirers commissioned a mausoleum. Before his eternal resting place was sealed,
though, his middle finger—that's right, the middle one—was
removed and given to Florence's Museum of the History of
Science for display.

## 3. WHO'S BURIED IN GRANT'S TOMB?

It's an old joke and a trick question. Technically speaking, the
18th president of the United States is not buried in his tomb,
he's entombed there, since Grant's Tomb is a building and not a
plot of ground. And Grant's wife, Julia, resides forever next to
him.

---

# BURN, BABY, BURN

*Some of the worst tragedies in American history have led to regulations that keep us safe today. If you've ever wondered why we have fire drills, brightly lit exit signs, and emergency doors, these headline-grabbing fires had a lot to do with it.*

## 1. THE IROQUOIS THEATER FIRE

Chicago's Iroquois Theater was the epitome of elegant, old-world design. On December 30, 1903, the audience was packed with women and children for the holiday matinee performance of Mr. Bluebeard, a vaudeville comic revue. The house seated 1,724, but some estimates put the number of people inside at more than 1,900; people were standing in the aisles and were packed in four deep behind the last row of seats.

**Fire in a Crowded Theater.** The revue used more than 280 scenery backdrops—thin expanses of oil-painted canvases that hung above the stage when not in use. That's where the fire began: one of the canvases touched a hot light, and caught fire. A stagehand tried to put it out, but couldn't reach the flames in time. This wasn't the first fire during a performance of Mr. Bluebeard—there'd been a similar incident in Cleveland, but that fire had been quickly put out. Not this time.

**Setting the Stage.** The Iroquois Theater had only been open a month or so, and was supposedly fireproof. The architect claimed to have studied many theater disasters before designing it, but deadlines and budget constraints forced cutbacks on the promised safety features; the fire escape was unfinished and there were no sprinklers. The theater didn't even have a fire alarm box. Ventilation shafts over the stage were incomplete and had been nailed shut. A thin asbestos curtain was supposed to drop down on the stage in case of fire, but it had never been tested and the theater's ushers had never had a fire drill. Later investigations revealed that city fire inspectors had been bribed to allow the theater to open on schedule.

**What Price Ambience?** The theater had plenty of exits, but they weren't marked—and many were hidden behind drapes. The architect had chosen not to have exit signs because he thought they ruined the theater's ambience. Even worse, it was the theater's policy to bar the exits from the balcony to prevent those patrons from sneaking downstairs to the more expensive seats in the orchestra section.

**The Show Must Go On.** On December 30, as the fire quickly spread above the stage, the dancers continued their number, even as flaming scenery rained down on them. Stagehands tried to lower the asbestos curtain, but it caught on a tightrope that was supposed to be used later in the show. The audience began to panic. Eddie Foy, the show's headliner, rushed from his dressing room, dressed ridiculously in drag, to plead with the audience to remain calm as they exited the theater. But many of the exits were locked, and others had complicated latches that only the ushers knew how to open.

**No Escape.** Meanwhile, the nearly 400 people in the cast and crew rushed out of the theater through the backstage area. All but one—the tightrope artist—survived. As they rushed out of the theater, they opened the large backstage doors. The influx of oxygen turned the blazing fire into a fireball that rushed into the audience, incinerating everyone left in the orchestra section. Firefighters entered the building less than 15 minutes later, but there was no one left to save. Six hundred and five people died, making it the most lethal single-structure fire in American history and killing more than twice as many as the Great Chicago Fire of 1871.

**A Lot, but Too Late.** In the aftermath, the mayor of Chicago shut down 170 theaters for reinspection. New York's theaters eliminated standing-room-only tickets. Fire codes were changed to require theaters to conduct fire drills and install steel fire curtains. New laws required that doors could be opened from the inside and that, no matter how dark it was, the glow of the exit signs always be visible.

## 2. THE TRIANGLE SHIRTWAIST FACTORY FIRE

On March 25, 1911, the Saturday shift was just ending at the Triangle Shirtwaist Factory, which occupied the eighth, ninth, and tenth floors of the Asch Building near New York's Washington Square. Shirtwaists (light cotton women's shirts) were the fashion of the time, and the factory floor was dotted with bins full of cotton waste scraps. Fabric was draped over sewing tables, and tissue-paper patterns hung from clotheslines. The fire started in one of the waste bins on the eighth floor and spread quickly to the tables, then the patterns, engulfing the room in minutes.

**Unlucky Number 9.** Most of the workers on the eighth floor escaped. A bookkeeper called up to the offices on the tenth floor to warn the owners, who immediately fled, along with almost everyone on the floor. But no one thought to warn the workers on the ninth floor. As the fire spread below them, the ninth-floor workers, mostly young immigrant girls, were closing shop for the day and collecting their pay. One survivor said that "all of a sudden, the fire was all around."

**Violations Aplenty.** There were plenty of garment factories in New York at the time; many of them ignored labor regulations. The Shirtwaist Factory owners, Max Blanck and Isaac Harris, were two of the worst violators. When the Asch Building was built in 1901, an automatic sprinkler system would have cost $5,000, but it was omitted. The building's fire hose wasn't maintained—a manager tried to use it to put out the flames, but found that the hose was rotted and the valve rusted shut. Some workers knew there was a fire escape, but those who climbed out onto it found that the drop ladder, which was supposed to extend down to the alley, had never been installed. The weight of workers on the narrow fire escape tore it from the building, plunging two dozen people to their deaths.

**No Way Out.** Worst of all was the fact that only one of the doors to the two stairwells was unlocked—the other was kept locked to prevent employee theft. The one stairwell that was open was quickly blocked when a barrel of machine oil that was kept in the stairwell exploded; there was no other way out. In fact, the fire spread so fast that many workers never left their sewing machines. Those who couldn't get out were faced with an impossible choice. Helpless onlookers watched in horror as dozens jumped to their deaths.

**Rescue Operation.** Law students at New York University who were watching from a neighboring building saw hundreds of people, mostly from the tenth floor, on the roof of the building. The students laid ladders across the gap between roofs and rescued over 150 people. Firemen arrived at the scene within minutes and quenched the blaze half an hour after it started, but in that time, 146 people died. The Asch Building, which had been certified fireproof, was almost completely intact. It lived up to its billing—it didn't burn, but everything inside did. It still stands, and was renamed the Brown Building in 1929; it's now part of the New York University science department.

**Changes Across the Board.** The city soon sent inspectors to other factories to ensure that they weren't violating city codes. New York passed comprehensive building codes and fire safety laws within a few years—at the time, the best in the nation. You can thank the Triangle fire for the fire drills at your office. The tragedy was a turning point for the safety of all American workers. It empowered the unions (and increased popular support for them) so they could force the garment industry into improving working conditions. New York state reorganized its Department of Labor so it could more effectively regulate factories. These changes were imitated by other states, and served as the groundwork for the eventual passing of a federal minimum wage.

**Justice Unserved.** The owners were charged with manslaughter for locking the stairwell, but were acquitted. The insurance claims they put in for the fire made them a tidy profit of $400 for every victim. The victims' families received $75 for each life in a civil suit. Two years later, one of the owners was arrested for locking an exit door in another factory he owned. This time he was found guilty—and fined $20.

## 3. THE COCOANUT GROVE FIRE

Boston's Cocoanut Grove nightclub had been a speakeasy during Prohibition. By 1942, it was a popular nightspot for locals and soldiers on leave. Fake palm trees filled the rooms and fabric on the ceiling gave the impression of a tropical night. The club was so popular that the owner opened a new room, the Melody Lounge, in the basement. As a result, on November 28, 1942, there were 1,000 people in the club, well over the legal occupancy of 500.

**Let There Be Light.** The fire started in the Melody Lounge. Witnesses say they saw a busboy light a match to see while changing a lightbulb, and this started the fire, but others say it wasn't his fault. Whatever the cause, a spark flew onto an artificial palm. Amused patrons watched for a few seconds as waiters tried to douse the fire with pitchers of water. But then the whole lounge went up. The lights went out and the basement went dark—lit only by the fire.

**A Highly Flammable Situation.** Everything in the club was flammable—the fake trees, the ceiling, the table linens, and the imitation leather on the walls. Flames spread so fast that some patrons were burned to death while seated at their tables. Those who fled weren't much luckier. Running down a hall out of the basement, they came to an exit door, but found it locked. One survivor from upstairs recalled that the first indication that something was wrong was a girl running screaming through the club, her blazing hair lighting tablecloths as she went. Then the flames came, someone recalled, like a "great wave."

**Fire Trapped.** The patrons rushed to the main entrance of the club—but it was a revolving door, and the crush of bodies jammed it shut. Two other doors led to the street, but they opened inward and were quickly wedged shut by the crowd. Some people managed to escape via service entrances or windows, but in the dark confusion, with no exits marked and the main doors useless, most were trapped inside.

**Putting Out the Flames.** Firemen were a few blocks away attending to a minor fire at the time of the alarm, so they got to the Cocoanut Grove quickly and doused the flames. Only 12 minutes had passed since the first spark. That was all the time it took to kill 492 people. A Boston firefighter and researcher showed years later that the fire's lethal speed likely came from a highly flammable propellant in a refrigeration unit.

**Safety First and Last.** Surpassed only by the Iroquois Theater fire, the Cocoanut Grove fire is the next deadliest structure fire in U.S. history. It resulted in an overhaul of fire codes, particularly in determining legal occupancy of public spaces, and in the design of exit doors. Revolving doors must be flanked by regular doors, or have a safety feature that allows the panels to be pushed flat in an emergency. And ever since Cocoanut Grove, exits of public buildings have to open outward.

---

...A. The Angkor Wat Temple, the country's prime tourist attraction.

# THE ENVELOPE, PLEASE

*The red carpet, the glittering gowns, the tearful thank-yous…
what would we do without entertainment awards? Here's
the story of how the five major entertainment awards
ceremonies morphed into prime-time galas.*

## 1. THE OSCARS

Close to 300 movie bigwigs gathered at the Hollywood Roosevelt
Hotel on May 16, 1929, for the first Academy Awards ceremony.
Since the winners had already been announced three months
earlier, there was no suspense, and the statuettes were doled out
in a fifteen-minute ceremony.

Who won? *Wings*, a blockbuster World War I flick produced
by Paramount Pictures, took home Best Movie. Janet Gaynor won
the first Best Actress award for her work in three different films
(*Sunrise*, *Seventh Heaven*, and *Street Angel*), and Emil Jannings
(who became the Academy's first no-show) won Best Actor for
starring in *The Way of All Flesh* and *The Last Command*. Jannings
had recently left Hollywood and returned to Europe, perhaps
realizing that his thick German-Swiss accent would not be well
received in the new talkies. He later made Nazi propaganda films.

## 2. THE GOLDEN GLOBES

In 1944, when eight journalists calling themselves the Hollywood
Foreign Correspondents Association decided to host an award ceremony of their own, the Golden Globes were born. A luncheon
was held at Twentieth Century Fox's studio, which had produced
*The Song of Bernadette*—the first Golden Globe winner for Best
Picture. Jennifer Jones won Best Actress for portraying Bernadette,
and Paul Lukas was named Best Actor for *Watch on the Rhine*. No
statues, only commemorative scrolls, were handed out that day.

## 3. THE GRAMMYS

The National Academy of Recording Arts and Sciences was two
years old when it launched the first Grammy Awards on May 4,
1958. The awards snubbed Elvis Presley and his new rock 'n' roll
music, instead recognizing an Italian ballad called "Volare" with

---

**First American novel to sell more than a million copies: *Uncle Tom's Cabin*.**

the Best Single and Record of the Year awards. Henry Mancini, Ella Fitzgerald, Count Basie, and Perry Como all won awards, too. The ceremony was held in the Grand Ballroom of the Beverly Hills Hotel, and it wasn't televised until the early 1970s.

Why are the awards called Grammys? The name is short for "gramophone"—an early record player in which sound came out of a trumpet-shaped device.

## 4. THE TONYS

These awards honor theatrical plays and musicals, and they're named for actress-director Antoinette Perry. After her death in 1946, the idea of an award named to honor Perry caught on, and the top names in American theater voted on the nominees. On Easter Sunday in 1947, after an evening of dinner and dancing at the Waldorf-Astoria Hotel in New York City, the first Tonys were presented at midnight. The list of winners would thrill any theater lover: Helen Hayes, Fredric March, Jose Ferrer, Ingrid Bergman, Patricia Neal, Agnes de Mille, Arthur Miller, Elia Kazan, and Kurt Weill, just to name a few.

## 5. THE EMMYS

The Academy of Television Arts and Sciences originally called their awards the "Immys"—short for "image-orthicon camera tube." But the statue—a graceful, winged woman holding an atom—looked so feminine that by the first ceremony, everyone was calling it the Emmy. On January 25, 1949, at the Hollywood Athletic Club, the first Emmy was given to Shirley Dinsdale, for Outstanding Personality—Dinsdale hosted the kiddie show *Judy Splinters*. The Most Popular Program for 1949 was a game show: *Pantomime Quiz Time*. The show wasn't broadcast on network TV until 1955.

\*     \*     \*

"No matter how rich you become, how famous or powerful, when you die the size of your funeral will still pretty much depend on the weather. "

—**Michael Pritchard**

The rocks excavated for the Hoover Dam would be enough to build the Great Wall of China.

# SNAPSHOTS OF HISTORY

*Certain photos capture a moment in time you will never forget. Uncle John studied hundreds of iconic 20th-century photos to select a dozen of the most memorable—with apologies to Ansel Adams. These remarkable shots span the century and endure in memory: two words and a date are usually all you need to recall them. Drum roll, please...*

## 1. FIRST FLIGHT, KITTY HAWK, NORTH CAROLINA, DECEMBER 17, 1903

On a cold December 14, with wind blowing off the Atlantic Ocean, two bicycle mechanics from Ohio felt the moment was right to fly a motorized "aeroplane" for the first time in history. They chose the sand dunes of Kitty Hawk, North Carolina, in order to soften the landing of what was expected to be a short, bumpy flight. Brothers Orville and Wilbur Wright flipped a coin to see who would go first. Wilbur won the toss, but their attempt to launch the biwinged plane that day failed.

Three days later, with a photographer and other witnesses standing by, the twin propellers roared to life with Orville lying facedown on the center of the lower wing, rudder controls firmly in hand. The fixed-wing plane roared off twin rails and became airborne. The flight lasted all of 12 seconds and covered 120 feet. Proof of flight came in the photo taken by John Daniels showing the plane about four feet off the ground with Wilbur watching his brother Orville soar into history.

## 2. TSAR NICHOLAS AND FAMILY, YEKATERINBURG, RUSSIA, JULY 17, 1918

The family portrait of Russian tsar Nicholas Romanov II, his wife Tsarina Alexandra Feodorovna, their beautiful daughters Olga, Tatiana, Maria, and Anastasia, and male heir Alexei might seem fitting for one taken at their palace. But it is the knowledge of what came shortly afterward that made the photograph an icon of the 20th century. At 2:30 a.m. on July 17, 1918, the tsar—who had abdicated a year earlier—his family, and their physician and personal assistants were herded into the basement of the Siberian home they were residing in on the pretext of protecting them from revolutionary forces. There, Bolshevik officer Yakov Yurovsky announced that they were condemned to death. Stunned, the tsar asked, "What? What?" Executioners drew their revolvers and began shooting, killing Nicholas, his wife, their son, and the servants. The four sisters initially survived due to secreted diamonds embroidered into their clothing that deflected some of the bullets. Stabbed with bayonets and shot in the head, they too perished.

In order to prove that the royal family had been exterminated, Yurovsky delivered body parts and jewelry to the central committee of the communist party in Moscow. The massacre marked the end of the Romanov dynasty. In 1991, the remains of most of the family were recovered; in 2007, the missing remains of Alexei and one of his sisters were discovered in a grave near the first site. Apparently they were buried in separate graves because initially the jailers had attempted unsuccessfully to cremate two of the bodies. After DNA tests proved they were Romanovs, they were reinterred at the St. Peter and Paul Cathedral in St. Petersburg, where the tsar is considered Saint Nicholas the Passion-Bearer by the Russian Orthodox Church.

### 3. "MIGRANT MOTHER," NIPOMO, CALIFORNIA, MARCH 1936

At the height of the Great Depression, the federal Resettlement Administration hired San Francisco photographer Dorothea Lange (1895–1965) to document the plight of migrant workers pouring into refugee camps in central California from Oklahoma and other Dust Bowl states. One of her photos was of a woman with an expression of despair as two of her children buried their faces in her shoulders and another sat on her lap. That portrait of Florence Owens Thompson became the symbol of the Depression. The single image prompted the U.S. government to send food and supplies to the refugee camps—and made Lange famous.

The photograph was taken at a pea-pickers tent camp in the winter of 1936. Lange, 45, saw Thompson and, as she later recalled, went to her "as if drawn by a magnet." Thompson, the mother of seven, told Lange she had lost her husband to tuberculosis, and their car broke down, leaving the family stranded in the camp. They sold the tires and managed to survive on birds that her children killed, along with vegetables from local fields. By the time relief supplies arrived, she and her children had moved on. Lange's photo and others she took inspired author John Steinbeck to write *The Grapes of Wrath*.

## 4. AIRSHIP *HINDENBURG*, LAKEHURST, NEW JERSEY, MAY 6, 1937

Nothing shook the world like the explosion and destruction of the great German zeppelin *Hindenburg* in Lakehurst, New Jersey, on May 6, 1937. A photo taken by Murray Becker of the Associated Press immortalized the disaster as the lighter-than-air craft docked at the naval air station south of New York City. Perhaps the most famous news photo ever taken, it shows a fireball of hydrogen gas erupting from the tail, framed by a gantry tethering the ship. A sequence of photos shows antlike passengers as they leap from the conflagration and crumple to the ground.

Dirigibles, considered the safest form of air travel at the time, had conveyed passengers back and forth across the Atlantic throughout the 1920s and most of the 1930s without incident. Even when the navy's airship USS *Akron* crashed in the Atlantic in 1933 and the accident killed 73 of the 76 passengers aboard, public support for dirigibles didn't waver. But the photographic record of the *Hindenburg* disaster four years later incontrovertibly shattered public faith and ended the use of rigid airships in commercial transportation, even though 62 of the 97 people onboard survived.

## 5. MOUNT SURIBACHI, IWO JIMA, FEBRUARY 23, 1945

The most reproduced photo in American history was taken by Associated Press photographer Joe Rosenthal during the bloody World War II battle by U.S. Marines to wrest the Pacific island of Iwo Jima from the Japanese. The heavily fortified island included underground bunkers linked by 16 miles of tunnels that advance airstrikes had not destroyed. Just five days into the fight, the marines captured the crest of the atoll's highest mountain, 554-foot Mount Suribachi. It was there that Rosenthal photographed five marines and one navy corpsman struggling to plant the American flag, signaling the anticipated triumph over a Japanese garrison that had no means of escape. Ultimately, it became a symbol of American patriotism.

But the fierce struggle went on for another 30 days. Though hopeless, the enemy was determined to impose such a terrible toll on the marines that the United States would be dissuaded from invading Japan itself. By the time the battle ended on March 26, the United States and its allies had suffered 28,000 casualties, including approximately 6,800 dead. Three of the six men in Rosenthal's famed photo were killed. Of the 22,785 Japanese troops on Iwo Jima, 21,570 died in combat or through ritualistic suicide. Only 216 were taken prisoner. The epic battle symbolized by Rosenthal's photo earned him a Pulitzer Prize for photography, the only one ever awarded in the same year the winning photo was taken.

## 6. THE KISS, NEW YORK CITY, V-J DAY, AUGUST 14, 1945

Edith Shain was an attractive young nurse in a white uniform standing in Times Square on August 14, 1945, as news spread that Japan had surrendered. Suddenly, out of the crowd spilling into the street came an ecstatic navy sailor. A complete stranger, he swept her into his arms, then dipped her in an impassioned kiss as she clutched her skirt and purse. Photographer Alfred Eisenstaedt happened to be close by and snapped the picture.

Eisenstaedt didn't know who he had photographed that day, but his photo became a cultural icon when published in *Life* magazine a week later. The identity of the sailor has never been established, although 12 men later tried to claim the title. As for the nurse, Shain was anointed by the editors of *Life* in 1970 as that woman (although two others also claimed to be the woman in the photo). Shain said she was working at Doctor's Hospital in the city when she heard on the radio that the war was over. She rode the subway to Times Square to celebrate, and after stepping onto the street saw the sailor going from one woman to another kissing them, young and old. He then came to her and planted the immortal kiss. At age 90 in 2008, Shain returned to the city as grand marshal of its Veterans Day Parade. Looking back to that moment in Times Square in 1945, she said her only regret was not getting the sailor's telephone number.

*The story continues on page 286.*

# KNOW YOUR BARBARIAN HORDES

*The barbarian hordes conquered the Roman Empire,*
*but do you know your Goths from your Vandals?*

## 1. VISIGOTHS AND OSTROGOTHS

In the fourth century AD, the Goths (a name given to them by the Romans) lived just across the Danube River from the Roman Empire. Fearing the invading Huns, they asked to cross the Danube and were granted permission, provided they serve in the Roman army. This proved to be disastrous for the Romans—Alaric I, a Gothic general in the Roman army, led the first sack of Rome, in 410. What's the difference between a Visigoth and an Ostrogoth? Timing. The Visigoths entered Roman territory in the late fourth century; the Ostrogoths entered later. After the last Roman emperor was deposed in 476, barbarian groups set up kingdoms in what used to be the Roman Empire. The Visigoths settled in Spain, and the Ostrogoths in Italy.

The Goths give their name to the word "gothic," which initially meant barbarous or uncouth.

## 2. VANDALS

While the Romans were busy dealing with increasing unrest from the Goths, they pulled guards away from their borders. The Vandals took advantage of this lapse, along with an unusually cold winter in 406 that froze the Rhine River, to cross into Roman territory. They went on to sack Rome in 455. The Vandals initially settled in Spain, but were kicked out by the Visigoths. They moved on to conquer northern Africa, taking the city of Carthage and establishing a kingdom that lasted for only a century before being reconquered by the Romans.

The English word "vandal" comes from these people and, unsurprisingly, means a person who wrecks things.

## 3. FRANKS

The Franks—and a number of other barbarian groups—landed in

---

*Nosferatu,* the first vampire film, was released in Germany in 1922.

France after the fall of the Roman Empire. Their first kingdom, called Francia, was in modern Belgium, but they soon moved into the province of Gaul. The first great king of the Franks was Clovis, who conquered much of the rest of France and modern Spain. Many French kings after him have taken his name—Louis. The Franks were never conquered by outsiders, and gave their name to the modern country of France.

## 4. ANGLES AND SAXONS

When Roman soldiers withdrew from Great Britain in the fifth century, Germanic hordes began raiding and then settling there. The most prominent of these groups were the Angles, who give their name to England, and the Saxons, or simply the Anglo-Saxons. The local Celtic populations resisted the invasion. In fact, some historians contend that one Celtic general, who led his people to a brief victory against the Anglo-Saxons at the Battle of Mount Badon, was named Arthur—the origin of the myth of King Arthur and Camelot. However, this rebellion was unsuccessful, and the Anglo-Saxons stayed for good, bringing their language as well, which became Old English.

\*     \*     \*

## ANAGRAMS

Anagrams have been around since the fourth or sixth century depending on which historian you ask. Louis XIII employed a royal anagrammist, Thomas Bilon, to entertain his court with the word puzzles. Here are some fun ones:

**1. Emperor Octavius:** "Captain over Rome"
**2. Halley's Comet:** "Shall yet come"
**3. Chairman Mao:** "I am on a march"
**4. Mother-in-law:** "Woman Hitler"
**5. Madame Curie:** "Me, radium ace"
**6. Election results:** "Lies—let's recount"
**7. Osama bin Laden:** "A bad man (no lies)"
**8. The Morse code:** "Here come the dots"
**9. Leonardo da Vinci:** "Did color in a nave"

In 1846, Belgian musician Adolphe Sax invented the saxophone.

# GANGLAND

*Are you a joiner? If so, read this before you
start hanging around with the wrong crowd.*

Some people who have social justice as their goal will sit down
and write an essay, or hold a fund-raiser, or get involved in
politics. That's not what these guys were interested in doing.

## 1. ROBERT CATESBY AND GUY FAWKES

Back in the 1500s, when Henry VIII yanked England away from
Catholicism because he wanted a divorce to marry a younger
woman, the people who stayed with the Catholic Church were
accused of being traitors. When James I inherited the throne in
1603, the persecution continued. Priests were expelled from the
country, and Catholics who didn't attend Anglican services were
fined. One fed-up Catholic, Robert Catesby, launched a plot to
change all that. In 1604, he gathered a band of followers that
included Guy Fawkes, a formidable soldier and explosives expert,
and rented a cellar in the Parliament building. The idea was,
while the king addressed the legislators, Fawkes would blow up the
building. The others would kidnap James's young daughter Elizabeth and force her to rule as their puppet (and Catholic) queen.

**The Plot Thickens.** By October 1605, Guy Fawkes had hidden 36
barrels of gunpowder in the cellar and the conspirators were all set
to give the king an explosive surprise on November 5. But an
anonymous letter alerted a member of the House of Lords to stay
away from Parliament that day, so instead of blowing up the building on November 5, Fawkes was captured and tortured until he
finally admitted to the plot. Catesby and his men were hunted
down, and those who weren't killed were drawn and quartered
while still alive.

King James made November 5 a holiday because uncovering
the plot saved his life, so everyone was supposed to be happy.
Today, the English still celebrate Guy Fawkes Night with bonfires
and fireworks, but history remembers it as one of the world's most
famous fizzled terror plots.

## 2. THE RIGHTEOUS HARMONIOUS FISTS

At the turn of the 19th century, China's costal province of Shandong was famous as the birthplace of the Yi He Quan, which translates as the "Righteous and Harmonious Fists," a secret organization whose members came from the ranks of the poor. A religious organization, they also practiced martial arts, including forms of kung fu and shadow boxing. When Westerners saw the Yi He Quan fight, they called them "Boxers."

**The Magical Military Tour.** The Boxers celebrated Chinese traditions and resented the "foreign devils" who were gaining power in China because they had superior weapons. The Boxers also believed that with proper practice of the martial arts and the use of magical charms, they could develop supernatural powers to deflect foreign bullets. China's Empress Tzu-Hsi had at first seen the Boxers as enemies, but she too feared foreign domination and became their ally.

**Making an "Empression."** The Boxers roamed the countryside in 1898, attacking foreign businesses, embassies, and Christian missionaries. Sympathizers joined up and the Boxers' ranks swelled to as many as 100,000 members. The Boxer Rebellion spread across China, and in 1900 the empress's Imperial Army joined them in their war against the foreign diplomats working in Peking (now Beijing).

Eight countries (including the United States, Germany, France, Russia, and Japan) sent soldiers into China to put down the rebellion. The Boxers' "magic" powers proved to be no match for the international forces and their modern weapons. The uprising was crushed, and the empress had to give up even more power—paving the way for the overthrow of her grandnephew Puyi (better known as "the Last Emperor") and the establishment of the Republic of China in 1912.

## 3. THE PRETTY BOY FLOYD GANG

In 1924, Charles Arthur Floyd was 20 years old, married, and working hard picking cotton in Atkins, Oklahoma, when he became friends with John Hildebrand, a practiced thief who taught Floyd how to make much better money robbing gas stations and small stores. One of Floyd's theft victims described him to police as "a pretty boy with apple cheeks," so he was given a nickname he hated: Pretty Boy. Floyd was arrested in 1925 and sent to prison, where he learned a lot more about the crime trade.

**Bank Robbin' Hoods.** Paroled in 1929, Floyd went to Kansas City, where he met up with criminals like himself and soon became head of America's most successful gangs, robbing banks from Ohio to Oklahoma. With the Great Depression came even more success: Floyd became a criminal philanthropist, tearing up mortgages so that people wouldn't lose their homes, or throwing wads of money to people from the window of one of his many get-away cars. According to some historians, he sent this message to the government: "If you ain't gonna do nothing to help the little guy, 'Pretty Boy' Floyd will!"

**I'll Get You, My Pretty!** Floyd had killed more than one police officer during his crime sprees, so not everyone considered him a hero. In 1933, when four officers were killed in what became known as the Kansas City Massacre, J. Edgar Hoover made Pretty Boy Floyd a prime suspect, even though historians don't all agree on the truth of the FBI charge—Floyd was more into making money than murder, and used his gun only in self-defense. This had been a shootout with no bank money involved. The FBI caught up with Floyd in 1934 and chased him for two days through Ohio before finding him and killing him when he tried to run again.

Floyd's body was returned to Oklahoma; the thousands of people who attended his funeral made it the largest in Oklahoma history.

## 4. THE BAADER-MEINHOF GANG

The 1960s were famous for student protest marches and lifestyles of sex, drugs, and rock and roll. In 1968, in West Germany, student Gudrun Ensslin and her boyfriend Andreas Baader added violence to the mix. In their anger at what they saw as the sins of capitalism, they set fire to two department stores. Baader went to jail, but escaped with the help of an antiestablishment journalist, Ulrike Meinhof. In 1970, Baader, Ensslin, and Meinhof, along with their young, middle-class followers, launched a "revolution." They called themselves the Red Army Faction (RAF), though to

In 1900, only 10% of teenagers aged 14 to 17 went to high school.

most people they were simply the Baader-Meinhof Gang.

**The Cause of It All.** Professing support for the Palestinian cause and for bringing an end to the Vietnam War, the RAF robbed banks, kidnapped people, bombed military buildings, and murdered anyone who got in their way. They even blew up the offices of a newspaper that gave them some bad press. By 1976, Meinhof had hanged herself in prison, and Baader and Ensslin were both behind bars. But that only spurred more violence as the rest of the gang desperately tried to free their leaders.

In 1976, the battle went international as the "German Autumn." In September, the RAF kidnapped Hanns-Martin Schlever, a powerful businessman with a Nazi past, and demanded their leaders' release in exchange for Schlever's life. On October 13, their Palestinian allies hijacked a German Lufthansa 757, threatening to blow up the plane and passengers unless the RAF's demands were met. After a grim five-day standoff, a unit of German commandos managed to kill the hijackers and liberate the passengers.

**From Baader to Worse.** When Baader and Ensslin learned that the hijacking had failed, they took their lives in a suicide pact—one by gunshot, the other by hanging (though the government's role in their deaths remains controversial). The RAF pulled off more bombings and assassinations, but its power diminished and support from students faded. In 1998, the RAF formally dissolved with this message: "The revolution says: I was, I am, I will be again."

*　　*　　*

## TOM SWIFTIES

• "The propulsion systems were used by NASA on moon rockets," said Tom apologetically.

• "Don't let me drown in Egypt," said Tom, deep in denial.

• "This is the real goose," said Tom, producing the propaganda.

• "I'd better repeat that SOS message," said Tom remorsefully.

The average human digestive tract is about 30 feet long.

# REST IN PIECES

*In this story one man loses his
head, and another his heart.*

## THOMAS MORE AIN'T GOT NO BODY

When Sir Thomas More refused to attend the coronation of
Anne Boleyn in 1533, Henry VIII of England got annoyed and
had More beheaded in 1535. To add further indignity to the situation, More's body was buried in an unmarked grave in the
Tower of London and his head was parboiled, placed on a pike,
and displayed on London Bridge for all to see...and, perhaps, for
all to learn that you don't mess with the king.

Later, possibly by bribing a sympathetic official, More's foster
daughter acquired the head, which is now thought to be lying in
a family crypt in St. Dunstan's Church in Canterbury. Nobody
knows what happened to his body. Centuries later, Sir Thomas
More became Saint Thomas More after beatification by the
Catholic Church in 1980. Still no body, though.

## LORD BYRON GETS PICKLED

If drowning your sorrows in drink sounds appealing, consider
this: it's not going to help you achieve immortality. It's only
going to make a stinky mess. When Lord Byron, poet and leading figure of Britain's Romantic movement, died of a fever in
Greece in 1824, his innards were removed and his body
embalmed in alcohol and put in a leaky coffin. A few weeks
later, undertakers tried to preserve his body a second time by
sealing Byron plus the old coffin and its contents inside another
barrel of alcohol, and they sent the whole works to England.
Once there, Byron was removed from the barrel and given a
funeral but was refused burial in two different churches because
of his bad-boy reputation. His body was eventually taken to a
family plot in Nottinghamshire.

Legend says that Byron's heart is in Greece, but the truth is
that his heart and most of his other organs accompanied him to
his grave. According to sworn affidavits, though, Byron's lungs
are still in a jar in a Greek church.

---

At his birth, Elvis Presley's family was so poor that their house was unpainted.

# OH, BABY!

*Six ways to make history before
you're even toilet trained.*

## 1. FALL INTO THE CLUTCHES OF A MAD SCIENTIST

John B. Watson was a behavioral psychologist at Johns Hopkins University when he performed an experiment that still has people guessing at the results. Watson believed that people are the way they are based solely on their environment. In his view, environmental conditioning is what makes a baby brave or fearful; it can also influence him or her to grow up to become virtually anything from a biologist to a burglar, regardless of natural talents or tendencies. In 1920, he set out to prove his theory. The unfortunate subject of his experiment was a nine-month-old known only as "Little Albert" or "Albert B."

**Little Crybaby.** Albert showed no fear when he was allowed to play with a white rat—until Watson's experiment. Every time Albert touched the rat, Watson or his assistant made a loud clanging noise that scared the baby and made him cry. Albert learned to associate the scary sound with the rat, and eventually, even without the sound, he was afraid of the rat. This fear carried over to any furry creature that reminded Albert of the rat. Success! Watson had just conditioned a phobic toddler.

**Taking Baby for a Walk.** It's still not known if Albert's mother (a single woman employed as a wet nurse) knew every single detail of the experiment, or where she took her little boy, but take him away she did—before Watson could reverse his conditioning—if he planned to.

**Later in Life.** Watson's findings created an uproar: How could he have preyed on an innocent child—and would Little Albert ever recover from his ordeal? Decades later, researchers discovered that Little Albert's real name was Douglas Merritte. But we'll never know if Douglas continued to live in fear of furry animals—he died of an illness when he was six years old.

## 2. FALL INTO THE CLUTCHES OF A MAD SCIENTIST WHO'S YOUR FATHER

B. F. Skinner was a behavioral psychologist like Watson. His early experiments with rats and pigeons showed that they could learn quickly with rewards, otherwise known as "positive reinforcement." His success encouraged him to try the process on a human being. And who better than his own daughter, Deborah?

**All the Amenities.** Skinner had performed his animal experiments in a controlled chamber that he called the "Skinner Box," so when Deborah was born in 1944, he created a similar item: a glass-enclosed combination of crib, playpen, and diaper-changing station into which warm air circulated so that she could sleep and play comfortably in her diapers, without the confinement of clothing or blankets. Deborah seemed to enjoy the arrangement, and her mother liked doing less laundry. But then came the urban legend.

**No Way to Treat a Baby.** It all began in 1945 when Skinner wrote an article about his "air crib" for *Ladies' Home Journal.* Unfortunately, the photo that ran with the article depicted the baby in a smaller, portable box that was different from her usual box and was captioned "Baby in a Box." Eventually, the legend grew to horrific proportions, to the point that a 2004 book titled *Opening Skinner's Box* claimed that Skinner kept his baby in a Skinner Box while running experiments that left Deborah so deranged that she later killed herself.

**Later in Life.** The urban legend made baby Deborah famous—and the book made grown-up Deborah furious. In fact, she'd grown up to be a well-adjusted adult. She countered the stories about her father's experiments with a newspaper article entitled "I Was Not a Lab Rat," in which she angrily refuted the book's claims.

## 3. SELL STRAINED PEAS

Since 1928, the Gerber baby has graced labels that are printed in 16 languages and pasted on products sold in at least 80 countries. The topic of the chubby-cheeked baby's true identity has been argued for years: famous names have been bandied about, including Humphrey Bogart, Richard Nixon, and Jane Seymour. But according to company history, Gerber went looking for a baby mascot in 1928. By then, Bogart was already a grown man, Nixon was a teenager, and Seymour wasn't even born. So whose face was it that launched a billion jars of strained peas?

**The Baby in Question.** The baby's name was Ann Turner; she was five months old when artist Dorothy Hope Smith did a rough charcoal sketch of her. The following year, after a search for the perfect baby face to use in its ads, Gerber bought Smith's charcoal sketch for a flat fee of $300. The image worked out so well that in 1931, Gerber made the portrait its official trademark.

**Later in Life.** Ann grew up, married, raised four children, and after retiring from her career as an English teacher authored a mystery series under her married name, Ann Turner Cook. Sometimes she displays her innocent baby portrait at the bookstore while autographing her novels.

## 4. SHARE MOM'S WOMB

On May 28, 1934, the Dionne quintuplets were born in a farmhouse in Corbeil, a small village in Ontario, Canada. Annette, Cecile, Emilie, Marie, and Yvonne were identical, born from a single egg; the odds of that occurring were one in 57 million. The tiny preemies arrived in the middle of the Great Depression to a poor farm family that already had five children, so when the quints were four months old, their father accepted an offer from the Chicago World's Fair to exhibit his daughters. Even though he canceled it a day later, the public was outraged, and the Ontario government took custody of the babies, isolating them in a specially built hospital that became known as "Quintland." Their parents were discouraged from visiting.

**Five Little Goldfish.** Quintland had strict "scientific" routines for meals, bathing, and sleeping, but part of their rigid schedule took the babies to a corridor where visitors gawked at them through a one-way screen three times a day. The girls were on display for nine years while their doctors got famous for raising them in a controlled environment, the locals prospered from hordes of tourists (estimated at 6,000 a day), and the Ontario government and businesses made an estimated $500 million off endorsements and merchandise like dolls and books. (The girls' father partook of their fame, too, with a souvenir and concession shop across the street.) The quints didn't receive any profits and were raised in a manner they later described as "inhuman" and "like a circus."

**Later in Life.** In 1943, their parents won back legal custody and the sisters came home. But they left again at age 18, claiming that they were treated unfairly because their parents resented what their birth had done to the family. Emily died in 1954 and Marie in 1970, and in 1998 the three surviving sisters won a $4 million judgment against the Ontario government. They urged multiple-birth parents to keep the lives of their children private.

## 5. ENTER THE WORLD AS A SCIENTIFIC BREAK-THROUGH

Louise Joy Brown got famous as a fetus. For nine years, John and Lesley Brown of Bristol, England had been trying to have a child, but Lesley's Fallopian tubes were blocked, thus preventing a pregnancy. In November 1977, Lesley underwent in vitro fertilization (IVF), in which an egg was extracted from her uterus, placed in a lab dish, and fertilized with John's sperm. Two and a half days later, after cells of the egg divided to become an eight-celled embryo, the egg was carefully replaced in Lesley's uterus.

**The Mama and the Paparazzi.** IVF had been tried before, but had never resulted in a pregnancy that lasted more than a few weeks. When Lesley Brown's closely monitored pregnancy lasted months, the media went crazy over the possible birth of the first "test-tube baby." The relentless British press forced the Browns into hiding; when Lesley was ready to deliver, reporters tried everything—including a bomb hoax—to get into her hospital room.

**Mrs. Brown, You've Got a Lovely Daughter.** On July 25, 1978, at 11:47 p.m., Louise Joy was born via Cesarean section; she weighed 5 pounds 12 ounces. As the world's first baby conceived outside of the womb, Louise was a scientific milestone. Religious and ethical controversies over IVF continued to rage, but that didn't stop infertile couples from turning to the new procedure—especially since the blond, blue-eyed Louise was a normal, healthy baby.

**Later in Life.** By the time Louise had her 30th birthday, she was just the first among millions of in vitro babies. Today, she's married with a son who was conceived the old-fashioned way.

## 6. GET RESCUED ON TV

On October 14, 1987, 18-month-old Jessica McClure and three other children were playing in the yard of her aunt's home in

Midland, Texas. Jessica stumbled down an abandoned well shaft and fell 22 feet—leaving her alive but wedged in so tightly underground that she couldn't be pulled up. The shaft was only eight inches wide in places, but widening it could result in a fatal cave-in. Rescuers brought in drilling equipment to sink a parallel shaft about five feet from Jessica and then planned to dig a horizontal tunnel to reach her. Meanwhile, fresh, heated air was piped down the well to keep Jessica breathing and safe from hypothermia.

**Drill, Baby, Drill.** Millions of viewers kept a vigil, watching CNN's 24-hour coverage of the rescue attempt. The occasional rescuer would tearfully report how Jessica sang for them, recited nursery rhymes, or cried for her mother. After 58 hours of digging, two paramedics reached the toddler, slathered her with petroleum jelly, and yanked her out of the well—breaking her leg in the process. By that time, the entire country was cheering for "Baby Jessica." Her teenaged parents, who had been struggling to make ends meet, received so many donations that they bought a small house and established a trust fund for their daughter.

**Later in Life.** Jessica's injuries left her with scars and an injured right foot. She claims she has no memories of the incident, and grew up happily. She'll be even happier when she collects on that trust fund—said to be worth over $1 million—when she turns 25 in March 2011.

\*    \*    \*

### THE POLITICIAN VERSUS THE GENERAL

Can you believe a politician? Can you believe a general? Contrasting views offer choice irony to Uncle John's readers looking back in the rear view mirror of World War I:

• The Democratic slogan used to elect President Wilson during the 1916 general election was, "He kept us out of war." Wilson declared war on Germany the following year.

• French Marshall Ferdinand Foch, Supreme Allied Commander during World War I, had this choice comment after viewing the final draft of the peace treaty in 1919: "This is no peace. It is an armistice for 20 years." World War II began in 1939 when Germany invaded Poland.

---

As of 2008, 138 pyramids had been found in Egypt—most were built as pharaohs' tombs.

# WHO SAID THAT?

*Shhh…don't you hear it? That voice inside your head. It's
saying, "You will love this story." And don't worry, these
historical figures heard voices inside their heads too.*

## 1. PSST! HEY, SOCRATES!

**Who:** Socrates (470–399 BC)

**Voice:** A daimon (a "divine" or "supernatural" voice)

In 399 BC, at his trial for "impiety" and "corrupting youth"
with antidemocratic teachings, Socrates spoke of a voice outside
of himself that warned him of dangers and errors. "This is something that I have had since childhood," Plato quoted him as saying. "It is a voice that comes to me and forbids me from doing
something I'm intending to do. However, it never tells me what to
do, just what not to do." Supposedly, when the voice spoke, the
philosopher would stop whatever he was doing and stand motionless, sometimes for the better part of a day.

Unfortunately, Socrates' daimon failed him during his trial.
According to an account by the Greek historian Xenophon, it
told him to stay obstinately silent for most of the trial's duration
and loudly defiant during the rest of it. If the goal was to save
Socrates, that approach didn't work. The philosopher was found
guilty, and he (and presumably his daimon) was executed by hem-
lock.

## 2. VOICES IN THE DARK

**Who:** Joan of Arc (1412–31)

**Voices:** God and various saints

Joan of Arc had been a simple farm girl until, around the age of
16, she heard voices that told her to raise an army and liberate
France from British rule. Joan had been hearing voices since an
early age, but this was the first time they'd told her to go to war.
Dutifully, Joan appealed to the dauphin prince (the future French
king Charles VII) for men and equipment, claiming that God was
talking to her. The king was a little worried that Joan might be a
witch, but he gave her what she asked for. Joan led her army

January 15, 1919: A huge molasses tank exploded in Boston, creating a "tidal wave"…

offensively, attacking the British at unexpected places and times, a contrast to the typically cautious French army. With this approach, she managed to win many battles and rally the French army, but that didn't help her out in the end.

After ordering her outnumbered army to attack a force from Burgundy that was sympathetic to the British, she was captured and sold to the British, who sentenced her to death. According to popular accounts of the story, before being burned at the stake for heresy, Joan blamed the voices for misleading her.

## 3. VOCAL CHORDS
**Who:** Ludwig van Beethoven (1770–1827)
**Voice:** Musical instruments

Hearing loss can bring on auditory hallucinations, including voices, as the mind tries to fill the silence with familiar sounds. So we're all lucky that Beethoven suffered from a musical form of this, in which the "voices" were musical instruments he had long connected with. Beethoven contracted tinnitus as a young man, and it caused a painful, constant ringing in his ears. Over time, his hearing began to fade. Yet music still came vividly to him, and he wrote many of his major works in the last 13 years of his life, when he was completely deaf.

## 4. VOICE OF A NIGHTINGALE
**Who:** Florence Nightingale (1820–1910)
**Voice:** God

Florence Nightingale—the creator of modern nursing—suffered from recurring depression and bouts of mania throughout her life. She also heard voices. At 17, she said that God told her to go against the wishes of her family and refuse a life as a housewife. Seven years later, God told her to go into nursing. Nightingale "heard" from God at least once more—in 1850, while traveling in Cairo, Egypt, God told her to "do good for him alone without reputation," leading her to take a job as a hospital superintendent. Despite (or perhaps because of) her conversations with God, Nightingale was not a dogmatist. Even though she was raised a Unitarian, she demanded her sectarian hospital drop its requirement of caring only for Protestants and its attempts to convert dying members to its denomination. Instead, she insisted that Catholic, Jewish, and Muslim patients be admitted and granted their requests for visits from whatever clerics they preferred.

## 5. MATH INSANITY
**Who:** John Forbes Nash Jr. (1928–)

**Voices:** Assorted

John Nash's contribution to game theory and mathematics won him a Nobel Prize in 1994, and he was the subject of a much-fictionalized 2001 movie biography, *A Beautiful Mind*. That film showed Nash as suffering from visual and auditory hallucinations, but Nash maintained that he only heard voices. He'd suffered from schizophrenia since the late 1950s, but eventually Nash (called a true genius by many in the math and science world) learned to "outthink" the voices. He said in an interview that he dealt with them by "rejecting them and deciding not to hear them…you're really talking to yourself is what the voices are."

\*　　\*　　\*

## HE DIDN'T STAND A FIGHTIN' CHANCE

The Got Milk? advertising campaign has been going since October 29, 1993—a pretty good run in advertising history. The first ad featured actor Sean Whalen in a TV commercial. It opens with his character slathering a slice of bread with peanut butter in time to some classical music. He sits back to enjoy his repast, and the camera pans his tasteful home decorated with historical artifacts, especially ephemera pertaining to Alexander Hamilton.

As the music ends, a radio deejay breaks in to announce that a random listener will be called and given the opportunity to answer a $10,000 question. Whalen the history buff takes a big bite of his peanut butter bread just as his phone rings. When he picks it up, the deejay asks him to answer: "Who shot Alexander Hamilton in that famous duel?" Whalen smirks and answers correctly, but his reply is muffled because of the peanut butter. He reaches for something to wash it down with, only to upend an empty milk carton. He cannot make himself understood—so he loses the contest.

# THE LADY'S NOT A TRAMP

*For most of recorded history, women had just a handful of options
open to them: they could marry (hopefully to men of means,
they could teach, they could join convents, or they could do
something a little more exciting…like become mistresses to
the rich and famous. These eight are among history's
best known high-class ladies of the night.*

## 1. PHRYNE (FOURTH CENTURY BC)

As a child, she was called Mnesarete (Greek for "virtue"), but
because she was born with sallow skin, she was called Phryne (Greek
for "toad"). Still, Phryne became the most successful and sought-after
courtesan in ancient Greece, commanding 100 times the going rate.
Supposedly, she was even the model for a sculpture called *Aphrodite
of Cnidus*, one of the most famous works of Greek art.

**Lust Rewards:** Phryne became incredibly rich thanks to her
liaisons with powerful men in Athens. According to legend, she
even offered to pay to rebuild the city walls of Thebes, which
had been destroyed by Alexander the Great in 336 BC, but there
was a condition: the new wall had to contain the inscription
"Destroyed by Alexander, restored by Phryne the courtesan."
Her offer was declined.

Around 340 BC, Phryne was accused of affronting the gods by
appearing nude during a religious ceremony. At her trial, the ora-
tor Hyperides—her defender and also one of her lovers—ripped
open Phryne's robe and exposed her to the court. Why? He considered it a legitimate defense. She was, after all, the most beautiful woman in Athens, and someone that gorgeous must be on
good terms with Aphrodite, goddess of love and beauty, no matter
what codes of conduct she appeared to have broken. It worked.
The judges ruled in Phryne's favor.

## 2. THEODORA (497–548)

Theodora's father died when she was young, so her mother sent
the girl to work, first as an actress and then as a prostitute.

---

Abraham Lincoln's 1860 presidential campaign slogan: "Vote Yourself a Farm."

Theodora became the mistress to a politician named Hecebolus and then caught the eye of Justinian I, the emperor's nephew. Justinian was so enamored with Theodora that he wanted to marry her, but Byzantine law forbade royals from marrying mere actresses (and prostitutes, presumably), so his uncle changed the law and Justinian and Theodora became husband and wife.

**Lust Rewards:** Justinian ascended to the throne in 527, and together he and his wife ruled Byzantium (also known as the Eastern Roman Empire). Theodora proved to be a gifted politician—she helped to create a new constitution to curb corruption, expanded the rights of women in divorce, closed brothels, and founded convents for former prostitutes. When she died at around the age of 50, she had been empress of Byzantium for more than 20 years. Historians consider her to be the most influential and powerful woman in the empire's 1,100-year history.

### 3. VERONICA FRANCO (1546–91)

Like mother, like daughter: Veronica Franco was the privileged offspring of Venetian courtesan Paola Fracassa. She studied Greek and Roman literature and learned to play the lute. After marrying and divorcing a doctor, Franco consorted with politicians, artists, philosophers, and poets. She became an accomplished poet herself and celebrated her sexual prowess in her writing—her book *Familiar Letters* (published in 1580) was a collection of 50 letters written to her lovers, including King Henry III of France and the Venetian painter Jacopo Tintoretto.

**Lust Rewards:** In the 1570s, Franco lost most of her money to thieves, but it was her overt sexuality that was her undoing. In 1580, she was charged with immorality and witchcraft by the Roman Inquisition courts. She managed to avoid conviction by giving an eloquent speech in her own defense, and then a wealthy patron named Domenico Venier came to her aid. She never regained her former glory, though: Veronica Franco lived out the rest of her life in a section of Venice populated by destitute prostitutes.

### 4. NELL GWYNNE (1650–87)

Eleanor "Nell" Gwynne had a troubled childhood in London: Her father left the family when she was young, and her mother drowned in a pond after a drinking binge. Young Nell sold oranges to get by, but by the time she was 15, she'd also started working as an actress. Famous playwright John Dryden wrote roles for her, and she proved to be a comedic talent. With fame came wealthy men—eventually, Gwynne became a courtesan, cohabiting with members of the English nobility, including Charles Sackville, the sixth Earl of Dorset, and King Charles II.

**Lust Rewards:** Gwynne's main man was King Charles II, and she was his mistress exclusively from about 1670 until he died in 1685. They had two sons, and Charles built her a mansion near Windsor Castle. On his deathbed, Charles pleaded with his brother, James II, to "let not poor Nelly starve." James II carried out those wishes, providing for Nell Gwynne until her death two years later in 1687.

### 5. CORA PEARL (1835–86)

Emma Crouch was born in Plymouth, England, to a British musician and womanizer who deserted his family and moved to America. At around the age of 20, Emma worked as a milliner, dabbling in prostitution to augment her low wages. During this time, she met Robert Bignell, owner of a dance hall, and became his mistress. He took her to Paris, where she was enamored with the 19th-century Bohemian atmosphere. When Bignall returned to England, Emma stayed behind, changed her name to Cora Pearl, and became the city's most famous courtesan.

**Lust Rewards:** Cora Pearl had a series of lovers in high places, including the French statesman the Duc de Morny, the half brother of Napoleon III, and the Prince of Orange, heir to the throne of the Netherlands, who gave her a string of black pearls that became her signature ornament.

Pearl was known for her decadent ways—she once had waiters carry her naked on a silver plate into a fancy dinner, and she sometimes bathed in a tub of champagne in front of her dinner guests. But a shooting at one of her mansions led to her expulsion from France. She ended up indigent, living in a boardinghouse, where she died at age 51 of stomach cancer. In her memoirs, she left no regrets: "I am far from posing as a victim; it would be ungrateful of me to do so. I ought to have saved, but saving is not easy in such a whirl of excitement as that in which I have lived."

## 6. MADAME DE POMPADOUR (1721–64)

When Jeanne-Antoinette Poisson was nine years old, her mother took her to see a fortune-teller, who said the little girl would grow up to the be the mistress of a king. That seemed unlikely for the daughter of a disgraced French financier and a courtesan, but Jeanne-Antoinette eventually made good on the prophecy. In 1745, she was invited to a costume ball at the Palace of Versailles. Jeanne-Antoinette dressed as a shepherdess—King Louis XV was dressed as a tree. Within a month, she was his mistress.

**Lust Rewards:** Louis gave Jeanne-Antoinette her own coat of arms and the title of "Marquise de Pompadour," or Madame de Pompadour. Louis doted on her, and Madame de Pompadour spent fortunes on gems, art, and ornate porcelain. She also became one of Louis's foreign-policy advisers, even encouraging him to fight the Seven Years' War with England, which ended in France's defeat. The public blamed her for the war's devastation, but Louis remained loyal to her. She died in 1764, still a member of the royal court.

## 7. MATA HARI (1876–1917)

By the time Margaretha Geertruida Zelle MacLeod was 18, she'd married a Dutch colonial army officer who was twice her age and had moved with him to the Dutch East Indies. They had two children, but their marriage was on the rocks from the start—Margaretha liked the company of other men, and he liked to drink. Eventually, they divorced, and with little money and no skills, Margaretha turned to dancing and prostitution to make ends meet. In 1903, she moved to Paris, where she gained fame as an exotic dancer. Two years later, she was a sensation, flaunting her sexuality with Indonesian-derived dance and a new name: Mata Hari.

**Lust Rewards:** Mata Hari became the mistress of wealthy industrialist Emile Etiennne Guimet, and she was famous for a cabaret striptease in which she was left wearing only a bejeweled bra and an ornamental headdress and armbands. But she still had ties to the Netherlands, which allowed her free entry to Germany. And as the Germans and French got entrenched in World War I, she became an object of concern for the French military.

No one has ever proved that Mata Hari was (or wasn't) a German spy. According to some researchers, she took money to spy on the French because she was drowning in debt, but never actually participated in any espionage. Others claim she was a German operative with the code name of H-21. Whatever the truth, she was arrested and executed by firing squad in 1917 at the age of 41. Documents concerning her trial have been sealed, not to be opened until 2017. Stay tuned.

## 8. SHADY SADIE (1861–1944)

The closest thing the wild American West has to a famous courtesan is Josephine "Sadie" Marcus. At 18, Josephine ran away from home to join a traveling theater company as a dancer. While on tour, she romanced Tombstone, Arizona, deputy sheriff Johnny Behan; she liked the area so much that she moved there and became a prostitute, earning her the nickname "Shady Sadie."

**Lust Rewards:** In her early 20s, Sadie met famed lawman and gambler Wyatt Earp, who already had a common-law wife named Mattie Blaylock. But Blaylock was addicted to laudanum—an opiate used to treat headaches—and Shady Sadie won Earp's heart. No marriage records exist, but Sadie had adopted the last name Earp by 1882, and the couple traveled the West, gambling, hunting for gold and silver, operating saloons as far north as Alaska, and running horse races in San Diego.

Wyatt Earp died in 1929, but Shady Sadie lived until 1944. When she passed away, she was cremated, and her ashes were interred with Wyatt's remains in Colma, California.

\*     \*     \*

## ONE LAST THOUGHT BEFORE I GO—LAST WORDS

"How were the receipts today at Madison Square Garden?"
—P. T. Barnum, entrepreneur (d. 1891)

"I should never have switched from Scotch to Martinis."
—Humphrey Bogart, actor (d. 1957)

"That was a great game of golf, fellers."
—Bing Crosby, singer/actor (d. 1977)

"Moose . . . Indian . . . "
—Henry David Thoreau, writer (d. 1862)

In 1769, Dartmouth College received its royal charter from King George III.

# OLD SPORTS RULES

*Get off the sidelines and into the game as we examine*
*some of the most bizarre sports rules of yesteryear.*

## BASEBALL

• Until the 1920s, pitchers could coat the ball with anything at their disposal, including spit, mucus, and even petroleum jelly.

• Pitchers needed all the help they could get because, until 1883, they were required to throw underhanded, as if tossing a horseshoe. Pitchers were also required to keep both feet firmly planted on the ground during their delivery and were prohibited from stepping toward the plate.

• Batters were allowed to call for a high or low pitch from 1867 to 1887. This helps account for some of the unusually high batting averages from that era.

• Called strikes did not exist until 1858. Batters stayed at the plate until they put the ball in play, regardless of whether it took one pitch or a hundred. A new rule change in 1879 declared that nine balls made a walk. This rule changed several more times until 1889, when it was reduced to the now-standard four balls.

## GOLF

• When one player's ball blocked the path of another player's ball on the green but was at least six inches away, the obstructing player's ball was not lifted. Instead, the player who was farthest away from the hole had to curve or chip their putt around their opponent's ball. The "stymie rule," as it became known, was officially abolished in 1952 when the United States Golf Association and the Royal and Ancient Golf Club of St. Andrews established a new joint set of rules.

• Golf courses haven't always had a standard number of holes. That changed in 1764 when the Royal and Ancient Golf Club converted from 22 holes to 18 holes because the club thought the first four holes were too short.

• Golf holes used to come in many sizes. That changed in 1891 when the Royal and Ancient Golf Club determined that the hole should have a diameter of exactly 4.25 inches. The precise size was chosen in order to comply with a popular Scottish hole-cutter that had been invented 62 years earlier.

• The Royal and Ancient Golf Club introduced another important rule change in 1759 with the invention of stroke play. The new rule granted victory to the player with the fewest strokes over a set number of holes. This replaced match play, whereby each hole was treated as a separate competition and the player who won the most holes won the match.

## TENNIS

• During tennis's infancy, the game took place indoors, where the ball was played off the walls with a player's bare hands. As the game progressed, some players started using gloves with webbing to protect their hands before eventually upgrading to a primitive form of today's tennis rackets.

• The first indoor tennis courts had nets that rose to five feet high at the ends and drooped to 3½ feet in the middle.

• Tiebreakers were not introduced until 1970. They occur when the games are deadlocked at a score of 6–6.

• Some early tennis balls made from wood barely bounced at all.

## SOCCER

• Tripping, shin-kicking, and even carrying the ball all used to be allowed. Following the implementation of a new set of rules in 1863, these practices resulted in penalties.

• Prior to Charles Goodyear's invention of vulcanized rubber in 1836, soccer players kicked around "balls" made from human and animal skulls, stitched-up cloth, and inflated pig and cow bladders.

• According to an early set of rules established in Sheffield, England, in 1857, the ball could be caught off another player's pass, provided it had not touched the ground. A free kick then ensued.

• Cleats were once forbidden. According to a set of 14 rules established by England's Football Association in 1863, "No player shall be allowed to wear projecting nails, iron plates, or gutta percha on the soles or heels of his boots."

# OLYMPIC ALSO-RANS

*Dozens of eccentric events have been introduced and
discontinued since the dawn of the modern Olympics
in 1896. Here are some of the most peculiar.*

## 1. TUG-OF-WAR (1900, 1904, 1906, 1908, 1912, 1920)

Think tug-of-war is child's play? Think again! This popular
backyard game was an Olympic staple from 1900 to 1920, when
it appeared as both a four- and eight-man event within the track-
and-field program. As its name suggests, tug-of-war was a highly
contested affair that often brought out the worst in athletes and
fans alike. Fights frequently broke out in the middle of matches,
and it was common for spectators to jump out of the stands and
help their respective teams pull. However, the sport's most memorable controversy occurred in 1908 when the heavily favored U.S.
team lost in the first round to a group of Liverpool policemen
whom they accused of wearing enormously heavy boots complete
with illegal cleats, spikes, and grooved heels. The Americans'
protests ultimately fell on deaf ears, and the Liverpudlians went on
to capture the silver medal for Britain.

## 2. ROPE CLIMB (1896, 1904, 1906, 1924, 1932)

The Olympic motto of "Swifter, Higher, Stronger" applies
perfectly to the rope climb, a challenging gymnastic event that
was contested on five occasions between 1896 and 1932. Competitors began in a seated position on the floor and used only
their hands and arms to climb a rough-hewn rope that stretched
from 25 to 46 feet. The event was so grueling that many competitors never even made it to the top—and that's why we're still in
awe of George Eyser. The burly American won the event in 1904
despite having a wooden leg. Eyser went on to take five additional
gymnastics medals that day, including two more golds, two silvers,
and a bronze.

## 3. 200-METER OBSTACLE RACE (1900)

No obstacle is too great for a determined athlete. At least that was
the theory behind the 200-meter obstacle race. Held just once in

---

*Psycho* (1960) was the first movie to show a woman in just a bra and slip.

1900, this imaginative event took place on Paris's famed Seine River and required competitors to climb a pole, scramble over a row of boats, and then swim under another row of boats. Oh, and they had to do it while contending with the river's strong current and steady flow of raw sewage. The event was won by Australia's Frederick Lane, whose final time of 2:38.4 was just 13 seconds slower than his time in the regular 200-meter freestyle swimming event, which was also held in the Seine.

## 4. DUELING PISTOLS (1906, 1912)

Despite what the name suggests, the Olympics never allowed athletes to engage in live duels. Instead, the dueling pistols event required competitors to shoot at life-size mannequins dressed in fancy frock coats at distances of 20 and 30 meters. Fittingly, the athletes themselves were also dressed to the nines in elegant morning coats with pocket watches and top hats. According to the *New York Times*, "A polite atmosphere accompanied the activities, which involved many good wishes on the part of all of the participants."

## 5. LIVE PIGEON SHOOTING (1900)

There are some mistakes you only make once. Take live pigeon shooting, for instance. Introduced in 1900, this bloody event required competitors to shoot and kill as many pigeons as possible without missing. Marksmen were eliminated if they missed twice. By the end of the day, more than 300 birds had been slaughtered or maimed, and the spectators who showed up to observe the grisly event left covered in blood and stray feathers. Olympic organizers wised up when they saw the carnage, and for the next Olympics, the pigeons were replaced by clay disks.

## 6. CROQUET (1900)

You know your sport is destined for failure when the official Olympic literature describes it as having "hardly any pretensions to athleticism." That's how organizers classified croquet in 1900, when it was included in the Olympics for the first—and only— time. The event attracted a paltry 10 competitors from two countries (France and Belgium) and was attended by a single customer.

The oldest known food recipes are on cuneiform tablets from Mesopotamia (now Iraq).

### 7. BASQUE PELOTA (1900)

It seems fitting that Basque pelota is known as "the fastest game in the world." After all, this Spanish court sport was bounced out of the Olympics faster than nearly any other event in history. Making its debut (and exit) in 1900, two-man basque pelota disappeared after a single game when Spain defeated France in the event's only scheduled match. The game later returned as a demonstration sport in 1924, 1968, and 1992, but has yet to be invited back as a full-fledged medal event.

### 8. EIGHT-METER, 60-FOOT, AND OPEN CLASS MOTORBOATING (1908)

Olympic organizers learned a valuable lesson in 1908: if you're going to include a motorboating event, don't hold it off the coast of Southampton. The English region's foul weather led to the cancellation of six of the nine scheduled races, and thick fog prevented fans from having a good view of the other three races despite the fact that competitors failed to go much faster than 19 mph. Motorboating has since been banished by the Olympic charter due to its reliance on "mechanical propulsion."

### 9. UNDERWATER SWIMMING (1900)

Looking for another great event? Don't hold your breath. Olympic organizers came up with a colossal dud in 1900 when they introduced underwater swimming. Participants in this short-lived sport began by taking a plunge into the deep end of a pool and were rewarded points for distance swum and time spent underwater. The event was ultimately won by France's Charles DeVandeville, who swam 60 meters in 68.4 seconds. Curiously, the bronze medal was won by Denmark's Peder Lykkeberg, who stayed underwater 30 seconds longer, but didn't go as far because he swam in circles.

### 10. PLUNGE FOR DISTANCE (1904)

The plunge for distance made its sole appearance in 1904. Competitors were required to dive into the pool and remain completely motionless for 60 seconds, or until their heads broke the water's surface. Their dive distance was then measured and recorded. The event was won by William Dickey, an American salesman who "traveled" 62 feet 6 inches before coming up for air.

## 11. 100-METER FREESTYLE FOR SAILORS (1896)

Greece found a unique way of padding their medal count in 1896 by creating the 100-meter freestyle for sailors, a swimming event restricted to members of the Royal Greek Navy. The event was won by Ioannis Malokinis, whose time of 2:20.4 was nearly a minute slower than the winning time posted by Hungary's Arnold Guttmann in the regular 100-meter freestyle race.

## 12. ART, MUSIC AND LITERATURE (1912, 1936, 1948)

Beginning in 1912, competitions were held in the arts, mostly because the founder of the Olympics—Pierre de Coubertin—insisted on it. The inspiration—even for the music composi-tions—had to be sports. De Coubertin believed in melding mind and muscles, and he couldn't be persuaded that objective judging of artistic talent by the Olympic committee was difficult to achieve. But the problem became particularly obvious during the 1936 Olympics in Germany. Hitler (a failed artist himself) gave nearly all the art prizes to Austrians and Germans. By 1948, the art competitions were quietly dropped.

## 13. SYNCHRONIZED SWIMMING (1984)

In Los Angeles in 1984, the Summer Games introduced the event of solo synchronized swimming. Many people scratched their heads at this: how can you do synchronized swimming when there's no one to swim in synch with? Apparently the Olympic Committee thought swimmers could do their moves synchronized to music, but the fans disagreed and the event was dropped.

\*     \*     \*

"Holding an Olympic Games means evoking history."

—Pierre de Coubertin

# WORDS AT WAR

*War. What is it good for? Maybe the fact that
it introduced these words into the language.*

## 1. BIKINI

So far, no one we know of has worn a bikini to go to war, but a year
after the Japanese surrender ended World War II, the United
States began nuclear testing by dropping an atom bomb on the
chain of Marshall Islands in the Pacific known as Bikini Atoll.

The media hype inspired French fashion designer Louis Réard
to name his new skimpy two-piece bathing suit the bikini in hopes
that it would have a similar explosive effect. On July 5, 1946, the
designer's top model, Micheline Bernardini, paraded down a Paris
runway in the first bikini swimsuit. The name stuck, and today it
is still used for the itsy-bitsy swimsuit as well as for a style of briefs
worn by both men and women.

## 2. HAVERSACK

The canvas haversack was an essential piece of equipment for soldiers in the 18th century. Originally a shoulder bag used by the
cavalry to carry feed for horses, the name was derived from German and Old Norse words for "oats" and "bag." During the American Revolution, a British regular's haversack typically contained a
tin cup, dinner bowl and utensils, tobacco pouch, pipe, and cigars.
Later the name was extended to similar bags carried by civilians,
including letter carriers, hikers, and students.

## 3. HOOKER

Poor General Hooker: it's long been believed that the slang word
for prostitute alludes to the Civil War general of the same name:
Joseph "Fighting Joe" Hooker. Some said it came from the fact
that he confined prostitutes to one area of Washington, D.C.,
near Union Station. Others thought it alluded to Hooker's own
questionable behavior; Washington's seediest area was named
"Hooker's Division" in recognition of his reputation. But actually,
the earliest written record of "hooker" in this sense dates from
1845; the term probably comes from the idea of a prostitute

hooking a customer the way an angler hooks a fish. But apocryphal or not, the association with the general persists.

## 4. PANACHE

Today, "panache" means great flamboyance or swagger. Derived from the French *pennache*, for "tuft of feathers," in the 16th century it designated a plume or feathers ornamenting a military helmet. In the late 1800s, it began to be used figuratively, first by Edmond Rostand in his wildly popular play *Cyrano de Bergerac*, the title character of which—despite his humongous nose—overcomes obstacles in love and war by displaying his panache in the form of reckless, admirable courage.

## 5. SHRAPNEL

As a lieutenant in the Royal Artillery in the late 18th century, British Army officer Henry Shrapnel (1761–1842) invented a hollow cannonball filled with shot and a timed charge that made it explode in midair.

The British Army was slow to adopt the new antipersonnel weapon, but finally did so in 1803 and named it the "shrapnel shell." Its success during the Napoleonic campaigns led to Shrapnel's promotion. The shell was used until the end of World War I when it was replaced by high explosive rounds, but the term, "shrapnel" continues to be used for any shell fragments.

## 6. SIDEBURNS

Union general Ambrose E. Burnside (1824–81) lent his name to a number of items that haven't survived—the Burnside blouse, a loose-fitting shirt; the Burnside hat, a low-crowned felt hat; Burnside stew (hardtack soaked in water and then fried); and the Burnside carbine, a firearm that Burnside patented in 1856 and that was much used during the Civil War.

But his name is immortalized in a facial hair style he popularized: side whiskers that ran from the hairline to below the ears. In America, they were first called "burnsides" (they were known simply as "side whiskers" in Britain). In the 1880s, the word was changed to "sideburns." Since then, sideburns have come in and out of fashion and today are worn mostly by Elvis impersonators.

Canned sardines aren't popular in India—they like 'em fresh or fried.

## 7. STONEWALL

Confederate Civil War general Thomas Jonathan Jackson earned
the nickname "Stonewall" for his dogged defense at the First Battle
of Bull Run. It was Brigadier General Bernard E. Bee who said, on
July 21, 1861: "There is Jackson, standing like a stone wall." Jackson believed that Bee was referring to his brigade rather than to
him personally, but since Bee was killed in the battle, he never had
a chance to clarify the point. In any event, the name not only
stuck to Jackson but continues to be used as the verb "to
stonewall," meaning to obstruct or stall.

## 8. TURNCOAT

The noun "turncoat" first appeared in English in the mid-1500s,
but the practice probably originated earlier. Legend has it that a
duke of Saxony, whose castle lay between French and Saxon territory, had a reversible coat made of blue (the Saxon color) with a
lining of white (the French color). The side he wore facing out
depended on which monarch he needed to appease at the time.
The practice was originally referred to in French as *tourne-côte*,
meaning "turn side." In time, the idea was applied figuratively to
anyone who changed sides, whether in the military or in politics,
as it is today. The term has been applied to recent political "turncoats" like Senator Joseph Lieberman, who changed from the
Democratic Party to run as an Independent, and Senator Arlen
Specter, who abandoned the Republicans for the Democrats.

\* \* \*

### THE "SPEEDY WEENIE"

The microwave oven was discovered by accident around 1946
when Dr. Percy Spencer was testing a new vacuum tube called a
magnetron. When turning on the magnetron, Spencer noticed the
candy bar in his pocket had melted. He performed further testing
on popcorn and an egg. Spencer concluded that his experiments
resulted from exposure to low-density microwave energy. This ultimately became the basis of the microwave oven. However, he and
his associate P. R. Hanson referred to it as "the Speedy Weenie,"
meaning "a quick hot dog"!

Rene Laennec invented the stethoscope in 1816.

# BIG BANGS

*Natural disasters can cause explosions far greater than anything made by humans, but few blasts come close to the power unleashed by these three.*

## 1. THE YUCATÁN PENINSULA METEOR

It took something big to wipe out the dinosaurs 65 million years ago, and scientists continue to debate what that "something" was. But the prevailing theory is that a meteorite, about six miles across, struck the Yucatán Peninsula in Mexico, leaving a crater more than 100 miles wide. The meteorite likely came from the asteroid belt between Mars and Jupiter, where a large asteroid had just broken apart. Parts of the same asteroid are thought to be the cause of the Tycho crater on the Moon.

The piece that hit Earth struck with the equivalent force of 100 trillion tons of TNT—2 million times greater than the largest nuclear bomb ever tested. The impact threw up a cloud of dust that plunged Earth into a "freezing blackout," according to scientists. But even that wasn't enough to cause the global extinction that followed, as the dust settled within a few weeks. The real culprit was the 100–500 gigatons of water and sulfur dioxide also thrown into the atmosphere. These caused a global coating of aerosolized sulfuric acid, blocking the Sun's rays for up to a decade and bathing the Earth in acid rain. Large creatures didn't stand a chance, but some smaller animals managed to make it through.

## 2. TUNGUSKA

The Siberian forest is one of the least populated places on Earth—luckily. In the early hours of June 30, 1908, trappers near the Tunguska River in Siberia saw the sky ripped in half by fire. In czarist Russia, only a few years before the Bolshevik Revolution, no one was sent to investigate. The first expedition to the blast site arrived 19 years later and found 800 square miles of forest—over 80 million trees—flattened in a circle, with the felled trees pointing away from ground zero. At the focal point, trees were ripped of their bark and branches so quickly that they still stood upright. But there was no crater to show what had done the damage. So what was it? Scientists think it was a low-density asteroid that entered Earth's atmosphere at about 33,500 miles per hour, heating the air to 44,500°F. Under the heat and pressure, the asteroid disintegrated, releasing the equivalent force of 10–15 million tons of TNT (185 Hiroshima bombs) without leaving a crater. One person died in Tunguska as a result of the impact, but had that asteroid hit in a populated area—or the ocean, where it would have caused tidal waves—it would have been a night everyone (at least, those who survived) remembered.

### 3. GRB 090423

On April 23, 2009, telescopes all over the planet recorded a 10-second burst of gamma rays. To us, that may not mean much, but to an astrophysicist, this was an echo of the biggest explosion ever recorded. Gamma rays are given off when a star, in this case one 30 to 100 times larger than the Sun, collapses into a black hole. This particular burst came from over 13 billion light-years away, meaning that what the telescopes saw had happened not too long after the big bang. This explosion was the oldest, farthest, and largest thing ever recorded—an event so big, it could be seen anywhere in the universe. In the few seconds it took this star to collapse, it released a million times more energy than our Sun will release in its entire lifetime.

\* \* \*

### ROGER WILLIAMS: UNDER THE APPLE TREE

In 1631, Roger Williams left England in search of religious freedom and founded his own colony in what became Rhode Island. On his death in 1683, he was buried in an unmarked grave in Providence. In 1739, a gravedigger accidentally broke the side of Williams's coffin. Some 121 years later, local officials wanted to memorialize Williams and went in search of his grave. What they found astonished them. Near Williams's coffin (in a highly advanced state of decomposition) stood an apple tree. The tree had sent roots into the coffin and through the skeletal remains to form an exact replica of the body. Townspeople had been eating the fruit of the tree that was nourished by the long-dead Williams. The roots are on display at the Rhode Island Historical Society, and the soil containing molecular leftovers from the coffin were interred near a commemorative statue sometime in the late 1930s.

# WAR AND PEACE QUIZ

*Historical figures have a lot to say about war—and about peace as well. We've given you the first part of some of their most famous quotes. Can you guess the second half of the quote?*

**1. Albert Einstein:** "I know not with what weapons World War III will be fought, but..."
- **a.** "there is no doubt the result will be terrible beyond imagining."
- **b.** "World War IV will be fought with sticks and stones."
- **c.** "hopefully I'll be very far underground when it starts."

**2. General Robert E. Lee:** "It is well that war is so terrible..."
- **a.** "otherwise we would grow too fond of it."
- **b.** "it then makes peace all the more sweet when it comes."
- **c.** "because if I were enjoying this, what would it say about me?"

**3. General Ulysses S. Grant:** "The art of war is simple enough..."
- **a.** "Find out where your enemy is. Get at him as soon as you can. Strike him as hard as you can, and keep moving on."
- **b.** "It is the practice of it that is the true test of a leader and his men."
- **c.** "And let me tell you, I am an artist."

**4. Aristotle:** "We make war..."
- **a.** "so our children will breathe the free air."
- **b.** "that we may live in peace."
- **c.** "because it beats the hell out of farming."

**5. General George C. Marshall:** "If man does find the solution for world peace..."
- **a.** "it will be the most revolutionary reversal of his record we have ever known."
- **b.** "let us hope he finds the courage to employ it."
- **c.** "we'll still have soccer riots to keep us busy."

Answers: 1. b; 2. a; 3. a; 4. b; 5. a

---

# THE ROAD TO DISASTER

*You've heard the saying that to err is human? Well, we've got four disasters that could have been prevented if only the humans involved hadn't been so impetuous, stubborn, greedy, sloppy, indifferent, or just plain incompetent.*

## 1. THE JOHNSTOWN FLOOD

**The Error:** Cutting corners

In 1889, a group of investors planning the South Fork Fishing and Hunting Club purchased some acreage that included a reservoir and dam in the hills above Johnstown, Pennsylvania. The idea was to turn the reservoir into a lake for fishing and boating, with comfortable cabins and a clubhouse along the shore. It would be a resort for some of the wealthiest men in the country, including industrialists like Andrew Carnegie and Andrew Mellon. But to create the lake, the old dam had to be rebuilt, and that was an expensive proposition. To save money, the club built a new dam, but made it a cheap knockoff of the original.

The original dam had cost $240,000 to build: it was carefully engineered, solidly built, and had a spillway for water runoff. The shoddy $17,000 reconstruction was a few feet lower than the original, sagged in the middle, and its spillway was partially blocked with iron grates that prevented game fish from escaping from the newly created lake. There was also no way to drain the lake to repair the dam below the waterline, so any wear and tear or damage only got worse.

**The Disaster:** On May 28, 1889, the area experienced one of the worst rainfalls in its history. The poorly designed dam was no match for the swollen lake; on May 31, it broke open and 20 million tons of water rushed through the opening to form what became known as the "terrible wave." Thirty-five feet high, the rushing wave decimated the hillside neighborhoods, picking up houses, barns, a church, a bridge, and a train, as well as trees and stones, as it roared down the valley. Filled with deadly debris by the

---

Daniel D. Emmett, the man usually credited with writing "Dixie," the unofficial...

time it hit Johnstown, the wave destroyed 1,600 homes and four square miles of the city's downtown area. The flood killed more than 2,200 people; until the World Trade Center attack in 2001, the Johnstown Flood remained the worst loss of U.S. civilians in a single day.

## 2. THE ABERFAN TIP AVALANCHE

**The Error:** Bungling ineptitude

Beginning in the 1910s, Britain's National Coal Board (NCB), which ran the Merthyr Vale Colliery in southern Wales, had been dumping piles of loose rock and mining slag (called "tips") against the side of Merthyr Mountain, all perched around 700 feet above the village of Aberfan.

Slides in 1944 and 1963 kept the locals in a constant state of nervousness; old-timers knew that the tips had been piled on underground springs that could flood and cause an avalanche at any moment. But NCB officials denied that the tips were a danger to the town or that there were engineering problems. In 1964, a waterworks engineer made an official complaint that Aberfan's elementary school was in direct danger, but the NCB ignored him.

**The Disaster:** On October 21, 1966, in a heavy rainstorm, the springs overflowed to create what one official called "a water bomb." At 9:15 a.m., the force of water dislodged the saturated dirt of a large tip, pushing it down the hill in a 40-foot avalanche of mud and rock. The slide demolished a farm and several hillside houses as it raced toward the elementary school. Children sitting in their classrooms heard a roar like an approaching jet plane before the tons of coal waste enveloped the building.

Continuing landslides coming off the mountain hindered the efforts of rescue crews, and after the first few hours, no one was pulled from the rubble alive. In all, 144 people died, including 116 children. An official investigation concluded that the disaster was caused by "bungling ineptitude," but no one who ran the NCB or who was employed by it was held responsible. The powerful NCB even refused to remove the remaining tips; part of the public donations made to a disaster fund intended for the people of the village went to pay for the removal of the tips instead.

## 3. THE CRASH OF JAPAN AIRLINES 123

**The Error:** Incompetence

In 1978, a Boeing 747 flown by Japan Airlines suffered what's called a "tail strike" accident at Osaka International Airport. The plane's tail hit the runway, damaging the rear bulkhead, which controls pressurization. After the accident, the airline sent the plane back to Boeing for repairs.

According to regulations, the repair splices were to be covered with a doubler plate fastened by triple row of rivets. Instead, the repair was completed with two doubler plates attached with only one row of rivets. For the next seven years, the plane flew with a faulty repair that wasn't corrected—even when its pilots reported hearing "whistling noises" coming from the rear of the plane.

**The Disaster:** On August 12, 1985, at 6:12 p.m., JAL flight 123 took off from Tokyo Airport carrying 524 people. Twelve minutes into the flight, the damaged rear bulkhead finally ruptured. It caused an immediate decompression of the cabin followed by a surge of pressure that went off like a bomb. The plane's vertical stabilizer and rudder fell into the sea. The auxiliary power unit and hydraulic lines were suddenly useless, making the plane almost impossible to control. The plane crashed into Mount Osutaka, where another bad decision made a horrible disaster even worse.

Twenty minutes after the crash, a U.S. Army helicopter spotted the wreckage and radioed for rescue teams, offering to guide them to the site. Japanese officials compounded the disaster by ordering the helicopter to return to base, and sending out their own rescue forces—who didn't evacuate survivors until the following morning. By then, some of the injured had died from exposure and lack of care. Only four people survived; all 15 crew members and 505 passengers died. JAL 123 remains the deadliest single plane crash in history.

## POSTSCRIPT

If you've enjoyed these stories about disasters caused by human error—and let's face it, most of us do—check out "Two Fires, One Day" on page 436.

---

The anemometer, which measures wind speed, was invented by Leon Alberti in 1450.

# OUCH!

*These teams got hurt by Major
League Baseball's worst
losing streaks.*

## 1. THE LONGEST LOSING STREAK IN A SEASON

The Cleveland Spiders were a winning National League team
until 1888, when their owners bought a team in St. Louis in
1889. Spider fans saw most of their team's best players sent to
St. Louis to improve that franchise. Thanks to the decision to
weaken the Spiders, in 1889 the team lost 24 games in a row.
It's the longest losing streak in Major League Baseball history.

## 2. 10,000 LOSSES

Playing their first game in 1883, the Philadelphia Phillies are the
oldest Major League Baseball franchise in the country. They've
been dubbed the losingest team, too. During their first season,
they lost 81 of 98 games. In 1961, they lost 23 games in a row—
the longest losing streak in modern (post-1900) baseball history.

On July 15, 2007, they lost to the St. Louis Cardinals,
becoming the first team to lose 10,000 games. Fortunately for
the Phillies, that record was their "loss bottom." They rallied in
2007 to win the National League East title, and the next year
they won the World Series.

## 3. THE MOST LOSING SEASONS

The Pittsburgh Pirates' have a dismal record unmatched by any
major North American professional team, not only in baseball
but in hockey, football, and basketball as well. From 1993 to
2009, the Pirates had 17 consecutive losing seasons, a record
unmatched by any other team in professional sports.

\*       \*       \*

"Show me a good loser, and I'll show you an idiot."

—Leo Durocher

---

**June 25, 1950: The Korean War began. It ended on July 27, 1953.**

# LAUGHTER, THE BEST MEDICINE?

*Heartache, rage, frustration, and depression usually top the list of emotions that'll kill you. But hey—wouldn't you rather die laughing?*

### 1. OMG, LMAO!
**Who:** Chrysippus (c. 279–206 BC)
**Death by...**laughing at a drunken ass
Chrysippus was a respected philosopher in ancient Greece who famously claimed that there are no accidents and everything has a cause. Interesting, considering that he went down in history as having died during a laughing fit, which was brought on by first getting his donkey drunk, and then watching it stumble around trying to eat fruit.

### 2. BELLY LAUGH
**Who:** Martin of Aragon (1356–1410)
**Death by...**laughter mixed with indigestion
Martin of Aragon ruled over the kingdoms of Valencia, Sardinia, Sicily, and Corsica until his death in 1410. His unsuccessful struggle to provide an heir—along with the swiftly shifting political landscape—left him the last of what was known as the House of Barcelona, a family of kings and queens that had been in power for centuries. With problems like that, what can you do but laugh? And he did. Accounts say he fell into a fit of laughter (the subject, lost to history) while simultaneously struggling with a lousy case of indigestion. He died instantly. (One of the symptoms of heart attack is the feeling of indigestion, so historians surmise his heart was giving out and laughing brought on a sudden coronary.)

### 3. HE WHO LAUGHS BEST...
**Who:** Pietro Aretino (1492–1556)
**Death by...**"laughing too much"
Death threats were not unfamiliar to Italian satirist Pietro Aretino. He continuously pushed the envelope, writing blistering

---

An earthquake that measures 8 on the Richter scale is 10,000 times stronger than a 4.

political satire about the Roman Catholic Church, which kept him in trouble with the law. One of his more daring works was a Catholic series of provocative sonnets published in 1524 with a group of pornographic engravings by a well-known printmaker named Marcantonio Raimondi. The book, called *Sonetti lussuriosi* (*Lewd Sonnets*), garnered attention, but there was a price: when the pope threw Raimondi into prison, Aretino fled Rome for Venice to avoid the same fate. There, he continued to skewer the powers of Rome. According to accounts, Aretino suffocated to death from "laughing too much."

## 4. SOME CHEERED AND LIVED, SOME LAUGHED AND DIED

**Who:** Thomas Urquhart (1611–60)
**Death by...**laughing in delight and celebration
Writer and Scottish aristocrat Thomas Urquhart was on the losing side of the 17th century's English Civil War—he'd supported Charles II in defending his throne. For that, Urquhart was sent to the Tower of London for a year before being paroled. Finally, in May 1660, Charles II recaptured his throne, but by this time, Urquhart was back home in Scotland, living a quiet writer's life. When word came in to him that Charles II had been reinstated as king, Urquhart fell into a fit of joyful laughter and promptly died.

\*     \*     \*

"Assassin!"
—**Arturo Toscanini to his orchestra**

"This book fills a much-needed gap."
—**Moses Hadas**

"Better to have loved and lost a short person than never to have loved a tall."
—**David Chambless**

"You can always tell a Texan, but not much."
—**Unknown**

"I think the world is run by C students."
—**Unknown**

---

**May 1937: Jean Harlow was the first film actress to grace the cover of *Life* magazine.**

# WHISTLE-BLOWERS

*Long ago in England, when police noticed a crime being committed,
they blew their whistles to alert other officers and the general public to
the danger. In today's lexicon, a whistle-blower is an informant who
exposes wrongdoing in an organization in an effort to stop it.*

## IT'S THE LAW

In 1863, the False Claims Act was passed by Congress to fight
rampant fraud among government suppliers during the Civil
War. To inspire people to come forward under the act, whistle-
blowers stood to receive a percentage of any money recovered by
the government in fraud cases. The law protected informants from
being fired or demoted, awarded double back pay for any time lost
on the job, and paid reasonable legal fees. The law was strengthened in 1986 and again in 2009. Many states also got into the act
with their own whistle-blower protection laws. There is a long
honor roll of whistle-blowers who have risked their careers and
even their lives to expose fraud. Here are Uncle John's favorites.

## 1. THE TOILET SEAT WHISTLE-BLOWER

A. Ernest Fitzgerald, a top civilian air force auditor in the Defense
Department, testified before Congress in 1968 that $2 billion in
cost overruns had occurred in the military's Lockheed C-5A cargo
plane program. He'd been reporting this to his superiors for two
years, but they took no action and pressured him not to testify.
When he did testify, they retaliated by stripping him of his civil
service tenure, saying it had been awarded to him erroneously due
to a computer error. His department was restructured to eliminate
his position, and he was demoted to minor investigations, including cost overruns at a bowling alley in Thailand.

Fitzgerald, a navy veteran, fought back by filing suit and, after
a four-year battle, was finally reinstated to his original position.
He continued to report cost overruns and fraud. When the Reagan
administration threatened employees with loss of their jobs and
security clearances unless they signed a gag order, Fitzgerald
refused and beat back the order, which was withdrawn. His greatest fame as a whistle-blower came in the 1980s when he revealed

---

The red, yellow, and dark blue Renaissance uniform worn by the Vatican's Swiss Guard...

that the air force was being billed $200 for hammers, $7,622 for coffee pots, and $640 for toilet seats. He wrote *The High Priests of Waste* (1972) and *The Pentagonists: An Insider's View of Waste, Mismanagement and Fraud in Defense Spending* (1989) before retiring from the Defense Department in 2006.

## 2. THE HACKER WHISTLE-BLOWER

Shawn Carpenter was on the technical staff at Sandia National Laboratories in New Mexico in 2003 when he discovered that hackers based in China were gaining access to sensitive information in hundreds of computer networks operated by U.S. defense contractors, government agencies, and various military installations. He informed his bosses, only to be told not to share the information with anyone outside the organization. Nevertheless, he alerted the U.S. Army and the FBI and worked with them to stop the cyber attack by the Chinese group known as Titan Rain. When Sandia discovered that Carpenter had shared his information with other agencies, they revoked his security clearance and fired him in 2005.

Carpenter sued in the New Mexico state court and he was awarded $4.7 million in damages from Sandia in 2007. The jury ruled that the corporation's actions involving Carpenter were "malicious, willful, reckless, wanton, fraudulent, or in bad faith," given the threat to national security by the hackers.

## 3. THE LUNCHROOM WHISTLE-BLOWER

Michael J. Nappe was a financial manager at the University of Medicine and Dentistry of New Jersey when he became suspicious about the payment of millions of dollars for telecommunications contracts that weren't put out to bid. He also discovered that the technology department at the school overcharged other departments by using "dummy invoices" that were almost indistinguishable from real invoices. For four years, Nappe reported what he had found to the school's office of corporate compliance, but nothing was done. Meanwhile, university officials retaliated by harassing him, denying him promotions and pay raises, stripping him of his staff, and moving his office to a university lunchroom. He became known as "the Man in the Lunchroom" to students and staff. Guards also routinely escorted him from the building.

Nappe filed a lawsuit in 2006 while he was on administrative leave as the billing scandal exploded. The lawsuit resulted in multiple investigations by law enforcement that revealed a widespread pattern of corruption at the university. Nappe's experiences were detailed in the best-selling book *The Soprano State: New Jersey's Culture of Corruption* (2008), by Bob Engle and Sandy McClure.

## 4. THE PENTAGON PAPERS WHISTLE-BLOWER

At the behest of Defense Secretary Robert McNamara, Daniel Ellsberg, a Rand Corporation and Defense Department analyst, compiled a top-secret study of U.S. decision making from 1945 to 1968, in the lead-up to the Vietnam War. The 7,000-page study revealed a long series of presidential failures and public deceptions regarding Vietnam and left Ellsberg deeply disillusioned. A summa cum laude graduate in economics from Harvard and a former U.S. Marines infantry commander, Ellsberg made photocopies of the report and turned them over to the Senate Foreign Relations Committee in 1969 in hopes of altering the course of the war. Lawmakers refused to act. When nothing happened and the fighting escalated, Ellsberg leaked the so-called Pentagon Papers in 1971 to the *New York Times*, the *Washington Post*, and 17 other newspapers. The publication of the Pentagon Papers was the beginning of the end of public support for the war.

The Nixon administration, in an attempt to muzzle and threaten Ellsberg, created a secret team known as the "Plumbers," who broke into the office of Ellsberg's psychiatrist in Los Angeles to search for his medical records. Subsequently, the administration filed espionage charges against Ellsberg that carried a 115-year prison term. Because of the break-in (and an attempted bribery of the judge), however, a federal judge dismissed the case. In 1972, the infamous Plumbers carried out the Watergate burglary of the Democratic National Committee headquarters, which led to the conviction of several White House aides and the resignation of President Nixon.

## 5. THE FBI WHISTLE-BLOWER

In the 1990s, Frederic Whitehurst became the first agent to successfully blow a whistle on misconduct in the FBI. Whitehurst, who held a doctorate in chemistry from Duke University, was the

The Japanese once used kites to send bricks to workmen at the top of high buildings.

senior explosives expert in the FBI's crime lab. When the FBI concluded that the suspects in the first World Trade Center bombing
of 1993 had manufactured a urea nitrate explosive, Whitehurst
saw irregularities in the report. He conducted his own investigation and concluded that there was no proof, and that urea could
have come from 80 gallons of sewage scattered over the bomb
wreckage. Contrary to Whitehurst's analysis, the FBI put an
unqualified lab technician on the stand to testify that it was a urea
bomb. Whitehurst performed a double-blind test to show a urea
nitrate mixture made from fertilizer had properties identical to
those of urine. When Whitehurst's analysis was submitted to the
court, the lab technician who testified conceded that he could not
tell the difference.

Though the suspects were convicted, the episode embarrassed
the FBI, which relieved Whitehurst of his duties and assigned him
to another section of the lab. He filed suit, charging violation of
whistle-blower statutes; the suit was settled out of court for a
reported $1.16 million. In 1997, Whitehurst achieved vindication
when the inspector general of the U.S. Department of Justice
ordered a major revamp of the crime lab based on the 1993 case.
As a result, the lab implemented 40 major reforms, including an
accreditation process to prevent future lapses.

## 6. THE WATERGATE WHISTLE-BLOWER

William Mark Felt is perhaps the most famous whistle-blower of
all time for his role in exposing the break-in of the Democratic
National Committee headquarters at the Watergate office complex in Washington, D.C., which led to the resignation of President Richard Nixon. In 1972, Felt was the FBI's associate director,
working at the agency's headquarters in Washington. He met clan-
destinely with *Washington Post* reporter Bob Woodward, providing
him with critical leads that would unwind the Watergate scandal
and Nixon's involvement in the cover-up of the break-in. The
*Post's* coverage of the break-in and its ties to the White House
eventually led to hearings before the U.S. Senate and the jailing
of White House chief of staff H. R. Haldeman and presidential
adviser John Ehrlichman.

Woodward's anonymous key source came to be known as
"Deep Throat," a moniker given to him by *Post* editor Howard

---

What European town gave its name to health resorts everywhere? Spa, Belgium.

Simons; the nickname was a reference to a controversial pornographic movie. Woodward refused to reveal the identity of his informant for 33 years. On May 31, 2005, Felt, who was then retired, revealed that he was Deep Throat; he died in 2008 at the age of 95.

## 7. THE NIGHT GUARD WHISTLE-BLOWER

In 1997, Christoph Meili was employed as a night guard by an outside security firm responsible for protecting the Union Bank of Switzerland headquarters in Zurich when he discovered that bank officials were destroying documents related to the assets of Nazi Holocaust victims. Meili took home some files that were to be shredded; he intended to save the documents and expose the bank's activities. At the time, investigations were underway concerning Switzerland's activities during World War II, in particular what happened to the dormant bank accounts of Holocaust victims. By law, those records were supposed to have been turned over to the victims' heirs. Meili gave his files to a Jewish organization, which revealed to the public what the bank was trying to do. In 1998, Swiss banks and Jewish officials agreed to a $1.25 billion settlement, of which Meili received a reported $750,000. Meili was vilified by many in Switzerland for violating the laws of bank secrecy, and was granted political asylum in the United States.

\*     \*     \*

### KING FOR LIFE

Who were the longest-reigning monarchs in history?

• Tops on Uncle John's list is Pepi II. He ruled Egypt for 94 years, from 2278 to 2184 BC. The secret formula for Pepi was not discovered in his tomb, however.

• Coming in a close second is Taejo, the king of Korea from AD 53 to 146—a reign of 93 years.

• On our European list, King Louis XIV managed to rule France for 72 years, from 1643 to 1715. Can this longevity be explained by the French penchant for wine with supper?

---

Twelve U.S. presidents owned slaves—eight while serving as president.

# HITTING THE HEIGHTS

*If you're a man, you have to be at least 6 feet 2 inches to be considered tall—but that's shrimplike compared to the tallest of the tall. To reach the stratosphere of tall lists, you have to stretch to the benchmark set by the biblical Goliath. At 9 feet 9 inches, the Philistine warrior would have had to stoop to get inside a typical modern-day building.*

**O**H, THE HUMANITY
Goliath's height most likely was exaggerated. But who are the tallest documented famous men? Uncle John paged through the world's archives and came up with six of the world's most celebrated giants. Here are their stories.

### 1. THE GENTLE GIANT

In medical history, Robert Pershing Wadlow holds the record for tallest man, according to the *Guinness Book of World Records*. He continued to grow until the time of his death at age 22, reaching 8 feet 11 inches and 439 pounds.

When Wadlow was born in Alton, Illinois, in 1918, he was a rather normal 8 pounds 6 ounces. But when he was four years old, an undiagnosed pituitary gland tumor (something that has afflicted many extraordinarily tall men) caused a growth spurt that lasted for the rest of his life. By age eight, he was 6 feet 2 inches. At 14, he was the world's tallest Boy Scout at 7 feet 4 inches. By the time he was 18, while studying law at Shurtleff College, he reportedly wore size 37AA shoes and had reached 8 feet 4 inches.

Wadlow, known as the "Gentle Giant," became famous in 1936 by touring with the Ringling Brothers Circus and launching a series of promotional tours and public appearances. He had the largest and broadest hands in recorded history—they were so large, he could hide an entire quart bottle of soda in his hand. He died in 1940 when a bad infection in his ankle spread. At his funeral, it took 12 pallbearers to carry his half-ton coffin; 40,000 spectators attended. A life-size bronze statue of Wadlow stands on the Shurtleff campus, which is now a part of Southern Illinois University.

---

In 1929, 60 percent of American families had an annual income of $2,000 or less.

## 2. BIG JOHN

His name was John "Bud" Rogan and he was the second-tallest male in recorded history and the tallest African American. Rogan reached an imposing 8 feet 9 inches, which was revealed only upon his death in 1905, when his body was laid out and he was measured.

In his lifetime, he was known as the "Black Prodigy of Sumner County" in Tennessee. He was of normal size until age 13, when he developed a pituitary illness that led to rapid growth. Though Rogan had difficulty walking, he had very large hands that he used skillfully to build harnesses to hitch two billy goats to a wagon that carried him daily to the Gallatin city train depot. There, the strange spectacle encouraged passengers on the Louisville and Nashville Railroad to get off the train and talk to Rogan, who sold postcards of himself. From these sales as well as from donations, he was able to sustain himself.

## 3. THE WILLOW BUNCH GIANT

If you are one of 20 children, you need something to set yourself apart. Edouard Beaupré did it by growing to 8 feet 2½ inches. Born in 1881 in Willow Bunch in Saskatchewan, Canada, he reached 7 feet 1 inch by the time he turned 17. As a teen, he was a skilled equestrian who dreamed of becoming a cowboy. Sadly, it was impossible; his legs soon touched the ground even when he was astride the tallest horse. Calling himself the "Willow Bunch Giant," he turned to the circus to make a living. He toured North America, taking on challengers in wrestling matches and performing feats of strength. His showstopper was lifting 900-pound horses over his shoulders or head.

After contracting tuberculosis, Beaupré died in 1904 at the World's Fair in St. Louis. His father arrived from Canada to retrieve the body, but the expense of shipping his son home was too great. Beaupré's father hoped the circus would bury his son. It didn't. Rather, it embalmed Beaupré and put him on display. Three years later, the University of Montreal claimed the body for medical research. Relatives convinced the university to cremate the body in 1989. Subsequently, an urn carrying the Willow Bunch Giant's ashes was buried in his hometown in 1990.

---

**No actual rhinoceros is ever seen on camera in the 1974 film *Rhinoceros*...**

## 4. THE MIGHTY SCOT

Angus Mòr MacAskill (1825–63) was known in his lifetime a the world's largest "true" giant at 7 feet 9 inches. What made him a textbook giant is that he was perfectly proportioned, with no growth abnormalities. A native of Scotland, MacAskill was reared in Englishtown, Nova Scotia, and his legendary feats of strength included lifting ship anchors weighing 2,800 pounds to the height of his chest. In 1849, he went to work for P. T. Barnum's circus, where he performed alongside General Tom Thumb, the smallest person in the world according to Barnum.

After retiring from the circus, he returned home to Englishtown and took over a general store. The story making the rounds was that he would ask customers buying expensive tea, "Will you take a pound or a fistful?" Inevitably, they would go for the pound, thinking they would get more tea that way—but his fist could hold more.

In 1981, listings for MacAskill in the *Guinness Book of World Records* included "tallest natural giant," "strongest man," and "largest chest measurements of any nonobese man." Today, the Giant Angus MacAskill Museum near Englishtown is a tourist attraction.

## 5. THE MONGOLIAN HERDSMAN

Until 2009, Guinness recognized Bao Xishun as the world's tallest living man, tipping the tape at 7 feet 9 inches. (Recently, Guinness recognized Sultan Kösen of Turkey as the world's tallest living man at 8 feet 1 inch.) Bao grew up in Inner Mongolia in China, working as a herdsman.

In December 2006, Bao earned notoriety by helping veterinarians retrieve shards of plastic lodged in the stomachs of two dolphins. The dolphins, who had accidentally swallowed the plastic, lost their appetites as a result. The physicians tried without success to remove the obstructions with a variety of instruments. Enter Bao. Using arms that stretched more than 3 feet long, he wiggled them down the gullets of the dolphins and into the creatures' stomachs, where he grabbed hold of the plastic pieces and dragged them out.

## 6. FATHER FIGURE

At 6 feet 3 inches, George Washington is the shortie on Uncle John's tall list. As commander in chief of the Continental army during the American Revolution and the first president of the United States, his story is well known by most Americans. Here's what's not as well known. In Washington's time, the average male stood 5 feet 8 inches. Washington was much taller, putting him at odds with painters who depicted him as being of average height. Washington inherited 10 slaves at age 11 and owned 317 at his death. One visitor to his Virginia plantation in 1798 noted he treated slaves "with more severity" than his neighbors. Though he had misgivings privately, he never criticized the practice of slavery in public.

On the lighter side, early biographer Parson Weems invented the story of a young Washington cutting down a cherry tree and confessing the deed to his father. Likewise, the Potomac River is so wide that it would have been impossible for young Washington to skip a silver dollar across, as legend has it. The president never wore a wig; nevertheless, famed portraits show him wearing one. And Washington's teeth were not made of wood; they were made from the teeth of various animals.

\*   \*   \*

### THAT'S ONE TALL WOMAN!

Until her death in 2008, Sandra Elaine Allen was the tallest living woman in the world at 7 feet 7¼ inches. Born in Chicago in 1955, she developed a tumor in her pituitary gland that caused extreme growth. At 22, she had an operation to remove the tumor and cap her size.

Allen achieved success as an author with her autobiography, *Cast a Giant Shadow*, and appeared in the Italian film *Il Casanova di Federico Fellini*, which won an Academy Award. She also appeared in the television movie *Side Show* and the documentary *Being Different*. She was immortalized in the popular 1982 song "Hello Sandy Allen" by the New Zealand band Split Enz.

Late in her life, Allen was unable to walk due to her size and lived in a retirement home in Indiana.

In 1985, player Anne White shocked Wimbledon by wearing only a white body stocking.

# TRAFFIC TALK

*Firsts in parking meters, tickets, accidents, and lights.*

**1. Parking Meter.** Oklahoma City merchants were tired of cars parking in front of their stores for hours on end, so they enlisted the help of the head of the Oklahoma City Chamber of Commerce traffic committee, Carl C. MaGee. On May 13, 1935, MaGee filed a patent for his coin-controlled parking meter—the Park-O-Meter. The first one was installed on July 16 in downtown Oklahoma City. Of his parking meter, MaGee wrote, "This gadget treats all alike. It knows no favorites. The public will like it."

**2. First Parking Ticket.** No one knows for sure who got the first parking ticket, but the earliest one on record went to Reverend C. H. North. Just one month after MaGee's meters were installed in downtown Oklahoma City, North parked his car at a meter and read that it required a nickel. He had none, so North went to the nearest store to get change. When he returned to his car, he found a ticket on his windshield for parking at an expired meter. Eventually, though, North fought the ticket in court and won.

**3. First U.S Traffic Accident.** On May 31, 1896, New York City motorist Henry Wells hit bicyclist Evelyn Thomas with his brand-new car (a Duryea motor wagon). Thomas suffered a broken leg, and Wells spent the night in jail.

**4. First Traffic Lights.** In 1868, too many horses were clogging up the streets in London, so the city installed a signal to control the traffic near the Houses of Parliament. In 1917, when cars began taking over the streets, Detroit, put up the first traffic tower in the United States. Three years later, Detroit upgraded to a red, green, and yellow traffic controller invented by a local police officer named William L. Potts. Although several different versions of the traffic light were invented in the early 1900s, Potts was the only one to use a yellow light.

---

Unlike patents, trademarks can be renewed forever as long as they're used in commerce.

# THE SECRET LIVES OF SODA POP

*In the 19th century, most people got their fizzy carbonated drinks at a soda fountain inside the local drugstore. Why is this important to know? You'll understand as we explain the origins of some classic soda pops.*

### 1. COCA-COLA: THE BIG RED ONE

It's a well-known fact that the original formula for the world's most popular soft drink featured cocaine—but did you know that the original also contained alcohol? The carefully guarded secret formula for Coca-Cola is derived from "Pemberton's French Wine Coca," a concoction of coca leaf, kola nut, and damiana, a fragrant flower often used to make a stimulating tea. Its creator was Atlanta pharmacist Dr. John Pemberton, who touted the wine coca's medicinal qualities for anyone who was "devoted to extreme mental exertion."

However, in 1886, when temperance laws went into effect in Atlanta and Fulton County, Pemberton had to change the tonic's formula so it was alcohol-free—although it still contained cocaine, and would until 1905. The result: Coca-Cola was marketed as a nerve tonic as well as a temperance drink.

### 2. PEPSI-COLA: WE TRY HARDER

Beyond its carbonation and cola flavor, Pepsi shares something in common with its main competitor, Coca-Cola. Pepsi also was originally formulated by a pharmacist—North Carolina's Caleb Bradham, who in the 1890s began selling the concoction as "Brad's Drink." He touted the drink's medicinal properties: indeed, the name Pepsi-Cola, introduced in 1898, implies its origin as a health tonic: "Pepsi" is taken from pepsin, a digestive enzyme used in Bradham's original formula. Just as Coca-Cola no longer contains cocaine, Pepsi no longer includes pepsin. In 1898, Bradham wisely bought the rights to the trade name "Pep Cola" from a bankrupt competitor. He trademarked the new name in 1903.

In 1900, 225 million tons of coal were mined in England.

## 3. DR PEPPER: WACKY IN WACO

Was there a doctor involved in the creation of Dr Pepper? No, but there was yet another pharmacist who, while not actually named Pepper (his name was Charles Alderton), invented the drink in Waco, Texas, in 1885. And if you're guessing that "Dr Pepper's Phos-Ferrates" was originally touted as a health tonic, just like Coke and Pepsi, you'd be correct in that as well. Indeed, one ingredient in Dr Pepper's early formulas was pepsin, the same digestive enzyme that gave Pepsi its name. (However, prune juice, commonly rumored to be an ingredient, is not and never was part of the formula.)

Interestingly, no one—including the folks at Dr Pepper or the Dr Pepper Museum in Waco—knows exactly how the soda pop got its name; theories range from a nod to pepsin to the soda being named in honor of the former owner of the drugstore where the drink was invented. None of these theories is verified. (And for you editorial types, there is no period after the "Dr" in "Dr Pepper"; it was removed sometime in the 1950s.)

## 4. HIRES: A ROOTING GOOD DRINK

Another soda pop, another pharmacist inventor. In this case it was Philadelphia's Charles E. Hires. While on his honeymoon in 1875, Hires was served a "root tea" he liked so much that when he got back home, he set to work replicating the taste experience. By the next year he was selling root tea packets, which people could take home to brew their own drinks. By 1884, Hires decided people would buy more of the stuff if they didn't have to make it themselves. He'd also decided to take the suggestion of a friend who said the working class would like it more if he called his root concoction a beer rather than a tea. Smart friend.

## 5. VERNOR'S: AN OLD-TIME FAVORITE

Vernor's Ginger Ale is generally accepted as the oldest American soda pop brand still in existence. It got its start just after the Civil War when Detroit's James Vernor—a pharmacist, of course—discovered that a ginger-ale syrup he'd left to age in an oak cask ended up with a distinct flavor thanks to the wood. The company legend is that the syrup had aged from 1862, when Vernor left Detroit to fight in the Civil War, until 1865, when he returned.

**The song "Happy Birthday to You" is still protected by copyright.**

Vernor originally sold the soda pop in his drugstore, but by 1896, the drink was so popular that he was able to close the drugstore and focus purely on selling the soda.

## 6. 7-UP: THE OTHER SOFT DRINK

This classic lemon-lime beverage is the first and only soda on our list that wasn't invented by a pharmacist—it was created by businessman Charles Leiper Grigg in 1929. However, like our previous pops, it was originally marketed for its health benefits; its original formula featured lithium citrate, a chemical still used today as a mood stabilizer. And while 7-Up is one of the shortest soda brand names today, the drink's original name was more of a mouthful: "Bib-Label Lithiated Lemon-Lime Soda." Grigg changed the name of the soda pop shortly thereafter, and then changed the name of his business from the Howdy Corporation to the Seven-Up Company in 1936. Another good call.

\*     \*     \*

## FLUSH WITH SUCCESS

After all of that soda, we feel a trip to the bathroom is in order.

• The flushing toilet came into being in 1596 in England. It was invented by Sir John Harrington for Queen Elizabeth I.

• Thomas Crapper capitalized on the invention, establishing a plumbing company to manufacture them for the British public. Given a royal warrant, Crapper's name was forever associated with flush toilets.

• British King George II died falling off a toilet in 1760.

• *Psycho* was the first movie to show a toilet being flushed, a scene that drew indecency complaints.

• Statistics show that more Americans flush their toilets at half-time during the Super Bowl than at any other time of the year.

Q. What American diversion did the *London Times* label a "menace" in 1924...

# WHO WROTE THAT?

*Throughout history, for one reason or another, authors have tried to protect their identity by using pen names.*

What do Lewis Carroll, Ellery Queen, S. E. Hinton, and Lemony Snicket have in common? They all wrote their most popular books using pseudonyms (did you really think there was a Lemony Snicket?) just like the authors of these writings.

## 1. PRIMARY COLORS

Okay, so everyone knows that Joe Klein wrote it now, but back in 1996, Washington, D.C., was abuzz with rumors about who penned this searing and wildly entertaining expose of Bill Clinton's race for the presidency in 1992. Sorry, did we say Bill Clinton? What we meant was "Jack Stanton," the novel's ruthlessly charming and cheerfully amoral Southern Democrat governor and presidential candidate.

Given that the book appeared while Bill Clinton was still our commander in chief, it was no surprise that Klein neglected to put his name on the book. As a well-connected *Newsweek* and CBS News journalist, Klein was a D.C. insider. By naming and shaming Clinton...oops, Stanton...as such a ruthless political operator, Klein was risking career suicide. But as the book's popularity grew—topping the *New York Times* best-seller list for two months—the campaign to unmask the author gained momentum.

**The Secret of His Success.** Several of Klein's peers named him publicly, but when confronted he flat-out denied everything. But six months after *Primary Colors* was published, Klein finally caved in and unmasked himself.

Did Joe become the outcast of the beltway? Hardly. In December 1996 he bagged himself a political column in the *New Yorker*, and in early 2003 moved on to *Time*. He also published a sequel to *Primary Colors* in 2000: *The Running Mate*. In 2002, he climbed back on board the Clinton gravy train for one last ride, the result being *The Natural: The Misunderstood Presidency of Bill Clinton*. He even put his name to that one and on *The Running Mate*.

## 2. BELLE DE JOUR

Subtitled *The Intimate Adventures of a London Call Girl*, this book began as a diary-style blog written by an anonymous British working girl in 2003. The world was shocked that English people even had sex, never mind that they wrote about it. As the blog's popularity grew, it was quickly parlayed into book form. As both blog and book, *Belle de Jour* was the ultimate kiss-and-tell, a rollicking ride through the higher end of London's sex-for-sale industry. It's a world of five-star hotels, expensive limos, country estates—and lots and lots of sex. You name it, Belle does it and then recounts it all to her dirty diary. *Pretty Woman* it ain't. What saves Belle's bacon is the sheer joi de vivre she brings to her job. More than anything, *Belle de Jour* is funny. More than anything, it's about the sheer absurdity of being a high-class hooker.

Published in 2005, the book was an instant smash. Women (and not a few furtive, pasty-faced young men) flocked to Britain's bookstores to snap it up. Two more volumes followed, as did a regular column in Britain's hitherto stuffy and conservative Sunday *Telegraph* newspaper.

**Exposed in Public.** Inevitably, what everyone wanted to know was: Who is Belle? In late 2009 the book's author was outed as 34-year-old Brooke Magnanti, a research scientist at Bristol University in the west of England. While studying for her PhD in 2003–4, Magnanti supplemented her income working as a £300 per hour escort (around $462 per hour). In some ways it's a depressingly familiar tale: college girl enters the sex trade to pay her way through school. The difference was that Magnanti transformed her experiences into a popular blog, a best-selling book, and, from 2007 on, a successful TV series. Her call-girl past behind her, Magnanti now happily continues her scientific studies and—last we hear—is working on a novel.

## 3. THE FEDERALIST PAPERS

A series of 85 eloquent essays published from 1787 to 1788, *The Federalist Papers* were a call to arms to Americans to ratify the Constitution. Each was signed by the anonymous author "Publius," who turned out to be Alexander Hamilton, James Madison, and John Jay—the American Revolution's three amigos.

Hamilton penned 52 of the Papers. An illegitimate child born on the Caribbean island of Nevis around 1755–57 (no one really knows), Hamilton was also bright and ambitious. He arrived in New York in time for the War of Independence, becoming George Washington's aide-de-camp and America's first secretary of the treasury. His stellar career ended in 1804 when he was killed in a duel with Vice President Aaron Burr over their political differences.

James Madison (1751–1836), by contrast, was the scion of Virginia plantation aristocracy. Known as the father of the American Constitution, Madison contributed 28 of the Papers, his aim being to persuade his fellow Americans to accept the Constitution he himself had written. He was also a hugely successful and popular two-term president between 1809–19.

Last—and least—was statesman and diplomat John Jay (1745–1829). Responsible for just five of the Papers, Jay doesn't fit into the what-happened-next thrust of this story, so let's put him to one side for the moment.

**Estranged Bedfellows.** Once the Constitution was ratified in 1798, Hamilton and Madison wasted no time in becoming bitter political enemies. Hamilton favored strong central control with a powerful president and an influential national bank. Madison, meanwhile, supported Thomas Jefferson's Democratic-Republicans, who were all about states' rights. When Madison became president in 1809, it seemed the small-is-beautiful argument was won. And it was—by Hamilton. As president, Madison found he liked the idea of big government after all—especially when he was at the head of it.

## 4. GO ASK ALICE

This is one where you think, "They couldn't make it up." Except someone did. Published in 1971, *Go Ask Alice* was a literary sensation. The diary of a troubled 15-year-old anonymous girl, the book describes in grim detail her moral, emotional, and physical decline. The book sold millions of copies and was translated into almost 20 languages. It was even made into a TV movie starring William Shatner (not as Alice).

At the start of the diary our heroine is an all-American girl, happy in her suburban idyll with mom and pop. Everything changes after she unknowingly takes LSD at a party. Within a matter of weeks—and pages—she's smoking marijuana, doing speed, and mainlining heroin. Sexual assault and prostitution follow, as the by-now-homeless teen drifts from town to town in search of her next fix. When her inevitable death comes, the reader is left in no doubt that drugs are really bad for you.

**Unmasking Alice.** As powerful a work as *Go Ask Alice* is, many claimed from the start that it was too powerful. A 15-year-old couldn't have written that, could she? No. In 1979, it was revealed that *Go Ask Alice* was written by one Beatrice Sparks. Far from being a drug-addled prostitute in 1971, Sparks was a 53-year-old Mormon social worker and youth counselor. Confronted with her authorship, Sparks claimed Alice was in fact inspired by her work with troubled teens and was based on an actual diary that she had since inadvertently mislaid. Following her unmasking, Sparks went on to publish several other diaries based on consultations with her young charges. These include *Jay's Diary*, dealing with a boy lured into the occult, and *Annie's Baby*, themed around teen pregnancy.

\* \* \*

### FAMILY FEUD
**Scotland's Campbells vs. McDonalds**
Property raids and skirmishes between the Campbells and the McDonalds fed a feud that was almost 200 years old in 1692. Yet that year the McDonalds welcomed Campbell men into their Glencoe home because hospitality was considered a moral obligation. The Campbells responded by killing their hosts, burning their homes to the ground, and leaving women and children to die of exposure. The English government had ordered the "Glencoe Massacre" because the McDonalds hadn't shown proper allegiance to the crown.

In 2000, the *Guardian* reported on this sign in a Glencoe pub: "No Hawkers or Campbells."

In 1747, surgeon James Lind discovered that citrus fruits prevented scurvy...

# AND THE SECRET INGREDIENT IS...

*There is a reason for the saying "Necessity is the mother of invention." In the past, some people were quite inventive...and not too squeamish.*

## 1. CROCODILE DUNG

The ancient Egyptians used crocodile dung as a birth-control method. They made vaginal suppositories out of the dung, honey, sour milk, and sodium carbonate.

## 2. URINE

Ancient Romans did not let urine go down the drain. Their laundries had collection vats for urine, and they mixed it with potash, carbonate of soda, and fuller's earth (a claylike substance) to form a detergent that was used to wash all those white togas. Romans also used urine as a mouthwash and tooth whitener. (Eww!) The Romans imported Portuguese urine for their dental hygiene. Portuguese urine was thought to be more potent than Roman urine. Whether Portuguese urine actually freshens breath is questionable, but urine does contain ammonia and urea, which kill germs and would have helped fight gingivitis.

## 3. ANTLERS

Roman women loved exotic face creams. One cream for removing wrinkles consisted of honey mixed with Libyan barley, narcissus bulbs, and crushed antlers from a healthy young stag.

## 4. LEECHES

Roman women dyed their hair darker with a mixture of crushed leeches and vinegar.

## 5. COCHINEAL INSECTS

The lipstick used by women of the Elizabethan era was made from a mixture of ground cochineal insects—which produces a vibrant

---

...As a result, by 1795, lemon juice was a standard supply on all British ships.

red color—and egg whites. The insects were first used by the Mayans and Aztecs for dyeing fabrics between 1,500 and 4,000 years ago, before being exported to Europe. In fact, the carminic acid from these insects produces such a good dye that it is still used today in lipsticks, candy, yogurt, fruit juices, and ice cream.

## 6. BAT GUANO

Bat guano was used in the United States as early as the War of 1812 to make gunpowder. Bat guano is largely saltpeter, a necessary ingredient in gunpowder. At the start of the Civil War, every bat cave in the South was raided for guano after supply lines were cut and the Confederacy became desperate for gunpowder.

## 7. BIRD GUANO

Hundreds of years ago, Japanese geishas were renowned for their soft, luminescent skin. The secret was an ancient facial treatment made from *uguisu no fun*—the droppings of the Japanese bush warbler, a type of nightingale. The droppings were ground into a powder and used to remove the geisha's white makeup. The urea in the droppings helped hold in moisture, and the guanine created a shimmering effect. Buddhist monks also used the bird poop to clean and polish their bald scalps. Facial treatments made of this product are still sold in high-priced salons around the world.

## 8. CAMEL DUNG

During the North Africa campaigns in World War II, the Germans discovered that fresh camel dung cured dysentery, which was affecting many German soldiers. They observed that the Arabs also came down with dysentery, but could usually cure it within a day. The Arabs followed camels around until the camel dropped fresh dung—then the Arabs ate the dung immediately, while it was still warm. In order for the remedy to work, the camel dung had to be fresh and warm. Laboratory analysis has shown that the dung was teeming with powerful bacteria that ate harmful microorganisms in the intestinal tract to produce the cure. The Germans soon developed a method of drying these bacteria and placing them in capsules, removing the need to ingest a steaming bowl of fresh camel dung.

The practice of agriculture in India had started by 9000 BC.

# IT'S CONTAGIOUS!

*One day you're in, the next day you're out. So goes the life of a fad.*

## 1. DANCE MARATHONS

On the heels of World War I, the Roaring Twenties ushered in the freewheeling days of flappers and bobbed hair, raccoon coats and roadsters, and fads like kissing marathons, drinking marathons, rocking-chair marathons, and flagpole-sitting marathons. But the one that's lasted in our collective memory is the dance marathon.

The first day or two of a dance marathon were relatively easy: as soon as the band struck up the first note, a couple was required only to keep moving; fancy steps weren't necessary and would only tire them out faster. Dancers took regular breaks to rest their feet and catch a catnap. But as the dancing continued, so did the difficulty. Dancers were allowed mere minutes of rest every few hours. Sleeping while dancing was allowed; one partner would stay awake and hold the sleeper up.

Though dance marathons faded from popularity by the late 1930s, they employed thousands of people—from nurses to ticket takers to bouncers—during the Depression. Dancers who flirted with death (at least one actually died of exhaustion) became minor celebrities and made extra income by selling autographs and promotional cards. And, yes, there was the prize money to be considered: according to *Guinness World Records*, the longest dance marathon lasted 214 days, and the winners took home $2,000.

## 2. SWALLOWING GOLDFISH

Though most fads seem to spring up from nowhere, goldfish swallowing can be traced back to one individual and one specific date: on March 3, 1939, Harvard student Lothrop Withington Jr. swallowed a live fish to win a $10 bet. Days later, not to be outdone, a college student in Pennsylvania downed three fish seasoned with salt and pepper. When a fellow classmate upped the ante to six goldfish, the gauntlet had been thrown down and the fad spread like wildfire on campuses across the country. Before the goldfish craze faded a few months later, thousands of goldfish had met their gruesome ends and even coeds had taken up the challenge. Gulp!

To stay in shape, French statesman Cardinal Richelieu jumped over furniture.

## 3. PANTY RAIDS

Following World War II, 1950s college students were ready for some silliness. The first documented panty raid—in which a mob of underclassmen "broke into" an all-female dorm and stole a few pairs of panties—took place in 1949 at Augustana College in Illinois. The next panty raid was three years later at the University of Michigan, but this time news of the raid traveled fast and far.

Before long, marauding young men at colleges around the country were assisted by coeds who helpfully opened the doors of their dorms and/or tossed panties and bras out of their windows. Panty raids became a spring ritual on dozens of campuses, but the craze came to an end in the 1960s. The fad lost its mojo when women's panties became easier to come by thanks to more permissive attitudes toward sex, as well as the addition of mixed dorms on campuses in the early 1970s.

## 4. PHONE BOOTH STUFFING

It started in South Africa in the mid-1950s when students there claimed to have fit 25 people in a space approximately three feet square and eight feet high. British students tried, but couldn't outdo the South Africans. American and Canadian college students had a go at it, and the craze spread across the continent, with increasingly elaborate "rules" (someone had to make or answer a call; phone booths had to be of standard size; a certain percentage of the body had to be inside to count, and so on). Lots of variations were tried, too, like stuffing people in a car or in a booth underwater. One of the shorter-lived fads of the 1950s, phone booth stuffing lost its steam by the end of the decade.

## 5. HULA HOOPS

When Wham-O founders Richard Knerr and Arthur Melin learned that Australians—like the Greeks centuries earlier—were using large hoops as exercise equipment, they never imagined that their new idea would end up circling the globe. Hula hoops took the world by storm in 1958 and became a near-obsession in many countries.

Made of plastic and weighing just a few ounces, the first hula hoops sold for $1.98; Wham-O sold 20 million of them at that

June 6, 1933: The first drive-in theater opened in Camden, New Jersey.

price in the first four months. In Great Britain, newspapers published step-by-step instructions on how to hoop, and the toys were briefly banned in Japan for causing "obscene movements." Anyone with a modicum of skill could use a hula hoop, but kids seemed to be best at it. As with most fads, contests and competitions sprang up and records were set and broken daily. The fad died out relatively quickly, but it resurfaces now and then, mostly when someone makes a hoop out of a new material.

## 6. MOOD RINGS

The original mood rings, as marketed through a sensitivity training center in New York, were sold as a biofeedback aid. The ring had a stone made of quartz or glass filled with thermotropic liquid crystal that changed color in response to fluctuations in one's body temperature, from violet at the warmest temperature (which supposedly meant that the wearer was happy) through blue (calm), green (feeling okay), yellow (tense), and brown, gray, or black (which signaled serious agitation or that the ring had been damaged in some way).

The ring caught on like wildfire in the summer of 1975. Society columnists sang the praises of the ring and other media passed the word. Within a few days, hundreds of rings were sold for a pricey $45. After a few weeks, everyone who was anyone owned one. Joe Namath, Muhammad Ali, and Steve McQueen wore them. Sophia Loren reportedly had dozens of them shipped to Italy.

The liquid crystal technology was real, but mood rings weren't all that reliable. No scientific correlation between a particular mood and a specific color was ever established. The people who bought them figured out that they didn't need a ring to tell them how they were feeling, and by early 1976, the fad was laid to rest at the bottoms of thousands of jewelry boxes around the world. However, as with all things old, there has been a resurgence in mood rings for new generations, often incorporating the crystal in more fanciful designs like the body of an animal.

## 7. STREAKING

The fad of streaking began on college campuses in the warm regions of California and Florida in early 1974. A streaker's task was to dash—completely naked—from point A to point B without

---

Gelett Burgess, author of *The Purple Cow*, invented the word "blurb."

being arrested for indecent exposure. Most of the streakers were men, but by March of that year, mixed streaking was common. The craze wasn't confined to campuses, either; your average Joe and Josie began to strip and zip through restaurants, stores, or wherever the streaker could be sure of an audience. At the height of the fad, radio stations in Los Angeles broadcast "streaker alerts," and a streaker even showed up onstage during the Academy Awards ceremony in 1974. The presenter, the late actor David Niven, had the last laugh when he commented about the inevitably of this happening and went on, "But isn't it sad that probably the only laugh that man will ever get in his life is by stripping off and showing his shortcomings." Although incidents of streaking continue to this day, the fad has not regained the popularity it enjoyed in the mid-1970s.

## 8. PET ROCKS

Advertising exec Gary Dahl was in a bar in Los Gatos, California, in 1975 listening to his friends complain about their pets. He joked that a rock didn't need to be fed or walked, and would never die. He took the idea home with him that night. He bought a bunch of gray stones at a building supply store (and eventually imported them from Mexico for a penny apiece), put each in a straw-lined box that was designed like a pet carrier, threw in a 32-page manual on the care and training of a pet rock, and started selling his rock-in-a-box for $3.95. The fad lasted six months, from mid-1975 to the Christmas season, just long enough to make Dahl a millionaire. He used the money to open his own bar in Los Gatos.

\* \* \*

## ANOTHER FAMILY FEUD: THE WAR OF THE ROSES

King Edward III had two sons: the Duke of Lancaster (crest of a red rose) and the Duke of York (crest of a white rose). From 1455 to 1487, the two duked it out over who would be king. The War of the Roses started when York's Edward IV defeated Lancaster's cousin, King Henry VI, and took the throne. Hundreds died in battles between red and white before both families lost out to the Tudors. Today, the dysfunctional family warfare lives on in *Alice in Wonderland*, where roses get painted white or red, and monarchs yell "Off with her head!"

# ASSASSINS

*The killing goes on… part one of this story is on page 31.*

*The killing goes on… part one of this story is on page 31.*

## 1. RAMÓN MERCADER

On August 20, 1940, Leon Trotsky, architect of the Russian Revolution of 1917, was fatally stabbed in the head with an ice axe as he worked in his study in the Mexico City suburb of Coyoacan. The man who killed him was Ramón Mercader, Spaniard and fellow communist. But why?

**A One-Way Ticket to Mexico.** Trotsky, born Lev Davidovich Bronstein in 1879, was at Vladimir Lenin's side when the Russian Revolution broke out in 1917. After the revolution was won, he set up the Red Army to "save" it. Lenin died in 1924, and everyone thought Trotsky would take over—everyone, that is, except Joseph Stalin. Somehow, the dull and plodding Stalin overcame the more fiery and flamboyant Trotsky to become the country's leader. Trotsky was banished and settled in Mexico in the late 1930s. Cozying up to new friends such as artists Diego Rivera and his wife Frida Kahlo (with whom he had an affair), Trotsky set about denouncing Stalin in a series of articles and books.

**Traveling in the Red Zone.** Born in Barcelona, Spain, Ramón Mercader was a communist student in Paris's Sorbonne University when he was recruited by the Soviets to kill Trotsky. His cover story was that he wanted to marry one of Trotsky's close confidantes, Sylvia Ageloff. He gained access to Trotsky's inner sanctum—and promptly brained him with an ice pick. Mercader told police that Trotsky was killed because he'd refused to bless the marriage. Mercader was released in 1960 and spent the remaining 18 years of his life in Havana, Cuba, and the Soviet Union, where he was awarded a Hero of the Soviet Union medal for his skills at handling an ice axe.

## 2. NATHURAM GODSE

For millions of Indians, Mahatma Gandhi (1869–1948) is a hero, the man who won their country independence from Britain. And he did it by following a principle of nonviolence and peaceful civil disobedience.

At a time when the British Empire was the mightiest superpower the world had ever seen, the people of India were hopelessly divided among conflicting races and religions, including Hindus, Sikhs, Muslims, Christians, Buddhists, and countless others. But at midnight on August 15, 1947, India became an independent nation, thanks in no small part to Gandhi's efforts.

**A Moving Experience.** But not even the saintly Gandhi could avoid the political horse-trading that came with freedom. Part of the independence deal was that India's Muslims be given their own independent homeland, to be named Pakistan. This looked good on paper, but more than 14 million people had to be uprooted from their homes—7 million Muslims to Pakistan from India and the same number to India from Pakistan—and hundreds of thousands were killed in the process.

**Time to Kill.** Gandhi's most vocal critic was the Hindu nationalist party Rashtriya Swayamsevak Sangh (RSS), which believed that India was one and indivisible. RSS member Nathuram Godse was a high-school dropout who was drawn to Hindu nationalism for the sense of belonging that it gave him. This is why he felt Gandhi's "betrayal" so keenly. On January 30, 1948, Godse approached Gandhi as he was going to evening prayers and shot him three times with a pistol, killing him instantly.

**A Fitting End?** Godse's trial for murder became a political battleground. He openly admitted his guilt, but some claimed he was mentally unfit for trial. Then there were those—including Gandhi's sons and his political protégé, prime minister Jawaharlal Nehru—who said that Godse was merely a pawn of the RSS, whose leaders should really have been on trial. Inevitably, Godse was found guilty. He was hanged at Ambala Jail outside New Delhi on November 15, 1949. Godse's end was, of course, ironic. Gandhi would never have sanctioned the execution of the man who killed him.

### 3. LEE HARVEY OSWALD

Who was Lee Harvey Oswald, and why did he assassinate President John F. Kennedy? The first question is easier to answer than the second, so let's start there. Born in New Orleans on October 18, 1939, Oswald was raised by his mother. They moved around a

---

Logical lingo: The word "lobster" in Chinese translates literally as "dragon shrimp."

lot. By the time he was 17, Oswald had lived in 22 houses and attended 12 schools—excelling academically at none of them. He joined the U.S. Marines just a week after his 17th birthday—he needed some stability in his life.

**From Marines to Marina.** Sadly, though, Oswald and military discipline didn't get along. For one, he was a contrary character: delusional and passive-aggressive, according to one school psychiatry report. Second, he was a loud and vociferous communist. (In the Marines! During the Cold War!) Perhaps his superiors were relieved when the truculent young soldier defected to the Soviet Union in 1959. They were less delighted 32 months later when he "un-defected" back to the States—this time with a newly acquired Russian wife and child in tow.

Oswald drifted around Dallas and New Orleans looking—mostly unsuccessfully—for work. By the spring of 1963, Lee Harvey Oswald was a certified failure. In yet another desperate attempt to fit in, Oswald became involved in New Orleans's pro-Castro Fair Play for Cuba Committee.

**Theories Abounding.** Somehow, within the next six months, this involvement would lead Oswald to the sixth floor of the Texas School Book Depository building in Dallas, from where, on November 22, 1963, he shot and killed President John F. Kennedy. Some say the Mob put him up to it, others blame the Cubans. For many, Oswald's "puppet-masters" were a rogue cell of right-wing CIA agents. One credible source even blames the Vietnamese. Or maybe Oswald was just an old-fashioned loner with a grudge.

Whatever the answer, we'll probably never know. Two days after the Kennedy killing, Oswald was himself assassinated as he was being transferred to the Dallas County Jail. The killer was Jack Ruby, a nightclub owner with suspected Mob links. "I'm just a patsy," Oswald had declared when he was arrested. Maybe he was. But whose patsy?

## 4. JAMES EARL RAY

On April 4, 1968, Martin Luther King Jr. was killed by a sniper as he stood on the second-floor balcony of the Lorraine Motel in Memphis, Tennessee. Two months later, James Earl Ray—petty crook, armed robber, forger, and prison escapee—was arrested at

Heathrow Airport in London, trying to leave England on a forged Canadian passport. He was extradited to the United States and indicted for the murder of King. Case closed? Hardly.

**Cold-blooded Killer.** James Earl Ray was not a nice man. Born in 1928, he left the army after World War II and drifted into crime. In 1959 he was given a prison term of 20 years for armed robbery and other offenses. In 1967, he escaped from jail by hiding in a bread truck. An admitted racist, Ray was a man with a grudge against the world in general and high-profile African Americans like King in particular. No one doubts Ray took part in the assassination of King. The argument is whether he acted alone or with conspirators.

**A Different Story.** When tried for King's murder, Ray pleaded guilty—but only in return for avoiding the death penalty. As soon as his life sentence began, Ray announced his innocence. He claimed that after he broke out of jail in 1967, he fled to Canada and encountered a shadowy underworld character he identified as "Raoul" who wanted Ray to help him kill King. What Ray didn't know, some say, is that Raoul was acting on behalf of either the U.S. government or the FBI (or both), who wanted King silenced. Even the Reverend Jesse Jackson, who was with King when he died, accepts the theory that Ray didn't act alone and the government may have been involved. James Earl Ray died in prison in April 1998, leaving a lot of questions behind him.

## 5. SIRHAN SIRHAN

To this day no one, including Sirhan himself, has been able to plausibly explain why he shot and killed Robert F. Kennedy on June 5, 1968. So let's start with what we know. Sirhan Bishara Sirhan was born in Jerusalem on March 19, 1944, to a Palestinian Christian family. His family emigrated to the United States when he was 12, and settled in California.

**Stranger in a Strange Land.** As an Arab growing up in America, it's fair to say that Sirhan was conflicted. His family clung to their Middle Eastern way of life, speaking Arabic at home, reading Arabic newspapers, and mostly keeping to themselves. Schoolmates remember Sirhan as pleasant but withdrawn. By the mid-1960s, he was adrift in American culture. Was he an Arab or an American?

---

Felix Frankfurter is the only naturalized American to serve...

And what position should he take on Israel's ongoing conflict with his Arab brothers in the Middle East, especially when he wasn't even a Muslim?

**A Legend Out of His Own Mind.** There are some who claim Sirhan was an overt anti-Semite and that somehow the Arab-Israeli Six-Day War of June 1967 sent him over the edge into a kind of anti-Israeli, anti-American frenzy. The truth, whatever it is, is undoubtedly more complex. When Sirhan Sirhan marched into the Ambassador Hotel on June 5, 1968, he surely intended to kill Robert Kennedy, but even he has never been able to give a satisfactory reason for why he did it—which probably points to mental illness as at least a contributing factor.

Sirhan was convicted of murder and sentenced to death in the gas chamber, a penalty that was later commuted to a life sentence. He now resides in California's Pleasant Valley State Prison.

\*     \*     \*

## FAMILY FEUD—THE PLEASANT VALLEY WAR

In the 1880s the Tewksburys and Grahams were neighboring cattle ranchers in Arizona's Pleasant Valley. Their quarrels over boundaries and missing livestock escalated when the Tewksburys allowed sheep into the valley. Since the Grahams feared sheep would graze until there was no grass for cattle, the feud became a range war that involved the entire community and eventually killed 20 people.

By 1892 each family had only one survivor. When the surviving Graham was murdered, the surviving Tewksbury was suspected, but never convicted. In 1904 the death of the last Tewksbury marked the end of the feud.

# OH, WHAT A DAY!

*July 4, 1826, started out with a bang, and as the day wore on, things started happening that seem more than a little coincidental.*

## 1. THE BIG 5-0

**Who:** The United States of America

**What:** A bicker-free golden anniversary

In 1776, John Adams famously predicted that Americans would annually celebrate Independence Day with "pomp and parades, with shows, guns, bells, bonfires, and illuminations." He was wrong. Instead, for its first 40 years, America "celebrated" the Fourth of July as a political holiday with divisive gatherings—the country's two main political parties at the time (the Federalists and the Democratic-Republicans) excluded each other from their July 4th speeches and meetings. Why? They had very different agendas. The Federalists (founded by the wealthy Alexander Hamilton) believed in a strong federal government, a national bank, and an alliance with England. On the other hand, the Democratic-Republicans (founded by the country's favorite well-off everyman, Thomas Jefferson) favored state governments, the interests of common folk over those of the moneyed class, and an alliance with France.

The Federalists had held solid control of the government through the 1700s. In 1800, things started changing when the Democratic-Republicans took over Congress and got Thomas Jefferson elected as president. That did little to stop the partisan bickering or make July 4th a fun holiday, though. It wasn't until 1816 and the election of James Monroe as president that the bickering dissipated...and it was only because Monroe soundly defeated the last remaining Federalist candidate, making that party irrelevant in American politics.

Finally came the Era of Good Feelings (1816–1824), as James Madison united the country with a post-politics presidency. July 4th began turning into a nonpartisan celebration of the nation's founding instead of merely an opportunity for divisive politicking. Without all the partisanship, Americans were free to celebrate their golden anniversary as a unified nation.

---

**July 11, 1798: The U.S. Marine Corps officially formed. Semper fi!**

## 2. DEATH OF A PRESIDENT I

**Who:** John Adams

**What:** Death

After serving as vice president during George Washington's administration, Federalist John Adams was elected the second president of the United States in 1797, beating Thomas Jefferson. Under the Constitution at the time, the second-place candidate became vice president, so the Adams/Jefferson administration forged ahead. The two were trusted friends and allies, even though they were also members of two warring parties.

That changed in 1801 when Jefferson again ran against Adams for president and beat him. In the days before Jefferson's inauguration, Adams made scores of last-minute appointments in an effort to thwart the new president. Jefferson perceived the behavior as pettiness, and it ended their friendship for the next 10 years. A mutual friend finally reconnected them in 1811, and the two, separated by hundreds of miles, began sending each other long letters discussing science, philosophy, and politics.

When Adams received his invitation to the jubilee in 1826, he hoped to see Jefferson in person again after 15 years of correspondence, but realized that, at 90 years of age, he wasn't in good enough shape to travel to Washington, D.C., from his home in Massachusetts. So Adams reluctantly declined the invitation.

On June 30, neighbors came to visit the former president. He was so frail that he had to be lifted into his coach, but still felt that politeness required him to return the visit the next day. When he got home on the night of July 1, he went to bed feeling ill and never fully recovered. On July 4, visitors came to see Adams again and asked him about the 50th anniversary celebration. He responded, "It is a great day. It is a good day." However, as the day wore on, he sunk into semiconsciousness—a doctor was called, and Adams said only a few recognizable words and phrases. (One of them was "Thomas Jefferson survives.") By the evening, John Adams was dead.

## 3. DEATH OF A PRESIDENT II

**Who:** Thomas Jefferson

**What:** Death

---

In 1981, Neva Rockefeller became the first woman ordered to pay her husband alimony.

Unfortunately, Adams was wrong: Thomas Jefferson did not survive. He had died a few hours earlier in his home outside Charlottesville, Virginia. Jefferson's health had been deteriorating for years and had taken a turn for the worse in the spring of 1826, so when he received his invitation to the Washington, D.C., celebration, Jefferson sent his regrets…in a note so eloquent that the jubilee's organizers sold copies of it.

On July 2, 1826, Jefferson had awoken feeling ill and retired to his bed, drifting in and out of consciousness. On July 3, he was lucid long enough to ask, "Is it the Fourth?" Told it would be soon, he began refusing the mind-dulling opiates that he'd been taking to ease his pain. Then, just after noon on July 4, 1826—as brass bands played and cannons resounded across the nation—Jefferson passed away.

## 4. A STAR IS BORN

**Who:** Stephen Foster, "America's first great songwriter"
**What:** Birth

On July 4, 1826, William and Eliza Foster couldn't make it to the celebrations either. They were too busy welcoming their ninth child, Stephen Collins Foster, at their home near Pittsburgh, Pennsylvania. Foster published his first song at 18 and, three years later, found fame with his first hit, "Oh, Susanna." At the time, minstrel shows (variety shows that starred white actors in blackface) were the biggest market for songs, and Foster wrote several songs for these shows. However, many of his minstrel songs seemed to empathize with the slaves' perspective. (On the other hand, most minstrel songs depicted them as ignorant caricatures.) Of Foster's ballad "Old Uncle Ned," abolitionist Frederick Douglass wrote that it would likely "awaken sympathies for the slave."

Over the next 15 years, Foster wrote such classics as "Camptown Races," "Nelly Was a Lady," "Jeanie with the Light Brown Hair," "Hard Times Come Again No More," and "Way Down Upon the S'wanee River (Old Folks at Home)." His music earned him the title of "Father of American Music," but it never made him enough money to provide for his family. In January 1864, at the age of 37, Stephen Foster died in New York City. He had just 38 cents in his pocket.

---

The last descendant of the musical Bach family died on Christmas Day, 1845…

# EXIT, STAGE LEFT

*Playwrights have given humanity some of the finest moments of
tragedy and farce—and not just in their works. A surprising
number of the world's most prominent stage writers have
shuffled off this mortal coil under unusual circumstances.
Life imitating art, or just plain old bad luck?*

## 1. THE BIRTH—AND DEATH—OF TRAGEDY

**Act I:** Aeschylus invented drama. Born around 525 BC, he was a
national hero in Athens. From his mid-20s on, he wrote some 90
plays and won more awards than you can shake a stick at. All in
all, one of the immortals.

**Act II:** Only seven of his dramas survive, but they are towering
achievements, especially the Oresteia trilogy, which charted the
decline and fall of the great Greek king Agamemnon and his offspring at the hands of their evil mother, Clytemnestra. The first
soap opera? You bet.

Anyway, that's enough culture. What you want to know is:
How did Aeschylus meet his maker?

**The End:** No one really knows what happened to Aeschylus, but
around AD 78, Roman philosopher Pliny the Elder offered this
"explanation": An eagle soared overhead, a terrified turtle
clutched in its talons. "How," the eagle thought, "am I going to
break into this turtle shell? I'm starving." Suddenly, something
glinted in the Hellenic sunlight. "Hey, I'll crack the shell on that
rock down there." But it wasn't a rock. It was the polished bald
dome of old Aeschylus. So the eagle dropped the turtle, the turtle
brained the playwright, and the playwright became legend.

## 2. THE MAN WHO WASN'T SHAKESPEARE

**Act I:** English playwright Christopher "Kit" Marlowe was born in
1564—the same year as William Shakespeare. For a time, his fame
threatened to eclipse that of the Bard. Until, that is, death itself
eclipsed Marlowe at a tragically young age.

**Act II:** Unlike the brainy-but-dull Shakespeare, Marlowe lived.
He drank, gambled, and brawled—and no one was safe from his
roving eye. Kit wrote like an angel and lived like a demon. His

greatest work, *The Tragical History of Doctor Faustus* (written, we think, in 1592), dealt with murder, ambition, subterfuge, and Satanism.

**The End:** On May 30, 1593, the 29-year-old scrawler and brawler was stabbed to death in a dingy London inn, allegedly after arguing with his drinking partner over the bar bill. The truth of the event is suitably shady. It's thought that Marlowe had been a government spy and was bumped off by agents of the state who were worried about his unreliable temperament. This legend is borne out by the fact that Ingram Frizer, the man who killed Marlowe, was an Elizabethan G-man and was pardoned for his blatant act of murder just a few weeks after the offense.

Whatever the truth, the boy wonder left behind a beautiful body of work and, lying on the floor of a London tavern, a good-looking corpse.

## 3. FRENCH FARCE

**Act I:** Ah, the French. They're so *dramatique*. Just like Jean-Baptiste Poquelin, better known to the world and to posterity as Molière. Born in 1622, he is France's greatest playwright and the author of such timeless classics as *The Misanthrope* and *The School for Wives*.

**Act II:** A favorite of France's royal family, Molière's company of actors was known as the King's Troupe, and in 1661 he had been appointed as the official producer of court entertainments. But Molière's satirical plays and comic exposés of French pomposity (an easy target, then and now) earned him powerful enemies, including the Catholic Church, especially after his play *Tartuffe* attacked what he saw as religious hypocrisy.

So, was there some shadowy plot to do away with the troublesome author? Afraid not. What really happened was less sinister—but loaded with delicious irony.

**The End:** Molière was so pleased with what would be his final work—a play about a hypochondriac titled *The Imaginary Invalid*—that he took the lead role. During a performance one evening in 1673, the 51-year-old Molière, who suffered from pulmonary tuberculosis, was seized by a coughing fit. Completely unaware of the maestro's sickly nature, the audience applauded his "realistic" performance to the rafters. They cheered as the poor

---

In Korean folklore, the magpie is associated with good fortune.

playwright turned blue. "Encore!" they cried. But there was no encore. And no more Molière. He died a few hours later.

## 4. BANZAI!

**Act I:** Yukio Mishima. Never heard of him? Well, in Japan he's a legend as a playwright, novelist, and bodybuilder.

Born Kimitake Hiraoka in Tokyo on January 14, 1925, he was raised at first by his aristocratic grandmother, who instilled a sense of superiority and artistic integrity in the young writer. She also made him play with dolls, a fact not appreciated by Kimitake's dad, who reentered the boy's life in 1937. The elder Hiraoka was all about military discipline and tried to beat any girlie tendencies out of his boy on more than one occasion.

**Act II:** Artistically, socially, and sexually conflicted, Kimitake Hiraoke emerged after World War II as one of Japan's most interesting writers, adopting the pen name Yukio Mishima and espousing an extreme romantic nationalism in plays and novels like *Patriotism* and *My Friend Hitler.* He took up martial arts, believing the body was just as important as the mind. And as his body developed, so did Hiraoke's belief that he was destined to "save" Japan from the modern world. In 1968, he formed his own militia group, the Shield Society.

**The End:** On November 25, 1970, Hiraoke marched on the Tokyo headquarters of the Self-Defense Force (a kind of national guard, but with fancier uniforms) with a few handpicked Shield Society acolytes. After tying the force's commander to his chair, Hiraoke stepped out onto the balcony to command the troops below to rise up and restore the ancient samurai warrior code of Japan. His audience, not knowing how to react, broke into laughter. As the hoped-for coup d'etat failed to materialize, Hiraoke, having severely lost face, did what any goof Japanese warrior would do. He took out his sword and committed ritual suicide.

## 5. SWEET AND CRAZY

**Act I:** Thomas Lanier Williams won everlasting fame as Tennessee Williams, whose steamy, Southern-set melodramas have entranced generations of theatergoers since *A Streetcar Named Desire* exploded onto the American stage in 1947.

As with many artists, Williams didn't have what you'd call a balanced and carefree childhood. Born in 1911, he grew up gay in the Deep South, with a much-loved sister who was a paranoid schizophrenic. While this gave him plenty of material for future plays such as *Streetcar* and *The Glass Menagerie*, it didn't exactly make for a happy family life.

**Act II:** Williams wrote his way out of those emotional and familial difficulties to become a national institution—as proven by his two Pulitzer Prizes and a Tony Award, not to mention the Presidential Medal of Freedom he received in 1980. And we all know what happens to national institutions: they die old and much loved, surrounded by friends and family, before being whisked off to lie in state, followed by a huge official funeral.

**The End:** But that's not what happened to Williams. In fact, it was pretty much the opposite. Aging and alone, his eyesight failing, Williams sat in his New York hotel room on the evening of February 25, 1983. An habitual user of optical ointments, he took out his eyedrops, popped the lid in his mouth to avoid misplacing it, and leaned his head back to administer the medicine. In doing so, he accidentally swallowed the lid and choked to death. As a final insult, Williams's family insisted that the dead writer be buried in St. Louis—one of his least favorite places on earth. (In the trade, that's what they call "dramatic irony.")

\*　　\*　　\*

### WHEN IN DOUBT, CHANGE YOUR NAME

That's what the royal family of England did during World War I, according to records retrieved by Uncle John. The current royal family was known as the Saxe-Coburg and Gotha clans in 1916 as war brought on by the Germans engulfed Europe. Worried about this German lineage and any connotations the public might draw from it, the family decided a break from the past was needed posthaste:

• The Saxe-Coburgs and the Gothas adopted Windsor at the suggestion of a royal family staff member.

• Cousins of the newly minted Windsors changed their family name from Battenburg to the now hallowed Mountbatten to follow the tradition set by the royals.

---

In 1439, the English government banned kissing to stop germs from spreading.

# 7 MODERN WONDERS

*Sure, sure...the Great Pyramid of Giza and the Colossus of Rhodes are ancient wonders, but haven't humans built anything extraordinary since? Well, as a matter of fact, the American Society of Civil Engineers has a list of candidates.*

## 1. PANAMA CANAL

**Location:** Isthmus of Panama, a narrow strip of land that links North and South America

**Purpose:** The canal joined the Atlantic and Pacific oceans to create an easier and cheaper way to travel and ship goods between the two oceans. Before the canal was built, ships had two options: 1) they could unload their cargo, transport it across the isthmus, and reload it onto new ships; or 2) they could go around Cape Horn at the tip of South America, a long and dangerous journey.

**History:** Construction began in 1880 and lasted until 1914. More than 25,000 workers died during the building years, mostly of malaria and yellow fever. The French were the first to work on the canal, but abandoned it in 1889 when they ran out of money.

When the United States took over in 1904, they took significant steps to protect workers from disease. Since mosquito larvae live just below the water's surface after they hatch, most places where stagnant water collected were destroyed. Where that wasn't practical, the government dumped about 700,000 gallons of oil every year into standing water in an effort to kill the mosquitoes.

In order for ships to pass through the canal and traverse Lake Gatun, which reaches 85 feet above sea level in the Isthmus of Panama, three massive locks were built. Each lock must be filled with 26.7 million gallons of water so that a ship can reach the height of the next gate. When the locks were completed in 1913, they were the largest concrete structures ever made.

• The sanitation effort over the years the United States spent building the canal cost about $20 million.

• The final canal was 50 miles long, and today, more than 14,000 ships pass through it every year.

• An expansion project will double the canal's capacity by 2014.

## 2. CN TOWER

**Location:** Toronto, Ontario, Canada

**Purpose:** The Canadian National Railway came up with the idea for the CN Tower in 1968 because it wanted to erect an antenna high enough to prevent broadcasting interruptions when signals bounced off Toronto's many tall buildings. Canadian National also wanted to show off the strength of Canadian industry by building the tallest structure in the world. The CN Tower was surpassed by Burj Khalifa in Dubai, United Arab Emirates, which officially opened in 2010.

**History:** It took 1,537 people working 24 hours a day, five days a week, for 40 months to build the tower. The tower was finished on February 22, 1974, and stretched to a height of 1,500 feet at the roof. The antenna came next and was completed on April 2, 1975. With that addition, the CN Tower reached a record-breaking height of 1,815 feet 5 inches.

• Today the tower serves more than 16 local Canadian television and FM radio stations.

• In April 2008, the CN Tower introduced the world's highest glass elevator. It travels at 15 miles per hour, taking riders up the 1,136-foot glass-fronted elevator shaft in 58 seconds.

## 3. EMPIRE STATE BUILDING

**Location:** New York City

**Purpose:** During the early years of the Great Depression, millionaires Walter Chrysler (owner of the Chrysler Corporation) and John Jakob Raskob (a financial executive at Dupont and General Motors) started a competition to build the world's tallest building. Chrysler's team finished New York City's Chrysler Building in 1930 and it was the tallest for a year...until construction was completed on the Empire State Building.

**History:** Construction began on March 17, 1930, using 60,000 tons of Pennsylvania steel. Seven million work hours later, the building was finished on November 13, 1930. At 1,454 feet high (including the antenna), the Empire State Building is currently the tallest building in New York City (after the destruction of the World Trade Center's twin towers in 2001). It is 102 stories high and has observatories on the 86th and 102nd floors.

---

**Q. What did Mahatma Gandhi say when asked what he thought of Western civilization?...**

- The building has five entrances, 73 elevators, 1,860 steps, and 6,500 windows. Each month, city sanitation workers haul away 100 tons of garbage.

- The building is used today solely as an office building. There is no livable space inside it because, according to city building assessments, there are "inadequate bathing facilities."

## 4. GOLDEN GATE BRIDGE

**Location:** San Francisco, California

**Purpose:** Engineer Joseph Strauss wanted to make it easier to get across San Francisco Bay. The Golden Gate Bridge connects the city of San Francisco to Marin County in the north. Before the bridge opened, you had to take a ferry, which was time-consuming and inconvenient.

**History:** Construction lasted from 1933 until 1937. The men building the Golden Gate Bridge had the benefit of some of the most rigorous safety precautions of the time: they were required to wear hard hats and were not allowed to drink on the job (a rule that was often ignored at construction sites). But most important, Strauss had a safety net suspended under the entire floor of the bridge to catch anyone who slipped accidentally. In all, that net saved 19 lives, but even with the net in place, 11 men died during the bridge's construction.

- It's 8,981 feet (1.71 miles) long and is the second-longest suspension bridge in North America. (The double-decked Verrazano-Narrows Bridge in New York is the longest in North America. The Akashi Kaikyo in Japan is the longest in the world.)

- The bridge is painted orange because the architect didn't like black or gray—he thought that orange blended better with the landscape.

- More than 1,250 people have jumped to their deaths from the Golden Gate Bridge since 1937. The first incident occurred just three months after the bridge opened. An estimated 26 people are known to have attempted suicide from the Golden Gate and lived to tell the tale.

- A seismic retrofit of the Golden Gate Bridge is due to be completed in 2012. The retrofit should enable the bridge to withstand a magnitude 8.3 earthquake with only minimal damage.

## 5. ITAIPU DAM

**Location:** Paraná River, along the border of Brazil and Paraguay

**Purpose:** In the 1960s, Brazil and Paraguay both wanted to find a new, renewable energy source. They agreed to dam the Paraná River, build a power plant there, and share the electricity it created.

**History:** To build the dam, engineers had to change the course of the Paraná River. They moved more than 50 million tons of rock to create a channel. About 40,000 people worked on the project between 1975 and 1978. Nine thousand houses and a hospital were built to accommodate them.

• The Itaipu Dam is the largest operating hydroelectric power plant in the world—it's 4.8 miles long and 643 feet high. The amount of steel used in the dam could build 380 Eiffel Towers.

• In 2009, the Itaipu Dam generated 91,651,808 megawatt-hours, the fourth-highest power production in its history. That's enough electricity to supply the entire world for two full days.

## 6. ZUIDERZEE WORKS (NETHERLANDS NORTH SEA PROTECTION WORKS)

**Location:** Friesland, Netherlands

**Purpose:** The Netherlands is below sea level, so flooding has always been a concern. As early as the 1700s, people talked about damming the Zuiderzee, a shallow inlet of the North Sea, to protect the country from surging water. The technology didn't exist back then, but by the early 1900s it was a real possibility.

**History:** In 1916, after an especially bad storm flooded low-lying areas, the government decided to go ahead with a massive dike and dam project. Building started three years later and continued on and off until 1975. The first step in the Zuiderzee project was damming the inlet, first with a small wall and then a larger one. Next, the engineers created new agricultural land out of boulder clay, found along the bottom of the inlet. During World War II, the unfinished agricultural land provided many hiding places for the Dutch Resistance fighters who were battling the Nazis. The Dutch Resistance also intentionally bombed the dikes to flood them and drive the Germans out.

• The Zuiderzee Works wasn't strong enough to protect the

---

**What does the letter E on the left side of Spanish license plates stand for?** *España*

Netherlands from "the storm of the century" in 1953. More than 1,800 people and hundreds of thousands of livestock died as water surged over the seawalls. More than 370,000 acres of farmland were lost. This tragedy led to the Delta Project, a new series of dams, dikes, and storm surge barriers that connected to the Zuiderzee Works.

## 7. ENGLISH CHANNEL TUNNEL

**Location:** Connects Folkestone, Kent, England, to Sangatte, Pas-de-Calais, France, underneath the English Channel

**Purpose:** Crossing the English Channel—the strip of water that connects the Atlantic Ocean and the North Sea—has always been difficult. Storms are common, and the sea is rough. So a tunnel that went underwater would be ideal...so thought French engineer Albert Mathieu as early as 1802.

**History:** It wasn't until 1986, though, that the English and French governments agreed to begin construction on the Channel Tunnel (a.k.a "the Chunnel"), and the actual work got underway a year later. There are actually three tunnels under the English Channel: two full-size ones that run trains back and forth, and one smaller service tunnel that can be used as an escape route in an emergency.

Trains speed along the 32 miles of track through the tunnels at up to 100 miles an hour. About 23 miles are actually underwater, which means the Chunnel has the longest undersea portion of any tunnel in the world. England's Queen Elizabeth II and French president François Mitterrand officially opened the tunnel on May 6, 1994.

• The rock and rubble removed to build the Chunnel was deposited in southern England and increased the country's overall land area by about 90 acres (equivalent to about 87 soccer fields).

\* \* \*

"Architecture aims at eternity."

—**Christopher Wren**

# WHAT'S FOR DINNER?

*Ever wonder what dignitaries eat when they gather
to celebrate? A historic event calls for a historic
menu. Here are three that made history.*

## 1. THE MIDAS TOUCH

His legendary golden touch was the stuff of mythology, but there really was a King Midas, and archaeologists can tell you what he ate. The legend of Midas derives from the life of King Mita, who ruled the state of Phrygia, in what is now Turkey, around 700 BC. University of Pennsylvania archaeologists discovered his tomb in the Turkish city of Gordion in 1957, and the site captured the world's imagination when it yielded textiles, wooden furniture, and clay jars containing food residue. Organic materials such as these typically decompose, especially after 2,700 years, so finding a large number of them in such good condition was rare indeed.

Judging by the types of items they found, and how many were present, the archaeologists determined that the ancient Phrygians had gone to the tomb site to give their king a send-off banquet fit for…well…a king.

Midas probably would have enjoyed the feast—maybe the menu featured his favorite foods. From samples of the residue left in the 18 pottery jars found in the tomb, chemists detected traces of a spicy goat or lamb stew made from meat that had been marinated in honey, wine, and olive oil. They figured that lentils were probably served with it, and it might have been eaten with flatbread instead of utensils. To wash it down, the mourners drank barley beer, wine, and mead—a fermented beverage made from honey, water, malt, and yeast. And even though the mourners drank from vessels made of bronze and not gold, when the 150 bronze goblets found at the tomb were polished, they shone as if they had been touched by the Midas of myth.

## 2. A NOBEL MENU

When Swedish industrialist Alfred Nobel died in 1896, his will stipulated that a substantial part of his estate be used to establish annual prizes given "to those who, during the preceding year, shall

---

First Lady Eleanor Roosevelt once held a toga party to poke a little fun at…

have conferred the greatest benefit on mankind" in the five fields of physics, chemistry, physiology or medicine, literature, and peace. Each prize would have amounted to nearly $1 million in today's currency. No wonder Nobel's heirs balked and tried to prevent his wish from being executed. It took five years before the conflict was resolved and the first Nobel Prizes were awarded.

The first Nobel Prize ceremony, where the prizes for physics, chemistry, medicine, and literature were awarded, took place in Stockholm on December 10, 1901, the anniversary of Nobel's death. At the banquet following the ceremony, the laureates and their guests dined on hors d'oeuvres, poached fish with truffles in white wine sauce, filets of beef, breasts of grouse in Madeira sauce, ice cream parfaits, and pastries.

In the more than 100 years since the first Nobel Prizes were awarded, the menu has evolved and changed ever so slightly each year. In 1954, for instance, American chemist Linus Pauling and his fellow laureates dined on smoked brook trout with creamed spinach; filet of beef with artichokes, mushrooms, and potatoes; and pears Roberta for dessert. As the Nobel laureate for literature that year, Ernest Hemingway would have enjoyed the meal, but he didn't attend the ceremony or the banquet.

While most of us won't come close to being named Nobel laureates, it's still possible to dine like one. The restaurant at Stockholm's city hall, where the banquet takes place each December, will prepare sample Nobel Prize banquet menus for diners who request them in advance.

### 3. HIS MAJESTY'S HOT DOGS

When you're entertaining royalty, it's difficult to provide them with a meal they'll always remember. Yet Franklin Delano Roosevelt managed it, and made history in the process. In 1939, FDR sent a personal and private note to King George VI of England—via his ambassador to the Court of St. James, Joseph P. Kennedy—inviting him and the queen to visit the United States, and even suggesting that they bring their children along. (That would be Princess Elizabeth, now Queen Elizabeth II, and her younger sister, Princess Margaret Rose.) The king agreed, and plans were put into action for a June visit.

The visit by King George and Queen Elizabeth (without the

kids) was a history-making occasion in its own right. Amazingly, it was the first time that a reigning British monarch had ever set foot in the United States. And with Hitler gaining power in Germany and Europe edging closer to World War II, the two leaders had a lot to discuss.

The royal couple went to the White House for a formal state meeting, but knowing that they would have a better opportunity to bond in a relaxed atmosphere, FDR invited them to join him at his home in Hyde Park, New York, for a more leisurely visit. And there, on the front porch of the cottage, the Roosevelts hosted their most memorable meal: they served the king and queen hot dogs!

The grilled hot dogs were presented to the royals on a silver platter, but that didn't keep the queen from being perplexed. "How do you eat it?" she asked the president. The king, on the other hand, reportedly dived right in, thoroughly enjoyed the hot dog, and washed it down with a beer. And for a few hours two of the most powerful men in the world enjoyed a barbecue on a sunny Sunday afternoon. The official menu for the event follows.

### Menu for Picnic at Hyde Park
### Sunday, June 11, 1939

Virginia ham

Hot dogs (if weather permits)

Smoked turkey

Cranberry jelly

Green salad

Rolls

Strawberry shortcake

Coffee, beer, soft drinks

**The first capital of ancient Egypt was Memphis, which means "white walls."**

# ONE-ARMED BUT ABLE

*It's amazing what some people can accomplish,*
*even if they've been "disarmed."*

Fans of the hit TV series and movie *The Fugitive* know that the one-armed man was not a real nice guy. In contrast, here are some real heroes who lost an arm but gained the admiration of their peers for their courage and accomplishments in the face of increased odds.

## 1. THE NAVAL HERO

At age 12, he was a midshipman on an Arctic expedition. At 15, he was patrolling the West Indies on an English man-of-war. In 1780, at 21, Horatio Nelson had cemented his reputation as the brave captain of the HMS *Hinchinbrook*, which captured a Spanish fort in Nicaragua after Spain and France decided to support the American colonies in the Revolutionary War. It also made Nelson the arch nemesis of Emperor Napoléon Bonaparte.

**You Win Some, You Lose Some.** In 1794, Nelson helped secure Corsica from a French army invasion and lost his sight in one eye from enemy fire. Three years later, as a rear admiral, Nelson captured a Spanish treasure ship in the Canary Islands. On landing, a cannon blast shattered his elbow; when he returned to his ship, his arm was amputated. But Nelson wasn't sidelined for long. By the turn of the century, he'd won the Battle of the Nile, ending Napoléon's threat to Egypt; defended Naples from French invasion; and had taken on a coalition of northern European powers in the Baltic. After the Battle of Copenhagen, Nelson dictated the terms of an armistice, thus ending any challenge to English naval supremacy.

**Nelson 27, Napoleon 0.** After a brief four years at home, Nelson became commander in chief of the Royal Navy. When it looked like Napoleon was readying an armada to seize control of the English Channel, Nelson sailed south with 27 ships, found Napoléon's fleet of 33 Franco-Spanish ships off Cape Trafalgar in southern Spain, and decimated the enemy fleet without losing a single ship. The victory ended the threat to England, but came at a tragic

---

**Some scenes in Disney's *Bambi* (1942) are unused footage from *Pinocchio* (1940).**

price. A sharpshooter on the French ship *Redoubtable* fired a bullet that struck Nelson in the shoulder and passed through his spine. He died on the deck of the HMS *Victory*; his last words were, "Thank God I have done my duty."

**The Nelson Touch.** Unlike many admirals who demanded silence and obedience from subordinates, Nelson was the opposite. He cared for his men and sought feedback from everyone aboard. His enthusiasm and hatred for the French was energizing. He gave a sense of empowerment to every man who served under him— lessons in military and business leadership that are taught to the present day. The hero of Trafalgar was a complex individual—on one hand vain, insecure, and craving recognition while on the other courageous and patriotic. Though married, he had a well-publicized affair with Lady Emma Hamilton, who was also married. Nelson and his wife separated amicably in 1801, and that same year Lady Hamilton bore him a daughter, Horatia.

## 2. THE HALF-MAN
They called him *Mediohombre*, or "Half-man," and for good reason. Spanish midshipman Don Blas de Lezo lost his lower left leg at the Battle of Velez Malaga in 1704 when he was 15; in 1707, he lost his left eye in the siege of Santa Catharine Castle in the port of Toulon, France; and as captain of a frigate in 1713—while capturing 11 British ships—he lost his right arm in the siege of Barcelona.

**A Full Force to Be Reckoned With.** Despite the loss of his limbs, Blas de Lezo was the scourge of English and Dutch pirates along the Pacific coasts of North and South America for the next decade. Leading Spain's Mediterranean fleet in 1730, he bombarded Genoa, Italy, and successfully recouped two million pesos owed to Spain. He also battled Islamic Algerians in North Africa and commanded 54 ships and 30,000 troops that recaptured the city of Oran from the Ottoman Empire in 1732.

**Half a Man Is Better Than One.** In 1741, Blas de Lezo defended the port of Cartagena, Colombia, from a British invasion force of 180 warships and 28,000 men commanded by Admiral Edward Vernon. Some of Vernon's enlisted men came from the American colonies under the leadership of a half-brother to George Washington, Lawrence Washington (who, incidentally, named his family estate Mount Vernon after the admiral). Vernon was so confident that he urged Blas de Lezo to surrender before the invasion even began. The Spaniard sent him a frosty reply and prepared to do battle.

**Forewarned Is Forearmed.** Fortunately, Blas de Lezo had more than a year to get ready. He depended on a small fleet to safeguard Cartagena's harbor and approximately 6,000 troops behind fortifications. Starting on March 13, 1741, and for 67 days, the Spanish and English fought from ship to ship, from ship to shore, and in skirmishes on land. In every case, Blas de Lezo rallied defenders with his stubborn courage and tactical brilliance. On April 20, Vernon ordered a marine assault on the key fort overlooking the harbor where Blas de Lezo and 600 defenders were holed up. Blas de Lezo ordered a do-or-die bayonet charge as the British landed. Eight hundred of the invaders died and a thousand were captured. On May 20, a dejected Admiral Vernon retired with his fleet to Jamaica. He'd lost an estimated 18,000 soldiers, half of them to injuries and the rest to disease.

**Good News, Bad News.** Spain managed to preserve its empire in the Americas, but Blas de Lezo died a few months later from the plague and was buried at an unknown site. A statue of him, with missing arm and leg and with a patch over one eye, overlooks Cartagena's port. The figure holds high a sword with its one arm.

### 3. CIVIL WAR HERO AND GRAND CANYON PIONEER
Nearly 24,000 of the 110,000 soldiers who fought in the two-day Battle of Shiloh died. Second Lieutenant John Wesley Powell, an enlisted engineer serving with the 20th Illinois Volunteers, survived—but his right arm didn't. Powell endured lifelong pain from raw nerve endings where the arm was amputated, but he returned to his regiment to fight in the Battles of Champion Hill and Big Black River Bridge around Vicksburg, Mississippi.

**Way Out West.** After the war, Powell—35 years old and now a major—led a three-month geologic expedition down the Green and Colorado rivers in 1869. Financed by the Smithsonian Institution, the trek involved nine men in four small wooden boats. Six

---

The earliest known thimble, made of bronze, was Roman; it was found at Pompeii.

men, including Powell, completed the journey, which included the first known passage through the unexplored Grand Canyon. The other three left the expedition and were reportedly killed by Native Americans.

**It's Grand, All Right.** Powell later became the first head of the U.S. Geological Survey and founded the Smithsonian's Bureau of Ethnology. He wrote of the Grand Canyon: "It is a region more difficult to traverse than the Alps or the Himalayas, but if strength and courage are sufficient for the task by a year's toil a concept of sublimity can be obtained never again to be equaled on the hither side of Paradise."

*For the rest of the story see page 387.*

\*     \*     \*

## THE MAN WHO DESIGNED AMERICA

During his seventy-year career, French-born Raymond Loewy designed everything from fashion illustrations to advertising logos to sleek automobiles. In New York, Loewy freelanced as a window designer for the big department stores and worked as a fashion illustrator for *Vogue* and *Harper's Bazaar*. Later in his career—besides creating now-familiar logos for brands like Lucky Strike cigarettes, Nabisco, Shell Oil, Exxon, and Greyhound—Loewy was busy streamlining the designs of 20th century products like these:

- Sears Coldspot refrigerator (1935)
- Pennsylvania Railroad's T1 Locomotive (1937)
- Greyhound Scenicruiser (1946)
- Greyhound Double-Deck Coach (1951)
- Studebaker Commander (1953)
- BMW 507 (1957)
- Studebaker Avanti (1961)
- The livery worn by attendants on Air Force One (1962)
- The 5¢ John F. Kennedy stamp (1964)

Hawaii imports 90 percent of its food.

# NOMS DE PLUME

*Why go to all the trouble of writing a book and then put someone else's name on it? Here are some of the best-known writers who didn't want to be known.*

## 1. MARY ANNE EVANS (A.K.A. GEORGE ELIOT)

The British author, Mary Anne Evans, better known as George Eliot (1819–80), wrote such classics as *The Mill on the Floss* (1860), *Silas Marner* (1861), and *Middlemarch* (1872). So why the name—and gender—reassignment?

Simple. Evans wanted to be taken seriously as a writer, and in Victorian England, that was impossible for a woman. But that wasn't her only reason for keeping a low profile. By 19th-century standards, she was a "loose woman." From 1854, she openly conducted a 20-year affair with the philosopher and intellectual George Henry Lewes, who was married. This was scandalous stuff, and Evans and Lewes were both snubbed by polite society.

Equally contentious was her literary output. In 1856, she penned an essay titled "Silly Novels by Lady Novelists" that took her fellow female writers to task for their frivolous and romantic plots, breathless heroines, and square-jawed heroes. Evans declared that a new, more realistic, and psychologically insightful type of novel written by a woman was needed—and that she was, so to speak, the man for the job.

In 1858, as George Eliot, she published *Scenes of Clerical Life*, followed a year later by *Adam Bede*. The latter was such a huge best seller that she was unable to keep her identity secret, and George Eliot was outed as Mary Anne Evans. Even so, for more than 20 years she continued to write under her pen name. This is why some readers were confused when "George Eliot" published *The Mill on the Floss* in 1860 with the dedication "To my beloved husband, George Henry Lewes." (To add to the confusion, Evans and Lewes were never legally married.)

Lewes died in 1878, and two years later, the 60-year-old Evans courted controversy once more by marrying John Cross, who was 20 years her junior.

When she died on December 22, 1880, Evans/Eliot was one of

---

Archers at the ancient Olympic Games used tethered doves as targets.

Britain's most celebrated authors, and her reputation has grown steadily ever since. She is appreciated for her keen insights into small-town prejudice and for her sharp eye and even sharper pen that gently but firmly skewered Victorian England's social and sexual double standards. Man, what a woman!

## 2. WILLIAM LUTHER PIERCE (A.K.A. ANDREW MACDONALD)

If you wrote *The Turner Diaries*, you'd probably keep your identity secret, too. That's why William Luther Pierce used the name Andrew Macdonald in 1978 when he published the book dubbed "the bible of the racist right" by the FBI.

A bizarre, racist sci-fi adventure, *The Turner Diaries* is set in the year 2099. In diary form, its protagonist, Earl Turner, describes how he and fellow members of a terrorist group known as "The Organization" have brought down the American government and instituted a worldwide race war that ultimately eliminated all Jews and nonwhites. It's unhinged, paranoid stuff—and it's sold about 500,000 copies to date. Many bookstores won't touch it, but it can be bought online—and at many gun shows.

So this William Luther Pierce—he's your classic lives-with-his-mom-and-doesn't-get-out-much nerd, right? Wrong. Pierce was in fact Dr. William Luther Pierce III (1933–2002), an assistant professor of physics at Oregon State University in the 1960s and onetime leader of the National Alliance, a white separatist group associated with the American Nazi Party, whose racist rhetoric made the Ku Klux Klan look tame. Pierce was also the founder of Cosmotheism, a religion based on white racial superiority and eugenics.

In case there was any doubt, in 1984 Pierce/Macdonald wrote *Hunter*, a novel in which the hero is Oscar Yeager, a Vietnam vet who murders mixed-race couples. Showing his sentimental side, Pierce dedicated the book to the serial killer and fellow racist Joseph Paul Franklin.

Among other things, *The Turner Diaries* is credited with influencing many libertarian and right-wing acts of violence and terrorism, including the 1995 Oklahoma City bombing by Timothy McVeigh, a known admirer of the book. When Pierce died of cancer in his West Virginia home in July 2002, he was hailed as a prophet by some and as an inflammatory racist scaremonger by others. For a man who saw life in black and white, he wouldn't have expected anything less.

## 3. ANNE DESCLOS (A.K.A. "O")

It's unlikely you've heard of this author, who sometimes also wrote under the pen name of Pauline Réage—or that you'd admit it. In *The Story of O*, Desclos penned one of the filthiest books of all time. There, that's got your interest—so read on.

Originally published in 1954 in France as *Histoire d'O*, the novel describes in very graphic detail the sadomasochistic sexual adventures of "O" and her innumerable partners. O is portrayed as the willing victim in her sexual subjugation, which is one reason why some say the book is a celebration of feminine empowerment. Others revile it as self-hating, antifemale propaganda. In a typically French move, in 1955 the novel was awarded the prestigious Prix des Deux Magots literary prize.

In the 1970s, several film adaptations of the book were made. Most were from directors involved in the adult movie industry, but there were "art house" versions too, most notably the confrontational Danish filmmaker Lars von Trier's *Menthe—la bienheureuse* in 1979. In 1992, a 10-part miniseries based on the book was inflicted on the presumably more sexually liberated Brazilians.

All in all, not bad for a book written as a dare. In the early 1950s, Anne Desclos was an editor at the prestigious Parisian publishing house of Gallimard. She also wrote "proper" novels under the pseudonym Dominique Aury. Her boss and married lover, Jean Paulhan, an avid fan of erotic fiction, bet Desclos that no woman could write anything as racy as his beloved Marquis de Sade. Desclos rose to the challenge.

The result was a huge and controversial best seller. It was also, in effect, a job application to continue as Paulhan's submissive mistress. Perhaps shocked by the book's reception, Desclos did not reveal her identity as the author for another 40 years, when she was in her 80s.

The ancient Sumerians were the first to charge interest for loans, around 3100 BC.

# SETTLE DOWN

*Old maps that show the first North American settlements include such future large cities as Boston, New Amsterdam (later New York City), Philadelphia, and Charleston. But other settlements didn't succeed on the same scale—or failed altogether. Yet each was important to the early colonization of the New World. Here's what happened to them.*

## 1. PORT ROYAL, SOUTH CAROLINA (1526)

For more than a century, Spain, France, and England wrangled for a toehold in coastal Carolina. Spaniard Lucas Vázquez de Ayllón established San Miguel de Gualdape in October 1526 near the site of today's Port Royal, South Carolina. Ayllón, a prosperous sugar planter in Hispaniola, sailed there with supplies, livestock, and 600 settlers, including perhaps the first African slaves. Many colonists—including Ayllón—succumbed to disease, hunger, and hostile Indians. With winter approaching, 150 survivors left the settlement after just six weeks and sailed back to Hispaniola.

The next attempt at settlement came in 1562 when French explorer Jean Ribault arrived. He and his men constructed a fort near the first settlement, which they named Porte Royall. Ribault left behind 30 settlers and sailed back to France for supplies and more colonists. When he didn't return soon, the settlers feared the worst and persuaded Indians to help them construct a ship to return home. The poorly constructed vessel sank, but an English ship rescued the colonists.

In 1566, the Spanish returned and constructed their own fort, which they called St. Elena. A century later, however, Spanish interest in the Carolinas had weakened due to war with the English, so King Charles I of England staked a claim. Among the new arrivals was Lord Cardross of Scotland, who brought 148 settlers to build Stuart Town near Port Royal in 1684. The satellite colony lasted only two years before it was destroyed by a Spanish naval patrol. Despite the setback, the English prevailed and built the town that would last—Port Royal, South Carolina.

## 2. ST. AUGUSTINE, FLORIDA (1565)

Spanish explorer Juan Ponce de León first sighted the North

American mainland in 1513. He claimed it for Spain and called it Pascua Florida, meaning "flowery Easter" (because he landed in the spring), but did not establish a settlement. Fifty years later, with the French threatening to colonize Florida by sending a garrison to the St. John's River on the Atlantic coast, Spain's King Phillip II responded by deploying Admiral Pedro Menéndez de Avilés with 1,500 soldiers and settlers to establish a colony and drive out the French. The Spaniards came ashore in 1565 near an Indian village about 30 miles south of modern-day Jacksonville.

Menéndez de Aviles seized the village, erected ramparts around it, and called the new Catholic settlement St. Augustine. He then set out on the St. John's River, located the French garrison, and destroyed it. Later, Menéndez de Aviles chased and overtook the garrison's French fleet led by Jean Ribault, Porte Royall's founder. Ribault and his men surrendered, but were put to death as heretics. Menéndez de Aviles's bloody reign had its intended outcome: Florida was secured for Spain. However, the settlement came to epitomize Catholic cruelty to the French and English, who occasionally attacked the city in retribution. Nevertheless, St. Augustine survived and is today known as the oldest permanent European settlement in North America.

## 3. ROANOKE ISLAND, VIRGINIA (1585)

The first attempt by England to colonize North America consisted of 100 people chartered by Sir Walter Raleigh to establish a settlement in Virginia under the auspices of Queen Elizabeth I. Two ships transported the settlers to Roanoke Island, about 25 miles below the mouth of Chesapeake Bay, and then made haste back to England for supplies. The ships were delayed, however, and by the time they returned, the settlers were nearly starved to death and wanted nothing more to do with America, so they returned home.

Not to be dissuaded, Raleigh organized a second expedition that landed in 1587. The new settlers—117 men, women, and children—went to work clearing land, planting crops, and building shelters. John White, the leader of the colony, had returned to England to bring back supplies, but armed conflict between Spain and England delayed him for three years. By the time he made it back, there were no traces of the settlers of what came to be known as "the Lost Colony," a mystery that persists to this day.

...in the Southern Hemisphere. The iconic structure opened in 1997.

## 4. JAMESTOWN, VIRGINIA (1607)

Twenty years after the failure at Roanoke Island, three ships carrying 104 English settlers sponsored by the Virginia Company of London arrived at Chesapeake Bay in 1607 to find a place for a settlement to be called Jamestown. It was all part of a plan by England's King James I to raise enough cash to settle Virginia, the area between French Canada and Spanish Florida. Though Spain had declared ownership of the entire coast, it had not been colonized.

The English colonists chose a peninsula on the James River 40 miles inland from the bay's entrance for its fledgling settlement. Hardships due to Indian attacks and disease plagued Jamestown at first. After two years, only 60 settlers remained. Just in time, English supply ships arrived, and the colonists were convinced to stay. The marriage of Pocahontas, daughter of the Algonquin chief Powhatan, to colonist John Rolfe helped usher in several years of peace and prosperity that made Jamestown the first successful permanent English colony on the coast of North America. By 1619, Jamestown became the capital of the territory of Virginia. After the capital was moved to Williamsburg in 1699, Jamestown began a precipitous decline and all but disappeared. It passed into federal ownership in 1934 and has since been restored as a National Historic Site operated by the U.S. National Parks Service.

## 5. POPHAM, MAINE (1607)

Founded in the same year as Jamestown, Popham was established by the Virginia Company of Plymouth, the second group of investors in England chartered by King James I to settle Virginia. The plan was to establish this settlement as a shipbuilding colony just south of French Canada.

Popham was located in present-day Maine, 10 miles south of what is now the city of Bath. The colony managed to survive its first year, though half of the 125 settlers returned to England as winter set in. A change in leadership brought on by the death of founder George Popham discouraged the rest. After just one year, the remaining colonists went back to England. Popham left a legacy, however. The settlers completed the construction of a 30-ton ship and christened it the *Virginia*, the first ship built by

Europeans in North America. The ship was well constructed and returned the colonists to England. It then made another Atlantic crossing—this time to Jamestown.

## 6. PLYMOUTH ROCK, MASSACHUSETTS (1620)

It is more legend than fact that the Pilgrims stepped off their ship onto Plymouth Rock. It was about 150 years after they arrived that writers began to designate a granite boulder deeply embedded in the sand as "Plymouth Rock" and the site where the Pilgrims came ashore. The boulder's top half split off while being jacked up. It then got rolled around the area for a century as a show rock, losing about half its size before being reunited with its base.

What is known historically is that 102 passengers—73 males and 29 females—embarked from England on the *Mayflower* in 1620, hoping to reach Virginia. Because of storms, landfall was instead made at the tip of Cape Cod. There the immigrants drafted the Mayflower Compact, the first governing document for an English settlement in the New World. A few months later, the settlers crossed Cape Cod Bay and arrived on the mainland at a clearing where the ship could be anchored close to the shore. No mention of any rocks was made in diaries kept at the time. Also, none of the refugees were known as "Pilgrims." Most were English Calvinist Separatists who believed that life was a pilgrimage to find heavenly bliss. It was a few years later that a leader of the group, William Bradford, referred to the settlers as "pilgrims" in his journal, which was published in 1856. The name caught on.

Captain John Smith named the site of the embarkation Plymouth Colony after the town where the *Mayflower* left England, Plymouth in Devon. People lived aboard the ship while men scouted the region for an appropriate place to build homes. That was found about three miles south, at a place that came to be known as Plimoth Plantation. As more settlers arrived, the colony expanded but was formally dissolved on May 14, 1691, and annexed by the Massachusetts Bay Colony to the north.

The original plantation settlement has been restored as an historical site. The city of Plymouth that we know today is located about half a mile north of Plymouth Rock. The rock itself exists on the edge of the bay; it is protected by a privately built portico and is cared for by the state government.

According to fossil records, wildfires have occurred on Earth for over 420 million years.

# TREES OF HISTORY

*If a tree falls in the forest and there's no one around to tell
its tale, does it still deserve a place in the history books?
Fortunately, these trees never had to find out.*

### 1. THE LIBERTY TREE

In 1765, the British government imposed the Stamp Act on the
American colonies. The law required that all printed materials
be produced on paper that had an embossed revenue stamp.
The only way to get the stamp was to pay a tax to the British
government that helped to pay for its military presence in North
America. The colonists didn't like this. For one, they didn't
appreciate being forced to pay for a British military presence they
didn't want in the first place. But also, they saw the stamp as a
form of censorship. Since all printed materials had to include it—
from newspapers to books to leaflets—the stamp tax essentially
determined what people in the colonies could read. If you couldn't
afford the tax, you couldn't publish your materials.

To protest the law, a group of colonists calling themselves
the Sons of Liberty gathered under the biggest tree they could
find—it happened to be growing near Boston Common in
Massachusetts—and hung two dummies (representing tax
collectors) from it. From that day forward, the tree was known
as the Liberty Tree. Colonists decorated it with banners and
lanterns and people regularly gathered under it to complain,
usually about the British.

The British government, however, thought the tree was
ridiculous...and a threat. In August 1775, a group of British
loyalists defiantly cut down the Liberty Tree and used it as firewood. Thereafter, the Liberty Tree became the Liberty Stump
and for many years was a reference point for locals. Today a
bronze plaque in Boston Common, near where the tree once
stood, commemorates it.

### 2. THE GENERAL SHERMAN TREE

This giant sequoia was enjoying a peaceful and rather obscure
existence until 1879 when naturalist James Wolverton discovered

---

The *hypocaust* was an ancient Roman system of central heating. It used an...

it and named it after Civil War general William Tecumseh Sherman, under whom he'd once served. In 1931, the General Sherman was named the oldest and largest tree in the world. Located in California's Sequoia and Kings Canyon National Park, it's estimated to be a whopping 2,300 to 2,700 years old and 274.9 feet tall, with a base circumference of about 103 feet. Its largest branch is almost seven feet in diameter. No one knows the exact age of the oldest giant sequoias; some say they could be up to 3,500 years old. The General Sherman's status as the world's largest tree is based on its volume in cubic feet.

## 3. THE GENERAL GRANT TREE

The General Grant Tree, also in Sequoia and Kings Canyon National Park, is the only living object to be declared a memorial to those who have given their lives in service to their country. The tree—named for Civil War general and U.S. president Ulysses S. Grant—became a memorial on March 29, 1956, via a declaration by President Dwight D. Eisenhower. But it was famous long before that: on April 28, 1926, President Calvin Coolidge called it the "Nation's Christmas Tree," and Christmas services have been held at its base ever since. At about 268 feet high and with a circumference of 108 feet, the General Grant is the world's third-largest tree.

## 4. THE BODHI TREE

According to legend, the Bodhi Tree in Bihar, India, grows on the spot where the founder of Buddhism—Siddhartha Gautama (a.k.a. Buddha)—found enlightenment after 49 days of meditation. The tree got its name because *bodhi* means "enlightenment" in Sanskrit.

The ancient Indian emperor Ashoka (circa 304–232 BC) regularly paid homage to the tree, so much so that, according to legend, his wife got jealous and tried to "kill" it by stabbing it with thorns. It didn't work. The tree survived the attack, and a shrine was built near its base. It did die eventually, though— Buddha lived more than 2,000 years ago—and Buddhist tradition says that the current Bodhi Tree is a direct descendant of the original, planted from a branch collected by Emperor Ashoka's daughter.

...underground furnace and tile flues to distribute the heat.

# FIRST THINGS FIRST

*Some of the first accomplishments of the English language are perennial favorites of English teachers. Others are all but forgotten— but each reveals a little bit about the history of literature.*

## 1. FIRST ENGLISH POEM: CAEDMON'S HYMN

For centuries after the fall of the Roman Empire, Latin remained the language of record across much of Europe. It was the language of court and official documents, and of literature and creative expression, even in far-off Britain. In the seventh century, residents of Britain spoke what we now call Old English—a Germanic language brought to the island by invaders. Sometime between 657 and 680, a cowherd named Caedmon lived in Northumbria, a kingdom in northern England. Though we have none of his original documents, and it's likely that he was illiterate, his story was later recorded by the scholar Bede.

An angel was said to have appeared to Caedmon in a dream, and asked him to sing a song of the creation of the world—in Old English, "sing me frumsceaft." The hymn that Caedmon was inspired to compose, which he later recited for others, is the first known English poem. It doesn't look like much of a poem to modern English speakers—Old English is so different from modern English that it needs to be translated. And there is no rhyme or meter. In Old English, poetry was expressed through alliteration and creative nouns. Caedmon's facility with language came to the attention of an abbess, who saw in him a way to preach the Christian gospel to a population that did not speak Latin, and so Caedmon's hymn became the cornerstone of English literature.

## 2. FIRST ENGLISH EPIC: *BEOWULF*

Scholars hotly debate the origin of the epic poem *Beowulf*, placing its creation anywhere from 675 to 1100. But it was likely written in the seventh century by a nobleman in one of England's middle kingdoms. But the story's hero isn't English—he's Scandinavian. The story takes place in either Denmark or western Sweden. Not only that, but the story is set sometime in the sixth century. In the saga, the glorious hero Beowulf arrives at the court of the Danish king Hrothgar from across the sea to fight the monster Grendel. Once Grendel is defeated, Beowulf then has to fight Grendel's even more fearsome mother. If that wasn't enough, Beowulf then takes on a dragon, all the while drinking and boasting.

Why would the first English epic be about Scandinavians? Many settlers of England had come from Scandinavia or Germany, so their ancestors would've been raised on legends of Norse gods. And England was repeatedly attacked by Vikings in the ninth and tenth centuries, leading to a wave of Viking settlers. Beowulf was a throwback to a time before these people came to England.

## 3. FIRST ENGLISH BOOK: *RECUYELL OF THE HISTORYES OF TROYE*

In 1066, the Normans, who came from northern France and were descendants of the Vikings, invaded England and put a French-speaking king on the throne. This started the long antagonism between France and England, but it also changed the English language, with the influx of French vocabulary. So it is not surprising that the first book ever printed in the English language was originally written in French. *Recuyell of the Historyes of Troye* by Raoul le Fevre was a courtly romance about the fall of Troy.

At the time, Homer's *Odyssey* and *Iliad* were almost entirely unknown, so the tale bears little resemblance to what would be familiar to modern readers. It was translated into English by William Caxton in 1474. Caxton brought the printing press to England in the 1470s and began the first great effort to put vernacular English into print, standardizing spelling and creating an official version of written English along the way. The result may be the bane of many schoolchildren, but at the time it was necessary. Caxton told a story of a London merchant who asked a farmwife in Kent for eggs—but their dialects were so different, the farmwife answered that she didn't speak French. So Caxton began his efforts to standardize English with *Recuyell of the Historyes of Troye*. Why that book first? It was a special request of his patron, the Duchess of Burgundy.

## 4. FIRST ENGLISH SHORT-STORY COLLECTION: *THE CANTERBURY TALES*

Written in the late 14th century, *The Canterbury Tales* by Geoffrey

Chaucer is a collection of stories supposedly told by a group of pilgrims engaged in a contest to see who can tell the best tale. While most medieval works were written either in French (the language of the nobility) or Latin (the language of the church), *The Canterbury Tales* was written in the same Middle English spoken on the streets of 14th-century London.

Chaucer can be credited with other English firsts, as well. Before *The Canterbury Tales*, Western stories focused on religion, the clergy, or aristocrats. Chaucer's pilgrims are the first characters taken from every walk of medieval life. Another first is that the tone of each tale matches the social status and human eccentricities of the pilgrim who narrates it. For example, a romantic knight tells a tale of two knights desperately in love with the same woman. But the lusty Wife of Bath tells a much earthier tale about a knight accused of rape who can avoid execution only by discovering what women really want.

The characters are so realistic, and they have so many psychological quirks, that they are still entertaining and illuminating seven centuries later. Chaucer's work also is the first collection of short stories in the English language to become a classic.

## 5. FIRST ENGLISH NOVEL: *LE MORTE D'ARTHUR*

There is a lot of contention over which book can claim to be the first English novel (depending on one's definition of "novel"), but one contender is Sir Thomas Malory's *Le Morte d'Arthur* (*The Death of Arthur*). Malory began the massive work (507 chapters, originally published as 21 books, and over 300,000 words) while in prison in the 1450s. He finished it in 1469, and William Caxton published it in 1485. Despite its French title, the book was written mainly in English.

Courtly romances—tales of chivalric knights, unrequited love, and great deeds—were popular at the time, and none were more popular than stories of King Arthur and his court at Camelot. *Le Morte d'Arthur* is a compilation of these stories, with some originals added by Malory, and it has become the bible of Arthurian legend. These are the stories of Arthur, Guinevere, Sir Lancelot, Merlin, and dozens of others that are still adapted every few years into new movies, TV series, and musicals. It's fair to say that the first English novel was a best seller.

# CSI: MUMMIES

*Everyone knows that the ancient Egyptians mummified their dead,
but they weren't the first or the only people to do it. Here are four
mummies that tell us a lot about their times and cultures.*

## 1. OTZI THE ICEMAN

**Claim to Fame:** Europe's oldest naturally formed mummy

**When:** Otzi was discovered in 1991 by two hikers. Scientists think
he lived between 3350 and 3300 BC.

**Where:** Otzi was bent at the waist and sticking out of a glacier in
the Otztal Alps along the border of Italy and Austria.

**Getting to Know Him:**

• Otzi's stomach still contained the contents of his last meal: ibex
meat and a crackerlike bread. There were also bits of charred rock,
as though the food had been cooked on a hot stone.

• His tools were typical Copper Age fare: a bow, a quiver of arrows,
a flint, and an ax with a copper blade. The fact that Otzi was carrying the copper-bladed ax gave scientists a better sense of when the
Copper Age began—about 1,000 years before they'd thought it did.

• Otzi had whipworm, a parasite that causes diarrhea and malnu-
trition. Fossilized whipworm eggs were found inside his stomach.

• There was also pollen from a tree called the hophornbeam in
Otzi's stomach. Because the tree blooms between March and June,
scientists were able to figure out that Otzi probably died in the
early summer.

• DNA evidence from Otzi's tools and clothes showed blood from
four different people, leading scientists to theorize that he died in
some kind of fight. There was blood on his arrows and ax and an
arrowhead in his shoulder. Plus, there was blood on his goatskin
coat—some researchers think that means he had a wounded companion whom he carried before they both died.

## 2. GINGER

**Claim to Fame:** Oldest Egyptian mummy

**When:** Ginger lived between 3400 and 3200 BC.

**Where:** He was buried in a pit in the Egyptian desert.

---

**In India, a "Himalayan blunder" means a very serious mistake.**

**Getting to Know Him:**
• He got the name Ginger from the bits of red hair still attached to his head.
• The Egyptians didn't perfect their mummy-making techniques until about 2700 BC, but Ginger shows that they had the idea for it long before that. Ginger was buried in hot, dry sand, which absorbed most of his moisture and mummified the remains. How do we know he was put there on purpose? His grave contained pieces of pottery that probably originally held food and drinks that the Egyptians thought he might need in the afterlife.

### 3. THE BEAUTY OF LOULAN
**Claim to Fame:** The oldest of the famous Tarim mummies
**When:** She was found in the 1980s and probably lived about 4,000 years ago.
**Where:** The Beauty was found in western China's Tarim Basin, near the modern-day city of Xinjiang.
**Getting to Know Her:**
• The Beauty of Loulan (so named because of her delicate bone structure) and the other Tarim mummies had European/Caucasian features: recessed eyes, long bodies, even blond and red hair. The discovery of these mummies told researchers that Caucasians had moved into China, Mongolia, and the surrounding regions earlier than originally thought. So where did the Tarim people come from? Based on DNA, probably eastern Europe.
• The Beauty was buried in a cloth shroud and was wearing a hat decorated with feathers. Those feathers indicate that she was probably from a wealthy family, since only the upper classes could afford extras like that.

### 4. TOLLUND MAN
**Claim to Fame:** Best-preserved body from prehistoric times
**When:** He was discovered in 1950, but probably lived during the fourth century BC.
**Where:** Tollund Man was buried in a peat bog—an acidic wetland filled with tannins that preserve human skin by essentially turning it into leather. He hails from Denmark's Jutland Peninsula.

**Getting to Know Him:**

• The head and face of Tollund Man (named after a local village) are remarkably well preserved. His mouth, nose, closed eyes, forehead wrinkles, even the stubble on his chin are all visible. When scientists did a scan of his skull, they discovered that his brain was also intact. His clothes, however, are mostly gone. He was found naked except for a leather belt, sheepskin cap, and braided leather rope still attached to his neck.

• Hundreds of mummies (called the "bog bodies") have been found in peat bogs throughout Denmark, Ireland, England, and other parts of northwestern Europe. The existence of the rope attached to Tollund Man's neck gave researchers some solid evidence that bog bodies were purposely killed, probably either as human sacrifices or as executed criminals.

• His last meal was entirely vegetarian: barley, flaxseed, and other grains, leading researchers to believe the last thing he ate was some kind of porridge.

• Peat bogs only preserve bodies buried during cool weather. That—and the fact that most Iron Age people usually ate porridge or gruel when livestock and other fresh food were scarce—tell us that Tollund Man was likely killed in the winter or early spring.

\*　　\*　　\*

## FOUR MORE MUMMY FACTS

**1.** The word "mummy" comes from the Arabic term *mumiyah*, meaning "embalmed body."

**2.** The ancient Egyptians didn't just mummify people—cat, ram, and even alligator mummies have been found in various tombs.

**3.** The world's oldest mummy comes from an area of Libya called Uan Muhuggiag. In 1958, scientists found the body of a boy who probably lived about 5,500 years ago.

**4.** It took 70 days to make an Egyptian mummy. Priests removed all the internal organs except the heart, which the Egyptians thought housed a person's intelligence and personality. Then they covered the body with salt and let it sit until all the moisture was removed. They added false eyes, puffed out any sunken-in parts with linen, covered the body with resin, and then wrapped it in a shroud.

# SWEET STARTS

*Some familiar candy brands have been in production for more
than a century, while some others reach back even further.
How did these sweet treats get their start? We've
got their sugar-coated beginnings right here.*

## 1. NECCO WAFERS
The oldest mass-produced candy brand in the United States,
NECCO wafers got their start in 1847 when Oliver Chase, a
candy-making English immigrant, went into business selling the
wafers with his brother Silas. (Chase also invented the machine
the wafers were stamped out on.) Their company became the basis
for the New England Confectionery Company, which rebranded
the candy as NECCO Wafers around 1910 or 1912.

## 2. SQUIRREL NUT CHEWS
Adults today might be more familiar with Squirrel Nut Zippers as
an eclectic rock band active in the 1990s, but the candies the band
took their name from reach back a full century earlier to 1890,
when the first of the excessively chewy taffy candies known as
Squirrel Nut Chews rolled off the line of the Austin T. Merrill
Company in Massachusetts. The "zippers" candy arrived in the
1920s. Since 2004, the candies have been made by NECCO.

## 3. HERSHEY'S CHOCOLATE BAR
The quintessential American chocolate bar got its start in 1900
when Milton Hershey perfected a formula to mass-produce milk
chocolate, which until that time had been a confection limited
primarily to the upper classes. The bar's widespread success helped
Hershey to found what is now the Milton Hershey School, in
1909, which provides education for disadvantaged children.

## 4. TOBLERONE
This famously triangular bar of Swiss chocolate with nougat, almonds, and honey got its shape and name (a combination of the
last name of inventor Theodor Tobler and *torrone*, the Italian word
for "nougat") in 1908. Given the image of the Matterhorn on the
wrapper, you may be forgiven for assuming the triangular shape is a

---

**There are 261 "dry" counties (which prohibit the sale of alcohol) in 13 states.**

tribute to the Alps, but the company Web site maintains the shape was actually inspired by "a red and cream-frilled line of dancers at the Folies Bergères in Paris, forming a shapely pyramid at the end of a show."

## 5. GOOGOO CLUSTERS
A regional favorite from Nashville, Tennessee, where it was invented in 1912, this circular candy bar's claim to fame is that it was the first "combination" candy bar—that is, the first made with more than one type of candy (in this case marshmallow, caramel, and roasted peanuts), all covered in milk chocolate. In the 1930s, the Standard Candy Company advertised the GooGoo Cluster as "a nourishing lunch for a nickel!"—a claim that they'd be unlikely to get away with today.

## 6. MARY JANE
These pocket-sized taffies made from molasses and peanut butter were named for the aunt of Charles N. Miller, who invented the candy in 1914 and inherited the candy company his father had founded in a house originally belonging to Paul Revere. Mary Janes eventually became so popular that the Miller Company stopped making other candies to focus on that brand alone. At the moment, however, the candy is being made by NECCO.

## 7. CLARK BAR
This crispy, peanuty chocolate bar was the signature bar of the D. L. Clark candy company, named for Irish immigrant David Clark, and founded in what is now the north side of Pittsburgh in the early 1900s. The Clark Bar came into existence in time to become a favorite for U.S. soldiers fighting in World War I, and its popularity carried over after the boys came home. Like so many early candy favorites, this one is also currently produced by NECCO.

## 8. BABY RUTH
A popular misconception about this chocolate-covered bar of caramel and peanuts, created in 1920, is that it was named for baseball player Babe Ruth. While disputed, it has never been proven false. But Baby Ruth candy maker Curtiss Candy Company sued another candy maker who put out a "Babe Ruth Home Run Bar," on the grounds that the candy names were too similar. The

In 2007, China became the world's largest salt producer, surpassing the U.S.

official line from Curtiss Candy, echoed to this day from contemporary producer Nestle, is that the bar is named after Ruth Cleveland, daughter of U.S. president Grover Cleveland. Some sources allege that Curtiss Company made up the Ruth Cleveland story in order to win the lawsuit and that it was actually named for the baseball player. Skeptics note that "Baby Ruth" died in 1904—16 years before the creation of the candy bar.

### 9. MOUNDS
The Mounds bar was created in 1920 by the Peter Paul Candy Manufacturing Company and was originally a single bar of chocolate-covered coconut instead of the current two smaller bars. Although the Peter Paul Company would later produce a number of coconut-based treats (including Almond Joy), during World War II the company faced severe coconut shortages. Rather than ration its top product, the company temporarily discontinued several other candy brands to ensure Mounds would stay in production.

### 10. MILKY WAY
Mars, Inc., one of the largest privately held companies in America, got its start with this candy bar in 1923, when candy maker Forrest Mars developed the candy to approximate the taste of a malted milk drink in chocolate bar form. In 1926, the bar was offered in chocolate and vanilla flavors, with the vanilla version becoming the Forever Yours bar for over fifty years before becoming the Milky Way Dark bar (now Milky Way Midnight).

\*    \*    \*

### BEST-SELLING CANDY BY COUNTRY
**1.** United States: M&M's
**2.** Australia and United Kingdom: Cadbury Dairy Milk bar
**3.** Germany: Milka milk chocolate bar
**4.** Brazil: Trident chewing gum
**5.** Japan: Meiji chocolate bar
**6.** France: Hollywood chewing gum
**7.** Russia: Orbit chewing gum
**8.** Mexico: Trident chewing gum
**9.** Thailand: Halls cough drops

---

In 1977, the Supreme Court ruled it was unconstitutional to ban lawyers from advertising.

# GOING GLOBAL

*The United States consisted of a measly 17 states before it started gobbling up real estate in 1803. Five of the acquisitions became a part of the union; the last didn't work out so well.*

## 1. THE LOUISIANA PURCHASE (1803)

Napoléon Bonaparte's big plans for building his empire included North America. New Orleans, as the gateway to the Mississippi River with its vast sources food and trade, was one of his key acquisitions. He planned to open trade with Hispaniola, the Caribbean island that's now made up of Haiti and the Dominican Republic, but his hopes were dashed when Haitian slaves rebelled and seized power in 1801. Facing war with Great Britain in Europe, Napoléon needed troops and money more than he needed possessions in North America, so he offered to sell Louisiana to the United States.

**That's Unconstitutional!** President Thomas Jefferson had his hopes, too: he wanted the French off the continent. In 1803, he sent future president James Monroe and Robert R. Livingston to Paris to negotiate the purchase of New Orleans and West Florida, or, failing that, at least a guarantee of free navigation on the Mississippi. Americans had been using the port of New Orleans for exporting flour, cotton, pork, and other products, but they were allowed to do so only under treaty agreement. Napoléon surprised the envoys by offering to sell the entire territory. Nothing in the Constitution empowered the federal government to acquire new territories, but Jefferson said the practical benefits—getting rid of the French—outweighed the silence of the Constitution. Congress ratified the agreement on October 20, 1803. A month later, France turned Louisiana over to the United States.

**The Deal of the Century.** The selling price of $15 million for 828,800 square miles of land included nearly $4 million in reparation payments for American claims against the French. In one stroke, the United States doubled its size; the new territory encompassed all or part of 15 present-day states, and included small parts of Alberta and Saskatchewan that were later traded to

---

In medieval Europe, sugar was so rare that it was kept under lock and key.

Great Britain. Americans had little idea of the richness of the vast territory purchased by Jefferson until the Lewis and Clark expedition returned to St. Louis in 1806 after three years in the West. According to the 1810 census, only 97,000 Americans occupied the entire area, and most of them lived along the Mississippi.

## 2. FLORIDA (1819)

At the end of the American Revolution, Britain signed over the colonies of East and West Florida to Spain. American settlers ignored the change of ownership, continued to immigrate to West Florida, and in 1810 declared independence from Spain. President James Madison, aware that Spain had been weakened by war, claimed that West Florida was part of the 1803 Louisiana Purchase. Secretary of State James Monroe began negotiations for all of Florida with Spanish foreign minister Luis de Onis in 1815. When Monroe became president in 1817, he made John Quincy Adams secretary of state, and handed over the Florida negotiations to him.

**Heading South.** The situation intensified in 1818 when General Andrew Jackson invaded West Florida in a raid against outlaws, runaway slaves, and Seminole Indians from East Florida. Jackson seized Spanish forts at Pensacola and St. Marks and executed two British citizens convicted of aiding the Seminoles. Monroe praised Jackson's action and cited the necessity of restraining the Seminoles and fugitive slaves because Spain had failed to protect American settlers.

**The Final Frontier.** Jackson's military action paved the way for Adams to demand that Spain either control the inhabitants of East Florida or give it up, along with West Florida. In the ensuing agreement, all of Florida was ceded to America in exchange for $5 million in compensation for damages supposedly inflicted by American citizens rebelling against Spain. Under the Adams-Onis Treaty of 1819, Spain and the United States also defined the western limits of the Louisiana Purchase, Spain gave up its claims to the Pacific Northwest, and the United States recognized Spanish sovereignty in present-day Texas and all the land to the west of the Louisiana Purchase except the Oregon country. The United States now controlled the entire East Coast from Maine to Florida and all of the Gulf of Mexico from the tip of Florida to the Sabine River, the eastern boundary of Spanish Texas.

## 3. THE TREATY OF GUADALUPE HIDALGO (1848)

Mexico had invited Anglo-Americans to populate the wide-open spaces of its northern frontier in Mexican Texas in the early 1820s. The immigrants soon became the majority and in 1836 Texas declared its independence from Mexico, becoming the Republic of Texas. The annexation of Texas in 1845 brought on the Mexican-American War, but other factors had contributed to strained relations. Americans had long-standing property and chattel claims against Mexico, and the U.S. government was looking for ways— peaceful or otherwise—to infiltrate and acquire California.

**An Offer They Couldn't Refuse.** After the annexation of Texas, President James K. Polk sent John Slidell to Mexico with an offer to assume American claims in exchange for a boundary adjustment and the acquisition of New Mexico (which at the time included present-day Arizona) and California. When the offer was refused, the United States officially declared war on Mexico in May 1846, and 16 months later, General Winfield Scott entered Mexico City and remained there with his army until the signing of the treaty.

**Nicholas Who?** You've probably never heard of Nicholas Trist. Aside from being chief clerk in the State Department, he had no other diplomatic credentials. He'd accompanied General Scott into Mexico as President Polk's representative and Scott's political adviser. Once there, he began negotiating with a special commission that represented Mexico's collapsed government. Polk wanted to hold the negotiations in Washington with State Department diplomats, so he recalled Trist. It took six weeks for the president's message to arrive. Deciding that the president didn't understand conditions in Mexico, Trist ignored the order and continued to negotiate.

**Have I Got a Deal for You, Mr. President!** Trist held the negotiations in the city of Guadalupe Hidalgo, where the Mexican government had fled as Scott's army advanced. Trist forwarded a copy of the treaty to Washington, forcing Polk to accept or reject his

In 1907, a German apothecary used camera-carrying pigeons for aerial photography.

extraordinary diplomatic work. Polk sent the treaty to the U.S. Senate for ratification, and it passed—but only after a clause guaranteeing the protection of Mexican land grants was deleted. The Mexican commission accepted the alteration and several other small modifications.

**Another Deal of the Century.** Trist's handiwork, for which he deserves most of the credit, ceded 525,000 square miles of Mexican territory to the United States in exchange for $15 million. The treaty also wiped out any claims by Mexico for Texas, which involved another 389,122 square miles. Trist's only concession was that the United States would assume responsibility for $3.25 million in debts and claims by Americans against Mexico. The treaty confirmed the southern boundary of Texas and regions now made up of California, Nevada, Utah, most of Arizona and New Mexico, and parts of Colorado and Wyoming.

*For the rest of the story, see page 390.*

\*       \*       \*

## PAYING THE PRICE FOR WAR

• Uncle John's review of casualties of World War I–"the war to end all wars," as it was called—reveals some surprising data.

• The conflict cost France 11 percent of its population killed or wounded compared to 9 percent of Germany's citizens and 8 percent of Britain's.

• For the United States, less that 1 percent (.37%) of its population was injured or perished in the war.

• Of all American soldiers serving in Europe during World War II, one out of every 10 contracted a sexually transmitted disease before returning home.

# LESSONS IN LARCENY

*Whether it's gold, jewels, painted masterpieces, or even
dead bodies—anything that's worth something is fair
game to miscreants with larceny in their hearts.*

## LESSON #1: ANYONE CAN BE TEMPTED
### Stealing the Crown Jewels (1303)

England's crown jewels were stolen from a literal fortress: a thick stone vault in Westminster Abbey, protected by heavy, iron-bound doors and guarded by the Church of England. When the robbers broke in, they found cash; gold crowns encrusted with pearls, sapphires, and rubies; fabulous rings; jewel-encrusted crosses and swords; and a collection of diamonds and precious stones. There were vessels, knives, and forks of gold and silver; it was a haul worth a fortune.

**Timing Is Almost Everything.** The robbery had been carefully timed for late April,1303, while England's wealthy and ambitious monarch, Edward I (the villain from *Braveheart*), was away waging war on Scotland. Fast-growing hemp had been planted early in the spring in the abbey's cemetery so that thick, tall plants concealed the tools and work leading up to the break-in. When Edward heard news of the theft in June, he was furious. He needed the money from his treasury if he was going to continue to torment the Scots. He ordered an immediate investigation.

**Finding Stolen Treasure.** The theft had been a success, but trying to fence the royal loot was a bust. Priceless objects kept turning up in pawnshops, houses of prostitution, and even the river Thames. By October, the valuables were traced back to an audacious ring of thieves whose mastermind was a butter, cheese, and wool merchant named Richard of Pudlicott.

**Is Nothing Sacred?** Pudlicott was a charmer who'd recruited plenty of help for his theft—goldsmiths, the palace's keeper of the gate, local prostitutes, and even some of the Benedictine monks who lived in the abbey: they'd helped with access, the transport of the treasure, and had even planted the hemp to help hide evi-

---

...made with chickpea flour, water, olive oil, salt, and pepper.

dence of the burglary. Dozens of people were arrested, including 40 monks who ended up being held in the Tower of London for two years. The crown jewels were moved away from Westminster Abbey to the Tower of London. Pudlicott was hanged, his body flayed, and his skin hung on the door of Westminster Abbey—perhaps as a warning to the monks that it was better to be pious rather than larcenous.

## LESSON #2: IT HELPS TO WEAR A DISGUISE
### The West's First Stagecoach Robbery (1856)

After gold was discovered at Sutter's Mill in California in 1848, some stagecoaches started carrying gold shipments along with their passengers. They traveled through the most remote country-side with no way to communicate for help, so it's surprising that it took eight years for someone—in this case one Tom Hodges, a.k.a. Tom Bell—to get the bright idea to rob one.

**Small-Time Crooks.** Born in Tennessee, Bell came to the gold-fields to strike it rich, but had no luck in that department, so he turned to petty theft and was caught. Bell escaped from prison in 1854 along with the handful of men who would form his gang. Their crime spree (which included robbing a vegetable delivery wagon) wasn't exactly making them rich, so when one of Bell's spies learned that Sam Langston's Express Company stagecoach was carrying a strongbox containing about $100,000 in gold dust, Bell decided to go after it.

**The Hold-Up Artists Get Held Up.** Late in the afternoon of August 12, Bell's gang waylaid the stagecoach near Marysville, California, but everything went wrong from there. The plan had been to surround the stagecoach, but while Bell and two of his pals came up on one side, the three other members of the gang were still far back down the trail. The stagecoach guard—with no guns at his back—fired point-blank at the bandits, and the passengers who were carrying guns joined in. The gang fell back and the stagecoach took off amid a hail of gunfire from both sides.

**Who Was That Unmasked Man?** Bell's gang never did get the gold, and although they might have improved at robbery, they never got the chance. A female passenger inside the stagecoach died of gunshot wounds, and no one had any doubt about the identity of her killers. Bell's disfigured face (he had a smashed-in nose from a bar fight) made him easy to recognize—and he and his gang had made the mistake of not wearing masks. By September, an intensive manhunt was in progress. One of the captured gang members gave Bell's hiding place away and in early October, Bell was caught and hanged from a spruce tree. His legacy and his pioneering enterprise of robbing stagecoaches lived on for another 60 years in the more capable hands of bandits like Jesse James, "Rattlesnake Dick" Bartar, and the infamous Black Bart.

\*　　\*　　\*

## PATENT PHILOSOPHY

Patents have been around since 15th-century Italy, when Venetian officials required that inventions be registered with the government. But before 1790, inventors didn't automatically own their creations. Anything they came up with belonged to their respective governments, which could grant ownership as it saw fit.

By signing into law Article 1, Section 8 of the U.S. Constitution, George Washington changed that and established the modern patent system. The law said: "Congress shall have the power...to promote the progress of science and useful arts by securing for limited times to authors and inventors the exclusive right to their respective writings and discoveries." Thus, Washington laid the foundation for the patent system we have today: inventors can register their creations (new or significantly improved products, processes, or designs) with the Patent and Trademark Office just outside of Washington, D.C., and receive a certificate identifying them as the first to come up with the invention. But patents always run out after a set period of time. Why? The government wants to prevent anyone from monopolizing a particular market forever.

### Two Milestones in Patent History

**1.** First American patent issued: In 1790, Vermont's Samuel Hopkins received a patent for a new way of making potash (a type of ash used to make soap, glass, and gunpowder).
**2.** Only U.S. president to get a patent: In 1849, Abraham Lincoln patented a part to help boats avoid getting stuck in shallow water.

# TO HILL AND BACK

*There always seems to be a perceived advantage to holding
the high ground in a battle, even though most famous hills
were little more than pimples on the landscape—and
most happened into history not because they were
targeted but just because they were there.*

## 1. BUNKER HILL: JUNE 17, 1775

Charleston, Massachusetts, rested on a small peninsula
jutting into the Charles River that was approached by a narrow
neck of land and that lay directly across from British-held Boston.
From there, colonists had placed Boston under siege; General
Thomas Gage, commander in chief of the British forces, planned
to assemble a garrison, cross the river, and drive the colonists off
the Charleston peninsula. He began the affair at daybreak with a
bombardment from shore and floating batteries, followed by 28
barges moving out from Boston with 2,500 British soldiers.

The grassy battlefield was about a mile long and half a mile
wide. The colonists made the mistake of fortifying Breed's Hill
instead of the higher Bunker Hill, which would have been a better
defensive position. (It might be they chose the hill closest in
range to Boston.) The British drove the colonists from Breed's Hill
and pursued them to Bunker Hill. During the last-ditch stand on
Bunker Hill, Continental army general Israel Putnam reportedly
gave the order, "Don't fire until you see the whites of their eyes,"
although some claim the order came from Colonel William
Prescott. The engagement should have been called the Battle of
Breed's Hill, which was where the heaviest fighting occurred. The
Americans succeeded in driving the British back on their first two
charges. During the third charge, they continued to fight even
after running out of ammunition. The British had to fight for
every inch of ground and suffered far greater casualties than the
Americans—226 killed and 928 wounded, or about 45 percent of
the men engaged. On the other hand, American casualties—mostly incurred while in retreat—were 139 killed, 278 wounded, and
36 missing. Although the British took possession of Charleston,
the aftermath of the battle created a groundswell of support for the

colonists and also led them to believe victory against the British was possible.

## 2. HENRY HOUSE HILL: JULY 21, 1861

Judith Henry, an 85-year-old widow, lived with her two sons on a quiet hill near the Warrenton Turnpike (now U.S. Route 29), which ran east across the meadows of Bull Run to Centreville, Virginia. When fighting erupted on July 21, she refused to leave her home, which by 2:00 p.m. stood squarely in the center of the First Battle of Bull Run. As the brigades of Confederate generals Thomas J. Jackson and Barnard E. Bee defended the hill, Union troops charged up the northern slope. It was during this action that Bee gave Jackson the nickname "Stonewall" because the latter's brigade stood stalwart in the battle "like a stone wall." The Confederates won the fight on Henry House Hill, but the widow who lived there heard no more after a Union projectile smashed into her bedroom and took her life.

This would not be the last time Henry House Hill came under fire. Jackson returned to Bull Run on August 29–30, 1862, passed by the hill, and positioned his men along an unfinished railroad cut. This brought on the Second Battle of Bull Run. On August 30, more than 100,000 Confederate and Union troops fought over and around the hill, further damaging the dwelling on Henry House Hill. The house and hill are now part of the Manassas National Battlefield Park.

## 3. CHAMPION HILL: MAY 16, 1863

Confederate general Joseph E. Johnston reached Jackson, Mississippi, on May 13 and on the following day ordered Lieutenant General John C. Pemberton, who was in nearby Vicksburg, to attack the rear of Union general Ulysses S. Grant's army. Before Pemberton arrived, Grant defeated Johnston and began moving toward Vicksburg. Pemberton, with 22,000 men, wasted two days before marching and encountered 29,000 troops from Grant's army posted on and around 75-foot-high Champion Hill, midway between Jackson and Vicksburg. The hill changed hands several times in the fighting, partly because officers on both sides did not expect an engagement and failed to follow orders promptly.

Major S. H. M. Byers of the Fifth Iowa Infantry wrote: "Grant's

...It honors Native Americans and promotes their rights.

crown of immortality was won, and the jewel that shone most brightly in it was set there by the blood of the men of Champion Hills...six thousand blue- and gray-coated men were lying there in the woods, dead or wounded, when the last gun of Champion Hills was fired." In 2007, the owners of the land granted the Civil War Preservation Trust a 147-acre easement to the family farm because of the overall role the battle played in the Vicksburg Campaign.

## 4. CEMETERY HILL: JULY 1–3, 1863

In the years before the Civil War, Cemetery Hill in Gettysburg, Pennsylvania, was a serene burial ground. On July 1, 1863, everything changed when fighting erupted on the Chambersburg Pike east of Gettysburg. By 10:00 a.m., the main Union army under Major General George G. Meade approached from the south. General Robert E. Lee put more Confederate troops on the road, and by afternoon Lieutenant General Richard Ewell's Second Corps arrived north of town. As fighting intensified, Meade began funneling troops onto Cemetery Hill, which stretched south from Gettysburg and ran for two miles in a nearly straight line down Cemetery Ridge. With hills guarding either flank, Meade seized the best defensive position; his action left Lee with Seminary Ridge, a less advantageous position more than a mile from Cemetery Hill.

Lee's army assaulted Meade's flanks for two days, and on the third day Lieutenant General James Longstreet sent 15,000 Confederates up a long, sloping incline in a desperate assault known as "Pickett's Charge." However, once the Union forces moved onto Cemetery Hill and Meade chose to fight defensively, Lee lost any chance of winning. More than 163,000 men fought at Gettysburg, and more than 51,000 were killed, wounded, or captured.

The following November, President Lincoln delivered his famous Gettysburg Address to dedicate the battlefield as the Gettysburg National Cemetery. Volunteers began to dig up the bodies of more than 3,500 soldiers from shallow battlefield graves to rebury their remains in the new cemetery.

*You may continue your climb of historic hills on page 303*

# MOVIE MILESTONES

*The first movie camera was patented in the late 1800s, and motion pictures have been dazzling us ever since. Here are 14 firsts in filmmaking.*

**1. First Movie Shown to a Paying Audience:** *Young Griffo v. Battling Charles Barnett* (1895)
**Fact:** It lasted four minutes and was of a real boxing match filmed on the roof of Madison Square Garden.

**2. First Striptease Caught on Film:** *Le Coucher de la Marie* (*Bedtime for the Bride*) (1896)
**Fact:** This French movie by Eugéne Pirou was also one of the first pornographic films ever made.

**3. First Censored Movie:** *Fatima's Coochie Coochie Dance* (1896)
**Fact:** Fatima was a well-known belly dancer of the time whose gyrating hips were covered up with a white grid in this short film.

**4. First Science-Fiction Film:** *Le Voyage Dans la Lune* (*A Trip to the Moon*) (1902)
**Fact:** This 14-minute film was loosely based on two novels: *From the Earth to the Moon* by Jules Verne, and *The First Men in the Moon* by H. G. Wells.

**5. First Feature-Length Film:** *The Story of the Kelly Gang* (1906)
**Fact:** Made in Australia, this movie tells the story of the outlaw folk hero Ned Kelly, who was captured and hanged by Australian authorities in 1880. It was originally 70 minutes long, but only about 17 minutes still exist today.

**6. First Movie Reviewed by the *New York Times*:** *Pippa Passes* (also called *The Song of Conscience*) (1909)
**Fact:** The film was based on Robert Browning's 1841 poem of the same title.

**7. First Film by an African American Director:** *The Homesteader* (1919)

---

April 30, 1900: Engineer Casey Jones died in the *Cannonball Express* train wreck.

**Fact:** Oscar Micheaux wrote, directed, and produced this movie about a doomed interracial romance at a time when it was illegal in most states for blacks and whites to marry.

**8. First 3-D movie:** *The Power of Love* (1922)
**Fact:** All copies of this movie have been lost to time.

**9. First Movie to Include a Swear Word:** *The Big Parade* (1925)
**Fact:** It was a silent movie—the word "damn" appeared on a dialogue card.

**10. First Feature-Length Talkie:** *The Jazz Singer* (1927)
**Fact:** Originally, the film was going to have only synchronized singing, not talking. But star Al Jolson ad-libbed the line "Wait a minute, wait a minute. You ain't heard nothing yet." The director liked it and left it in. Good thing—it appears as #71 on the American Film Institute's list of the 100 greatest movie quotes.

**11. First Commercially Successful Feature-Length Animated Film:** *Snow White and the Seven Dwarfs* (1937)
**Fact:** In the proposal for the film, writers suggested 50 names for the dwarfs. Some that weren't used: Blabby, Gabby, Gloomy, Gaspy, Hoppy, Hotsy, Jaunty, Nifty, and Shifty.

**12. First (and Only) X-rated Movie to Win the Best Picture Oscar:** *Midnight Cowboy* (1969)
**Fact:** This movie also includes the first use of the word "scuzzy" on film. (Its rating was later changed to R.)

**13. First Movie to Show an Actor on the Toilet:** *Catch-22* (1970)
**Fact:** Actors Martin Balsam and Anthony Perkins appear in the scene. In 1960, the first movie to include a shot of a toilet flushing was *Psycho*...which also starred Balsam and Perkins.

**14. First Movie Directed by a Woman to Win the Best Picture Oscar:** *The Hurt Locker* (2008)
**Fact:** To date, Kathryn Bigelow's story of the Iraq War is the lowest-grossing Best Picture winner ever.

---

In 1920, Joe Cartledge marketed the jockstrap (athletic supporter) under the name Protex.

# THE WORLD'S OTHER OLDEST PROFESSION

*We're talking about warfare. From history's earliest days, men have been driven to find ever more effective means of killing each other.*

The inventions that have shaped the way men go to war fall into three major categories: projectiles, fire, and locomotion. Here's how the earliest weapons got their start.

## PROJECTILES: TAKE THAT!

Throwing stuff dates back to the dawn of time. Even primates have been known to throw feces at their foes. Poop may be unpleasant and it may make a statement, but it's usually not fatal. It took the human brain to graduate to throwing things that could actually cause some damage. And as a bonus, sticks and stones were even more readily available than dung.

## 1. SLINGS

First came the sling, then came the slingshot. Nobody knows who invented the sling, but it was used practically everywhere throughout antiquity, in both the Old World and the New World, and is still in use today.

Most everyone knows the biblical story of David and Goliath. The young shepherd David, armed with nothing but his skill and his trusty slingshot, kills the hulking giant Goliath. But the weapon used by the future king of Israel wasn't a slingshot—it was a sling.

In its most basic form, a sling is composed of a length of string holding a stone. The string is then slung and when the projectile is released, it carries far more force than if it were merely thrown by hand. In this instance, the stone and string are thrown together. Eventually, someone came up with the idea of putting a leather pouch in the middle of the string to hold the stone. After the stone was thrown, the thrower is still in possession of his trusty sling and can reload quickly.

---

**Aunt Jemima pancake flour was the first ready-mix food to be sold commercially (1889).**

## 2. SLINGSHOTS

In contrast, the Dennis the Menace–type Y-shaped slingshot (which requires a string made of elastic material) came into widespread use only after the invention of vulcanized rubber. The simplest slingshots are made from forked sections of tree branches and the rubber strings are most commonly made from the inner tubes of used tires.

The low-tech gadget is still very much in use today. Survivalists and campers love the fact that it can be fashioned from simple materials easily found in the wild (well, maybe not the inner tubes). Guerrilla fighters with few resources at their disposal can inflict serious damage on far more technically advanced enemy forces with slingshots. The Irish Republican Army and Palestinian rebels have used them effectively, and it's been reported that Saddam Hussein, when faced with the likelihood of a U.S. invasion, released a propaganda video instructing his people on how to make and use a humble slingshot to defend themselves.

## 3. BOWS AND ARROWS

Scientists believe that bows and arrows date back to the middle of the Stone Age, more than 60,000 years ago. The mummified remains of a man with an arrow point shot through his lungs were found in Europe and dated to 3300 BC.

It's easy to see how the bow and arrow was an improvement over the sling—the bow is easier to aim and an arrow can inflict far greater damage. At its most basic, a bow is made of a bent (bowed) piece of wood with a taut string attached to either end. The first arrows were probably made from fire-dipped sharpened sticks. Later, animal bones and flint-tipped points were used. Ancient versions of flint points date as far back as 16,000 BC, during the Paleolithic period.

## 4. CROSSBOWS

The horizontally held crossbow, which the Chinese came up with more than 2,000 years ago, was a vast improvement over the simple bow. The difference between the two is the use of a crosspiece or stock, which does the work of pulling and holding the string; it provides more tension, so the arrow can travel a greater distance. A well-made crossbow was powerful enough to penetrate armor.

The crossbow came to Europe with the returning crusaders. In 1066, William the Conqueror brought it to England. In 1199, Richard the Lionhearted died of gangrene as a result of being shot by a crossbow bolt in France.

Because the crossbow required relatively less skill and strength to use than other weapons, Pope Innocent II banned it in 1139, calling it an "inhumane weapon" against Christians—though infidels, undoubtedly, were another matter. The ban did little to change things; the crossbow remained in use for several more centuries. Seventeenth-century improvements included a repeating crossbow, which could shoot several arrows in succession. Eventually, the crossbow was eclipsed by the invention of gunpowder.

## 5. CATAPULTS

A catapult is any kind of machine that causes a projectile to travel a great distance. The term covers a wide range of weapons—from the humble slingshot to the sophisticated assemblies that launch planes off the decks of aircraft carriers.

The catapult emerged in China around the third or fourth century BC as an offshoot of the crossbow. The best-known type of catapult is the trebuchet, a machine that uses a counterweight to hurl large projectiles over long distances. A popular weapon during the Middle Ages, it was used during sieges of well-fortified and previously impenetrable castles. In a hint of the germ warfare that was to come centuries later, catapult-wielding attackers liked to lob diseased corpses over castle walls—the more disgusting and infectious, the better—as well as pots of burning pitch. Some historians believe that it was the use of the catapult that signaled the end of medieval castles and fortresses made of stone.

*For the rest of the story about inventions that shaped warfare, go to page 318.*

\*        \*        \*

"My toughest fight was with my first wife."

—**Muhammad Ali**

---

**Noah Webster published the first American dictionary in 1828.**

# FIRSTS ON THE FIRST

*Uncle John founded the Bathroom Readers' Institute
on April . Here are some more historical events
that took place on the first of the month.*

## JANUARY 1

**404:** Rome held its last official gladiator battle.

**1958:** Twenty-year-old San Quentin inmate Merle Haggard heard Johnny Cash's first-ever prison concert and decided to become a musician.

**1965:** Cigarette packages had to carry health warning labels for the first time.

**1995:** The last *Far Side* cartoon by Gary Larson was published after it had been syndicated for 15 years.

## FEBRUARY 1

**1790:** The Supreme Court met for the first time in New York City.

**1884:** Great Britain's Philological Society published the first portion of the *Oxford English Dictionary*—it was just 32 pages long.

**1887:** Prohibitionist Harvey Wilcox registered the town of Hollywood with the recorder's office in Los Angeles. Wilcox named the area after the summer home of a friend, and it was originally supposed to be place for Christians to live peaceful, moral lives.

**1972:** Hewlett-Packard released the first scientific calculator (the HP-35)—it took three AA batteries, measured 3.1" x 5.8" x 1.4", and cost $395.

## MARCH 1

**1692:** The witch trials began in Salem, Massachusetts.

**1790:** The United States authorized its first census.

**1937:** Connecticut became the first state to issue permanent automobile licenses.

**1961:** President John F. Kennedy established the Peace Corps.

---

**November 24, 1859: Charles Darwin published *On the Origin of Species*.**

## APRIL 1

**1891:** The Wrigley Company sold its first products: soap and baking powder. (The company focused on gum the next year.)

**1970:** John Lennon and Yoko Ono sent an April Fool's press release announcing they'd both be having sex-change operations.

**1981:** The USSR used daylight saving time for the first time.

**2002:** The Association of Professional Animal Waste Specialists began International Pooper Scooper Week as a way to educate dog owners about the importance of cleaning up after their pets.

## MAY 1

**1873:** The United States issued its first postcard.

**1927:** Cooked airline meals debuted on an Imperial Airlines flight from London to Paris.

**1940:** The Japanese government canceled the Summer Olympics in Tokyo over concerns the games would distract from its military goals in World War II.

**1952:** New York City inventor George Lerner patented Mr. Potato Head as a cereal box prize.

## JUNE 1

**1869:** Thomas Edison patented the first electronic voting machine.

**1942:** The Polish underground newspaper *Liberty Brigrade* published the first news story exposing the Nazi death camps.

**1969:** Canada banned tobacco advertising on radio and TV.

**1974:** Dr. Henry Heimlich first described the "Heimlich maneuver" for rescuing choking victims in the *Journal of Emergency Medicine*.

## JULY 1

**1847:** The United States put its first two postage stamps on sale: the 5¢ Franklin and the 10¢ Washington.

**1963:** The United States got five-digit ZIP codes.

**1979:** Sony introduced the Walkman.

**2005:** Ford produced its last Thunderbird.

There is one chicken for every human being on earth.

## AUGUST 1

**1774:** British clergyman Joseph Priestley discovered oxygen, which he called "dephlogisticated air."

**1944:** Anne Frank made the last entry in her diary. The 15-year-old was arrested three days later and sent to a Nazi concentration camp, where she later died.

**1976:** Actress Elizabeth Taylor divorced Richard Burton...again. It was her fifth divorce.

**1995:** Lingerie giant Victoria's Secret held its first fashion show in New York City at the Plaza Hotel.

## SEPTEMBER 1

**1689:** The Russian government started taxing men who wanted to keep their beards in an effort to encourage clean-shaven faces as a way to modernize the country.

**1878:** Alexander Graham Bell recruited Emma Nutt to become the world's first female telephone operator at a Boston dispatch company; she was paid $10 a month for 54-hour workweeks.

**1980:** Canadian cancer victim Terry Fox's Marathon of Hope ended in Thunder Bay, Ontario. He raised $1.7 million for cancer research.

**1998:** Air bags became mandatory on all vehicles sold in the United States.

## OCTOBER 1

**1949:** China became a communist country under the rule of revolutionary Mao Zedong.

**1957:** "In God We Trust" appeared on American currency.

**1962:** Comedian Johnny Carson took over hosting *The Tonight Show* from Jack Paar.

**1971:** Walt Disney World opened outside Orlando, Florida.

## NOVEMBER 1

**1512:** The public saw Michelangelo's paintings on the ceiling of the Sistine Chapel in Italy's Vatican City for the first time.

**1896:** *National Geographic* published its first picture of an African woman with bare breasts.

---

Dutchman Cornelius Drebbel invented the first navigable submarine in 1620.

**1952:** The United States detonated a hydrogen bomb at Eniwetok Atoll in the Pacific Ocean. It was the world's first thermonuclear weapon.

**1968:** The Motion Picture Association of America introduced its first rating system for films: G (general audiences), M (mature audiences), R (no one younger than 17 admitted without an adult), and X (no one under 17 admitted at all).

## DECEMBER 1

**1913:** Henry Ford installed the first assembly line for mass-producing cars. Cars used to take more than 12 hours to build, but with the assembly line, a car could be built in just two and a half hours.

**1952:** The *New York Daily News* ran a front-page story called "Ex-GI Becomes Blonde Beauty" about the first widely known person to have gender reassignment surgery. New York–born George (Christine) William Jorgensen Jr. went to Denmark and got permission from the Danish minister of justice to be castrated.

**1955:** Rosa Parks, a seamstress and civil-rights activist, refused to give up her seat to a white man on a bus in Montgomery, Alabama, sparking a yearlong boycott that led the Supreme Court to declare that segregating buses by race was unconstitutional.

**1981:** The U.S. Center for Disease Control and Prevention officially recognized AIDS as a disease.

\*　　　\*　　　\*

## BENJAMIN FRANKLIN'S EPITAPH

"The body of Benjamin Franklin, printer (like the cover of an old book, its contents worn out, and stript of its lettering and gilding) lies here, food for worms. Yet the work itself shall not be lost, for it will, as he believed, appear once more. In a new and more beautiful edition, corrected and amended by its Author."

The movie *Pretty Woman* was almost called $3,000—the title of the original script.

# SNAPSHOTS OF HISTORY

*Our look at memory-making images continues. Part one is on page 160.*

## 1. WACKY GENIUS, PRINCETON, NEW JERSEY, MARCH 14, 1951

We all know that Albert Einstein's brain was preserved after his death. Fortunately, his tongue was preserved, too—on film—and made him everyone's favorite genius. The photo was taken on the campus of Princeton University as the famed physicist was celebrating his 72nd birthday. Asked to smile for the umpteenth time, he stuck out his tongue instead and photographer Arthur Sasse captured it in full extension.

Einstein was celebrated for the wild tangle of his long hair and his expressive face, or as one put it, "a cartoonist's dream come true." In fact, the scientist became the model of the mad scientist (or absentminded professor) as depicted in the film *Back to the Future*. But that pointed tongue, at full extension, became the iconic poster of countless college dorm rooms. We can't be sure, but perhaps it was inspiration for the rock group Kiss and bass guitarist Gene Simmons, whose "ten-foot tongue seen around the world" is the group's enduring symbol.

## 2. SEVEN-YEAR ITCH, NEW YORK CITY, 1955

Another photo to become a cultural icon is a picture snapped in the 1950s of Hollywood vixen Marilyn Monroe. Photographer Bernard Brujo photographed the famously blonde actress giving a come-hither smile as she gathered her billowing white dress around her while standing over a subway grate as a train passed underneath. The picture taken at Lexington Avenue at 52nd Street in Manhattan was intended to publicize the opening of *The Seven Year Itch*, in which Monroe was the star.

Director Billy Wilder refused to use the photo, however. He fretted that negative reaction from censors might affect the success of the comedy. He also didn't use motion picture footage taken at the same location because of an unruly crowd that began whistling

---

Q. What's a *gymnasticon?* A. Invented in 1796, it was a machine to exercise a person's joints.

over Monroe's see-through undergarments. The director arranged for another, more subtle publicity shoot on a soundstage and used that. As for Brujo, his still photo was published and became so famous that Mattel marketed a Barbie doll in a similar pose.

## 3. JOHN-JOHN, WASHINGTON, D.C., NOVEMBER 25, 1963

Perhaps no photo illustrates the nation's anguish after the assassination of President John F. Kennedy more than a freeze-frame of his three-year-old son watching his father's casket passing in Washington, D.C. John F. Kennedy Jr. stood solemnly saluting beside his mother Jacqueline Kennedy (veiled in black), his sister Caroline, and his uncles, Attorney General Robert Kennedy and Senator Edward Kennedy. The black-and-white photo has become the most reproduced of that scene.

Who took the famous photo of "John-John" has been debated over the years because it was seemingly taken by photographers on the government payroll, with no credit given. When White House photographer Joe O'Donnell retired in 1968, he began selling cropped versions of the photo. However, that close-in version of the president's son is identical to a larger frame picture taken by United Press International photographer Stan Steans, who is generally credited with the photo.

## 4. MOON MAN, JULY 20, 1968

Most people can tell you who was the first man to set foot on the moon. It was U.S. astronaut Neil Armstrong on July 20, 1968. As he lowered himself onto the lunar surface, Armstrong immortalized the moment with his famous words, "That's one small step for a man, one giant leap for mankind." When it comes to iconic photos of a man on the moon, however, one picture stands out from the rest. It isn't of Armstrong. Rather, he was the photographer. He snapped the photo of fellow moon man Buzz Aldrin, the second man to step on the surface.

Armstrong took the famous photo of Aldrin saluting the American flag firmly planted in the dusty surface, with a dunelike mountain rising up behind him into the ink-black cosmos. In the reflection of Aldrin's lowered helmet visor is the image of Armstrong and the lunar lander *Eagle*.

---

Papias the Lombard wrote the "first fully recognizable dictionary" in the 1040s.

## 5. BURNING GIRL, TRANG BANG, VIETNAM, JUNE 8, 1972

Huynh Công (Nick) Út was a photojournalist for the Associated Press covering the Vietnam War when he took a number of photos of villagers fleeing from a napalm attack on Trang Bang. One of those images was of a naked girl running down a dusty road with other terrified children, and it came to epitomize the horror and tragedy of the war. The black-and-white picture shows nine-year-old Phan Thi Kim Phúc running from the napalm attack after being severely burned on her back and left arm. It's among the most published of the war and earned Út the Pulitzer Prize for photography in 1973. The photo has three well-known titles: "Terror of War," "Vietnam Napalm," and "Children Fleeing an American Napalm Strike." But contrary to public opinion at the time, the attack on the village was mounted by South Vietnamese planes, not the U.S. Air Force.

After taking the photo, Út took Phúc to a hospital in Saigon, where doctors thought her injuries were too severe for her to survive. But after 17 operations over 14 months, she returned home, grew up, and later entered college in Cuba, where she met and married Bui Huy Toan, another Vietnamese student. On their honeymoon, they left their plane during a refueling stop in Gander, Newfoundland, and asked for asylum in Canada, which was granted. The couple took up residence in Ontario and have two children.

## 6. TANK MAN, BEIJING, CHINA, JUNE 5, 1989

First it was a hunger strike by 3,000 students camped in Tiananmen Square in Beijing. Then the protest grew over seven weeks until more than a million people jammed the square, demanding freedom and human rights from the totalitarian regime that ruled China. Finally, the government decided to act. Soldiers and tanks swarmed toward the square to end the protest. On the deserted Chang'an Avenue leading to the square, one man stood defiant to block the tanks. That man, known today only as the "Unknown Rebel," did not move as the tanks approached.

With arms holding shopping bags, he was steadfast, blocking four tanks that threatened to run him over but stopped just short. Associated Press photographer Jeff Widener was there and captured the moment. The lead tank followed by the other tanks tried repeatedly to get around the demonstrator. Each time, the Unknown Rebel moved in front and stopped their forward movement. At last the entire line came to a full halt, engines off. The protester climbed onto the lead tank's gun turret, where he appeared to converse with someone inside. He jumped down when the engines started up again and continued to stand defiantly in front of the idle tanks. At that point, two men in blue uniforms emerged from the crowd and took the demonstrator away. The tanks resumed their processional into the square to quash the student protest. No one knows what happened to the Unknown Rebel. But some historians believe that he was among the many who were executed in the aftermath of the Tiananmen Square uprising.

\* \* \*

## THE FIRST FASHION KNOCKOFF

Uncle John has always had a sense about fashion. So he took a look at the history of silk to see what he could find:

• The Chinese discovered about 5,000 years ago how to make silk from the cocoons of the silkworm. It quickly became a coveted commodity.

• The favorite fabric of ancient fashionistas willing to pay a high price was kept a closely guarded secret for the next 3,000 years to preserve its value.

• Not to be denied, poor folk who couldn't afford silk robes came up with a knockoff variety. They beat cotton with sticks to soften it, then rubbed the fiber against a stone to make it shine like silk. The resulting fabric was called "chintz" because it was cheap. Today, "chintzy" describes something that is cheap and not of good quality the world over.

...so they could provide care for their masters in the afterlife.

# EARTH'S CARETAKERS

*Our salute to nine people who made it their mission in
life to save the world. Well, somebody had to do it.*

To celebrate its 10th anniversary, the Environment Agency
in Britain invited a blue-ribbon panel of ecologists to list its
100 greatest "eco-heroes" of all time. Rachel Carson, whom
the panelists dubbed "the patron saint of the green movement,"
was number one on a list that included the ancient Greek philosopher Aristotle and St. Francis of Assisi, Catholic patron saint of
animals and ecology. Here's Uncle John's own winnowed-down list
of earthly crusaders with interesting stories.

### 1. JOHN MUIR

**Quote:** "Climb the mountains and get their good tidings. Nature's
peace will flow into you as sunshine flows into trees."

**Father Nature.** The man who's been called the "Father of Our
National Parks" started life in Scotland. In 1849, when he was 11,
his family emigrated to the United States to establish a farm in
Wisconsin. In 1867, a severe eye injury nearly blinded him; when
he recovered, he decided to pursue his first love: walking the
countryside. He trekked 1,000 miles from Indianapolis to Florida,
then sailed to New York, where he caught a ship to San Francisco
in 1868. He discovered the Sierra Nevadas and dedicated his life
to walking them and protecting them, especially the Yosemite Valley area. He helped found the Sierra Club in San Francisco and
wrote 10 books and 300 articles devoted to safeguarding the
wilderness.

**Parking, Lots.** Muir was a leading voice in convincing the government to establish Yosemite, Mount Rainier, and the Grand
Canyon as national parks, among others. Before his passing in
1914, he anguished over loggers cutting down sequoia redwoods:
"God has cared for these trees, saved them from drought, disease,
avalanches, and a thousand tempests and floods. But he cannot
save them from fools."

## 2. THEODORE ROOSEVELT

**Quote:** "In your full manhood and womanhood you will want what nature once so bountifully supplied and man so thoughtlessly destroyed; and because of that want you will reproach us, not for what we have used, but for what we have wasted."

**The Great Outdoorsman.** At 42, Roosevelt was the youngest man to serve as president. He earned the Nobel Peace Prize for negotiating an end to the Russo-Japanese War in 1905, wrote 35 books, and helped found the National Collegiate Athletic Association. But his first love was the outdoors. He spent his early years on horseback in the West, where he'd witnessed the decimation of buffalo and bighorn sheep in the Dakotas and the disappearance of grassland habitats. Many feel that his greatest accomplishment as president was giving voice to the conservation movement in the United States. From 1901 to 1909, he established 150 national forests, 51 federal bird reservations, 18 national monuments (including Chaco Canyon, Petrified Forest, Muir Woods, and Devils Tower), four national game preserves, 24 reclamation projects, and five national parks, including Oregon's Crater Lake. By the time he left office, he had placed under federal protection 230 million acres, an area as large as all the states along the East Coast, from Florida to Maine.

**Looking Ahead.** Seven years after leaving office, Roosevelt appealed to the nation to establish a consensus to preserve the wilderness. "Our duty to the whole, including the unborn generations, bids us restrain an unprincipled present-day minority from wasting the heritage of these unborn generations."

## 3. ALDO LEOPOLD

**Quote:** "We abuse land because we regard it as a commodity belonging to us. When we see land as a community to which we belong, we may begin to use it with love and respect."

**Junior Explorer.** Born in Iowa, Aldo Leopold grew up along the Mississippi River, and loved to explore the woods and streams near his home. After graduating from Yale, he went to work for the U.S. Forest Service for 19 years in the Southwest. He wrote a field manual for the government in 1933 called *Game Management*, which established the new field of wildlife ecology. When the

University of Wisconsin installed a new game management
department, they chose Leopold to head it. He purchased 80 acres
in Wisconsin's sand country that was once heavily forested. There
he put his land management practices to work, which he espoused
in *A Sand County Almanac*, completed just before his death in
1948. The book had a profound impact on America's budding
environmental movement and has been compared in importance
to Henry David Thoreau's *Walden* and Rachel Carson's *Silent
Spring*.

**It's Alive!** Leopold came to view land as a living organism that
mankind had to learn to live with in harmony and protect. To
that end, he noted, "Recreational development is a job not of
building roads into the lovely country but of building receptivity
into the still unlovely human mind."

### 4. ANSEL ADAMS

**Quote:** "It is horrifying that we have to fight our own government
to save the environment."

**Picture Perfect.** A native of San Francisco, Ansel Adams was four
years old when the 1906 earthquake devastated the city and one
of its aftershocks knocked him to the ground, breaking his nose.
Trained to be a concert pianist, Adams instead took a job as a cus-
todian at the LeConte Memorial Lodge in Yosemite Valley, the
headquarters of the fledgling Sierra Club headed by John Muir. By
1927, he'd developed a knack for photography and became the
club's official cameraman. A trip to Taos, New Mexico, inspired
him to become politically active in the club. Adams traveled the
West, producing black-and-white images of nature's grandeur that
established his reputation as the foremost nature photographer of
his time. His photographs in the book *Sierra Nevada: The John
Muir Trail* convinced President Franklin D. Roosevelt to establish
King's Canyon and its giant redwoods as a national park.

**Heavy Medal.** In 1980, Adams received the Presidential Medal of
Freedom, the nation's top civilian honor, for his work in preserving
wild and scenic places through his photographs. It was Yosemite
that always inspired him, and he established a studio there.

*For the rest of the story, turn to page 354.*

The term "go-go dancer" first appeared in print in 1965.

# EPITAPHS

"Good Frend for Jesus Sake
Forbeare to Digg the Dust
Encloased Heare. Blest Be Ye
Man Yet Spares Thes Stones
And Curst Be He Yet Moves
My Bone."
—**William Shakespeare**

"At Rest / An American
Soldier and Defender of the
Constitution."
—**Jefferson Davis**

'Steel True, Blade Straight."
—**Sir Arthur Conan Doyle**

"So Much to Do,
So Little Done."
—**Cecil John Rhodes**

"Everybody Loves
Somebody Sometime."
—**Dean Martin**

"Author of the Declaration of
American Independence of
the Statute of Virginia For
Religious Freedom and Father
of the University Of Virginia."
—**Thomas Jefferson**

"If I should die, think only this
of me: That there's some corner of a foreign field that is for
ever England."
—**Rupert Brooke**

"Cast a Cold Eye on Life, on
Death Horsemen, Pass By!"
—**William Butler Yeats**

"A Genius of Comedy His Talent brought Joy and Laughter
to All the World."
—**Oliver Hardy**

"For God And His Country
He Raised Our Flag In Battle
and Showed A Measure of his
Pride at a Place Called 'Iwo
Jima' Where Courage Never
Died."
—**Rene A. Gagnon**

"A Gentle Man And A Gen-
tleman."
—**Jack Dempsey**

"Sacred to the Memory of
William Bligh, Esquire F.R.S.
Vice Admiral of the Blue, the
Celebrated Navigator Who
First Transplanted the Bread-
fruit Tree From Otahette to
the West Indies, Bravely
fought the Battles of his
Country and Died Beloved,
Respected, and Lamented On
the 7th Day of December,
1817 Aged 64."
—**William Bligh**

"She Did It The Hard Way."
—**Bette Davis**

"Thank you for all the love you
gave me. There could be no
one stronger. Thank you for
the many beautiful songs. They
will live long and longer."
— **Hank Williams**

---

Alaska's Red Dog Mine, in the Brooks Range, is the world's largest source of zinc.

# COLD CASES

*Rumor has it that Amelia Earhart and the grassy-
knoll gunmen have been found in a bar on
Atlantis. Whew—three mysteries
solved. Now, on to these.*

## 1. THE BABUSHKA LADY

**The Mystery:** President John F. Kennedy was assassinated in Dallas, Texas, on November 22, 1963. Many people lined the motorcade route, filming the event with still and video cameras. In the days after the shooting, police and the FBI confiscated a lot of the footage, and someone interesting shows up in many of the images—a woman wearing what looks like a traditional Russian headscarf called a babushka tied beneath her chin. Her back is to the camera, but it looks like she's also filming the event, and even as the people around her run for cover or hit the ground when the president is shot, the woman stands her ground and continues to film. Who is she?

**Solved?** No. In 1970, a woman named Beverly Oliver came forward, claiming to be the babushka lady. She said that all the hoopla and conspiracy theories around Kennedy's assassination scared her into silence. She also claimed to have handed over her video footage to some mysterious men who identified themselves as FBI and CIA agents.

Most investigators, though, think Oliver's story is a hoax. Her account of the day contradicts those of the other people there, and the model of movie camera she claimed to have used wasn't on the market in 1963. No one else has come forward.

## 2. NEW JERSEY SHARK ATTACKS OF 1916

**Mystery:** You did not want to be a swimmer along the New Jersey coast in July 1916. Over 11 days that summer, five people were mauled by sharks in three different seaside towns—four victims died. Then, like now, shark attacks were rare; fatal attacks even more so. But newspapers sensationalized the story—nicknaming the shark the "Jersey Maneater"—and rumors about the type of shark and number of sharks terrified vacationers into staying away from the beach towns...which ended up costing businesses along the coast more than $200,000.

**Solved?** No one is sure. On July 14, a fisherman named Michael Schleisser produced a 325-pound great white shark that he said he'd caught near the town of Matawan, where the last three victims were attacked. When he gutted the animal, Schleisser found human bones in its stomach.

Most people were satisfied that the Jersey Maneater had been caught, and indeed, the attacks stopped after that. But as often happens, later research said "Not so fast." In 2002, the National Geographic Society released a report that questioned the species of shark implicated in at least three of the 1916 attacks. Two people were killed in the open ocean, but the three victims in Matawan were attacked in a creek fed by the ocean. According to National Geographic researchers, it's unlikely that the creek would have a high enough salt content to support a great white shark. Most sharks need to keep a consistent level of salt in their bodies at all times, and a mixture of fresh creek water and salt water wouldn't do the trick. So these scientists think that an unidentified bull shark was actually the culprit (bull sharks are unique in that they can move easily from salt water to freshwater environments). Whatever the species, the Jersey Maneater remains part of American lore, and it inspired one of the most successful movies of all time: *Jaws*.

## 3. RONGORONGO

**The Mystery:** Spanish explorers first visited Easter Island in the South Pacific in the 1770s. After they left, the indigenous people who lived there developed a type of picture writing now called *rongorongo* (which means "to recite" in the native language). They carved this "text" onto hundreds of wooden tablets, but by the 1860s, their descendants had lost the ability to read the rongorongo writing. Only a few dozen of the tablets are left today.

**Solved?** No. Scientists have been unable to decipher the writing.

## 4. THE MARFA LIGHTS

**Mystery:** Unidentified glowing orbs in the desert might sound like something out of the *X Files*, but they're very real to people in the town of Marfa, Texas. The first recorded sighting of the lights came in 1883 when a ranch hand noticed them and thought they were Indian fires. On further investigation, though, he found no ash from any fires or evidence that anyone had been there at all. And the story has been like that ever since. The lights glow red, orange, and yellow, appear on most clear nights, and bounce like balls in the sky near where Highway 67 and Highway 90 meet. But no one can actually identify where they're coming from.

Solved? Not really. People with an interest in ghosts and ghost stories claim that the Marfa lights are supernatural spirits (both friendly and harmful), while others claim they are aliens. But the most likely explanation is that they're some kind of mirage produced when warm and cold layers of air meet and bend light. The fact is, though, that no one really knows. You can't see the lights up close, only from far away, so no one has ever been able to truly identify what they are. Texas considers them a tourist attraction, and the highway department built a viewing area off Highway 90 so that curious visitors could see the Marfa lights for themselves.

\*       \*       \*

## THE GREATEST OF THE GREAT

What made Alexander the Great so...well...great was that he conquered most of the world. What's not so well known is his influence on these Roman leaders:

**1. Julius Caesar,** the future emperor, came across a statue of Alexander while leading his troops across Spain. Immediately, the 33-year-old general broke down, grief-stricken that he hadn't accomplished much while the Great One had conquered the entire known world.

**2. Caligula,** the schizoid Roman emperor, tried to emulate Alexander by riding horseback across a bridge of boats over Naples Bay while dressed in armor he stole from Alexander's tomb.

**3. Caracalla,** another Roman emperor, set out to reconquer lands once ruled by Alexander, and in so doing made a great public show of visiting Alexander's tomb in Alexandria, Egypt.

First film with Leo the Lion roaring as MGM's logo: *He Who Gets Slapped* (1924).

# READ ALL ABOUT IT!

*Here is Uncle John's list of print journalists who
were once as well known as Katie Couric,
Tom Brokaw, and Brian Williams.*

Before broadcast news and the Internet, there were newspapers—and they were the kings of communication. For hundreds of years, bylined stories made print journalists famous.

## 1. THE FIRST FEMALE WAR CORRESPONDENT

Margaret Fuller (1810–50), a well-educated native of Massachusetts, was in her early 30s when she joined the *New York Tribune* as its literary critic in 1844. The first female editor on the staff, she soon gathered a loyal readership that made her a celebrity in New England—so much so that she became the first woman allowed access to the library at Harvard College. Besides arguing for the right of women to have the same access to education as men and to be employed, she also embraced prison reform and abolition of slavery, writing about her views in the book *Woman in the Nineteenth Century*, published in 1845 and considered the first major feminist literary work.

**Love and Death Find Margaret.** In 1846, the *Tribune* sent Fuller to Europe as its first female correspondent, where she covered the democratic revolution in Italy led by Giuseppe Mazzini and fell in love with revolutionary Giovanni Ossoli. After bearing him a child out of wedlock, Fuller, Ossoli, and their child were en route to America in 1850 when their ship foundered off Fire Island, New York, drowning them. Her friend, writer Henry David Thoreau, searched the beach for Fuller's personal effects, but none were found.

Fuller's legacy was her fierce determination to set her own course in life. "A house," she famously said, "is no home unless it contains food and fire for the mind as well as the body." Many future feminists, including Susan B. Anthony, considered Fuller their inspiration.

---

Architect Frank Lloyd Wright coined the term "carport" in 1936.

## 2. THE WORLD TRAVELER

Like Mark Twain, Elizabeth Cochrane Seaman (1864–1922) was better known by a pseudonym. In 1880, "Nellie Bly" got her first writing job after sending an impassioned letter to the editor of the *Pittsburgh Dispatch*, rebutting an antifeminist article. The editor gave her the pen name Nellie Bly, from the Stephen Foster pop tune of the same name. After a brief stint at the *Dispatch*, she moved to New York City and persuaded Joseph Pulitzer to hire her as a reporter for his *World* newspaper. She accepted an undercover assignment in which she feigned insanity to investigate reports of brutality and neglect in the city's Women's Lunatic Asylum. The exposé made her famous and initiated a grand jury investigation that resulted in major reforms. She said of her experience, "It is only after one is in trouble that one realizes how little sympathy and kindness there are in the world."

**Whoa, Nellie!** In 1889, Bly convinced her editor to allow her to attempt to travel around the world in less than 80 days—beating the mark dreamed up by Jules Verne in his best-selling novel *Around the World in 80 Days*. Along the way, she filed short newspaper dispatches that included stories about meeting in France and touring a leper colony. Readers were mesmerized. After arriving in San Francisco, Bly boarded a private train arranged by Pulitzer that got her back to New York on the 72nd day, a record that stood for 23 years. In 1895, Bly married a wealthy businessman and became president of a steel company. In 1904, she invented and patented a 55-gallon steel drum that became today's industry standard. And Superman fans will be interested to know that Clark Kent's coworker Lois Lane was modeled after her.

## 3. THE CRIME REPORTER

Edna Buchanan, who was born in 1939, moved from her native New Jersey to Miami in the 1960s to pursue a career as a journalist at a small community newspaper. Her wit and flair for writing came to the notice of editors at the *Miami Herald*, and they hired her in 1973 as a crime reporter. She was enthralled with the job, covering thousands of violent crimes during the peak of the city's reputation as the center of the international drug trade.

**Murder, She Wrote.** Her gift was crafting opening sentences that grabbed attention. Thus, in a story about an ex-con who, when a fast-food place ran out of fried chicken, went a little crazy and ended up being shot by a security guard, she began, "Gary Robinson died hungry." She won a Pulitzer Prize for general reporting in 1986 and later, after retiring and devoting herself to writing mystery novels, she discussed her more memorable assignments in her books *The Corpse Had a Familiar Face* (1991) and *Never Let Them See You Cry* (1992). Asked how she could do the job of police reporter year after year, she said, "Nobody loves a police reporter. The job can be lonely and arduous. I have been threatened with arrest, threatened physically, had rocks thrown at me. I've gotten threatening letters, subpoenas, and obscene phone calls, some of them from my editors. It is tiring, haunting, and truly wonderful."

*To read about famous male journalists, go to page 342.*

\*　　　\*　　　\*

## THE FIRST NEWSPAPER

The Romans get the credit for their *Acta Diurna* (*Daily Events*), a handwritten news report posted daily in public places around 59 BC, but the first printed newspaper is credited to the Chinese in AD 700. The movable-type printing press, introduced circa 1450, was the breakthrough that helped spread the development of the newspaper, and Germany was circulating regularly published newspapers by the early 1600s. The *News-Letter*, America's first newspaper, was published in Boston in 1704.

---

Bodybuilder Charles Atlas had a son named Hercules, who grew up to be a math teacher.

# WHAT THEY WORE TO WAR

*What you're wearing right now may have been named
for a person, place, or thing that originated during any
of the thousands of wars fought throughout history.*

Among the following list of wearable items, you'll find a varied cast of characters and locales that includes the men in the trenches (literally), a chilly port on the Black Sea, a one-armed British nobleman, and an American sex symbol.

## 1. CRAVAT
During the Thirty Years' War in the 17th century, Croatian troops came to Paris dressed for battle in uniforms that included bright-colored scarves tied tightly around their necks. The fashion-conscious French civilians adopted the style as their own, looping the scarves more loosely and tying them in a bow with long, flowing ends. They called it *la Croate*, which was corrupted into *la cravate*. By mid-century the term entered English as *cravat*, which now refers to a scarf or band of fabric worn around the neck, mostly by men as wedding wear.

## 2. FATIGUES AND COMBAT BOOTS
As early as the 1770s and throughout the American Revolution, fatigues—loose uniforms worn as work clothes—were used for noncombat duties like digging ditches, which was called "fatigue duty." Similar work clothes were worn in both the British and the American armies. Much later, Fidel Castro's loose work clothes became popular with civilians, particularly young people, who wore them with the perfect accessory: combat boots, front-laced infantry footwear covering at least the ankles or higher, with thick rubber soles. In 2005, the U.S. Army changed the design of its fatigues for the first time in 22 years, and issued new ones with easy-to-use Velcro openings and a redesigned camouflage pattern. The new style hasn't caught on as widely in civilian life—but give it time.

### 3. WELLINGTONS

In his campaigns against Napoleon, Arthur Wellesley, First Duke of Wellington, sported high leather riding boots with the front part extending over the knee and the back cut away so he could bend his knee on horseback. The boot, named for his dukedom, came to be called the Wellington. When cobblers started making a shorter boot that came midway up the calf, it was dubbed the half-Wellington. In the early 1900s, the name Wellington began to be used for high waterproof boots made of specially treated leather, and later, rubber. Wellies (their nickname in Britain) are still a popular item given that nation's notoriously wet weather.

### 4. BLUCHERS

Wellington's defeat of Napoleon at Waterloo was ably assisted by a Prussian general, Field Marshal Gebhart Leberecht von Blücher, who also gave his name to two kinds of footwear. Originally, bluchers were half boots made of heavy leather; somewhat later the name was used for a man's leather shoe in which the vamp (the upper part of a shoe) and the tongue are made of one piece, and the sides with the lacing holes meet together over the tongue and tie over the instep. Bluchers are still popular as dressy men's shoes, and L. L. Bean sells what they call "leather blucher mocs" that look a lot like those preppy boat shoes.

### 5. SAM BROWNE BELT

Sam Browne sounds like he might have fought at the Alamo, but he was a British officer and a veteran of India's Sepoy Rebellion of 1857: Sir Samuel James Browne. His creation, the Sam Browne belt, was made of leather and supported by a light shoulder strap so that the sword it held wouldn't make the belt sag. At first there was a strap over each shoulder, but later it was changed to just one strap over the right shoulder, since swords were worn on the left side. The Sam Browne belt was compulsory wear for British Army officers until 1939 (after that, it was optional) and was adopted in many other armies. Today it's worn all over the world by police officers, cadets on parade, guards, and the like.

### 6. CARDIGAN

During the Crimean War of 1853–56 (Russia versus the allied

---

**The Academy Awards were televised for the first time in 1953.**

forces of England, France, and the Ottoman Empire, a light-cavalry brigade commanded by James Thomas Brudenell, Seventh Earl of Cardigan, met a disastrous end. Owing to a disputed error in orders—or possibly the commander's notorious incompetence—the brigade was ordered to charge a heavily fortified Russian position. To get there, the brigade had to ride down a ravine between two hills, with no backup in the rear. A third of the men—247 out of 637—were killed or wounded. Their gallantry was memorialized by Alfred, Lord Tennyson, in his poem "The Charge of the Light Brigade."

That same incompetent earl missed his calling as a clothes designer; he gave his name to the cardigan, a collarless button-down sweater he wore under his uniform for warmth. The style was adopted by British troops, and Queen Victoria allegedly praised the design, which makes us wonder if she ever wore one in drafty old Balmoral Castle.

\*     \*     \*

## WAR, BY THE NUMBERS

Uncle John was curious about history's wars and discovered some interesting facts:

• The shortest war between two nations was fought between Zanzibar and England in 1896. Zanzibar capitulated 38 minutes after the conflict began.

• The longest war in history, according to most experts, was between England and France. It lasted for 116 years, from 1337, when England invaded, to 1453, when the French threw them out.

• The longest war in the 20th century is the ongoing Sudanese civil war that began in 1955 and pits the Arab Muslim north against the predominantly black Christian south.

• The costliest war in history was World War II, in which an estimated 60 million people died.

# OVER HILL, OVER DALE

*To paraphrase a famous saying, "Hill is for heroes!"*
*If you missed part one it started on page 274*

## 1. SAN JUAN HILL: JULY 1, 1898

On July 1, 1898, there were 200,000 Spanish troops in Cuba but only a little more than 35,000 were near the city of Santiago de Cuba. Another 13,000 Spaniards garrisoned the city. However, the actual fighting occurred on San Juan Heights, not San Juan Hill, on a small, round rise in front of the ridge that the press named Kettle Hill. General Arsenio Linares, commanding Santiago, sent just 1,200 men to defend the ridge and another 500 to defend El Caney, a nearby hill on the Americans' right. Major General William R. Shafter, commanding the U.S. troops, planned to assault both positions simultaneously.

When Shafter's men were slow to get into position, Lieutenant Colonel Theodore Roosevelt lost patience and led his "Rough Riders" up and over Kettle Hill to attack the enemy on San Juan Ridge. In the fight that ensued, the Spaniards were defeated and the fate of Santiago was sealed. The press made Roosevelt a hero and the public demanded something be done for him, so the army awarded Roosevelt the Medal of Honor.

## 2. PORK CHOP HILL: MARCH 23–JULY 11, 1953

The action pertains to a number of small, violent battles fought near the 38th parallel for Hill 234 during the Korean War. This hill looked like a pork chop from the air, hence the name. On March 23, Chinese troops furiously attacked Pork Chop Hill and a nearby treeless hill called Old Baldy. The Americans gave up Old Baldy but tenaciously held Pork Chop. The Chinese captured the hill in a surprise assault on April 16 but lost it two days later. The decision to hold the worthless hill had more to do with political than military strategy—and to keep the Chinese from flaunting the victory. Sporadic fighting continued over the summer. In a way, the defense of Pork Chop Hill symbolized the last two years of the Korean conflict, which had deteriorated into a war of communist containment rather than of unconditional surrender. U.S. troops evacuated the hill two weeks before the armistice was signed.

### 3. HAMBURGER HILL: MAY 11–20, 1969

One of the bloodiest battles of the Vietnam War took place on Hill 937 during the Battle of Ap Bia Mountain. The Americans did not anticipate the enemy's fierce resistance; North Vietnamese regulars often withdrew from frontal attacks. This time they entrenched and fought back, creating a bloody landscape. U.S. troops called the blood-spattered scene "Hamburger Hill." After several unsuccessful assaults over three days, two American battalions and a battalion of South Vietnamese troops arrived as reinforcements. On May 18, a two-battalion attack reached the summit, only to be washed back down by a sudden downpour. Finally on May 20, after ten tries, a four-battalion assault drove the North Vietnamese off the hill and into Laos. In another perplexing episode of the Vietnam War—and after wasting lives to capture the hill—the U.S. troops received orders to abandon the area. The tagline for the subsequent movie about the event called it "war at its worst, men at their best."

### 4. LONGSTOP HILL: DECEMBER 22, 1942–APRIL 26, 1943

Djebel el Ahmera became one of the first strategic hills encountered by the Allies during World War II's North African Campaign. German and Italian forces had dug in on the fortified hill, which blocked the Allied advance to Tunis. The fight began in cold, heavy rain. Soldiers scaling the hill called it "infantry warfare at its worst." The British captured the hill on December 22 and turned it over to U.S. forces. The Germans counterattacked the following day and drove off the Americans. On Christmas Eve, the British recaptured the hill, but lost the summit the next morning. Frustrated by German resistance, General Dwight D. Eisenhower halted the advance on Tunis for four months—and so the massif became known among the Allies as "Longstop Hill."

On April 23, 1943, the British began opening the way to Tunis by assaulting Longstop Hill. Three days later, German resistance ended and the Allies forged ahead, restarting the Battle of Tunis, which resulted in an Allied victory less than two weeks later.

In Latin, the word *arena* meant "sandy place."

# NOMS DE PLUME

*Literature is replete with books that were published under pseudonyms. Here are more well known writers who didn't want to be known. Part one began on page 249.*

## 1. VICTORIA LUCAS (A.K.A. SYLVIA PLATH)

You've heard of her, right? The Grace Kelly of American poetry. The tortured, suicidal artiste. Her 1963 novel *The Bell Jar* is familiar to many readers today. But did you know that she originally published it under the name of Victoria Lucas?

The book is really a semiautobiographical account of Plath's own life. The novel's heroine, Esther Greenwood, is a young girl from the suburbs with an internship at a prestigious New York fashion magazine. Alone and adrift in the city, Esther slides into depression. After undergoing psychoanalysis, Esther makes several halfhearted suicide attempts and is then made to undergo electroshock therapy. Then, Esther has a life-changing event (she loses her virginity) and finally rejects the idea of death after a close friend commits suicide. At the end of the novel, Esther is able to face up to the future.

Many of the events in *The Bell Jar* echoed Plath's own life. Like Esther, in her youth Plath worked at a New York magazine, and she endured years of depression and therapy. But, unlike Esther, there was to be no happy ending for Plath. Just weeks after the novel was published, Plath committed suicide.

At the time of her death, Plath appeared to have it all. After a brilliant academic career in the United States, the budding young writer and poet was awarded a scholarship to Cambridge University in England. It was there that she met the dashing English poet Ted Hughes. After a rapid and explosive courtship, the couple were married in 1956. For the next six years, Hughes and Plath were the king and queen of Anglo-American poetry.

Plath developed a powerful style of confessional lyric poetry into which she channeled most of her emotional insecurities, beginning with her debut volume *The Colossus* in 1960. Yet, despite her marriage and growing critical success, Plath's ongoing mental health problems persisted. In 1962, after discovering that her husband was having an affair, Plath ended the marriage. Less than a year later, she ended her own life by gassing herself to death in her London flat. In a case of life superseding art, the suicidal Plath ultimately succeeded where her novelistic alter ego Esther failed.

## 2. DAVID CORNWELL (A.K.A. JOHN LE CARRE)

When British intelligence officer David Cornwell decided to write some espionage novels, he was required to publish under a pen name, and chose John Le Carré—a name that would earn him worldwide fame. However, it was only with the success of his third novel, *The Spy Who Came in from the Cold* (1963), that Cornwell was able to quit his day job with MI6 (Britain's version of the CIA) and write full-time.

Unlike the earlier James Bond novels of Ian Fleming, Le Carré's stories paint a downbeat picture of the espionage industry. No glamorous spies, fancy casinos, and speeding sports cars—just humdrum civil servants, smoky pubs, and suburban trains. Le Carré's books allowed readers to think that the man in the crumpled raincoat sitting next to them on the bus could just as easily have been a spy as an accountant.

By deglamorizing the Cold War, Le Carré showed, in books such as *Tinker, Tailor, Soldier, Spy* (1974) and the semiautobiographical *A Perfect Spy* (1986), that spying was a grim game where, on the British side at least, class prejudice and outdated pre–World War II thinking undermined the service's effectiveness. Following the fall of the Berlin Wall in 1989, Le Carré turned his attention away from the old enemy, Russia, and took on new targets—most notably the pharmaceuticals industry in *The Constant Gardener* (2001).

Unlike his novels, Le Carré's life was anything but low-key. He was born in 1931—his father was jailed for insurance fraud and appeared to be something of a con man. After studying at Oxford and teaching at the prestigious English private school Eton, Cornwell joined MI5 (Britain's FBI) in 1959. He ran agents, organized wire taps, and generally lived the secretive spy's life depicted in his books. In 1960, he transferred to MI6 and spent time running agents in Germany. But he has always denied he was a spy himself. "I sat behind a desk," he told one interviewer. Just as he does now.

## 3. ELLIS, ACTON, AND CURRER BELL
## (A.K.A. CHARLOTTE, EMILY, AND ANNE BRONTË)

Emily Brontë (1818–48), author of *Wuthering Heights*, suffered from the same grievance as George Eliot. Worried that she would not be taken seriously as a female writer, Emily submitted her one and only novel (but what a novel!) under the name Ellis Bell. The fifth of six children, Emily was one a trio of writing Brontë sisters, the other two being her older sister Charlotte (1816–55) and younger sister Anne (1820–49). All three adopted male pseudonyms: Charlotte was Currer Bell and Anne was Acton Bell. Their brother, Patrick Branwell Brontë, also wrote—but was not quite as talented.

The Brontë children's mother died when they were young, and they sought refuge by writing about fantasy realms they called Gondal and Angria. But it was not until her late 20s that Emily finally got into print when she, Charlotte, and Anne issued *The Poems of Currer, Ellis and Acton Bell* in 1846. A year later, Ellis Bell published *Wuthering Heights*. A wild, romantic Gothic masterpiece, the book's tortured romance between Catherine and Heathcliff disturbed and enthralled readers in equal measure.

At the same time, Charlotte was working on her magnum opus, *Jane Eyre* (1847). More restrained than *Wuthering Heights*, Charlotte's novel is considered by many the better literary work. Not to be outdone, in 1847 Anne published her first novel, *Agnes Grey*, followed in 1848 by *The Tenant of Wildfell Hall*.

The Brontë sisters' best year came in 1847, and from there things went rapidly downhill. Always a sickly bunch, Emily was first to go. In September 1848 she caught a cold while attending her brother's funeral. Two months later, she was dead (from tuberculosis or pneumonia—no one's sure which). Anne went next, dead at 29 from influenza in May 1849. Charlotte hung on until 1855. The cause of her death remains unclear. One theory is excessive vomiting brought on by severe morning sickness. Charlotte was pregnant when she died, and her unborn child died too.

All three Brontë sisters are now recognized as major writers, with perhaps the prize for biggest impact going to Emily for her remarkable *Wuthering Heights*. Today their childhood home in Haworth, on the wild and windy Yorkshire moors, is a museum dedicated to their memory.

---

...world's first pizzeria. It lines its ovens with lava rocks from nearby Mount Vesuvius.

# DEAR DIARY

*Diaries of the famous (and not so famous) provide a personal perspective on the great events of history.*

## 1. GEORGE WASHINGTON WROTE THIS

The first president of the United States was not known for his wit or talkative nature, but he was a dedicated diarist for much of his life. He titled his diaries "Where & How my Time is Spent" and, for the most part, that is what they detail.

His diary entries were terse and not always illuminating:

> "Saturday March 12th [1748]. This Morning Mr. James Genn the surveyor came to us. We travel'd over the Blue Ridge to Capt. Ashbys on Shannondoa River. Nothing remarkable happen'd."

Yet the simple fact of seeing how Washington expressed himself and what he chose to mention (or leave out) provides a unique insight into his personality. What's most remarkable is the fact that as activity increased prior to the Revolutionary War—meetings held and decisions made with regard to organizing the Colonial forces for the war with Britain—Washington's diaries grew even more brisk and superficial. His entry for May 4, 1775, says merely:

> "Set out for the Congress at Phila. [Philadelphia]. Dind in Alexa. [Alexandria, Virginia] & lodgd at Marlborough [Maryland]."

This was to be the Continental Congress at which Washington was commissioned as general and commander in chief of the Continental army, yet he doesn't mention this appointment, which was made on June 19, at all. He does, however, keep a separate diary entry of the weather for each day—ever the farmer.

There is a hiatus in the diaries from June 19, 1775, until 1781, and another from late 1781 until 1784. The diaries resume in 1784 and continue right up until the day before Washington's death on December 14, 1799. His last entry included sentences that were as simple as the first:

> "Morning Snowing & abt. 3 Inches deep. Wind at No. Et. & Mer.[cury] at 30. Contg. Snowing till 1 Oclock and abt. 4 it became perfectly clear. Wind in the same place but not hard. Mer. 28 at Night."

---

In ancient Rome, kisses were used to "sign" a contract.

## 2. MARY CHESNUT'S CIVIL WAR

Few stories of the American Civil War are as intimate or individual as that of Mary Boykin Miller Chesnut. The diaries she kept from November 1860—after Abraham Lincoln was elected president—to August 2, 1865, show wartime life from the perspective of a Confederate woman, and a well-connected woman at that.

Mary Chesnut was the wife of James Chesnut Jr., a South Carolina senator who resigned his congressional seat when Lincoln was elected, and who was instrumental in drafting the plan for the southern states to secede from the union. Among the couple's closest friends were Confederate president Jefferson Davis and his wife Varina. Many of the key members of the Confederacy appear in Chesnut's diaries as well, including General Robert E. Lee:

> "The man and horse and everything about him were so fine-looking; perfection, in fact; no fault to be found if you hunted for it."

Her accounts of events—from the trials of everyday life to the aftermath of General William T. Sherman's March to the Sea—are filled with detail and emotion. Following the death of Colonel Francis S. Bartow at the First Battle of Bull Run in July 1861, Chesnut wrote:

> "Witnessed for the first time a military funeral. As that march came wailing up, they say Mrs. Bartow fainted. The empty saddle and the led war-horse—we saw and heard it all, and now it seems we are never out of the sound of the Dead March in Saul. It comes and it comes, until I feel inclined to close my ears and scream."

Although her feelings were understandably partisan, her diaries are so enduring because they reflect universal thoughts and feelings. After Bull Run, she wrote:

> "They brought me a Yankee soldier's portfolio from the battle-field. One might shed tears over some of the letters. Women, wives and mothers, are the same everywhere."

Ken Burns quoted extensively from these diaries in his television series *The Civil War*. Mary Chesnut edited her diaries with the intention of publishing them. She died in 1886, and the diaries were not published until 1905, as *A Diary from Dixie*. Later, preeminent American historian C. Vann Woodward won a Pulitzer Prize for an edited version of what is now known as *Mary Chesnut's Civil War*.

---

Danish biologist Wilhelm Johannsen (1857–1927) coined the term "genes" in 1911.

## 3. SCOTT'S LAST ENTRY

Robert Falcon Scott led the first British expedition to reach the South Pole, although he and his team perished in the attempt. What happened to them is known in great detail because when a search party was sent to Antarctica to find Scott and his group, they recovered Scott's diary along with the team's bodies.

His diary included daily entries about the team's progress from their initial voyage to the establishment of their base camp, and mentions their scientific research and the geological samples they collected to bring home with them. (It's thought that Scott's reluctance to leave behind the heavy samples might have hindered the group's progress from the pole back to their camp.)

The story is a sad one, and not merely because there were no survivors from the expedition. When Scott learned that a Norwegian expedition led by Roald Amundsen had departed for Antarctica at the same time as Scott's own expedition, he realized that his quest to reach the South Pole had become a race. Scott's group arrived at the South Pole on January 16, 1912, only to discover that Amundsen's group had planted the Norwegian flag there a little more than a month earlier on December 14, 1911. Scott's diary entry for January 17 expresses his frustration:

> "The Pole. Yes, but under very different circumstances from those expected. Great God! This is an awful place and terrible enough for us to have laboured to it without the reward of priority."

Bitterly disappointed, Scott's group began their return journey to their base camp, only to be confronted with such severe weather that they had no hope of making it back alive. His last diary entry, written with a weak hand on March 29, 1912, reads:

> "We shall stick it out to the end, but we are getting weaker, of course and the end cannot be far. It seems a pity, but I do not think I can write anymore."

## 4. FROM THE MINISTER FOR PROPAGANDA

The diaries of Joseph Goebbels provide an insider's view of life in Germany during Adolf Hitler's rise to power and the events of World War II. As the Nazi minister for public enlightenment and propaganda, Goebbels naturally has a one-sided view of events—he was a classic spin doctor and much of the propaganda he disseminated to the public via films, broadcasts, pamphlets, and speeches was complete fabrication. Nevertheless, his diaries have proven to be remarkably candid about the personalities and inner workings of the Nazi Party, providing a view from "the other side."

Goebbels's diaries begin in 1923, when he was 26 years old and pursuing a career as a journalist. Things were not going well for him either professionally or personally.

"I'm so despondent about everything. Everything I try goes totally wrong. There's no escape from this hole here. I feel drained. So far, I still haven't found a real purpose in life. Sometimes, I'm afraid to get out of bed in the morning. There's nothing to get up for."

In 1925, he joined the Nazi Party. By 1926, he was in the party's inner circle and completely captivated by Adolf Hitler, whom he found to be a "fabulous man...witty, humorous, and spirited." On July 18, 1926, Goebbels describes Hitler as very few ever would:

"He is a dear and pure—a child."

Yet Goebbels does not have the same warm sentiments for Hitler's inner circle. Goebbels's favorite target was Hermann Göring, the enormously influential German Luftwaffe commander who was also his political rival. By 1945, when the Luftwaffe's lack of success appeared to be dooming Germany's entire war effort, Goebbels devoted page after page of his diary to excoriating Göring:

"February 27, 1945. [Göring] is no National-Socialist but a sybarite. [He has] as much to do with the Party as a cow with radiology... Bemedaled idiots and vain perfumed coxcombs have no place in our war leadership...[I]t is simply grossly bad style for the senior officer of the Reich...to strut around in a silver-gray uniform. What effeminate behavior in the face of present developments!"

On the same day, Goebbels notes that Hitler was pleased to hear Göring's wife had moved away "because she was a bad influence on him," adding:

"By contrast the Führer had high praise for the simplicity and purity of my family life."

Goebbels's diaries—29 printed volumes and more than 20,000 pages—end in April 1945. On May 1, 1945, Goebbels had a Nazi physician kill his six children with cyanide capsules; he and his wife then took their own lives.

# OLD SPORTS RULES

*Rules were made to be broken. Nowhere is that more apparent than in sports, where regulations are constantly revised to improve the quality of play and the safety of the participants.*
*For more rules see part one on page 184.*

## BASKETBALL

• From 1900 to 1921, players who were substituted were not allowed to reenter the game. In fact, it wasn't until 1934 that players were allowed to reenter the game more than once after coming out for a breather. Teams were finally allowed unlimited substitutions beginning in 1945.

• Coaches were prohibited from addressing their players during the game until 1949, when they were allowed to speak with them only during timeouts.

• Until 1911, players were disqualified from the game after collecting their second foul. This rule has since been amended to five fouls at the high school and college level and six fouls in NBA games.

• Time restrictions on ball possession weren't introduced until 1933. Until then, one team could legally hold onto the ball for the entire duration of the game after building up a comfortable lead.

• Believe it or not, dribbling was not originally part of basketball. The act of continuously pounding the ball into the hardwood did not come into vogue until 1909, when players were finally allowed to take more than one bounce before being required to shoot or pass.

• Until 1938, players and fans alike had to endure a jump ball at half-court after every made field goal. The rule was eventually abolished because it slowed the pace of play.

## HOCKEY

• Forward passing was not allowed until the 1929–30 season. Until then, a player could move the puck forward only by handling it with his stick.

---

**The Vatican's Papal Swiss Guard was founded in 1506.**

• Ice hockey borrowed many of its earliest rules from field hockey, including the use of the "bully," which required opposing centers to bang their sticks together three times before trying to control the face-off. This practice eventually fell out of vogue in 1913 when the modern face-off as we know it was introduced.

• Each team was allowed to play seven men at a time until the 1911–12 season. This septet included the goalie, two defensemen, three forwards, and a rover who switched from defense to offense as needed.

• Goaltenders were not allowed to drop to the ice when making saves and could, in fact, be penalized if they did so. This rule was eventually changed prior to the 1917–18 season.

• The game used to be structured quite differently. The 1910–11 season saw hockey change from two 30-minute periods to three 20-minute periods—the format we have today.

## FOOTBALL

• Football teams were originally allowed to take the field with 20 players per side. The number of participants was reduced to 11 in 1880 thanks to a series of sweeping changes championed by Yale graduate Walter Camp.

• Another change introduced by Camp in 1880 was the reduction of the size of the field by almost half, to 110 yards. In 1911, it changed again, to its current length of 100 yards.

• Gaining first downs was a lot easier in years gone by. From 1882 to 1906, players were given three attempts to advance the ball five yards for a first down. The distance was later changed to 10 yards, and a fourth down was added in 1912.

• Forward passing wasn't legal until 1905. The innovation was introduced after 18 players were killed and 159 were seriously injured on football fields across America earlier that year.

• Football has never been a genteel sport, but it was especially brutal in the 19th century, when players were encouraged to score touchdowns by any means necessary. Punching, eye-gouging, and tackling around the neck were all legal.

# FLY THE FLAG, BOYS!

*Either India or China invented them. The Roman Empire helped
popularize them. Armies and soldiers used them to identify who was
in charge, and everyone from pirates to military ships have flown
them to proclaim their loyalties. Every nation has its own flag.
Here are five sovereign banners with interesting histories.*

## 1. SWITZERLAND: THE NEUTRALITY OF BEING SQUARE

It seems only appropriate that Switzerland, with its neutral position in international conflicts, should share similarities to the
international rescue group the Red Cross. Both have similar flags.
Switzerland's flag is unique for being square rather than rectangular. Its stubby white cross on a red background evokes the Red
Cross, which employs the same design but with the colors
reversed.

The Swiss flag, which is one of only two square national flags
(the Vatican has the other one), traces its heritage to banners
used by the Holy Roman Empire and adopted by the cantons of
Switzerland after they were granted sovereignty. The flag has come
to represent peace, refuge, democracy, and neutrality. Though
Switzerland has had democratic traditions since 1291, political
struggles within the confederation of cantons and a French invasion in 1798 prevented the formal adoption of a national flag. The
creation of a constitution for a federal state in 1848 established
the national flag, which was formalized in 1889 by the Federal
Assembly.

## 2. NETHERLANDS: HOIST THE RIBBON! IT'S PARTY TIME!

The Dutch tricolor national flag has three horizontal stripes of red,
white, and blue, positioned from top to bottom. What's unique is
that the flag is festooned with an orange pennant whenever the
royal family has special occasions such as birthdays. And for families
throughout the kingdom, it is customary to place a schoolbag atop
the flagstaff to indicate students who have graduated.

Like the flags of many nations, the Dutch flag has roots on a

---

The earliest known knitted garments: pairs of socks discovered...

battlefield. It was used for the first time in the 16th century during the Dutch revolt against Spain, which was led by Prince William of Orange. His followers called the banner the *Prinzenvlag*, or "prince's flag." Orange, white, and blue at the time, the flag's orange stripe was eventually changed to red. The flag was officially recognized by the Netherlands Council in 1937.

## 3. FRANCE: THE HOLY TRICOLOR

Like that of the Netherlands, France's flag, created in 1790, is also distinguished by a tricolor design in red, white, and blue, but in this case the stripes are vertical. The colors come from the city flag of Paris that was used the day French radicals stormed the city's Bastille prison in 1789 to usher in the French Revolution and overthrow the aristocracy of King Louis XVI. The Marquis de Lafayette is said to have designed the flag, which fell out of favor after French emperor Napoléon Bonaparte was defeated at the Battle of Waterloo in 1815. However, it came back into vogue in 1830 and has flown over France ever since (except for two weeks in 1848 when it was changed, then changed back). The colors represent three religious figures important to France: blue for St. Martin of Tours, a French-Roman officer who gave his cloak to a peasant suffering in the cold; white for the Virgin Mary; and red for St. Denis, the patron saint of Paris.

## 4. TURKEY: THE MOON STAR FLAG

The Turkish national flag is mostly red, with a white star and crescent in the center, and dates back 700 years; Sultan Selim III formalized the look in 1793. The crescent and star have been adopted by many other Muslim nations since then. What is not so well known is that in Turkish history the crescent symbolizes Diana, the patron goddess of the ancient Turkish city of Byzantium, and the five-pointed star at the mouth of the crescent symbolizes the Virgin Mary, the patron saint of Byzantium after it became Constantinople in AD 330.

In 1453, when the city was conquered by the Ottoman Turks and renamed Istanbul, the flag remained unchanged, though other myths arose to explain the meaning of the star and crescent. One explains that the moon and star were conceived as the reflection of the moon and Jupiter in a pool of blood from the sultan Murad I, who was assassinated after the Battle of Kosovo in 1389. Another says it came about as a dream of the first emperor of the Ottoman Empire. Today, citizens of Turkey refer to their seminal national flag as *ay yildiz*—the "moon star" flag.

## 5. NEPAL: THE LIVING FOSSIL

The national flag of Nepal is the only one that is neither rectangular nor square. It's in the shape of two pennants sewn to one another. The pennants are symbolic of the Rana dynasty's two branches that ruled the mountainous country from 1846 to 1951. In the 19th century, the two crimson pennants were joined to represent the nation of Nepal, and in 1962 the conjoined form was officially adopted by Nepal's constitutional government. To the Nepalese, the pennants denote the two religions of Nepal—Hinduism and Buddhism—existing side by side. Set against the red background are the shapes of the sun and moon, which represent permanence and the hope that the nation will last as long as these celestial bodies.

The shape of the flag is not odd in the context of Nepal's history and isolation. For centuries, pennants were the common shape for regional flags in Asia. The form of a rectangular flag that eventually took hold worldwide was European in origin. But in Nepal, the idea of a pennant flag never seemed unusual to citizens cut off from the world by the towering Himalayas. Today the outside world views the flag as "the living fossil flag."

## WHAT WERE THEY THINKING?
### 1. Mozambique: My Bullets Beat Your Sword and Machete.

Angola has a machete on its flag, Saudi Arabia a sword. The African country of Mozambique, however, goes a step further. It's got an AK-47 machine gun on its national flag. The weapon is superimposed over a crossed hoe and a book; the three symbols represent defense, production, and education. The emblems are centered over a red triangle on the left side jutting into three broad stripes of green, black, and gold.

Why the AK-47? It was the primary weapon used in 1964 when the nation began its bloody but successful war for independence from Portugal.

## 2. Bosnia and Herzegovina: I Raise You Half a Star.

It's difficult at a glance to decipher the meaning of the flag of Bosnia and Herzegovina. An upside-down yellow isosceles triangle juts through the center of a blue banner. A ribbon of white stars flows along the long edge of the triangle, with half stars at both ends. What does it all mean?

The flag of the newly formed nation (once part of the former Yugoslavia) was imposed on the country by the NATO armistice that ended the Bosnian War of 1992–95. Carlos Westendorp, international high representative to the peace talks, came up with the flag when the parliaments of the country couldn't agree on a design that would meld the passions of Bosniaks, Croats, and Serbs. Westendorp hoped that his design would emphasize unity among the nation's three primary constituents. The points of the triangle supposedly represent a theoretical union of each group. The yellow, the color of the sun, represents hope. The blue corresponds to the color of the European Union flag and, along with the stars, represents Europe.

## 3. Libya: Plain But Proud.

The flag of Libya is the only one in the world with a single color: green. That's it. Just green. No animals, no weapons, no dragons, no stripes, no stars, no moon. Just green. Adopted in 1977, green has long been the national color, representative of Libya's devotion to Islam. Libya went green after leaving the Federation of Arab Republics in 1977.

\*　　　\*　　　\*

## TWO WORLD WAR I FACTS

**1.** On the opening day of the Battle of the Somme, 58,000 British soldiers were killed and wounded. On that same day (July 1, 1916), the entire U.S. Army had fewer than 58,000 soldiers.

**2.** General John J. "Black Jack" Pershing, commander of the American forces in Europe, became the only six-star general in U.S. history during the war. Congress advanced him in rank to General of the Armies as a face-saving move to put Pershing on an equal plane with the haughty field marshalls of France and Britain.

In 1953, Elizabeth II was the first monarch to have a televised coronation.

# GOING PLACES AND BURNING THINGS

*In part one on page 279, we looked at the use of projectiles In war. We continue our look at how man built more effective fighting machines using fire and locomotion.*

## FIRE: FEEL THE BURN

The ability to tame fire changed civilization forever. While sitting around their campfire, maybe even dreaming of the day their descendants would invent s'mores, ancient cavemen must have recognized fire's ability to inflict harm, having undoubtedly observed the destruction that lightning and wildfires could cause. It didn't take long before they figured out ways to use this new technology against their foes.

**1. Flamethrowers.** The first recorded instance of military flamethrowing occurs in the Greek historian Thucydides's account of the Peloponnesian War (431–404 BC) between Athens and Sparta. At the Battle of Delium in 424 BC, the Athenians were holed up in a fort made of wood and vines. When the Spartans got tired of waiting them out, they hollowed out a great wooden log, lined it with an iron pipe, and stuffed it with a smoldering mixture of coal, sulfur, and pitch. They then attached a huge bellows to their end of the pipe, and were able blow (and burn) down the Athenians' fort.

It worked so well that the Spartan invention became an established weapon of war. The Byzantine Empire of the Middle Ages used it (under the name "Greek fire"—a nod to the Spartans) to particularly good effect during naval battles. By using oil-based combustible material that floated on water and continued to burn, they terrified their enemies and dominated the seas. The Chinese added a double-acting bellows with two pumps, which made the fire bursts continuous.

In 1942, at the height of World War II, Harvard researchers developed a combustible gel-like substance for flamethrowers, made of naphthenic acid and palmitic acid, and which they named "napalm" (from the first letters of its main ingredients). Napalm burned more slowly than previous incendiaries, could be projected farther, and clung to whatever it touched. It inflicted great damage in World War II and later in the Vietnam War.

**2. Gunpowder.** Gunpowder was invented by accident. In the ninth century, alchemists everywhere were looking for a potion that would confer immortality. The Chinese came up with a brew of saltpeter (potassium nitrate), sulfur, and charcoal. It isn't known whether they ever got around to tasting this elixir before they realized that what it did best was explode.

As early as the 10th century, the Chinese of the Song dynasty used gunpowder against their greatest enemy, the Mongols. At first they attached tubes of gunpowder to the shaft of an arrow (calling the result "flying fire"). Soon they graduated to rockets made of powder-filled bamboo tubes; from there, they learned to cast cannons out of metal. The use of gunpowder spread quickly via the Silk Road, along with all the other goods and ideas that traveled from Asia to Europe. The English first used it at the Battle of Crécy in 1346 during the Hundred Years' War, but still owed their victory there to the reliable old longbow.

When firepower was combined with locomotion, warfare advanced to a whole new level. Let's look at how war moved off the ground and out of the trenches.

## LOCOMOTION: GOING PLACES

The wheel was invented around 4500 BC, but it took a while for it to catch on as a means of locomotion. Its first use was as a potter's wheel. For some 300 years, the wheel lay around being used to make household utensils from clay, and then some unsung Mesopotamian came up with the idea of using it for transportation. Until the horse was domesticated, the first wheeled carts were pulled by donkeys, mules, oxen, or goats.

These animal-drawn conveyances weren't used to visit Grandma on Sunday—the lack of good roads delayed widespread domestic use of the wheel for centuries more. The vehicles were used for killing and warfare: they may have been heavy and cumbersome with their solid wooden wheels, but they could easily be driven into (and over) enemy ranks.

**1. Chariots.** After the Egyptians were introduced to war chariots by their enemies, the Hittites, they invented the spoked wheel, which was much lighter and more flexible. Their chariots had a curved front panel, an open back, and two spoked wheels. It was just large enough for two passengers—a driver holding the reins and an archer, whose hands were free to wield his bow. By the 15th century BC, Pharaoh Thutmose III had more than a thousand in his arsenal. Around 1000 BC, military commanders realized that cavalry mounted directly on horseback could fight even more effectively—and that marked the end of the war chariot.

**2. Ships.** Historians agree that the Battle of Salamis in 480 BC marked a monumental shift in the balance of power in the Middle East. Persia seemed poised to conquer the ancient world, but its defeat at Salamis turned the tide in favor of Greek civilization. The Greek victory is universally attributed to just one weapon— the trireme—a large warship 120 feet in length and propelled by 170 oarsmen distributed one per oar over three decks. It was built for speed and mobility, but was also powerful enough to ram enemy ships. With its fleet of more than 300 triremes, the Greek navy dominated the seas for years. In the United States, the trireme is considered the grandfather of today's Perry-class frigate.

**3. Tanks.** Leonardo da Vinci (1452–1519), who seemingly invented everything that the Chinese didn't, made a sketch of a round, tanklike wagon that was never built. In 1903, a short story by H. G. Wells included a description of a tanklike war machine. And although a number of lesser-known mortals had ideas about armored vehicles, it wasn't until World War I that actual tanks came into combat use by the British.

The tank was considered such a powerful weapon for breaking the deadlock of trench warfare that, during its development, Winston Churchill wanted to keep its true nature secret—even from the people who were building it. Factory workers were told that they were building water carriers for Russia. When someone pointed out that factory drawings would be titled "WC's for Russia," Churchill changed the name to "water tanks for Russia," which was later shortened to just "tanks."

---

At one time, people thought giraffes were a cross between a camel and a leopard.

# WWII JARGON

*World War II was an exhausting battle, so it makes sense that
people found short ways to say long things: Franklin Delano Roosevelt
was simply "FDR." General Dwight D. Eisenhower became "Ike."
Navy destroyers were "tin cans." And then there were these.*

## 1. FAT MAN, THIN MAN, AND LITTLE BOY

**Nicknames For:** The nuclear bombs made by scientists working
on the Manhattan Project in New Mexico

**The Story:** J. Robert Oppenheimer (often called the "Father of
the Atomic Bomb") usually gets credit for all of the nuclear suc-
cesses that came out of the Manhattan Project, but it was actually
a physicist named Robert Serber who came up with the bombs'
code names. Serber invented the first workable theory for how to
trigger a nuclear explosion, and he named the bombs built with
that technology after three characters in two Dashiell Hammet
detective novels: "fat man" Kasper Gutman and "little boy"
Wilmer Cook from *The Maltese Falcon*, and "thin man" Richard
Wynant from *The Thin Man*.

Thin Man and Little Boy were the first models—these long
and slender nuclear bombs were similar in design, but they used
different isotopes to trigger their explosions. Little Boy required
uranium, and Thin Man used plutonium. Eventually, the Manhattan Project scientists had to abandon Thin Man because its plutonium core became contaminated. Instead, they focused on Little
Boy and a third bomb, Fat Man, which also used plutonium, but
was shorter and stockier in design. On August 6, 1945, Colonel
Paul Tibbetts Jr. flew the bomber *Enola Gay* and dropped Little
Boy on Hiroshima, Japan. Three days later, pilot Charles W.
Sweeney led the mission that dropped Fat Man on the city of
Nagasaki. With hundreds of thousands of people dead or severely
injured in the bombings, Japan formally surrendered on September
2, ending World War II. Little Boy and Fat Man remain the only
two nuclear weapons ever used in war.

## 2. V-E DAY

**Nickname For:** Victory in Europe Day

**The Story:** On May 8, 1945, Winston Churchill made a public

---

National dish of Brazil? *Feijoada,* a stew of black beans with beef and pork.

broadcast announcing Germany's total surrender and declaring it "V-E Day." (Fighting in Europe had officially ended the night before when Germany signed the unconditional surrender document in Reims, France.) During the hours that followed, he rode through the streets of London in an open car—greeted everywhere by cheering crowds—and flashed a familiar "V" sign with his right hand, a gesture he'd used often through the six years of war. U.S. president Harry Truman dedicated the victory to his predecessor, Franklin Delano Roosevelt, who had died on April 12, less than a month before the war ended.

### 3. TOM, DICK, AND HARRY

**Nicknames For:** Three escape tunnels crafted by Allied prisoners at the German-run Stalag Luft III POW camp

**The Story:** The expression "Tom, Dick, and Harry" is usually used to refer to any group of unspecified people, especially nonentities with no distinguishing characteristics. At Stalag Luft III, enterprising servicemen turned the phrase into a security code name for three escape tunnels. Because the names are common in the English language, the soldiers could discuss the tunnels openly without the German guards getting suspicious.

Stalag Luft III was the third camp the Germans built to hold captured pilots. It was about 100 miles southeast of Berlin near what's now the town of Zaga, Poland. Ironically, the Germans chose the site specifically because its sandy soil discouraged tunneling. Little did they know that their efforts would be in vain.

The Germans did the best they could to secure the camp. Guard towers surrounded the entire fenced compound, which included about 18 wooden barracks for prisoners. German buildings were outside, facing the compound's two main gates. The guards tended to treat the airmen well compared to other camps and provided athletic fields, a theater, a library, and schools offering prisoners an opportunity to learn advanced degrees in languages, engineering, and other subjects. But the perks didn't impress RAF Squadron Leader Roger Bushell, who was the one to come up with a plan for a mass escape. Of the project, Bushell later said, "Three bloody deep, bloody long tunnels will be dug—Tom, Dick, and Harry. One will succeed!"

"Tom" began in a dark corner of one of the barracks. Tunnel crews used a drain sump in one of the washrooms to conceal the entrance to "Dick." "Harry" began under a stove. More than 600 prisoners participated in the project. In November 1943, the Germans discovered the Tom tunnel. Thinking it was a unique effort, they didn't bother looking for another.

Harry was completed in March 1944, and on the first moonless night (March 24), 200 flyers lined up to make their escape. Only 76 managed to crawl through the tunnel and make it into the woods before German guards figured out what was going on, and all but three of those were later caught. A second escape attempt followed with equally disastrous results.

Still, the tunnels became a symbol of the Allied resolve against the Nazis. In 1963, director John Sturges brought the story to the big screen as the film *The Great Escape*, starring Steve McQueen. It's still considered one of the best World War II movies ever made.

\*     \*     \*

## HEY, DOGFACE!

World War II wasn't known just for its nicknames—it also had some colorful slang:

**1. Whitewalled:** If you see a man with a typical close-cropped GI haircut, he has just been whitewalled.

**2. S\*\*t on a Shingle:** Also known as "SOS," it was a type of food usually served at breakfast. The mixture consisted of one stale slice of cold toast topped with a slurry of dehydrated cream sauce containing thin shavings of dried beef.

**3. Dogface:** This is the term for infantrymen because they lived in pup tents, dug foxholes, and were treated like dogs during training.

**4. Zulu:** The letters have no significance. Zulu simply refers to Greenwich Mean Time (GMT), the average solar time at the Royal Greenwich Observatory in Greenwich, England.

**5. Fubar:** It means "F\*\*\*\*d up beyond all repair." The word was used liberally by World War II mechanics.

Middle Ages fashion: Men and women wore a gownlike garment called a *houppelande*.

# WHAT'S THE RUSH?

*Thar's gold in them thar hills, or at least that is what the prospectors hoped.*

## 1. BLACK HILLS GOLD RUSH (1874)

**The Find:** The opening of the American West after the Civil War meant that new lands and opportunities were ready to be explored. In 1874, General George Armstrong Custer led an expedition into the Black Hills of the Dakota Territory, where their discovery of gold set off a gold rush that attracted thousands of prospectors who staked their claims along the creeks over the next four years.

**The Rush:** According to the 1868 Treaty of Fort Laramie, the area belonged to the Lakota Indian tribe. It should come as no surprise that tensions developed between the Lakota and the American settlers who wanted to claim the land and the gold for themselves. In 1876, these tensions sparked the Black Hills War, which led to the famous defeat of Custer's forces at the Battle of the Little Bighorn in June of that year. The U.S. forces regrouped and Lakota leader Crazy Horse was killed in September 1877; Sitting Bull surrendered in July 1881. The Americans took full control of the Dakota Territory, pushed the Lakota onto reservations away from the Black Hills, and set the course for South Dakota's admittance to the union in 1889.

Gold mining in the area was originally limited to placer gold in the creeks, but in 1876, four men staked a claim on the Homestake Mine and established the town of Lead (pronounced "leed"). The Homestake was the mother lode, the source of the placer gold that had been eroding into the creeks for thousands of years. Plus, the gold was relatively easy to extract from the rocks, and this bonanza would go on to produce 40 million ounces, almost 10 percent of the world's gold supply, during its 125 years of operation. Although the region saw plenty of boom-and-bust cycles related to the price of gold and the costs of extracting it, the Black Hills gold rush continued well past that first surge in the 1870s.

**Mined Out:** The Homestake Mine ceased operations in 2001, but was put to other uses. In 2007, the National Science Foundation selected the mine—the deepest in the United States at more than 8,000 feet—as the site for a new underground lab where

---

What's odd about Australia's wattlebird? Alas, unlike other wattlebirds...

researchers will be able to study neutrinos without interference from background radiation, a condition that's possible only at great depths below the earth's surface.

## 2. WITWATERSRAND GOLD RUSH (1886)

**The Find:** Unlike in the other finds, the gold of South Africa wasn't conveniently gathered in nuggets at the bottoms of riverbeds or even buried underground. The Witwatersrand ("white water ridge") is a range of hills near Johannesburg 62 miles long and 23 miles wide containing a layer, or reef, of low-grade gold ore nearly invisible to the naked eye. In 1886, an Australian gold miner named George Harrison discovered the gold-bearing reef on a farm. The low-grade nature of the formation meant that mining by individual prospectors was rarely worth the effort, but large companies with access to heavy equipment and methods for extracting the gold (which involves using cyanide to dissolve the gold from the rocks) could turn a tidy profit.

**The Rush:** Mining companies and workers soon flocked to the area; Johannesburg was quickly laid out as a small mining settlement but soon grew into the sprawling city that it is today—the nation's largest. With the increased number of foreigners, or *uitlanders*, came increased discomfort among the Boers whose ancestors had settled the Transvaal region in the 1830s and 1840s to get away from the British-dominated Cape Colony to the south.

The Boers saw the uitlanders as a threat to their autonomy; besides imposing harsh taxes on the miners, they demanded long periods of residency before the Transvaal government would grant them voting rights. The miners and the Boers came to blows in 1899, when the Second Boer War began. (The First Boer War of 1880–81 had resulted in a victory for the Boers, who maintained their independence from Britain.) But this time the winner would go home with the gold; the British sent more troops and greater resources to secure the region. The war ended in 1902 with a British victory, and the Union of South Africa was established eight years later as a dominion of the British Empire.

**Still Not Mined Out:** Production has slowed in recent years due to the difficulty of extracting the gold from greater depths underground, but the Witwatersrand—the source of nearly 50 percent of the gold ever mined on earth—is still very much in operation.

# MORE LESSONS IN LARCENY

*On page 271, we introduced you to the first batch of miscreants with larceny in their hearts. Here's the rest of the story.*

## LESSON #3: ALCOHOL CAN SCREW UP YOUR HEIST
### Stealing Lincoln's Corpse (1876)

Ben Boyd was famous in Illinois as a master engraver—a counterfeiter whose phony bills could pass for the real thing. James "Big Jim" Kinealy made good money passing Boyd's bills, but in 1875 the engraver was sentenced to 10 years in the slammer. Desperate to regain his source of income, Kinealy decided to steal Abe Lincoln's body and hold it for ransom. His terms were harsh: he would return the corpse in exchange for $200,000 and Ben Boyd's freedom.

**Casing the Joint:** Kinealy's gang scoped out Lincoln's mausoleum at the Oakfield Cemetery in Springfield, Illinois: a granite base decorated with a 117-foot obelisk. They learned where the burial chamber was and discovered that the tomb wasn't guarded at night. But before they could act, one of the conspirators got drunk and spilled the beans to a lady friend. Rumors spread that robbers were after Lincoln's body, and Kinealy fled to Chicago.

**Let's Have Another Round!** Undaunted, he found two new pals and decided to try again. They would snatch Lincoln's body during the distraction of November elections, spirit the corpse off in a wagon, then drive to Indiana, where they'd hide Honest Abe in the sand dunes near Lake Michigan. Meanwhile, they hung out in a Chicago tavern drinking whiskey, where they met ex-con Lewis Swegles—a tough guy and pleasant drinking companion who was brought into the plot. On November 7, the gang broke a padlock to enter Lincoln's tomb. They forced open the marble sarcophagus and sent Swegles to get the wagon while they pulled out the coffin.

**Two Strikes and You're Out:** As it turned out, their Chicago drinking pal was a paid informant. Swegles signaled to detectives hiding outside, who rushed to arrest the thieves. Kinealy's crew escaped that night but were soon captured, tried, and imprisoned.

---

In 2005, British comedian Tim FitzHigham was the first person to successfully...

Instead of being returned to its marble sarcophagus, Lincoln's body was secretly reburied inside the tomb. Finally in 1901, Robert Todd Lincoln laid his father to rest inside the tomb for the last time—covering a deep grave with concrete to discourage any more trouble.

## LESSON #4: YOU NEED THOSE STINKIN' BADGES
### The Gardner Museum Heist (1990)

At the turn of the 19th century, wealthy Bostonian Isabella Gardner decided to create a museum like no other in the United States. She had it designed to resemble the Palazzo Barbaro in Venice, where she'd often stayed on her world-traveling art collecting jaunts. She filled her museum with a highly valuable art collection that included masterpieces by the world's greatest painters, including Rembrandt, Vermeer, Titian, Botticelli, Manet, and Matisse. Today, museumgoers still see the same magnificent architecture and glass-roofed courtyard that visitors first admired in 1903. But now, along the museum walls there are empty picture frames or blank spaces with notes that describe the stolen masterpieces formerly on display.

**Cops and Robbers:** Just past midnight on the morning of March 18, 1990, two men showed up wearing Boston police insignias and flashing their badges. They informed the young, untrained security guard that they were there to investigate a reported disturbance. Instead of checking their identities, the guard buzzed them into the museum—a mistake that led to the largest property theft in U.S. history. Once inside, the Beantown "cops" found the security guard "suspicious" and put him in handcuffs. It all happened too fast for the first guard to notify the other guard in the building or to push the panic button that would notify the real authorities about a robbery. Both security guards wound up handcuffed, ducttaped, and imprisoned in the museum basement.

**The Art of the Steal:** Thanks to their bold impersonation, the Beantown burglars had the run of the museum. They didn't seem to know a heck of a lot about art, since it took them 81 minutes to loot 13 objects; most professional art thieves could have pulled off a similar heist in 15 minutes. They also devalued their haul by cutting some paintings from their frames and nabbing relatively common objects like a gilded eagle flag finial while leaving priceless masterpieces behind. The museum's (and Boston's) most significant painting, Titian's *The Death of Europa*, was ignored. Art-educated or not, they got away with an incredible haul—including the first painting Isabella Gardner ever purchased, Vermeer's *The Concert*, three prized Rembrandts, sketches by Degas, and a Manet. Today that stolen art is valued as high as $500 million.

**Still Looking.** A $5 million reward offered for the return of the artworks has led to plenty of leads. And there is even a fairly clear description of one of the burglars who, according to the first security guard, resembled "Colonel Klink on *Hogan's Heroes*." Suspects have been found among antique dealers, imprisoned art thieves, Boston's Irish Mafia, and even the Irish Republican Army, but there have been no arrests. And though several people claim they know what happened to the artworks, not even one piece has been returned. The FBI investigation remains ongoing.

\*      \*      \*

## WE'RE OUTTA HERE!

During the presidential election of 1860, the southern states pledged to secede if Abraham Lincoln (and his antislavery views) were elected president. Lincoln warned against this in his inaugural address, saying, "In your hands, my dissatisfied fellow countrymen, and not in mine, is the momentous issue of civil war. The government will not assail you...You have no oath registered in Heaven to destroy the government, while I shall have the most solemn one to preserve, protect, and defend it." But the Southerners weren't buying it. On December 20, 1860, South Carolina was the first to leave the Union. Ten states followed:

| | |
|---|---|
| Mississippi | Texas |
| Florida | Virginia |
| Alabama | Arkansas |
| Georgia | North Carolina |
| Louisiana | Tennessee |

The Southerners amassed an army of more than 75,000 volunteers, and on April 12, 1861, attacked Union forces at Fort Sumter, near Charleston, South Carolina. The Civil War had begun.

George Eastman patented the Kodak box camera in 1888.

# MIND YOUR K's AND Q's

*It's tough to keep all the kings and queens of England straight, but British schoolkids have to do it. So for generations, they've used this poem to remember all the monarchs in the proper order.*

William the Conqueror long
did reign,
William, his son, by an
arrow was slain;
Henry the First was a
scholar bright;
Stephen was king without
any right.
Henry the Second,
Plantagenet's scion;
Richard the First was as
brave as a lion;
John, though a tyrant,
the Charter signed;
Henry the Third had
a weakly mind.
Edward the First conquered
Cambria dales;
Edward the Second was
born Prince of Wales;
Edward the Third humbled
France in its pride;
Richard the Second in
prison died.
Henry the Fourth for himself
took the crown;
Henry the Fifth pulled the
French king down;
Henry the Sixth lost his
father's gains.
Edward the Fourth of York
laid hold of the reins;
Edward the Fifth was killed

with his brother;
Richard the Third soon
made way for another.
Henry the Seventh was
frugal of means;
Henry the Eighth had
a great many queens.
Edward the Sixth
reformation began;
Bloody Queen Mary
thwarted the plan.
Wise and profound were
Elizabeth's aims.
England and Scotland were
joined by King James.
Charles found the people
a cruel corrector;
Oliver Cromwell was called
Lord Protector.
Charles the Second was
hid in an oak,
James the Second took
Popery's yoke.
William and Mary were
offered the throne,
Anne succeeded and
reigned alone.
George the First from
Hanover came;
George the Second kept
up the name;
George the Third was
loved in the land,

---

**August 8, 1960:** The song "Itsy Bitsy Teenie Weenie Yellow Polka Dot Bikini" hit #1.

George the Fourth was
pompous and grand,
William the Fourth had
no heir of his own,
Victoria so young then
came to the throne.
When at last her long
reign was o'er,
Edward the Seventh the
nation's crown wore.
George the Fifth kept a
strict moral tone,
Edward the Eighth
relinquished the throne,
George the Sixth through
the war years was king,
Of Elizabeth the Second
her praises we sing.

\*     \*     \*

## HOW GOOD IS YOUR MEMORY?

**1.** Do you need to remember all the British royal dynasties, families whose heirs rule through succession? (Other royals came and went, but these are the main dynasties.) Use these mnemonics:

*"No Plan Like Yours To Study History Wisely" or "No Point Letting Your Trousers Slip Half Way!"*

The families: **N**orman (1066–1154), **P**lantagenet (1216–1399), **L**ancaster (1399–1461), **Y**ork (1461–1485), **T**udor (1485–1603), **S**tuart (1603–1714), **H**anover (1714–1901), and **W**indsor (1901–)

**2.** How about the fates of the wives of King Henry VIII (one of the Tudors)?

*"Divorced, Beheaded, Died, Divorced, Beheaded, Survived!"*

The wives: Catharine of Aragon (marriage annulled), Anne Boleyn (annulled, then beheaded), Jane Seymour (died following childbirth), Anne of Cleves (marriage annulled), Catharine Howard (annulled, then beheaded), and Catharine Parr (survived, lucky girl).

---

About 200,000 years ago: Homo sapiens first appeared on Earth. (That's you.)

# THE DEADLIEST AMERICAN WARS

*From the American Revolution through Iraq/Afghanistan, more than 650,000 American soliders have died on the battlefield. Here is the list of the deadliest American conflicts, ranked by deaths in combat.*

**1. World War II (1941–45):** America's "greatest generation" left 291,557 of its members behind on battlefields in Europe, Asia, and North Africa, with an additional 113,842 service members dying away from the battlefield and nearly 671,000 wounded.

**2. U.S. Civil War (1861–65):** The Union suffered 140,414 battlefield deaths, and the Confederacy 74,524, for a total of 214,938 killed in action. However, both sides suffered a combined 283,394 military deaths away from the battlefield, making the Civil War the number one deadliest American conflict overall.

**3. World War I (1917–18):** America's involvement in "The War to End All Wars" was brief relative to that of other combatants, but in the short time our armed forces served, they nevertheless suffered 53,402 combat deaths, and an additional 63,114 deaths in service. World War I was the last time noncombat service deaths exceeded combat deaths.

**4. Vietnam War (1964–75):** The Vietnam War is to date America's longest-running conflict, spanning 11 years, and saw 47,434 combat deaths, nearly 10,800 in-theater noncombat deaths, and 32,000 additional deaths in service.

**5. Korean War (1950–53):** In the four years of the Korean conflict, 33,739 Americans gave their lives in combat, and an additional 20,505 died in service.

**6. American Revolution (1775–83):** The United States' War of Independence saw 4,435 new citizens become the first Americans to lay down their lives for their country.

---

In the Persian Gulf in 1987, the U.S. Navy conducted the first military use of trained dolphins.

**7. Iraq/Afghanistan (2001– ):** As of March 27, 2010, the Department of Defense has registered 4,217 "hostile deaths" in Operation Iraqi Freedom and Operation Enduring Freedom, with an additional 1,179 deaths by nonhostile means.

**8. War Of 1812 (1812–15):** This last major struggle between the United States and the British Empire cost the young country 2,260 American lives in battle.

**9. Mexican-American War (1846–48):** This war secured the western third of what would become the continental United States, at the cost of 1,733 combat deaths.

**10. Spanish-American War (1898–1902):** This war is often forgotten by Americans, possibly because of the relatively few U.S. servicemen who died in combat during its prosecution: just 385. However, it's worth noting that the United States' involvement in this war led to its involvement in an even less well-known conflict (the Philippine Insurrection) between the U.S. and insurgents in the former Spanish possession of the Philippines, which lead to over 4,000 U.S. service deaths between 1899 and 1902.

*Sources: Department of Defense, Veteran's Administration*

\*     \*     \*

## OLD BOY'S CLUB

Uncle John looked at the history of U.S. currency and discovered that only three women have made it onto American money:

**1. Martha Washington,** the nation's first First Lady, is the only woman whose face has ever appeared on a currency note. Her portrait commanded the $1 silver certificate issued in 1186, 1891, and 1896.

**2. Susan B. Anthony** is one of two women whose image made it onto U.S. coins. The women's suffrage campaigner became the standard-bearer for the $1 coin minted from 1979 to 1981.

**3. Sacagewea,** the Shoshone Indian guide who assisted Lewis and Clark on their famous expedition to the Pacific coast in 1804, became the image for the $1 gold coin minted in 2000.

# TRAIL MIX

*These historic North American trails were major thoroughfares in their day. Whether they were used for moving people or goods or both, you can bet these trails were no walk in the park.*

## 1. THE NATCHEZ TRACE

**Route:** From Natchez, Mississippi, through the northwest corner of Alabama to Nashville, Tennessee

**Length:** About 440 miles

**Early History:** The "trace" (an Old French word meaning a line of footprints or animal tracks) was first formed by the movement of bison and other large animals and by early Native peoples, and was later used by the Natchez, Choctaw, and Chickasaw tribes.

**Travelers:** During the trace's heyday from about 1785 to 1815, boatmen known as "Kaintucks" (named for Kentucky, though they weren't all from there) floated goods down the Ohio and Mississippi rivers to sell in Natchez and New Orleans. Once there, they dismantled their boats, sold the lumber, and walked home. The first leg of the return trip consisted of the entire length of the trace, which took about a month to walk. From Nashville, other roads took them home to Ohio, Kentucky, or Pennsylvania.

In 1805, Aaron Burr, then vice president of the United States, was under indictment for the murder of Alexander Hamilton. He escaped west via the trace and was later arrested on suspicion of treason for allegedly trying to set himself up as the emperor of the Louisiana Territory.

Meriwether Lewis of the Lewis and Clark expedition was governor of the Upper Louisiana Territory when he died in September 1809 at Grinder's Stand, an inn 70 miles outside of Nashville, of a gunshot wound. The debate still rages as to whether it was murder or suicide.

In 1810, more than 10,000 people traveled the trace, often in large groups for safety. The trace was notorious for thievery and murder; even the innkeepers couldn't be trusted not to rob or murder their guests. At one point in its history, crime got so bad that local law enforcers cut off the heads of outlaws and staked them alongside the trace as a warning.

Andrew Jackson marched his army along the Natchez Trace from Nashville on his way to defeating the British at the Battle of New Orleans at the end of the War of 1812. And talk about highway robbery: George Colbert, who operated a stand and a ferry across the Tennessee River, reportedly charged $75,000 to ferry Jackson and his army across.

**Trail's End:** By 1820, the trace was falling into disuse, supplanted by steamships that carried folks and goods back upstream. Portions of the original Natchez Trace are preserved by the National Park Service along the modern Natchez Trace Parkway, which opened in 2005.

## 2. THE CHILKOOT TRAIL

**Route:** From Skagway, Alaska, to just north of Lake Bennet, British Columbia

**Length:** 33 miles

**Early History:** The trail originally served the coastal Tlingit people as a trade route to the interior. All that changed in 1897 when the Klondike gold rush began.

**Travelers:** Tens of thousands of gold seekers took the Chilkoot Trail to the goldfields in Canada's Yukon Territory. Don't be fooled by the shortness of the trail; it could take a prospector up to three months to complete the trek. First he had to slog up to the top of Chilkoot Pass, where he would be met by Northwest Mounties stationed there to make sure that anyone who entered Canada had enough food to last them a year, literally one ton of food supplies that included staples like 400 pounds of flour, 100 pounds of beans, and 200 pounds of bacon, among other necessary provisions. Since the trail was too steep for pack animals, the miners had to carry it all on their backs. A man could carry only 50 or 60 pounds at a time, so he had to make 30 to 40 trips while watching out for avalanches (one avalanche killed 60 people in 1898) and negotiating the 1,500 icy steps known as the "Golden Staircase." Once over the Chilkoot Trail, the fortune hunters still had a 500-mile boat trip to Dawson City and the goldfields. A few aerial tramways were built to make the process less grueling, but they were replaced before 1900 by the White Pass and Yukon Route railroad that ran from Skagway to Whitehorse, the capital of Yukon.

The first Bible printed in America was in Algonquin, an Indian dialect, in 1663.

**Trail's End:** The Klondike gold rush didn't last long. By August 1898, many of the prospectors were headed home, most of them broke. Today, items like shovel fragments and cookware that was discarded to lighten the load up the steep pass still litter the Chilkoot Trail.

## 3. THE IDITAROD TRAIL

**Route:** From Seward, Alaska, to Nome, Alaska

**Length:** 1,150 miles

**Early History:** It's a ghost town now, but in the early years of the 20th century, Iditarod, Alaska, was an outpost of one of the last gold rushes in the state—a halfway point on the southern portion of the trail to Nome, another gold-rush town. The trail was a winter route for the U.S. Postal Service, which used teams of sled dogs to make its deliveries.

**Travelers:** The route was made famous in January 1925 for the historic serum run. The port of Nome was frozen over during a severe outbreak of diphtheria, leaving dogsled teams as the only way to transport the antitoxin. A special train carried 300,000 units of the serum from Anchorage to Nenana. Then 20 mushers and 150 sled dogs carried the serum across 674 miles of the Iditarod Trail in temperatures that reached -60°F. It took them five days, but the dogs and mushers reached Nome in time to save the diphtheria victims.

**Trail's End:** Ten years after the serum run, airplanes replaced sled dogs for mail service along the trail. Because of the swampy ground, the trail is strictly winter use only. Today, the Iditarod Trail is known for the dogsled race from Anchorage to Nome, which follows part of the old dogsled mail route. The dogsled races have been run every March since 1973. In 1978, the Iditarod was designated a National Historic Trail.

*Continue on down the trail on page 397.*

\*       \*       \*

"I have never been lost, but I will admit to being confused for several weeks."

—**Daniel Boone**

---

At 86 years, nuns have the longest life expectancy of any group in the U.S.

# THE RUSH GOES ON

*The story of the rush for gold and wealth continues from page 324. Here are tales of strikes in two Golden States, followed by a thunder to rush Down Under.*

## 1. NORTH CAROLINA GOLD RUSH (EARLY 1800s)

**The Find:** On a lazy Sunday afternoon in the spring of 1799, 12-year-old Conrad Reed was fishing in a creek on his family's property in Cabarrus County, 20 miles outside of Charlotte. He returned home with a 17-pound gold nugget, which his father John—a German immigrant who had never seen gold before—used as a doorstop for three years before taking it to a jeweler to be appraised. The jeweler bought it for $3.50, a price that suited Reed just fine ($3.50 being a week's wages) until he learned that its true value was a thousand times that amount. A few years later, Reed established his own riverbed gold-mining operation, but worked it only during the seasons that he wasn't farming because he didn't know how to make the enterprise profitable.

**The Rush:** Twenty years later, prospectors were regularly panning the creeks and riverbeds around Charlotte for gold nuggets, but it wasn't until 1831 that an underground mine was established on the Reed property. The rush of immigrants to America in the 19th century included skilled mine workers from Europe, many of whom saw North Carolina as a good place to ply their trade. By the late 1830s, the state had 56 mines and was the nation's top gold producer; in fact, gold was the state's second-leading industry after agriculture. Although the North Carolina gold rush was small compared to later gold rushes, it established Charlotte as the state's leading business center (which it remains to this day) and served as a springboard to later gold rushes in California and elsewhere. New mining operations reaped the benefits of employing miners from North Carolina who shared their knowledge and skills so that others didn't have to learn the trade from scratch.

**Mined Out:** Gold mining in the original "Golden State" slowed to a trickle in the 1850s when underground mines began to yield less gold at greater depths and as prospectors scurried off to California in search of richer finds. The last great gold strike on

---

A baby's strongest sense is smell.

the Reed property was in 1896, when a 22-pound nugget was unearthed from a creek bed by Jake Shinn, a great-grandson of John Reed.

## 2. CALIFORNIA GOLD RUSH (1848)

**The Find:** John A. Sutter, owner of a sawmill on the American River in Coloma, California, was producing lumber to build a flour mill when an employee, James Marshall, returned from the field with a pea-sized gold nugget in January 1848. Sutter tried to suppress the news of the discovery from the public so that he could finish his flour mill, but word of the find spread like wildfire.

**The Rush:** The area was soon overrun by prospectors, who were free to set up camp wherever they liked and to keep every ounce of gold they found. The downside was that local merchants inflated their prices for food and supplies so much that the gold seekers had to find about an ounce of gold every day to break even. That still didn't prevent immigrants from invading California by the thousands. Passengers disembarked at the port of San Francisco (then a small settlement of 1,000 residents), and crewmen abandoned their ships in the harbor to join the stampede. By 1849, San Francisco had more than 25,000 residents and, owing to the sudden surge in population and the need to establish law and order, California was granted statehood a year later.

Panning for gold, or placer mining, was the method used by most prospectors, but the individual miners were eventually driven out by large companies that used more productive (and destructive) techniques such as sluicing, dredging, and hydraulic mining.

**Mined Out:** When the California gold rush ended in the late 1850s, thousands of men and their families were left without a source of income. Many of them turned to farming; the state's agriculture industry grew exponentially and, today, the (second) "Golden State" is the nation's leading agricultural producer, with farmland covering a third of its total land area.

## 3. AUSTRALIAN GOLD RUSH (1851)

**The Find:** Edward Hammond Hargraves was an English merchant marine who had spent time in Australia before joining the California gold rush in 1849. He'd come up empty-handed,

---

The human body contains enough phosphorus to make 2,200 match heads.

but returned to Australia in 1851 convinced that he could find gold there, owing to certain geological similarities between California and the area around Bathurst, New South Wales. Within a few weeks, he found his first gold nugget in a riverbed, and the news and gold fever spread quickly.

**The Rush:** When more gold was discovered to the south at Ballarat, Victoria, the port of Melbourne was inundated with gold seekers, especially the Irish and Chinese. Over the next ten years, Victoria's population increased from 76,000 to 540,000.

Unlike the general lawlessness in California, the frenzy in Victoria was regulated from the start. Administrators were appointed, hard liquor was banned, and monthly licenses were sold to prospectors for the right to dig at certain sections of a river.

In 1854, miners in Ballarat who were fed up with the rising cost of equipment and licenses staged a revolt known as the Eureka Rebellion. They demanded the right to vote and be represented (since they paid taxes) in the lower house of the Victorian parliament; they also wanted a voice in the reform of how the goldfields were administered. The authorities didn't take kindly to the miners' demands, and the ensuing skirmish resulted in the deaths of 22 miners and six British colonial soldiers.

The public outcry over the killings of the nearly defenseless miners forced the government to set up a commission to investigate. The commission's report concluded by recommending that all men (excluding Aborigines) in Victoria be given the right to vote and to be represented in the lower house of parliament, that mining licenses for individual plots be abolished in favor of annual mining fees, and that the administration of the goldfields be restructured. Some historians have called the Eureka Rebellion the birth of democracy in Australia, although full suffrage for all Australians didn't come to pass until 1962.

**Mined Out:** As in California, the Australian gold rush slowed after a decade. When most of the surface gold was claimed, large corporations with heavy machinery replaced individuals, who couldn't reach the underground gold. Although gold continued to be mined in earnest until World War I, the overwhelming influx of foreigners ended in the 1860s. The now-unemployed prospectors remained and laid the foundation for Australia's development in the 20th century.

# MORE WAR WEAR

*Among the following list of wearable items you'll find a varied cast of characters and locales that includes the men in the trenches (literally), a chilly port on the Black Sea, a one-armed British nobleman, and an American sex symbol.*

## 1. RAGLAN SLEEVES

FitzRoy James Henry Somerset, First Baron of Raglan, fought at Waterloo, too, where he lost an arm. Because of his handicap, he favored a loose, capelike overcoat with sleeves that extended from the neck rather than the shoulder. The coat, which came to be called a raglan, is no longer in fashion, but the sleeve style—the raglan sleeve—is still a popular design used mostly for women's coats, sweaters, dresses, and blouses.

## 2. BALACLAVA

The most memorable battle of the Crimean War took place on October 25, 1854, at the Black Sea port of Balaclava. When a large Russian force advanced on the Allies, the Turks fled in retreat toward the port, leaving 550 men of the 93rd Scottish Highlanders between Balaclava and the Russians. Because they were facing down in a line on the slope of a hillside, the Russians couldn't see the Scots as they advanced. Not realizing they were up against a mere few hundred men, the Russians retreated, thereby scoring a glorious victory for the Highlanders.

The harsh winter climate of Crimea forced troops to adopt various kinds of clothing to keep warm. One item was a knitted woolen hat that covered the head and neck, leaving only an opening for the face. Called a balaclava (a.k.a. ski mask), it's worn by just about anyone who has to brave the cold—or by various criminal types and terrorists who, by pulling up the neck portion to cover the mouth and nose, wear it as a face mask.

## 3. KHAKI

Remember the redcoats? Here's what happened to them. In the late 1840s, Harry Lumsden, a commander of a unit of Bengal irregular cavalry in India, decided that the traditional British redcoat uniforms were unsuitable in hot weather and also (hello!)

---

At six gallons per person per year, Americans are the leading consumers of ice cream.

made them too conspicuous to the enemy. Lumsden substituted coarse cotton smocks and pajamas, wrinkled cotton jackets and turbans, all dyed with plant juice that turned cloth a dull brownish gray and leather items more yellowish. Both colors were called khaki, from the Urdu words for "dust" or "dust-colored," from the Persian *khak*, meaning "dust." The style was eventually adopted by more regiments for their active-duty uniforms but wasn't generally introduced into the British Army until the Second Boer War (1899–1902). Today the color khaki is used for British and American soldiers' summer uniforms, which themselves are referred to as khakis, as are those comfy trousers that—if you're not wearing them—you've probably got hanging in your closet right now.

## 4. BELL-BOTTOM TROUSERS

Both British and American sailors have sported bell-bottom trousers, named for their wide flare at the bottom. In Britain they were introduced in 1857, supposedly to allow sailors to kick them off readily over their boots if they fell into the sea. Worn only by sailors, not officers, they were redesigned with a more modest flare in the late 1970s and abandoned entirely in 1994—at about the same time the U.S. Navy announced that bell-bottoms would be replaced by straight-leg pants. The American rationale for bell-bottoms was that wide-bottomed legs could be easily rolled up and kept dry when sailors scrubbed the decks. The fashion was immortalized in a World War II hit song, "Bell Bottom Trousers." Today, as fashion fluctuates, so do the flared or unflared bottoms of men's and women's pants and jeans. The wider they get, the more likely they'll be called "bell bottoms."

## 5. DUFFLE COAT AND PEA JACKET

Two World War II styles became popular in civilian life after the war. Both were first sold by military surplus stores and later imitated by designers. Britain's Royal Navy wore short duffle coats named for the town of Duffel, Belgium, where they were made. The coats were, and still are, fastened with toggles. European and American sailors wore pea jackets, hip-length double-breasted coats with notched lapels. It's thought that the "pea" comes from the Dutch word *pij*, a coarse cloth. Both styles—duffle and pea—are classics and seem to come in and out of fashion every few years.

---

Margaret Thatcher was the first European female prime minister (1979).

## 6. TRENCH COAT

The brutal trench warfare of World War I inspired the design of the trench coat, a water-resistant full-length coat allotted mainly to officers to protect against the miserable cold and wetness of the trenches. In civilian life, the trench coat has become one of those classic raincoat styles, worn by both men and women, that has yet to go out of fashion.

## 7. EISENHOWER JACKET

During World War II, General Dwight D. Eisenhower's name became attached to a popular style of jacket, but, according to historian Bradford Washburn, the Eisenhower jacket—but for a few alterations—might have been called the "Arnold jacket." Washburn served as a special consultant to General Henry H. "Hap" Arnold on problems related to high altitude and extreme cold, and had helped design a special battle jacket for the general. (General officers were the only army soldiers allowed to wear clothing of their own design, provided it was military in nature and made of standard material.)

Arnold had come to dislike the standard accordion-fold uniform jacket and thought it should be shortened, have slash pockets to warm the hands, and a plain back. It's not known when Eisenhower first saw the jacket, but he liked it, too, though he did have objections to the original's slash pockets, believing the hand-warming feature was unmilitary—no general should appear with his hands in his pockets—and had them removed. The removal of the pockets also removed General Arnold's claim to fame vis-à-vis the jacket. This modification alone made it the "Eisenhower jacket," which was widely imitated and adopted in civilian life.

## 8. MAE WEST

She didn't fight in any war that we know of, but her name (and her anatomy) live on in the name of the life jacket used by Allied airmen during World War II. The boys of the Royal Air Force dubbed the jacket the "Mae West" for its curvaceous resemblance to the American movie star (and some think for the Cockney rhyming slang of "West" and "breast" as well). Americans loved the name, and Miss West was apparently delighted, too, that her name would make it into the dictionary.

June 6, 1944: Gliders were used for the D-Day beach landings at Normandy.

# ON THE BEAT

*Earlier in this book you may have read about famous
groundbreaking female journalists. But in those days,
news reporting was mostly a male occupation. Here
are some memorable newsmen of the past.*

Before broadcast news and the Internet, there were newspapers—and they were the kings of communication. For hundreds of years, bylined stories made print journalists famous. In defense of his writings, one of them died at the hands of an angry mob. Another became the most famous and beloved of all American novelists.

## 1. THE ABOLITIONIST

Elijah Lovejoy (1802–37) died defending his right to freedom of the press. Born in Maine, he taught school for a while, then was ordained a Presbyterian minister in St. Louis in 1834. He published a religious newspaper, the *St. Louis Observer*, and wrote editorials calling for the abolition of slavery. Missouri was a slave state, so when Lovejoy criticized a local judge for not prosecuting the men who had hanged a free black man in May 1836, he might as well have drawn a target on his own back. Local opposition forced him to relocate across the Mississippi River to Alton in the free state of Illinois, where he set up the *Alton Observer*. He resumed his criticism of slavery over the next 15 months, inflaming mobs of slavery supporters who stormed his newspaper three times and threw his presses into the Mississippi.

**No Love, No Joy for Lovejoy.** Undeterred, Lovejoy got himself another press. When the pro-slavery mob found out that the new press was being stored at a local warehouse, they fired guns at the building, and Lovejoy shot back. After a brief exchange of gunfire, some of the agitators positioned a ladder alongside the building so they could climb up and set fire to the wooden roof. Lovejoy and his supporters managed to push the ladder over. When the ladder was repositioned and Lovejoy made a second attempt to overturn it, five blasts from a shotgun killed him. Martyrdom made him a cause célèbre among abolitionists, and helped fuel feelings about

---

In 1393, seven fat oxen were considered equal in value to one pound of nutmeg.

the coming war. Some even look back on the fight at the warehouse in Alton as the first battle of the Civil War.

## 2. THE GREAT AMERICAN NOVELIST

Samuel Langhorne Clemens (1835–1910) eked out a living in frontier America as a newspaper reporter who never let facts get in the way of a good story. As a writer for Virginia City's *Territorial Enterprise* newspaper in Nevada in 1863, he made up tales of train robberies that never happened. It was then and there that he discovered his true calling. Under the byline of his alter ego—Mark Twain—he told tales with drama and humor and parlayed his talent into a career at other California newspapers. It wasn't long before his humorous short story "The Celebrated Jumping Frog of Calaveras County" made him a writer of national repute.

**Sammy Reb.** It was his earlier life as a pilot on a Mississippi River steamboat and a stint in the Confederate army that provided Mark Twain with grist for his novels *The Adventures of Tom Sawyer* (1876) and *The Adventures of Huckleberry Finn* (1884). The latter is considered the "great American novel" by those who should know; William Faulkner called Twain "the father of American literature." His keen wit made him one of the world's most quotable authors:

- "A person with a new idea is a crank until the idea succeeds."
- "Against the assault of laughter nothing can stand."
- "All generalizations are false, including this one."
- "A man who carries a cat by the tail learns something he can learn in no other way."

## 3. THE CRITIC

The cigar-chomping Henry Louis Mencken (1880–1956) was the most prominent newspaperman of his era. His father owned Baltimore's Mencken Cigar Company and wanted his son to follow him into the business. But H.L. had other plans: he quit the business shortly after his father's death and became a cub reporter at the *Baltimore Morning Herald* in 1899.

By 1906, he was writing editorials at the *Baltimore Sun*. His acerbic wit and ultraconservative views made him famous. He also wrote for literary magazines and cofounded the commentary magazine *American Mercury*, which was hugely popular on college campuses.

---

**"Bless this house" and "Love is blind" are both phrases from Chaucer's writings.**

**An Opinion on Everything.** As a *Sun* columnist for four decades, Mencken attacked President Franklin D. Roosevelt, New Deal politics, democracy, World War II, scam artists, fundamentalist Christianity, intolerance, and even the practice of chiropractics. He expressed racist views against blacks but also outrage at violence toward them. In the case of a Maryland lynching, he wrote: "Not a single bigwig came forward in the emergency, though the whole town knew what was afoot. Any one of a score of such bigwigs might have halted the crime, if only by threatening to denounce its perpetrators, but none spoke. So Williams was duly hanged, burned and mutilated."

He admired the wit and humor of writers Ambrose Bierce and Mark Twain, and emulated them in his own writings. A frequenter of the nightclub scene, Mencken came up with one of his best-known turns of phrase when the famous stripper Gypsy Rose Lee asked him if he could think of a more dignified name for her profession. He coined the word "ecdysiast," from *ecdysis*, meaning "to molt or shed."

## 4. THE BEST-LOVED WAR CORRESPONDENT

Just two years out of Indiana University, Ernie Pyle (1900–45) was a staff reporter at the *Washington Daily News*, where was adept at doing what few other reporters dared: he took no notes except for the correct spelling of names and dates. It was a gift that enabled him, he said, to focus on the storytelling aspect of the day's events. He would hole up later and write and rewrite his accounts more than a half-dozen times to get the narrative just right—hard work that landed him a position as a roving reporter for the Scripps-Howard newspaper chain. He arrived in London to cover the Nazi bombings of the English capital at the end of 1940, and achieved lasting fame with a word-picture that began, "It was a night when London was ringed with fire."

**The Write Stuff.** Pyle's colorful writing during World War II made him a household name in the States. He cemented his reputation as the voice of the American GI while covering fighting in North Africa in late 1942 and early 1943. Known mostly for his depictions of life in the foxhole alongside a soldier, he also treasured friendships in high places, including relationships with generals Omar Bradley and Dwight D. Eisenhower. Pyle hated to cover invasions, but he landed on the beach at Normandy at General Bradley's request. His word picture of the D-Day landings helped inspire the opening scene in the movie *Saving Private Ryan* many years later.

Pyle earned the Pulitzer Prize in 1944 and then headed to the Pacific in 1945 for the landings on Okinawa. On the nearby island of Ie Shima on April 18, 1945, a Japanese machine-gunner fired on the jeep carrying Pyle, killing him instantly with a shot to the head. He died at the height of his fame.

\*     \*     \*

## THE RICHEST MEN IN THE WORLD

This ranking is updated annually, but often the people remain the same and just shift positions on the list.

1. William Gates III, $40 billion
(Microsoft/United States)
2. Warren Buffett, $37 billion
(Investments/United States)
3. Carlos Slim Hela, $35 billion
(Telecom/Mexico)
4. Lawrence Ellison, $22.5 billion
(Oracle/United States)
5. Ingvar Kamprad, $22 billion
(Ikea/Sweden)
6. Karl Albrecht, $21.5 billion
(Supermarkets/Germany)
7. Mukesh Ambani, $19.5 billion
(Petrochemicals/India)
8. Lakshmi Mittal, $19.3 billion
(Steel/India)
9. Theo Albrecht, $18.8 billion
(Supermarkets/Germany)
10. Amancio Ortega, $18.3 billion
(Fashion/Spain)

---

...baguette filled with meat (often sausage), salad, cheese, and French fries.

# VANISHED!

*How could a famous painting and three*
*lighthouse keepers simply disappear? Read on.*

## 1. THE FLANNAN ISLES KEEPERS

Off the western coast of Scotland, in the Outer Hebrides, are seven small, uninhabited islands called the Flannan Isles. Sailors passing through the area often complained about how difficult it was to navigate the islands' rocky coastlines, so in 1899, the British government built a lighthouse there, one of the most remote and isolated in the country.

The next year, three keepers were stationed at the lighthouse. They had no radio or telegraph system, and they relied on another keeper stationed on the island of Lewis, 18 miles away, to communicate with the outside world. The Lewis keeper watched for the light on the Flannan Isles—if he saw it, he considered it a sign that all was well. If he didn't see it, he was supposed to telegraph the main office in Edinburgh.

For some reason, though, the Lewis keeper never reported a problem with the Flannan Isles light. On December 15, 1900, a ship passing by the islands noticed there was no light on the shore and realized something was wrong. The ship's captain radioed in the odd occurrence, but bad weather stalled any investigation for more than a week. Finally, on December 26, a ship carrying the relief keeper Joseph Moore arrived at the Flannan Isles. The ship fired a warning rocket, but got no response. So Moore rowed ashore, and what he found was astounding: He found nothing. No keepers and no sign of distress. The light was prepped and ready to go, and the last notes in the entry logs (dated December 15) showed nothing out of the ordinary. The men had vanished.

The government launched investigations, but there weren't many clues. The only "oddity" was the weather. The same storms that had prevented the rescue ship from traveling to the lighthouse may have played a part in the keepers' disappearance. Eventually, investigators theorized that the men had somehow gotten caught outside in the bad weather and were washed out to sea. No bodies were ever found.

---

There are more statues of Sacajawea in the U.S.—at least 15—than of any other woman.

## 2. PORTRAIT OF DR. GACHET

In 1890, artist Vincent van Gogh wrote a letter to his brother Theo that said, "I've done the portrait of M. Gachet with a melancholy expression, which might well seem like a grimace to those who see it. Sad but gentle, yet clear and intelligent, that is how many portraits ought to be done." A lot of people agreed. The painting—of van Gogh's personal doctor in a suit, his head resting on his right hand, a vase of drooping flowers on the table in front of him—sold for a record $82.5 million at an auction in 1990. And then, as quickly as its price had climbed during the bidding, the painting disappeared.

The new owner was Japanese millionaire Ryoei Saito, who had his new purchase wrapped, sealed, and stored in a vault. Over the next few years, Saito got himself into trouble with the law. In 1993, he was accused (and later pled guilty and spent three years in prison) of trying to bribe government officials, and by the time he died in 1996, Saito claimed he was completely broke.

That's where the story gets tricky. Just before his death, Saito horrified the art world by proclaiming that he wanted *Dr. Gachet* to be cremated and buried with him. Later, he laughed the idea off as a joke, but...did he do it? After Saito died, his heirs went looking for the painting and discovered that it was nowhere to be found. Perhaps the millionaire had sold the van Gogh to pay his debts, but no collector has come forward with the painting, and *Dr. Gachet* remains missing.

Still, art lovers can take heart: Saito's *Portrait of Dr. Gachet* was one of two that van Gogh painted. The versions differ slightly in color and details, but the second one is on display at the Musee d'Orsay in Paris.

\*      \*      \*

The ancient Romans had a tradition: whenever one of their engineers constructed an arch, as the capstone was hoisted into place, the engineer assumed accountability for his work in the most profound way possible: he stood under the arch."

—**Michael Armstrong**

---

William Shatner made his Hollywood film debut in *The Brothers Karamazov* in 1958.

# 3 MUMMY MYSTERIES

*Mummies give clues to the past, but these corpses created mystery.*

## 1. THE YINGPAN MAN

In the early 1900s, mummified bodies, preserved by the climate of hot, dry deserts, were found in the Tarim Basin of western China. What stunned the archaeologists was that these mummies, one of which dated back 4,000 years, were of European stock. One of the most mysterious of these is the Yingpan man, who was buried with a gold foil death mask (a Greek funereal tradition) as well as gold-embroidered clothing—indicating great wealth.

**Mystery:** How did this successful European civilization come to China, and what happened to them?

## 2. THE LADY OF CAO

In 2006, archaeologists discovered a 1,500-year-old tattooed mummy in El Brujo on Peru's north coast. A member of the Moche tribe, she'd been in her 20s and was buried inside an imposing pyramid. Gold jewelry buried with her confirmed her high status. The Lady of Cao's tomb is the richest ever found for a female Moche. Among womanly weaving materials and sewing needles, archaeologists found war clubs and mechanisms for hurling spears.

**Mystery:** War implements have never before been found in female Moche tombs, so was the Lady of Cao a feminist princess warrior, or were these symbols of her power?

## 3. NEFERTITI

Two Egyptologists claim to have found the missing mummy of Egypt's famous Queen Nefertiti. Both say she's one of three mummies lying in a chamber of the tomb of Amenhotep II to protect her from grave robbers. Jennifer Fletcher identified Mummy 61072 as Nefertiti. In 2003, she used X-rays and computers to digitally reconstruct the face of the mummy, claiming it resembled the famous beauty queen. But Egyptologist Susan Page had used similar criteria to declare that nearby Mummy 61071 was Nefertiti.

**Mystery:** Which is the real Nefertiti, or is she (as most Egyptologists contend) still MIA?

---

Address of the first presidential mansion: 1 Cherry Street, New York City...

# DOWN ON MAIN STREET

*Before malls and megastores, you could walk down the streets of the town or city you lived in and take care of pretty much every aspect of your daily life. Here's how some of those small businesses and services got their start.*

### 1. SELF-SERVICE GROCERY STORE

As early as 1916, Piggly Wiggly gave us a peek at the shape of things to come. The first self-service grocery store opened on September 6 at 79 Jefferson Street in Memphis, Tennessee. Businessman Clarence Saunders built the chain to more than 1,200 locations in six years. Piggly Wiggly was also the first grocery store to:...

- Provide checkout stands.
- Mark every item in the store with prices.
- Use refrigerated cases to keep produce fresher longer.
- Dress their employees in uniforms.

### 2. DRUGSTORE

Some say the first drugstore was opened in 1823 in New Orleans by the first registered pharmacist in the United States. Others think it's the drugstore established in 1740 in Fredericksburg, Virginia, where Martha Washington was said to be a customer. The latter wasn't originally set up by a registered pharmacist, so the question remains open. The true golden age of drugstores didn't begin until the 1860s, when pharmacies began to base medications on scientific fact rather than popular antidotes.

### 3. CONVENIENCE STORE

In 1927, an employee at the Southland Ice Company in Dallas, Texas, started selling blocks of ice to refrigerate food, and eventually began selling milk, bread, and eggs on Sundays and evenings when grocery stores were closed. As the concept grew and automobiles became more popular, the company opened convenience outlets known as Tote'M stores because customers "toted" away their purchases. In 1946, Tote'M became 7-Eleven to reflect the stores' new, extended hours: 7:00 a.m. to 11:00 p.m., seven days a week. 7-Eleven was the first store to:

- Sell fresh coffee in to-go cups.
- Offer self-serve soda fountains.
- Offer super-size sodas—in 1980, the store offered the 32-ounce Big Gulp.
- Sell Slurpees, of which they sell 13 million per month, with the most sold in Winnipeg, Canada, followed by Detroit, Michigan.

## 4. SHOE STORE

Colburn Shoe Store has been located at 79 Main Street in Belfast, Maine, since 1905. Wood-rimmed glass cases preserve the history of the century-old business, displaying old pictures and vintage shoe advertisements, and rolling wood ladders are still used to reach shoe boxes stacked to the ceiling on long shelves.

## 5. MOVIE THEATER

The first public exhibition of projected motion pictures in the United States was at Koster and Bial's Music Hall on 34th Street in New York City in April 1896, but a few months later the world's first movie theater opened at the Ellicott Square Building upstate in Buffalo. Mitchell Mark, the man behind the operation, claimed that his 75-seat theater had more than 200,000 visitors in the first year, so to keep up with public demand, he kept the theater open 13 hours a day, seven days a week.

## 6. AUTOMATIC CAR WASH

You might guess that the first car wash was opened in Detroit—and you'd be right. Called Automated Laundry, it opened in 1914. The process took all day since the vehicle had to be pushed manually through brass wash components. The first automatic conveyor car wash, which opened in California in the 1950s, greatly speeded up the process.

## 7. BANK

Secretary of the Treasury Alexander Hamilton proposed the idea of a centralized bank in 1790. The Revolutionary War had left the new government in debt, and at the time, there were more than 50 different currencies in circulation, only a few of which were stable. Congress agreed to charter a bank—the First Bank of the United States—for 20 years, and that's exactly how long it lasted.

---

Aftershocks from Hawaii's largest earthquake in 1868, continue to the present day.

The bank was housed in Carpenters' Hall in Philadelphia from 1791 to 1795, when it moved to a new building of its own. The Second Bank of the United States was chartered in 1816, mostly to help relieve debts incurred by the War of 1812.

## 8. POST OFFICE

The first post office in America offered its customers more than stamps and mailing labels. Colonists who needed to send mail to England could use it as an excuse to pick up a pint or two of ale when they visited Richard Fairbanks's tavern—it was the first official postal service mail drop for overseas packages as established by the General Court of Massachusetts in 1639.

## 9. PAY PHONES AND PHONE BOOTHS

First came the public coin telephone, invented by William Gray and installed at a bank in Hartford, Connecticut, in 1889. Called a "postpay" machine because coins were deposited after the call was placed, it was replaced by the "prepay" phone in 1898. By 1902, there were 81,000 pay phones in the United States—all of them in high-traffic places like banks and railroad stations. The first outdoor coin telephone was installed in Cincinnati in 1905, but the open-air concept wasn't all that popular until the phone was encased in a phone booth. The first ones were made of hardwoods, with plush carpeting on the floors. The wooden booths were replaced by glass phone booths in the 1950s.

## 10. PUBLIC SCHOOL

Founded on April 23, 1635, in Boston, Massachusetts, the Boston Latin School was the first public school and is the oldest existing U.S. school. The school began with only a few students who met in the headmaster's home. To gain admission, students were required to read aloud a few Bible verses. The school was all male (including the teachers) until the first female was accepted in 1877.

## 11. AUTOMATED TELLER MACHINE (ATM)

The date that the first ATM in the United States opened for business is not recorded, but the patent was filed on September 2, 1969. One of the earliest known ATMs was at a Chemical Bank branch in Rockville Centre, on New York's Long Island. The machine, like most today, was built into a wall of the bank, facing the street, and under a canopy. The bank ran an ad in August saying, "On September 2, our bank will open at 9:00 a.m. and never close again!"

## 12. HOSPITAL

America's first and oldest hospital, the Pennsylvania Hospital, was founded in 1751 by Benjamin Franklin and a doctor named Thomas Bond to care for "the sick, poor, and insane who wander the streets of Philadelphia." The first patients were admitted in 1756. The hospital took a neutral stance during the American Revolution, taking care of injured soldiers from both the Continental and British armies.

## 13. INDOOR SHOPPING MALL

The first indoor shopping mall in the United States, the Arcade of Cleveland, opened in May 1890. It was modeled after the Galleria Vittorio Emanuele II in Milan, Italy, was built for $875,000, and was financed by several Cleveland businessmen, including John D. Rockefeller. For more than 100 years, the Arcade offered unique shops, restaurants, office space, and services in its two 10-story towers. It's still a bustling shopping center today.

\*     \*     \*

### MEDICAL TREATMENT, MIDDLE AGES STYLE

What were common treatments by physicians during the Middle Ages would stir a quizzical eye today.

• In the 14th century, doctors were unaware of what caused the deadly "Black Plague," but they did know it was contagious. As a result, they developed a suit to protect themselves while treating patients. It included a large, beaked head piece that made the physicians look like Big Bird's evil twin. The hats were filled with vinegar, sweet oils, and pungent compounds designed to counteract the stench of dead and dying victims.

• Barbers were also attending physicians back in the Middle Ages. Bloodletting, dentistry, bonesetting, wound treatment, and minor operations were routine treatments. The striped red pole familiar at today's barbershop originated back then and was the staff that patients gripped while blood was taken from them.

---

The term "booty" dates back to 1474. No, not that booty. Pirate's plunder, we mean.

# SLOGANS

*Companies work hard to craft catchy and memorable slogans to advertise, promote, and market their products. Here are some that have gone down in the history books.*

"You too can have a body like mine."　—Charles Atlas

"Beanz Meanz Heinz."
　　—Heinz Baked Beans

"Skim milk does not come from skinny cows."
　　—Alba Dry Milk

"Have it your way."
　　—Burger King

"The power to be your best."
　　—Apple Computers

"Does she or doesn't she?"
　　—Clairol Hair Coloring

"I can't believe I ate the whole thing!"　—Alka-Seltzer

"They're grrrr-eat!"
　　—Kellogg's Frosted Flakes

""It's the real thing."
　　—Coca-Cola

"It's what your right arm's for."　　—Courage Beer

"Let your fingers do the walking."　—Yellow Pages

"Put a Tiger in Your Tank."
　　—ESSO Gasoline

"Imagination at work."
　　—General Electric

"The best a man can get."
　　—Gillette

"Can you hear me now?"
　　—Verizon Wireless

"M'm M'm Good!"
　　—Campbell's Soup

"The best seat in the house."
　　—Jockey Underwear

"Finger-lickin' good."
—Kentucky Fried Chicken

"I'm Margie. Fly me."
　　—National Airlines

"It beats as it sweeps as it cleans."
—Hoover Vacuum Cleaners

"You can't resist the twist!"
　　—Twister

"Fun, anyone?"
　　—Playstation 2

"Just do it!"　　—Nike

"I'd rather die of thirst than drink from the cup of mediocrity."
　　—Stella Artois

"Don't live a little, live a lotto."
　　—The Lottery

---

**A U.S. Navy sailor in 1848 could receive 12 strokes of the whip for skulking.**

# EARTH'S CARETAKERS

*Our salute to people who made it their mission in life to save the world continues. If you missed part one, it started on page 290.*

## 1. CELIA HUNTER

**Quote:** "You're going to have to bite the bullet and really decide what kind of world you want to live in."

**Ahead of Her Time.** Growing up in Washington State's logging country during the Roaring Twenties, Celia Hunter was always told there were things only men could do. But that never stopped her. She worked in a logging camp as a young woman and later as a fighter pilot during World War II, ferrying aircraft and supplies to bases nationwide for shipment overseas. When she flew over Alaska, it was love at first sight.

**That's Life.** In the early 1950s, she established Camp Denali, a wilderness outpost near Mount McKinley where she preached conservation and showed visitors Alaska's natural wonders. She cofounded the Alaska Conservation Foundation, then the Wilderness Society, where she was the first female to head a major environmental organization. She lived with energy and purpose until her death in 2001.

## 2. DIAN FOSSEY

**Quote:** "When you realize the value of life, you dwell less on what is past and concentrate more on the preservation of the future."

**Gorilla Girl.** Dian Fossey's stepfather wanted her to go to college to get a business degree, but the San Francisco–born Fossey had other ideas, starting with her job as an occupational therapist at a Kentucky hospital. It was there that a lecture by anthropologist Dr. Louis Leakey turned Fossey's attention to Africa. By 1966, she'd gained Leakey's support to carry out research on the endangered mountain gorillas of the Virunga Mountains of Rwanda. She founded a research center dedicated to the primates and lived with them for 18 years, earning their trust. When one of her favorite gorillas was killed and beheaded by a poacher, she began a successful international campaign to stop the slaughter. After earning a PhD at Cambridge, she wrote the autobiographical *Gorillas in the Mist*, which became a movie in 1988. She then returned to the Virunga Mountains to continue the struggle to save the gorillas and their habitat.

**Tragic Ending.** On December 26, 1985, Fossey's body was found mutilated by a machete of the type used by poachers. Her murder remains unsolved, and poaching as well as logging continues in the gorillas' habitat. Fossey may have foreseen her own end: "The man who kills the animal today is the man who kills the people who get in his way tomorrow."

## 3. WANGARI MAATHAI

**Quote:** "It's a mater of life and death for this country. The Kenyan forests are facing extinction and it is a man-made problem."

**The Tree Lady of Africa.** Born in 1940 in Kenya, Wangari Maathai was the first woman in eastern or central Africa to earn a doctoral degree. As a veterinarian, she became a leader and later chairwoman of the National Council of Women of Kenya in 1976. Appalled by logging that had decimated so many of Kenya's forests, she introduced the idea of women's groups planting trees to improve the environment. Through her and her allies' Green Belt Movement, women's groups in Kenya have planted more than 20 million trees on farms and around schools and churches. Eventually the movement spread to other countries. Known as the "tree lady of Africa," Maathai has expanded her role into a variety of humanitarian causes as an ardent defender of democracy and human rights.

**A Little Big Thing.** In 2004, she and the Green Belt Movement received the prestigious Nobel Peace Prize. Maathai has addressed the United Nations on many occasions on behalf of women worldwide. She calls on citizens to start small, to take tiny steps toward a cause. As she put it, "It's the little things citizens do. That's what will make the difference. My little thing is planting trees."

## 4. CHICO MENDES

**Quote:** "A first I thought I was fighting to save rubber trees, then I thought I was fighting to save the Amazon rain forest. Now I realize I am fighting for humanity."

**Workers of the Forest, Unite!** As the son of a family of rubber tappers (workers who gather latex from rubber trees) in Brazil, Chico Mendes became a tapper when he was only nine years old. When prices for rubber collapsed in the 1960s, many Amazon landowners began auctioning their land to cattle ranchers, who promptly felled the trees to convert the acreage for grazing. Alarmed, Mendes campaigned to save the trees by running for local office. He proposed creating forest reserves managed by the people who lived there, and founded the Xapuri Rural Workers Union to unite rubber tappers and rally them to resist ranchers. In doing so, he raised environmental consciousness about the global dangers of deforestation. His effort led to 8 million acres of Amazon forests being preserved.

**Crime and Punishment.** In 1988, Mendes led a successful campaign to stop rancher Darly Alves da Silva from logging an area designated to become a reserve. Mendes was assassinated at his home on December 22, 1988, at age 44. The murder made headlines across the globe. Alves da Silva, his son, and one of their ranch hands were arrested, convicted, and imprisoned for the crime. Prior to his murder, Mendes said in an interview that he wanted to live, but "if a messenger from the sky came down and guaranteed that my death would strengthen our struggle, it would be worth it."

## 5. JULIA BUTTERFLY HILL

**Quote:** "We are all planetary citizens, and the ancient trees are living, breathing elders that remind us to respect and honor that which we cannot replace."

**The Tree Lady of California.** Julia Butterfly Hill was born Julia Lorraine Hill in Missouri, the daughter of a preacher who traveled the countryside with his family in the 1970s in a 32-foot camper. She loved exploring the rivers near the many campgrounds they stayed at. When Julia was six, a butterfly landed on her finger and stayed there, giving her the idea for her new name. In 1996, aged 22, she survived a near-fatal car accident; it was during a long recuperation that she began to discover her true calling in life. A visit to California and the sight of the sequoia redwoods finished the process. She went home, sold all her belongings, and moved to

California to devote her life to saving the giant trees. She built two six-foot-square platforms 180 feet up in the canopy of an endangered tree she called "Luna" and lived there for two years to keep loggers at bay. Her courage brought the plight of redwoods to the world's attention, helping protect them at a time when 97 percent had been cut down in just 100 years.

**True Believer.** Hill went on to write books about her Luna experience, and founded the Circle of Life Foundation. She lives by a simple mantra that came to her while she was living in the redwood: "I wake up in the morning asking myself what can I do today, how can I help the world today. I believe in what I do beyond a shadow of a doubt."

\*　　　\*　　　\*

## DOMES OF WONDER

Like others, Uncle John often is mesmerized when standing beneath a vast dome in a building, wondering how it's supported. Looking back in history, he found a few ancient forms that stir wonder even today:

• Lusty Emperor Nero liked elaborate parties, and what better way to celebrate than under a rotating dome over the main dining room? The roof of Nero's Domus Aurea was kept in motion, day and night, to coincide with the sky outside. Architects developed a unique turning mechanism powered by—you guessed it—slaves. As the dome revolved, perfume and rose petals descended from it on diners below.

• For nearly 1,000 years, the domed ceiling of the Pantheon in Rome was the largest in the world with no visible internal supports. Completed out of concrete in AD 125, the dome held the record until 1958, when the CNIT building in Paris surpassed it.

# GETTING BOARD

*Inventing a board game isn't for the easily discouraged.*
*Take a look at what these people had to go through*
*before their games hit the big time.*

## 1. SCRABBLE

In 1931, Alfred Mosher Butts was an unemployed architect with too much time on his hands. He read the entire *New York Times* every day, but even that didn't adequately occupy his brain. So one day he checked to see how often each of the English alphabet's 26 letters appeared on the newspaper's front page. His discovery? Vowels appeared more often than consonants, and "e" was the most commonly used vowel. Interesting...

Butts decided to use his discovery to create a game. He assigned each letter a point value and, using a percentage formula based on how often letters appeared on the front pages of various newspapers, decided how many of each letter would appear in the game. He also decided that each player should get seven letters at a time to work with. Butts created wooden letter tiles, called the game Lexiko, and started playing.

**The Long Road to Popularity.** Butts tried to sell his creation to several board game manufacturers, but none of them liked his idea. The most common criticism of the game was that it was "too intellectual." But Butts, who figured that all you needed to enjoy Lexiko was a love of reading and words, kept trying and improving his game. He came up with the 225-square game board and included premium squares—the ones that multiply the value of letters or words that land on them.

In the late 1940s, Butts made a breakthrough: He teamed up with a friend named James Brunot, and the two put a starting point (the star) in the middle of the board. Now the game wasn't just a word game; it required strategy, too. By 1942, Butts was making game sets by hand and selling them through Chester Ives, a Connecticut bookstore owner. Oh, and now the game was called Criss-Cross Words.

Brunot was a manufacturer, and in 1947, he and Butts made a

deal: Brunot would patent and manufacture the game, and Butts would get a royalty for each game sold. The men also brainstormed some improvements—they created a simple rule book, moved some of the premium tiles around, and changed the name...again. This time, though, they came up with the one that stuck: they called the game Scrabble, which means "to grope frantically," kind of like what players had to do in the midst of the game.

Still, sales remained unimpressive until 1952, when the partners got a lucky break. Jack Strauss, CEO of R. H. Macy & Co. (the company that owned Macy's department stores), had bought a Scrabble set on a vacation, and he enjoyed it so much that he put the game on sale in his store. That was it. Within a year, more than 300,000 Scrabble sets had been sold. By 1953, Brunot realized his small company couldn't keep up with the demand for the game, so he and Butts sold Scrabble to game manufacturer Selchow and Righter...which had rejected the original version of Lexiko many years earlier. Alfred Butts, who once admitted to a reporter that he was a terrible speller, got royalties from his game until he died in 1993 at the age of 93.

## 2. MONOPOLY

The story of Monopoly goes back to 1904, when a woman named Lizzie Magie got a patent for something she called the Landlord's Game. It was based on the ideas of American economist Henry George, who believed that people could own only what they created. Things found in nature (like land), on the other hand, should belong to everyone. With her game, Magie wanted to show how property ownership created upper and lower classes— i.e., rents made landlords rich and tenants poor. It didn't work. This was America, after all, and the dream of land ownership was strong. The game was distributed in several cities and people enjoyed playing it, but the Landlord's Game (later renamed Auction Monopoly) never caught on.

It would take another unemployed man and the Great Depression to bring Monopoly to the masses. In 1933, Charles Darrow, a former salesman from Pennsylvania, started an art project in his kitchen. He painted city streets on a tablecloth and built little hotels and houses to go on those streets. It wasn't long before the art project became a game and a way for Darrow's unemployed and underemployed friends and family to pass their free time: they "bought" pretend real estate and got fabulously rich with pretend money. Monopoly was so popular that Darrow's friends all wanted copies for themselves, so he made some more games and sold them for $4 each.

**Erring on the Side of Errors.** Pretty soon, Darrow decided that he should find a game manufacturer to produce the games for him instead. In 1933, he contacted the toy company Parker Brothers and pitched them his idea. They weren't nearly as enthusiastic as his friends. The suits at Parker Brothers told Darrow that his game was way too complicated, took too long to play, and didn't provide a clear goal for the winner. It had, in their opinion, at total of "52 fundamental errors."

Undaunted, Darrow hired a printer to produce 5,000 copies of the game and then sold them to department stores. One of those copies made it into the hands of a friend of the daughter of George Parker, the founder of Parker Brothers. The friend told the daughter, the daughter told her husband (Robert B. M. Barton, president of the company), Barton bought a game, and he was instantly hooked. In 1935, Parker Brothers bought the rights to Monopoly (and its earlier variations) and turned it into a best seller…just one year after someone else in the Parker Brothers organization had rejected the game.

## 3. TRIVIAL PURSUIT

In December 1979, Scott Abbott and Chris Haney got together to play a friendly game of Scrabble in Montreal, Quebec. Both were good with words: Abbott was a sports editor and journalist with the Canadian Press, and Haney was a photo editor for the *Montreal Gazette*. But several missing pieces ended their game quickly, and the two decided to create their own board game. Within just a few hours, they came up with Trivial Pursuit, a game about useless trivia on topics like foreign affairs, politics, music, television, and popular culture.

**Something Trivial Turns Out to Be Important.** The guys thought their game was something other people might want to play too, so they partnered with Chris Haney's older brother John and his friend Ed Werner, a former hockey player who was now a lawyer.

---

*Jai alai* means "merry festival" in Basque.

The foursome incorporated a company called Horn Abbot in January 1980 and started making the games themselves. Initially, the investment wasn't terribly profitable. Each Trivial Pursuit game cost $75 to manufacture, but sold for only $15. Even worse, in February 1982, the guys took their game to the American International Toy Fair in New York City and sold only a few hundred copies.

They kept at it, though, and finally hit the jackpot in 1983 when Selchow and Righter bought the rights to the game. The company saw potential and launched an extensive public relations and marketing campaign. By the end of that year, more than two million games had been sold in Canada, and one million in the United States. The next year, the game hit its sales peak: 20 million sold. Not a bad haul for a couple of guys who really just wanted to play Scrabble.

\* \* \*

## YOU'RE GONNA WANT TO BUY THESE

Mathematician Irvin R. Hertzel calculated the probability of landing on one Monopoly space more than another. The following is his list of the 10 most landed-on spaces.

**1.** Illinois Avenue

**2.** GO

**3.** B&O Railroad

**4.** Free Parking

**5.** Tennessee Avenue

**6.** New York Avenue

**7.** Reading Railroad

**8.** St. James Place

**9.** Water Works

**10.** Pennsylvania Railroad

---

**A typical carrot has to travel 1,838 miles to reach your dinner table.**

# TREES OF HISTORY

*Barbara Walters famously asked Katharine Hepburn in an interview, "If you were a tree, what kind of tree would you be?" The following trees mean a lot to many.*

## 1. THE ANNE FRANK TREE

On April 12, 1944, Anne Frank wrote in her diary, "The sun is shining, the sky is deep blue, there's a magnificent breeze, and I'm longing—really longing—for everything: conversation, freedom, friends, being alone." A month later, less than three months before she was sent to a Nazi concentration camp, Frank wrote, "Our chestnut tree is in full blossom. It is covered with leaves and is even more beautiful than last year." That tree still stands in the courtyard of the Anne Frank House, a museum located in the building where Frank and her family hid for two years during the Holocaust.

The Anne Frank Tree is now about 150 years old and has battled fungus, moth infestations, and a demand from the city that it be cut down for public safety. (City officials didn't want it falling on anyone.) After many appeals, a supporting structure was built around the tree in 2008, and it's expected to live for another five to 15 years. In the meantime, saplings and chestnuts from the tree have been sent to cities all over the world and planted as memorials in parks bearing Frank's name.

## 2. THE SURVIVOR TREE

On April 19, 1995, a terrorist bomb killed 168 people in or near the Alfred P. Murrah Federal Building in Oklahoma City, Oklahoma. The building was completely destroyed, and hundreds of nearby structures were damaged. The Survivor Tree stands today at the Oklahoma City National Memorial.

The force of the blast ripped most of the branches from the Survivor Tree and stripped it of its leaves. Burning cars parked beneath it scorched and blackened its wood. Debris embedded in its trunk nearly caused it to be cut down for evidence. The tree, an American elm, was located in the parking lot across the street from the Murrah Federal Building. Before the attack, commuters

---

In 1953, Lawrence Welk received a patent for an ashtray that looked like an accordion.

would arrive to work early to secure one of the few shady spots provided by the branches of the only shade tree in the lot.

The tree's low, forked trunk is tilted at an odd angle and its stature is modest, reaching only about 40 feet in height. Photos taken of the tree in the 1900s, when it resided in the backyard of a family home, indicate the tree is about 103 years old.

When the memorial was being designed, the survivors and surviving family members asked that the Survivor Tree be included in a prominent spot. Thus, the memorial's design mandated special measures to feature and protect the Survivor Tree. A forester was assigned to care for the tree's health. Beneath the decking surrounding the tree, an underground crawl space allows workers to enter through a secure hatchway and monitor and maintain the tree's health. Remarkably, about one year after the attack, the tree produced new growth. In its releafing, it became a symbol of resilience, renewal, and rebirth for the community and the nation.

The tree stands guard over a native stone plaza and its courtyard of 168 empty chairs. A memorial wall encloses a small plaza around the Survivor Tree. Inscribed on this wall is the following: "The spirit of this city and of this nation will not be defeated; our deeply rooted faith sustains us."

Seeds from the Survivor Tree are planted annually and the resulting saplings are distributed on the anniversary of the bombing. Saplings were sent to Columbine High School after the shootings there in 1999; to New York City after the September 11, 2001, attacks; and to Virginia Tech after the 2007 massacre.

## OTHER HISTORIC TREES

**1. Johnny Appleseed Apple Tree:** John Chapman, a.k.a. Johnny Appleseed, planted millions of trees in his lifetime. The apple trees he planted were a vital staple to new settlers moving west after the American Revolution. The last known apple tree planted by Johnny resides on a farm in Nova, Ohio. The farm's land grant was signed by John Quincy Adams in 1837.

**2. Gettysburg Address Honey Locust:** On November 19, 1863, President Abraham Lincoln arrived in Gettysburg, Pennsylvania, to dedicate a new Soldiers' National Cemetery for the men who had perished in the Union army's decisive victory over the Confederacy four and a half months earlier. He stood near a honey locust tree while he delivered his speech, which lasted just over two minutes. The tree, rooted on Cemetery Hill on the right side of the Union line, was a silent witness to the awful three-day battle. Gettysburg once was full of witness trees in 1863, but today only the honey locust tree and a few other witness trees remain. The others fell victim to storms, disease, insects, and old age. The honey locust itself suffered severe damage in a 2008 storm and only 20 percent remains intact—poor odds for survival.

**3. Andrew Jackson Southern Magnolia:** In 1828, newly elected president Andrew Jackson planted a large southern magnolia in honor of his deceased wife, Rachel. The old $20 bill depicts Jackson's magnolia to the left of the White House portico. Jackson began a tree-planting tradition that every president has followed since then.

**4. Texas Treaty Oak:** The lone survivor of the Council Oaks grove, a sacred meeting place for Native Americans that originally contained 14 trees, the Treaty Oak is estimated to be more than 500 years old. According to folklore, it is said to have witnessed Stephen F. Austin's signing of a treaty between white settlers and the Tejas, Apache, and Comanche tribes in 1824, which established the first boundary lines for what would become Texas.

**5. Tidal Basin Japanese Cherry Trees:** Japan gave these trees to the people of the United States as a gesture of goodwill and friendship. In 1909, Japan delivered 2,000 trees, but the U.S. Department of Agriculture found that they were diseased, so the trees were destroyed. In 1912, Japan donated funds to buy special seeds that were grafted onto understock, and delivered 3,020 trees. First Lady Helen Taft and Viscountess Chinda of Japan planted the first tree in 1912. Since then, the number of cherry trees has grown to 3,750 trees of 16 varieties.

**6. Prometheus and Methuselah:** The oldest known tree in the United States—a 4,900-year-old Great Basin bristlecone pine located in Nevada and known as Prometheus—was cut down in 1964. Supposedly, Methuselah, another tree of the same species and aged 4,800 years, is alive in a secret location in California.

*Bwana Devil,* the first 3D movie, opened in New York in 1953.

# ALL ABOARD

*Here's a list of ten famous historic trains. Choo choo!*

## 1. ORIENT EXPRESS, 1883
**Route:** From Paris to Istanbul, crossing six countries
Famous for luxury, five-course meals, and famous passengers—royalty, diplomats, government couriers

## 2. PERUVIAN CENTRAL RAILWAY, 1895
**Route:** From La Oroya to Limia, Peru
Considered the highest railway in the world, climbing to more than 13,000 feet.

A doctor is onboard to provide oxygen to passengers who succumb to altitude sickness. Maybe it is the zigzag route through 59 bridges and 66 tunnels, though, that makes people sick.

## 3. TRANS-SIBERIAN EXPRESS, 1898–1904
**Route:** From Moscow to Vladivostok
Covers almost 5,800 miles, making it the longest regular train trip in the world, which takes eight days and has close to 100 stops from end to end. During the Cold War, Westerners had to ride in compartments, where they were compelled to listen to propaganda played on loudspeakers.

## 4. THE 20TH CENTURY LIMITED, 1902
**Route:** From New York to Chicago
The phrase "red-carpet treatment" comes from the practice of this luxury train of rolling out a crimson carpet to welcome boarding passengers.

## 5. FLYING SCOTSMAN, 1928
**Route:** From London, England, to Edinburgh, Scotland
The Flying Scotsman was the first train to offer nonstop service. Its amenities included a hair salon, a Louis XVI–style restaurant and bar, and, for a while, a cinema coach.

### 6. BLUE TRAIN, 1939

**Route:** From Cape Town to Pretoria, South Africa

A luxury train named for its blue locomotives, railroad cars, and leather seats.

### 7. BULLET TRAIN, 1964 AND 1977

**Route:** Links most major cities on the Japanese islands of Honshu and Kyushu

The first train ran at a speed of 130 mph before being replaced in 1977 by the fastest train in the world, the second Bullet Train, which reaches speeds of up to 186 mph. In 2003, the train reached a speed of 361 mph on a test run.

### 8. INDIAN PACIFIC, 1970

**Route:** From Sydney to Perth, Australia

Distinguished by possessing the world's longest stretch of straight track, some 297 miles.

### 9. TGV, 1983

**Route:** From various cities, including Paris

The French electric train TGV (*train à grande vitesse*, or "high-speed train") travels at speeds of 130 mph and often reaches speeds of 186 mph. Set a world speed record of 357 mph.

\*     \*     \*

## GREAT BIG STUFFED ANIMALS

• The only survivor of Custer's Last Stand, a horse named Comanche, is stuffed and displayed in Lawrence, Kansas.

• Roy Rogers' horse, Trigger, is on display in Branson, Missouri.

• P. T. Barnum's famous elephant, Jumbo, was stuffed and donated to Tufts University (the actual carcass was destroyed in a fire in 1975, but Jumbo's ashes are still around in a jar, also at Tufts).

• One of behavioral scientist Ivan Pavlov's dogs still snarls, but somewhat stiffly, in a museum in Russia.

• And the last passenger pigeon, Martha by name, is firmly stuffed, mounted, and on display at the Boston Museum of Science.

---

**In 1955, Dorcas Reilly invented the green-bean casserole for Campbell Soup...**

# NAME YOUR SECOND

*Uncle John knows there's only one way to settle a score: water pistols at dawn. These guys took a more deadly approach.*

## 1. THAT'S NOT IN THE SCRIPT!

**Squaring Off:** Ben Jonson vs. Gabriel Spenser

**The Insult:** At the end of the 16th century, Ben Jonson was an up-and-coming playwright in London. He had been jailed briefly in 1597 for "lewd and mutinous behavior" in collaborating on a play titled *The Isle of Dogs*, so his record was not unblemished. For reasons lost to history, in 1598 Jonson and Spenser, an actor in his company, fought a duel to the death.

**Weapon of Choice:** Rapiers—Jonson later claimed that his was 10 inches shorter than Spenser's.

**Last Man Standing:** Jonson. However, "lewd and mutinous behavior" was child's play compared to the charges he faced for killing Spenser. England's monarch, Queen Elizabeth I, was a Roman Catholic and the church frowned on dueling to resolve conflicts. Jonson was arrested and thrown into prison, then tried on manslaughter charges. At his hearing, Jonson pled guilty but managed to avoid the hangman's noose through the benefit of clergy. In one fell swoop, the course of Jonson's life was altered—and most likely for the better.

**Aftermath:** Upon Jonson's release from prison, he was dismissed from his theater troupe, so the ex-con needed a new company to produce his play *Every Man in His Humour*, considered one of his finest. That company was the Lord Chamberlain's Men, for whom William Shakespeare was the principal playwright. This new relationship proved beneficial for Jonson, who was able to continue his career as a dramatist and poet. He went on to become England's unofficial poet laureate in 1616.

## 2. HONOR RESTORED, WITHIN INCHES

**Squaring Off:** Andrew Jackson vs. Charles Dickinson

**The Insult:** In 1806, Jackson was 39 and had already served in the U.S. Senate and House of Representatives, and was a plantation owner and horse breeder in western Tennessee. It was well known that he had married his wife, Rachel, before her divorce from her first husband was final (the result of a clerical error). Although the couple went through a second marriage ceremony, Jackson's opponents liked to use the incident to goad him. Charles Dickinson, a rival horse breeder—egged on by Jackson's political enemies—mentioned Rachel's adultery in a squabble with Jackson over a gambling debt. Jackson challenged Dickinson to a duel on the morning of May 30, 1806.

**Weapon of Choice:** Dickinson, as the challenged party, got to choose the weapon. Regarded as a crack shot, he selected pistols.

**Last Man Standing:** Jackson—but just barely. (Otherwise, who would have been the seventh U.S. president?) Jackson granted Dickinson the first shot from 24 feet, even though he knew of his opponent's prowess. Dickinson's shot struck Jackson inches above his heart, yet he did not fall. Jackson then proceeded to fire; his shot went into Dickinson's stomach, causing such injury that he bled to death later that day.

**Aftermath:** The bullet was never removed from Jackson's chest, and he coughed up blood and suffered pain from it for the rest of his life.

### 3. POETIC INJUSTICE

**Squaring Off:** Aleksandr Pushkin vs. Georges d'Anthès

**The Insult:** Pushkin, generally considered the finest poet in Russian history and the father of modern Russian literature, was outspoken, confrontational, and prone to dramatic mood swings. His wife, Natalya Goncharova, favored a lavish lifestyle and high society, which sent Pushkin into debt and worsened his mental state. When it was rumored that Natalya was having an affair with French military officer Georges d'Anthès, Pushkin was labeled a cuckold and became a target of derision. Enraged, Pushkin challenged d'Anthès to a duel, which was held on January 27, 1837.

**Weapon of Choice:** Pistols—not the best choice for a showdown between a poet and a military officer.

**Last Man Standing:** D'Anthès. As the challenged party, he fired first, hitting Pushkin in the stomach. Despite the wound, Pushkin managed to rise and take his shot, which hit d'Anthès in the chest—but the bullet was deflected by a button (some claim that d'Anthès was wearing armor under his coat) and grazed his arm. Pushkin died from his wound two days later, but not before he forgave d'Anthès of any wrongdoing.

**Aftermath:** Although Tsar Nicholas I pardoned d'Anthès, he stripped him of his rank in the Russian court and exiled him from the country. Pushkin's dramatic death cemented his legacy as a passionate artist who bridged the gap between high society and the common man. Sales of his works soared, and he has remained one of Russia's most revered writers.

## 4. SHOWDOWN OUT WEST

**Squaring Off:** David C. Broderick vs. David S. Terry

**The Insult:** In the 1850s, Broderick ruled politics in San Francisco, lining his own pockets with money garnered from government officials, who reportedly gave him half their salaries in exchange for their appointments. Broderick used these funds to mount a successful campaign for the U.S. Senate in 1857, running as a Democrat on the "Free Soil" platform, which was against the expansion of slavery into California. On the other hand, his friend David S. Terry, who favored slavery, lost a reelection bid for chief justice of the state supreme court—and bitterly blamed Broderick for the defeat. The two exchanged harsh words, tempers flared, and the situation came to a boil on September 13, 1859, when they met for a duel at Lake Merced, outside the San Francisco city limits.

**Weapon of Choice:** Pistols; both men were expert shooters, so it was a fair match—at least on paper.

**Last Man Standing:** Terry. Before the final count was called, Broderick accidentally discharged his pistol into the ground; the rules of dueling dictated that Terry be granted his shot at the unarmed and motionless Broderick. Terry's shot was true, hitting the senator in the chest, yet Broderick managed to hang on for three days before dying on September 16.

**Aftermath:** Terry was acquitted of any crime, but Broderick's popularity among San Francisco's largely Democratic citizens made the former chief justice the target of personal attacks and forced Terry to move away from San Francisco. As for Broderick, he may have been more effective in death than he was in life—he was hailed as a martyr for his stance against slavery; fellow politicians and the press lauded him as one who was willing to die for his beliefs. Talk of allowing slavery in California was quieted, and it remained a free state that lent its vast resources to the Union in the Civil War.

## 5. IN SEARCH OF LOST HONOR

**Squaring Off:** Marcel Proust vs. Jean Lorrain

**The Insult:** Well before he began work on his voluminous masterpiece, *In Search of Lost Time* (French title: *À la recherche du temps perdu*, originally translated as *Remembrance of Things Past*), writer Marcel Proust had come to terms with his own homosexuality, an issue usually kept private in the late 19th century. So when journalist Jean Lorrain wrote of an alleged affair between Proust and another man, Proust attempted to save face by challenging Lorrain to a duel. Ironically, Lorrain was also homosexual—and flamboyantly so, wearing corsets and blushing his cheeks with rogue. In February 1897, Proust and Lorrain met in a wooded area outside of Paris and stared each other down.

**Weapon of Choice:** Pistols; although Proust and Lorrain only wanted to put on a show to "restore honor," not kill one another, the guns were fully primed and loaded.

**Last Man Standing:** Both (or neither, if every fight needs a victor). Proust took the first shot, which exploded into the ground at Lorrain's feet. Lorrain's shot missed completely; witnesses described it as being discharged "in the general direction" of Proust. The duelists' seconds then convened and agreed that honor had been restored.

**Aftermath:** Everyone went home satisfied, and Proust later described the duel as being "one of my best memories"—even though neither man was ever in much danger of being killed.

*       *       *

"I thoroughly disapprove of duels. If a man should challenge me, I would take him kindly and forgivingly by the hand and lead him to a quiet place and kill him."

—Mark Twain

---

Italy was the first nation to use frogmen (military divers) in warfare.

# WHAT DID WE USE BEFORE...?

*Ever wonder how the world survived without the modern conveniences we have today? Here's how.*

## 1. ICE, ICE, BABY

German inventor Carl von Linde patented the first refrigerator in 1877. Before that, people used...

• **Iceboxes:** Starting in the early 1800s, to keep food cool, people relied on boxes made of metal or wood that held a 25- or 50-pound block of ice. The boxes were lined for insulation, and each box had a small drain so the melted ice could drip out of the box into a pan. During a typical summer, an ice block lasted one or two days, so housewives in cities and towns put "ice cards" in their front windows to place their orders for new ice blocks, which were regularly delivered by carts. The cards let the deliverymen know how much ice each woman wanted.

• **Cellars:** These dank, dark areas were dug into the ground under homes. Cellars were naturally cooler than houses but were made even cooler by insulating them with sawdust or straw. Sometimes they were also filled with snow and ice.

• **Ice Houses:** These were special rooms dug into the ground and used to store food for an entire community. They were insulated in the same way as cellars and were filled with ice and snow when available. Ice houses appeared in North America in the 19th century, but the Chinese had been using them since about 2000 BC.

## 2. SUDS AND SCRUBS

The first electric washing machine appeared in the United States around 1900. It used a motor to turn a tub that held dirty clothes. Before that, there were...

• **Fulleries:** Ancient Romans sent their clothes to laundry shops called fulleries. There, workers scrubbed the clothes in huge terracotta bowls. The bleaching agent of choice? Urine...mixed with clay, potash, and sodium carbonate. The clothes were then dried

---

Rodin's famous sculpture *The Thinker* was intended to depict poet Dante Alighieri.

on wire frames with burning sulfur underneath them.

• **Washboards:** The ancients also scrubbed or beat clothes against rocks to get them clean. Washboards showed up in the 1700s and served a similar purpose. Wooden washboards probably originated in Scandinavia, but the metal washboard was all-American—Stephen Rust of New York patented the first metal washboard in 1833.

## 3. I C U

Italian Salvino D'Armate invented the first pair of wearable eyeglasses around 1284. Before that, people used…

• **Water:** Seneca the Younger—a philosopher and playwright in ancient Rome—filled a small glass globe with water and used it to magnify words as he read.

• **Emeralds:** The Roman emperor Nero, who ruled during the first century AD and who was a student of Seneca the Younger, held emeralds in front of his eyes during gladiator games so he could better see what was happening in the arena. (The emeralds also worked like sunglasses to protect his eyes.)

• **Reading Stones:** These were the creation of Arab poet and inventor Abbas Ibn Firnas in the ninth century. They were basically little round rocks of clear, polished glass that magnified anything underneath them.

\*     \*     \*

## PRESIDENTIAL FIRSTS

Many of our presidents dared to be bold. Here are a few who trod where no other president had gone before:

• James K. Polk (1845–49) was the first president to have his photograph taken.

• Theodore Roosevelt (1901–09) was the first to ride in an automobile and the first to travel outside the country while in office by visiting Panama.

• Franklin D. Roosevelt (1933–45) was the first to ride in an airplane.

# FOREIGN AFFAIRS TO REMEMBER

*The affairs we're talking about aren't affairs of the heart. These three—our favorites from history—involved treachery, intrigue, and your basic clash of cultures.*

## 1. THE DREYFUS AFFAIR

Alfred Dreyfus was born into a wealthy family in 1859 in Mulhouse, Alsace. When Germany annexed Alsace in 1871, the family moved to Paris, where Dreyfus eventually entered the École Polytechnique, a military school. As a lieutenant in the artillery, he gained a reputation as an intelligent officer and in 1893 became the only Jew assigned to the French General Staff. That's where the trouble began.

**Talking Trash.** After a cleaning woman plucked sensitive documents from the wastebasket of the military attaché at the German embassy—unsigned papers that disclosed the location of French artillery emplacements—the General Staff began to believe that one of their officers with an artillery background was a spy. Some were quick to accuse Dreyfus, who, in addition to being the only Jew on the General Staff, had a continuous supply of money, courtesy of a stipend from his father. He didn't socialize, partly because he had few friends, but mostly because of his devotion to his family.

**His Day in Court.** Dreyfus was arrested in October 1894 on thin evidence provided by friends of Major Ferdinand Esterhazy, and was accused of high treason for divulging military secrets to the Germans. After a quick trial in a secret military court (in which strong anti-Semitic feelings prevented him from receiving a fair hearing), he was declared guilty and sentenced to life imprisonment on Devil's Island, the notorious penal colony off the northern coast of South America.

**The Wrong Man.** As the years passed, doubts of Dreyfus's guilt began to surface, and influential French intellectuals became involved. Writers Émile Zola and Anatole France and future prime minister Georges Clemenceau pressured the government to reopen

---

Bubble gum was invented in 1906. It's original name: "Blibber-Blubber."

the trial after handwriting experts agreed that Major Esterhazy, not Dreyfus, had stolen the damaging documents. When nothing came of it, Zola published an open letter to French president Félix Faure on January 13, 1898, entitled "J'accuse" ("I accuse"). It appeared on the front page of a daily Paris newspaper and accused the highest levels of the French army of obstruction of justice and anti-Semitism. The evidence became a national embarrassment when people learned that senior members of the General Staff withheld the truth. In 1899, the public, which for years had wanted to crush the arrogant and aristocratic military, forced a reopening of the case. Exonerated on July 12, 1906, Dreyfus returned to the army as a major.

**A Chestful of Medals.** The affair weakened the morale and solidarity of the French officer corps for years. Clemenceau tried to weed out anti-Semitism in France but never succeeded. Dreyfus continued to serve in the army, and was honorably discharged in 1907. He volunteered to serve in World War I, was elevated to lieutenant colonel, and earned several medals, including the Legion of Honor. He died in Paris in 1935 after a long illness. He is remembered as one of France's most tragic figures, but also as a hero.

## 2. THE XYZ AFFAIR

In 1792, Great Britain and France were at war for the umpteenth time. The issue at hand was the French Revolution, which the British thought they could keep from spreading across Europe by restoring France's deposed monarchy. America walked a delicate line between the two countries: When the British Royal Navy started to seize American ships en route to France, the Jay Treaty of 1794 eased tensions between the United States and Great Britain for a while. But the arrangement destabilized relations with France, which needed American financial and diplomatic support. The United States had been honoring a Franco-American commercial treaty from 1778, which France revoked in 1796 when the Jay Treaty went into effect. The French government claimed that the United States had reneged on its agreement of mutual support and began seizing American merchant ships.

**The Prez Steps In.** Wanting to avoid open war, President John Adams sent a delegation to France to negotiate a new treaty. Three commissioners—Elbridge Gerry, John Marshall, and Charles

Pinckney—headed the delegation. Vice President Thomas Jefferson's disagreed with Adams's pacification policy because he wanted France to win the war against England, bring down the British monarchy, and "republicanize" the country.

**Show Me the Francs!** On arriving in Paris, the American delegates found themselves working with three men who insisted on anonymity: Jean Conrad Hottinguer (X) and Lucien Hauteval (Z), both Swiss bankers, and Pierre Bellamy (Y), an American banker working out of Hamburg, Germany. The three bankers represented the interests of the French government, looking for collateral to back loans that France needed to carry on the war with England. But French prime minister Charles-Maurice de Talleyrand wanted something more. He sent a personal friend, Madame de Villette, to steer the opening discussions, in which she told the astonished Americans that Talleyrand wouldn't even speak with them about a treaty without a bribe of $250,000.

**Lost in Translation.** Talleyrand also demanded a formal apology from President Adams, who'd derided the French government in Congress, and a guarantee that France wouldn't be liable for damages inflicted by French privateers on American commerce. What Talleyrand didn't understand was that bribes worked in Europe, but did not work with Americans. Pinckney's answer was, "No, no, not a sixpence." When the XYZ trio subsequently demanded a loan of $10 million to get Talleyrand to speak with the delegation, Marshall returned home, leaving Gerry and Pinckney in France.

**You Want Freedom Fries with That?** Marshall reported the bribe to Adams, and a public outcry ensued in the United States. The XYZ affair scotched Adams's attempt to secure peace, but he refused to declare war on France. Talleyrand didn't want to declare war on the United States, either. Instead, from 1798 to 1800, the U.S. Navy fought the undeclared Quasi War with France, a conflict that took place entirely on the high seas. France finally relented and settled the matter by signing the Treaty of Morfontaine, also known as the Convention of 1800, and French privateering came to an end.

**Good-bye, Adams—Hello, Sailors!**
The two-year war and the loss of 2,000 merchant ships didn't help Adams at the polls in 1800; he lost the presidency to Thomas Jefferson. To his credit, Adams did establish a Naval Department in

1798 and built the first viable American navy during the Quasi War by putting to sea 27 armed warships and 365 privateers to battle the French navy, which lost 85 ships, mostly privateers, to the new U.S. Navy.

## 3. THE AFFAIR OF THE DIAMOND NECKLACE

French crown jewelers Boehmer and Bassenge spent years and much of their wealth collecting diamonds for a necklace commissioned by King Louis XV for his mistress, Madame du Barry. The king died in 1774, leaving the necklace, valued at 1,600,000 livres (or about $18 million today), undelivered and unpaid for. Four years later, facing bankruptcy, Boehmer and Bassenge appealed to King Louis XVI to buy the necklace for the queen, Marie Antoinette. The queen refused the gift and told the king that the funds would be better spent on equipping a warship. In 1781, the jewelers tried once more, after Marie Antoinette gave birth to the dauphin Louis-Joseph, but once again, the queen rejected the offer.

**Counting on Success.** Other attempts to peddle the necklace also failed, but eventually the plight of Boehmer and Bassenge caught the eye of Jeanne de Saint-Rémy de Valois, an attractive opportunist remotely related to the crown. Being a descendant of an illegitimate son of Henry II of France entitled Valois to a small pension from the crown, but she wanted more. To filch the jewels would require patience, connivance, and connections. Valois arranged to marry Nicholas de La Motte, who called himself Count La Motte, although his claim of nobility was dubious. Then, in 1784, to advance her plan—and in collusion with her husband—Countess La Motte became the mistress of Cardinal de Rohan, bishop of Strasbourg.

**The Cardinal Caper.** The cardinal wanted to mend broken relations with Marie Antoinette and set himself up as prime minister. The countess promised Rohan that she could get him back into the queen's good graces. Thus began an intimate correspondence between the cardinal and Marie Antoinette, with Countess La Motte as delivery girl. But instead of giving Rohan's letters to the queen, she gave them to an accomplice, Réteaux de Villette, who wrote warm and passionate responses that led the cardinal to believe that Marie Antoinette had fallen in love with him. La Motte arranged a rendezvous, hired a high-class prostitute who resembled the queen, and the surreptitious meeting took place in the Palace of Versaille gardens. The hooker promised that she would forget past differences and get the cardinal what he wanted.

**Le Sting.** Countess La Motte began to borrow large sums of money from the cardinal, supposedly for the queen's charities. Boehmer and Bassenge also got involved and commissioned the countess to sell the necklace. A few weeks later, she introduced the cardinal to the jewelers as the queen's intermediary. Rohan agreed to purchase the necklace for the original price, payable in installments, and showed Marie Antoinette's authorization, written, of course, by the phony letter writer. As soon as he got his hands on it, Count La Motte departed immediately for London, where he broke up the necklace and sold the stones. When the installments went unpaid, Boehmer complained to the queen, who said—in French, of course—"What necklace?"

**Ripple Effect.** On August 15, 1785, a crowd waited for the king and queen to arrive at the chapel for services officiated by Cardinal de Rohan. The gendarmes arrived first and conducted de Rohan, who'd begun to suspect foul play and had destroyed his letters, to the Bastille. Three days later, Countess La Motte, who had also destroyed all her papers, was arrested. After an investigation, the letter writer and the royal impersonator were also arrested.

The Parlement de Paris heard the cardinal's case, decided de Rohan had been duped by La Motte, and set him free. The court condemned Countess La Motte to the prostitutes' prison and ordered her whipped and branded. Count La Motte, though living comfortably in London, received a life sentence in absentia. The countess escaped from prison and went to England, where she wrote her memoirs and blamed the queen for the episode. The public tended to believe La Motte's account, which, combined with the acquittal of de Rohan, pointed to Marie Antoinette as the perpetrator of a scheme intended to embarrass Cardinal de Rohan.

**Let Them Eat Necklaces.** The affair of the diamond necklace discredited the Bourbon monarchy, especially Marie Antoinette. She became increasingly unpopular during the days leading up to the French Revolution in 1789. The affair didn't lead directly to her execution in 1793, but the French public continued to suspect her because of her reputation for careless extravagance.

# IT'S A (SPORTS) RIOT

*It's not whether you win or lose, but whether you can survive the game.*

### 1. BLUE VS. GREEN
Chariot racing fans were passionate at Constantinople's Hippo-drome. The city was divided between fans of the Blue and Green racing teams, and violence often broke out between sides. But in AD 532, both teams joined forces when Emperor Justinian—who'd ordered the execution of a Blue and also a Green driver because there had been deaths in their races—refused to pardon them. Yelling "Nika!" ("Conquer!"), the Blue and Green fans caused havoc in the stadium, set fire to the city, and laid siege to the palace. The riots killed about 30,000 people.

### 2. FOOTBALL HOOLIGANS
In 1314, King Edward II banned football (soccer) because two rival villages were physically brawling with each other. But foot-ball prevailed and so did that fighting village tradition that has became known as hooliganism. In 1885, a game between Preston North End and Aston Villa caused violence that saw both teams beaten and stoned and had one Preston player losing conscious-ness. A century later, in Brussels's aging Heysel Stadium, a riot broke out when Britain's Liverpool faced off against Italy's Juventus in the European Cup final. Italian and British fans fought until crowds ran for safety. Under the weight of panicked fans, a wall collapsed, killing 39 people and injuring 600.

### 3. HOCKEY HAVOC
Maurice Richard was the top player of the Montreal Canadiens, which made him a target for opposing teams. In 1955 at Boston, after being hit in the head once too often, Richard fought back with his hockey stick and fists. The NHL president suspended Richard for the season, which angered fans who'd counted on Richard to lead the team to the Stanley Cup. When the NHL president decided to attend the next Canadiens home game, enraged fans pelted him with eggs and debris until a tear-gas bomb forced them out of the arena. They then looted stores, overturned cars, and set fires until Richard was asked to calm the city.

# 10 PLACES YOU CAN'T GO

*Here are 10 places around the world closed to
the public that continue to provoke wonder:*

**1. Area 51.** This large, ultra-secret military airfield is 83 miles northwest of Las Vegas, Nevada. It is the test ground for experimental aircraft and weapons systems, and has been identified in popular culture with UFO sightings.

**2. The U.S. Bullion Depository.** Better known as "Fort Knox" (because it's adjacent to the town of Fort Knox, Kentucky), the depository's famous underground vault is classified, no visitors allowed. Why? It holds the United States's second-largest gold reserve: 147.3 million ounces. (The vault under the Federal Reserve Bank of New York is #1). Since it opened in 1937, the depository's vault—made of concrete, steel, and granite—has also stored important historical documents...everything from the Declaration of Independence to the Magna Carta.

**3. Mezhgorye.** This town, founded in 1979, is a forbidden zone except for the people believed to be working there on Mount Yamataw, the highest mountain in the southern Urals. Various Russians say it's a mining site, a repository for Russian treasures, a food storage area, or a bunker for leaders in case of nuclear attack.

**4. Room 39.** This secret organization established in the late 1970s in North Korea reportedly seeks foreign currency for Kim Jong Il, the country's leader. It is believed the group is involved in illegal weapons sales and uses bank accounts in China and Switzerland for illicit transactions.

**5. RAF Menwith Hill.** This top-secret British military base is reportedly the largest electronic monitoring station in the world. It is here with an array of white radomes that experts search for hints of terrorist attacks while filtering all telephone and radio communications in the United States, Britain and other host nations...privacy be damned.

**6.Vatican Secret Archives.** You can view documents from the archives, but you can't enter them. You can only see information

---

**October 4, 1931:** The comic strip *Dick Tracy* debuted in the *Detroit Daily Mirror*.

at least 75 years old. It's estimated the archive contains 52 miles of shelving.

**7. White's Gentlemen's Club.** Founded in 1693 by Italian Francesco Bianco (White), the club in England is famous for its "betting book," in which members place bizarre wagers like which of two raindrops will slide down the window first. No women are allowed. To join, you must be invited by a sitting member with the support of two other members.

**8. Mount Weather Emergency Operations Center.** If it's the end of the world, you might head to the center if you knew its location— but you wouldn't get in. Only a chosen few have access to avoid impending destruction. The center was established in the 1950s and is run by FEMA, which funnels telecommunications traffic through it.

**9. Moscow Metro-2.** Russian journalists have reported this parallel yet secret subway system in Moscow. It is reported to connect the Kremlin with the Russian Federation security service, the government airport, and the underground town of Remanki. But no one confirms any of this.

**10. Ise Grand Shrine.** This most sacred shrine in Japan has been around since 4 BC. The shrine is demolished and rebuilt every 20 years to live up to the Shinto belief in death and rebirth. The next reconstruction is scheduled for 2013. To enter, you must be a priest or priestess, as well as and be a member of the royal family.

\*     \*     \*

## MOST ENDANGERED U.S. HISTORIC SITES

**1.** America's state parks and state-owned historic sites, nationwide

**2.** Black Mountain, Kentucky

**3.** Hinchliffe Stadium, New Jersey

**4.** Industrial Arts Building, Nebraska

**5.** Juana Briones House, California

**6.** Merritt Parkway, Connecticut

**7.** Metropolitan AME Church, DC

*(Source: National Trust for Historic Preservation)*

Longest-lived twins: sisters Kin Narita (107) and Gin Kanie (108) of Japan.

# KODAK MOMENTS

*Today, just about anybody can take a great photo with a camera
as small as the one mounted inside your cell phone. But it has
been a march of 185 years to perfect how that could be done.
Uncle John recently cranked up the way-back machine
to examine the birth and development of photography.
Here is part one of his top photo firsts.*

## 1. OLDEST PHOTO, 1825

It was thought for nearly two centuries that the world's oldest
photo was taken in 1826 by Joseph Nicephore Niepce, a French
inventor known as the "father of photography." It was a rather
fuzzy eight-hour exposure of building architecture in the city of Le
Gras. But then an even older photo turned up in 2002—the image
of a man walking a horse. Who took it? Niepce in 1825. He did it
by covering a piece of copper with light-sensitive bitumen. Once
the metal plate was exposed to light, an image was created, which
Niepce transferred to paper. He called it heliogravure. As soon as
the discovery of the 1825 photo was announced, France declared
it a national treasure. It was sold at auction for $392,000 to the
French National Library.

## 2. FIRST STREET SCENE, 1838

French artist and chemist Louis Daguerre further developed
Niepce's process and took a picture of a busy Paris avenue; "Boulevard du Temple" is quite striking for its time. Taken from an elevation, the photo shows in exquisite detail a wide, curving boulevard
lined with tall buildings and a man standing in the foreground.
Amazingly, the street looks empty. Look more closely and you see
ghostly images—since traffic was on the move during a 10-minute
exposure, it virtually disappeared on film. The man in the photo,
however, stood still long enough to be seen clearly.

What Daguerre did was use silver-coated copper plates and
iodine to create a film of silver iodide. He next exposed the plate
to light from a scene and passed it through mercury vapor. Dip-
ping the plate in salt water "fixed" the image. The process became
celebrated as a daguerreotype.

The idea of the atom was introduced by ancient Greek thinker Leucippus of Miletus in 450 BC.

### 3. FIRST HUMAN FACE, 1839

Dutch chemist Robert Cornelius is credited with taking the first photograph a human face—his own—while standing outside his family's store in Philadelphia. As a silver plating and metal polishing specialist, Cornelius became intrigued with silver plates exposed to light that created an image, later known as a daguerreotype. With the help of chemist Paul Beck Goddard, he perfected the process and in October 1839 took a self-portrait. It shows Cornelius with tousled hair standing with crossed arms—showing clearly the first-ever photo of a human face.

Though the photographer made history and opened two of the earliest photo studios in the United States, he lost interest as other studios opened and competed with him. Instead, he committed himself to the family business: gas and lighting.

### 4. FIRST HUMAN SUBJECT, 1840

William Henry Fox Talbot of Britain is credited with inventing the negative-positive photographic process called photogravure. Talbot, a university-trained chemist and scholar, is credited with taking the first photo with a human as the main subject—a footman holding the door open to a royal carriage.

Talbot was dissatisfied with the daguerreotype process of fixing an image with salt water because it only partially stabilized an image. Talbot's friend, renowned scientist Sir John Herschel, suggested he use hyposulfite of soda to freeze the image during processing. It worked. "Hypo" as a fixer for black-and-white photography became the standard internationally.

### 5. FIRST UNDERWATER PHOTOGRAPH, 1856

William Thompson's niche in photo history came from a belief that he could take a picture underwater. He did it by mounting a camera on a tripod and then lowering it from a boat 18 feet to the bottom of Britain's Weymouth Bay, where it was fixed in an upright position. In doing so, he made a sacrificial lamb out of the camera—it leaked. But his second image survived on a plate exposed to light for 10 minutes. Thompson, a natural historian, later improved the camera but lost interest in underwater photography. However, a friend convinced him to submit an account of

---

There are 12 historic housebarns in the United States. As you might have guessed, a...

his experiment to the *Journal of the Society of Arts*. If it hadn't been published, no one would have known of Thompson's achievement.

His picture was of poor quality, showing nothing but seaweed and boulders at the bottom of the bay. Nevertheless, it was a first and gives Thompson an honored position on Uncle John's list.

### 6. FIRST COLOR PHOTO, 1861

Most people think of color photography as an invention of the 20th century. However, James Clerk Maxwell produced the first color photograph. It was of a tartan ribbon. The celebrated Scottish scientist filmed it three times, each time with a different color filter over the glass lens of his camera. The three images were developed, then projected onto a screen and aligned one on top of the other to produce a single color image.

Of course, you could see the color reproduction, but there was no way to print it until years later. The three plates are on permanent file in Maxwell's hometown of Edinburgh. The photographer's later and better-known claim to fame was his discovery of electromagnetic waves that led to radio, TV, radar, mobile phones, and many other modern conveniences.

*For part two, go to page 412.*

\*     \*     \*

### THE REAL LOST CITY OF ATLANTIS?

Since the time of the ancient Greeks, reports have persisted that a city was swallowed up by an earthquake and disappeared beneath the ocean. Greek writer Pausanias was the first to chronicle it, noting that in a single night the flourishing city of Helike was destroyed by an earthquake and a tsunami that swept over it.

Helike, according to Pausanias, was a Greek worship center devoted to Poseidon, the god of the sea. But no trace was ever found of the city until 1861, when a bronze coin with the head of Poseidon turned up at an archaeological site. Then, in 2001, two archaeologists discovered the supposed ruins of Helike buried by coastal mud and gravel. Work is now underway to uncover the real "Atlantis."

---

...housebarn is a building that combines a house and a barn.

# ART HISTORY 101

*Uncle John continues his review of historic works
of art that you should be familiar with.*

## 1. THE FARMER TAKES A WIFE
*American Gothic*
**Artist:** Grant Wood
**Where:** The Art Institute, Chicago, Illinois
**Medium:** Oil on beaverboard
**Appearance:** In an almost cartoonish style, a dour-looking couple—a farmer in bib overalls and dark blazer and a woman in an apron—stand in front of a farmhouse. He looks straight ahead, holding a pitchfork; she stands slightly behind him and looks past him, off to the side. A little bit bigger than the *Mona Lisa, American Gothic* comes in at just over 29 by 25 inches.
**Details of Interest:**
• The painting is named for the upstairs window of the house that appears in the background. Wood was inspired first by the house and the Gothic Revival–style window. He asked his sister, Nan, and his dentist to pose in front of it, and—tongue firmly in cheek—started painting them as an Iowa farmer and his unmarried adult daughter.

• When it was done, Wood entered it in a 1930 competition at the Art Institute of Chicago. One of the judges called it a "comic valentine," but a museum patron convinced the judges to take it more seriously: it ended up winning a bronze medal and $300 in cash. In another smart move, the patron also persuaded the museum to buy the painting.

• *American Gothic* is a cultural icon right up there with the *Mona Lisa* and *The Scream* as a target of parodies. You've seen variations of it in ads, magazines, cartoons, and on postcards, as well as on TV shows like *Pee-wee's Playhouse,* in the video of "Don't Go Breaking My Heart" (with Elton John and RuPaul portraying the couple), and in *The Rocky Horror Picture Show.*

---

**Sioux name for the Little Bighorn River: the Greasy Grass.**

## 2. THE ART OF WAR

*Guernica*

**Artist:** Pablo Picasso

**Where:** The Queen Sofia Museum, Madrid, Spain

**Medium:** Oil on canvas

**Appearance:** A Cubist depiction of the village of Guernica in Spain's Basque country in 1937 during the Spanish Civil War, it would be red with blood if it wasn't painted in black, white, and grayish blue. It's a chaotic scene of the aftermath of the bombing by German warplanes: a mother holds a dead child, a severed arm holds a broken sword, the dead and dying litter the ground. Technically, it's a painting on canvas, but it's the size of a mural: 11 feet 6 inches high by 25 feet 6 inches wide.

**Details of Interest:**

• About a third of the residents of Guernica (around 1,600 people) were killed or wounded in the three-hour bombing. The attack had been requested by General Francisco Franco, who came to power at the end of the war.

• Picasso (who was living in France along with most of the other artists of his day) had already been commissioned to depict the Spanish government's struggle in the Spanish Civil War when he read in a newspaper about the slaughter in Guernica. The painting was first exhibited in the Spanish Pavilion at the 1937 Paris International Exhibition.

• Picasso made sure that as many people as possible saw the painting, exhibiting it throughout Europe and North America between 1937 and 1939, at which point he gave the painting to New York's Museum of Modern Art on an extended loan, with the stipulation that it not be returned to Spain until the "reestablishment of public liberties." The painting was returned to Spain in September 1981. It was put on display in an annex of the Prado until it was transferred to its present home.

## 3. MMM, MMM, GOOD

*Campbell's Soup Cans* (a.k.a. 32 Campbell's Soup Cans)

**Artist:** Andy Warhol

**Where:** The Museum of Modern Art, New York

**Medium:** Synthetic polymer paint silk screen on canvas

**Appearance:** Thirty-two little canvases, each depicting a can of Campbell's soup, each 20 inches high by 16 inches wide, hung in four horizontal rows of eight each. All the classic Campbell's favorites are there, one of each of the varieties offered at the time: Tomato, Onion, Beef Broth, Split Pea with Ham—you name it.

**Details of Interest:**

• Warhol didn't show up the first time the paintings were displayed at the Ferus Gallery in Los Angeles, so the exhibitor lined them up straight across the wall on small individual ledges, as if in a supermarket display. The audience was mostly confused; the critics were critical. There was some interest, though: a few people (including actor Dennis Hopper) wanted to buy one of the 32 paintings for $100, but the exhibitor, Irving Blum, decided to keep them as a set. It was later that they were displayed as we see them today: four rows, eight across.

• Everyone had an opinion on why Warhol chose to turn mundane soup cans into iconic art: that he had it every day for lunch, or that his mother used to make flowers out of the cans when he was a kid, and so on.

• Warhol's first silk-screen production was of dollar bills, which was kind of prophetic since he was on his way to becoming the highest-paid living American artist.

\*　　\*　　\*

## FAMOUS PEOPLE WITH MÈNIERÉS DISEASE

Mènierés's disease is an inner-ear abnormality that causes a variety of symptoms including vertigo, a roaring sound, fluctuating hearing loss, and a sensation of pain or pressure in the affected ear. Here are some historic figures who suffered from this disease:

| | |
|---|---|
| Emily Dickinson | Mike Reilly |
| Andrew Knight | Alan Shepard |
| Martin Luther | Jonathan Swift |
| Les Paul | Vincent van Gogh |

# ONE-ARMED BUT ABLE

*It's amazing what some people can accomplish,*
*even if they've been "disarmed."*

## 1. THE SENATOR #1

Second Lieutenant Daniel Ken Inouye received the Medal of
Honor in World War II for extraordinary valor while leading a
charge up a heavily fortified ridge in San Terenzo, Italy, in April
1945. Directing his platoon against sustained machine-gun fire to
capture an enemy artillery and mortar post, Inouye crawled alone
up the slope when a crossfire of bullets halted the advance, and
got close enough to hurl grenades into not one, but two machine-
gun nests. Hit by a sniper's bullet, Inouye continued to engage the
enemy until a grenade exploded and shattered his right arm. He
refused evacuation and directed his platoon farther up the ridge,
where they overwhelmed the enemy.

**From Hospital to Senate.** Discharged in 1947 with the rank of
captain, the second-generation Japanese American gave up his
ambition to become a surgeon due to the loss of his arm. He
returned to college to study political science, entered politics as a
Democrat, and was elected U.S. senator from Hawaii in 1962. He
made history as a member of the Watergate Committee in 1974,
and later chaired the Iran-Contra hearings in 1987–89. As of
2010, Inouye has served eight consecutive terms and is the chairman of the powerful Senate Appropriations Committee.

## 2. THE SENATOR #2

In Khe Sanh, Vietnam, in April 1968, 25-year-old Captain Max
Cleland leaped to the ground from a helicopter to grab a live
grenade accidentally dropped by another soldier. It went off and
shredded both of Cleland's legs and his right forearm. Cleland was
awarded the Silver Star and Bronze Star, and made the long and
difficult recovery from his wounds at the Walter Reed Medical
Center in Washington, D.C. Back home in Georgia, he rebuilt his
life, winning a state senate seat in 1971 and later heading up the
Veterans Administration during Jimmy Carter's presidency.

**Broken Heart of a Patriot.** Cleland was elected to the U.S.

---

August 1, 1958: First-class U.S. postage became 4¢. It had been 3¢ for 26 years.

Senate in 1996 but was defeated for a second term when his opponent challenged his patriotism for opposing the Iraq War. The defeat wounded Cleland deeply—he lost his job, his income, and his fiancée. He reentered Walter Reed suffering from what was diagnosed as post-traumatic stress disorder. Surrounded as he was by a younger generation of veterans who were missing limbs just like he was, he came to realize that he'd never really dealt with his own wartime scars—the ones people couldn't see. After he was released from the hospital, Cleland detailed his life story in a memoir, *Heart of a Patriot*, which was published in 2009.

### 3. THE MOUNTAIN CLIMBER

Aron Lee Ralston didn't start out as a one-armed mountain climber, but he became America's most famous mountain climber when he was forced to amputate his right arm after it became pinned by a falling boulder near Moab, Utah, in May 2003. For five days, Ralston tried to work himself free. Dehydrated and growing delirious, he managed to pivot his arm against the rocks, breaking the bones in his forearm. He then used a pocketknife to cut away the tissue and tear through tendons to finally free himself.

**Highly Motivated.** He set himself a goal of becoming the first solo climber to reach the summit of all 59 mountains in the Rockies with an elevation of at least 14,000 feet. After his accident, Ralston wrote a book about his ordeal, *Between a Rock and a Hard Place*, and has since become a popular motivational speaker. He also returned to his passion of climbing solo. With the aid of a prosthetic arm, he completed his quest to climb all 59 "fourteeners" in the Rockies.

### 4. THE DRUMMER

Rick Allen had been the drummer for the rock band Def Leppard for six years when he had the accident that cost him his arm. On his way to a New Year's Eve party in Derbyshire, England, in 1984, the 21-year-old lost control of his speeding car. The resulting crash threw him from the vehicle, severing his left arm.

**The Thunder God.** A few weeks later, he rejoined the band and, after getting himself a new set of custom electronic drums, became known to his fans as the "Thunder God." In 2001, he established the Raven Drum Foundation, based in Malibu, California, which provides free educational programs to youths facing adversity. The foundation advocates "drum circles," where participants use rhythmic drumming to release frustrations and connect with others.

## 5. THE SURFER

Imagine the skill and balance it takes to pilot a surfboard over waves as tall as a three-story building. Now imagine doing that with only one arm—that's what American professional surfer Bethany Hamilton has accomplished. When she was 13 years old, she lost her arm to a shark attack on October 31, 2003, while surfing off Tunnels Beach in Kauai, Hawaii. A tiger shark ripped her left arm from a point just below her shoulder.

**The Comeback Kid.** Eight weeks later, Hamilton returned to surfing and became an international sensation. In July 2004, she earned cable sports network ESPN's annual ESPY Award for Best Comeback Athlete of the Year. Hamilton has been a full-time professional surfer since 2008.

\*     \*     \*

## "V" IS FOR VICTORY AND. . .

Emile Louis Victor de Laveleye was a Belgian Olympian, politician, and minister. On January 14, 1941, he asked his countrymen to choose the letter "V" as a rallying sign, He chose it because it was the first letter of *victoire* ("victory" in French) and also of *vrijheid* ("freedom" in Dutch). Although Churchill went on to get the credit for popularizing the "V" sign, this was its origin as the "V" for victory and freedom. Laveleye kicked off the "V" campaign, which saw "V" graffiti on the walls of Belgium and later throughout all of Europe.

The correct way to sign is with the palm outward (in the reverse, it has a derogatory meaning in Britain). The sign as a hand gesture is also known as the peace sign, not to be confused with the peace symbol. The latter was originally designed in 1958 by professional designer and artist Gerald Holtom for the nuclear disarmament movement in Britain. In the 1960s, the counterculture adopted it for the antiwar movement, and then it spread throughout popular culture.

# GOING GLOBAL

*Two big deals and one failure conclude the United States' nation-building and expansion plans. Part 1 is on page 267.*

## 1. THE GADSDEN PURCHASE (1853–54)

The Treaty of Guadalupe Hidalgo officially ended the Mexican-American War in February 1848, but it didn't end the tensions between the two countries. The railroad barons couldn't help but notice the large gap between the East Coast and California and they believed, quite rightly, that the territory that Mexico still held in the southern region of present-day New Mexico and Arizona would be better suited for building a transcontinental railroad than the mountainous land just to the north.

**Yankee, Go Home!** Afraid that colonists living in the disputed area would create conditions leading to another annexation, the Mexican government started evicting American settlers. Before the conflict could escalate, President Franklin Pierce sent James Gadsden, the new U.S. minister to Mexico, to negotiate a settlement with Mexican president Antonio López de Santa Anna.

**Gadsden Goes Shopping.** Pierce gave Gadsden a few options. He could offer Santa Anna up to $50 million for the peninsula of Baja California and a large portion of northern Mexico, or $15 million for a smaller section of land immediately to the south of the New Mexico Territory. Santa Anna needed money, but turned down the $50 million deal. On December 30, 1853, Gadsden and Santa Anna signed a treaty stipulating that the United States would pay $15 million for 55,000 square miles to expand the New Mexico Territory to the south. As part of the agreement, the United States would do what it could to prevent Native American raids along the new border, but it refused to take any financial responsibility for the attacks.

**Gadsden Makes a Purchase.** Congress initially ratified the treaty on April 25, 1854, but Gadsden continued to meet with Santa Anna to discuss boundaries while Congress debated whether or not slavery would be allowed in the new territory. A revised treaty reduced the acquisition price to $10 million and the area to 29,670 square miles. Private claims, including claims for Native

---

Do you think of Japan as a country of a few islands? It actually has 6,852 of them.

American attacks, were also excluded. Santa Anna, still stretched for money, signed the revised treaty on June 8, 1854. The coming of the Civil War disrupted plans for building a transcontinental railroad, but the treaty did establish the southern border of the United States as it stands today.

## 2. ALASKA (1867)

In the mid-19th century, the territory of Alaska was held by Russia, which had established a few small trading posts along the coast. But Tsar Alexander II needed money to finance his own plans for expansion into central Asia and the Transcaspian region. Because Alaska shared a border with British Columbia, Alexander was afraid that Great Britain, whose navy competed with his in the Pacific, would find an excuse to annex Alaska without compensating Russia, which had no way of defending the territory. When British settlers began moving across the border into Alaska, the tsar sent envoys to London and Washington to negotiate a sale in 1859. But Great Britain expressed no interest in purchasing Alaska, and the Americans were too distracted by the coming Civil War to take any immediate action.

**Here's Our Two Cents.** In early March 1867, Russian minister Eduard de Stoeckl visited the State Department and entered into negotiations with Secretary of State William H. Seward. Discussions continued until March 30 when, at 4:00 a.m. after an all-night session, Stoeckl agreed to Seward's offer of $7.2 million (about two cents per acre) for a territory that few Americans had ever heard of. At the time, Alaska's population consisted of about 2,500 Russians of mixed race, 8,000 indigenous people who worked as trappers and fur preservers for the Russian-American Company, and possibly 50,000 Eskimos and Native Alaskans living beyond the reach of the tsar's 23 trading posts.

**Not Fully a Folly.** When the acquisition was announced, most Americans learned for the first time that the territory consisted of 586,412 square miles. Because the area was remote and thought to be just a big chunk of ice, Americans mockingly referred to Alaska as "Seward's Ice Box" or "Seward's Folly." The press reviled Seward for buying useless land, but Seward was proved right in the end. The deal ended Russia's presence in North America and gave the United States complete access to the northern rim of the continent.

---

Chicago's Marshall Field's store created the first bridal registry in 1924.

**Laughing All the Way to the Gold Rush.** For three decades the United States pretty much ignored Alaska, which was administered mostly by the navy and the Treasury Department. Seward's final vindication came in 1896 when a major gold deposit was discovered in the Yukon, making Alaska the gateway to the Klondike. The strategic importance of Alaska was realized during World War II: air bases were established on the mainland along with air and naval bases on the Aleutians. These installations were used to drive the Japanese off the outer islands (Kiska and Attu) and bomb northern Japan. On January 3, 1959, the territory became the 49th state.

## 3. THE PHILIPPINES (1898)

In the 1890s, the United States began looking for ways to establish a stronger presence in the Pacific. Annexing Hawaii in 1898 gave them a foothold, but no bragging rights. Every other significant island in the Pacific was occupied by either a European country or Japan. Visions of imperialism came too late—unless another nation was silly enough to step on Uncle Sam's toes.

**Remember the *Maine*!** That opportunity came on February 15, 1898, when the USS *Maine* blew up in the harbor of Havana, Cuba. The cause of the explosion has never been resolved, but at the time, the press was quick to blame Spanish saboteurs, and President William McKinley demanded Spain's withdrawal from Cuba in reprisal. The Spanish refused and then declared war on the United States on April 23. Although most of the fighting took place in Cuba, the swift, victorious Battle of Manila Bay in the Philippines on May 1 produced the greatest reward and the biggest problem: the reward being the occupation and ceding of the islands and the problem being the perpetual difficulty of defending it against guerrilla insurgents, and in World War II against the Japanese.

**The Spanish Acquisition**

The Spanish-American War lasted less than four months; an armistice was signed on August 12, 1898. Four months later, Spain paid the price for its foolhardiness and signed the Treaty of Paris, which made the United States the protector of Cuba, with the understanding that it would not be annexed. The Spanish also ceded Puerto Rico and Guam and sold the Philippines to the Americans for $20 million. In one short war, the United States gained two possessions in the Pacific.

---

May 28, 1742: The first indoor swimming pool (43 feet long) opened in London.

**Not So Fast, Uncle Sam.** Unlike previous acquisitions that consisted of vast stretches of land, the Philippines was made up of 7,000 islands with a total land area of 114,830 square miles and a broadly distributed population estimated at around eight million. On February 4, 1899, Filipino insurgents opened fire on U.S. troops. From 1899 to 1913, there were several more uprisings. The United States maintained a strong military presence there for decades, but in 1941 the Japanese forced out General Douglas MacArthur's small army. Although MacArthur returned to liberate the islands in 1944–45, the United States decided to relinquish its sovereignty and granted the Philippines independence in 1946. It was the worst territorial investment ever made by the United States—and the last.

\*       \*       \*

## BIZARRE U.S. HISTORY

That are many unusual facts to uncover in the history of the United States. Uncle John antes up these gems:

• From 1784 to 1796, there was a colonial state called Franklin added to the original 13. It was the western portion of North Carolina, ceded to the government to pay off the state's Revolutionary War debt. Franklin eventually became the state of Tennessee.

• The familiar home of all presidents in Washington, D.C., was known as the "Presidential Palace" until President Theodore Roosevelt started referring to it as the "White House" on presidential stationery in 1901.

• The nickname "Uncle Sam" comes from a real man. Samuel Wilson was a meatpacker from Troy, New York, who supplied barrels of beef to the U.S. Army in the War of 1812.

In hot weather, Rome's Colosseum was covered by a huge canopy.

# FAMOUS LAST MEALS

*Some last meals are by special request, but others are purely accidental.*

I f you knew that your next meal was going to be your last, what would your menu look like? Some of these people knew that within a few hours they would be dead—others had no idea that last bite would indeed be their last.

## SPECIAL REQUESTS BEFORE THEIR EXECUTIONS:

**Gary Gilmore,** executed by firing squad for the murder of two men in 1976:

|  |  |
|---|---|
| hamburger | hard-boiled eggs |
| baked potato | coffee |
| three shots of whiskey | |

**Serial killer John Wayne Gacy:**

|  |  |
|---|---|
| bucket of original recipe KFC chicken | |
| deep-fried shrimp | French fries |
| strawberries | |

**Oklahoma City bomber Timothy McVeigh:**

two pints of mint-chocolate-chip ice cream

**Dobie Gillis Williams,** convicted of the stabbing murder of Sonja Knippers in 1984:

12 candy bars    ice cream

**Serial killer Theodore "Ted" Bundy** (no special request, so he was given this "traditional" meal):

|  |  |
|---|---|
| medium rare steak | hash brown potatoes |
| eggs over easy | toast with butter and jelly |
| milk, coffee, and juice | |

**Karla Faye Tucker,** executed in 1998 in Texas, for two murders that took place during a robbery:

|  |  |
|---|---|
| banana | peach |
| garden salad with ranch dressing | |

The first IMAX film was a short called *Tiger Child,* shown in Osaka, Japan, in 1970.

# ACCIDENTAL LAST MEALS:

**Jimi Hendrix** choked on a sandwich in the basement of a Paris apartment:

> tuna sandwich on white bread
> Vesperax (sleeping pills)
> wine

**James Dean** dined alone at a private table in the kitchen of the Villa Capri in Hollywood:

> pizza        spaghetti and meatballs
> dinner salad with Italian vinaigrette
> tiramisu        espresso

**Diana, Princess of Wales, dined with Dodi Fayed at the Ritz in Paris:**

> asparagus and mushroom omelet appetizer
> Dover sole with vegetables tempura
> champagne

**Mama Cass Elliot** choked on her last meal and died in bed at the apartment of singer Harry Nilsson in London.

> Ham sandwich
> Coca-Cola

Interestingly enough, drummer Keith Moon would die in the same bed, four years later, of an overdose of Heminevrin.

**Lynyrd Skynyrd's Ronnie VanZant, Steve Gaines, and Cassie Gaines** stopped for take-out before their private plane crashed after leaving a gig in Mississippi:

> fried chicken and ribs

**Marilyn Monroe** ate her last meal at a Brentwood restaurant:

> guacamole
> stuffed mushrooms
> spicy meatball
> Dom Perignon champagne

## THE LAST MEAL SERVED ON THE WHITE STAR LINE'S RMS *TITANIC*, APRIL 14, 1912:

First Course: Hors D'Oeuvres, Oysters
Second Course: Consommé Olga, Cream of Barley
Third Course: Poached Salmon with Mousseline Sauce,
Cucumbers
Fourth Course: Filet Mignons, Lili Saute of Chicken Lyonnaise,
Vegetable Marrow Farci
Fifth Course: Roast Duckling, Apple Sauce, Sirloin of Beef;
Chateau Potatoes, Green Peas, Creamed Carrots, Boiled Rice,
Parmentier & Boiled New Potatoes
Sixth Course: Punch Romaine
Eighth Course: Cold Asparagus Vinaigrette
Ninth Course: Pate de Foie Gras, Celery
Tenth Course: Waldorf Pudding, Peaches in Chartreuse Jelly,
Chocolate & Vanilla Eclairs, French Ice Cream

## THE LAST SUPPER

Undoubtedly the most famous last supper, a Passover Seder, was shared by Jesus and his twelve Apostles:

matzo (unleavened bread)
maror and chazeret (bitter herbs)
karpas (a vegetable dipped in salt water and vinegar)
z'roar (roasted lamb shank)
wine

\*     \*     \*

## MNEMONICS TO HELP WITH SHIP'S NAVIGATION

For remembering which side is Port and which is Starboard:

• Port wine should be left alone when it is red (port ([eft] red light, so starboard [right] green light).

• When on deck and facing the front of the ship, the "port" side is always to the left, just as after-dinner port wine is always passed around the table to the left and the port light is always red, just as port wine is always red.

Other simple ways to recall port and starboard sides are:

•StaRboaRd is Right. (i.e., 2R=Right) or

•The ship's left port or Port has less letters than Starboard as Left has less letters than Right.

---

Pistachios are known as the "smiling nut" in Iran and the "happy nut" in China.

# TREKKING ALONG

*More of the historic North American trails that served as major
thoroughfares in their day and helped populate the United States.*

## 1. THE OREGON TRAIL

**Route:** Various points in Missouri, through Kansas, Nebraska,
Wyoming, and Idaho to Oregon, along the Willamette River

**Length:** About 2,000 miles

**Early History:** In 1800, the American West was still wild and
untouched—except for the occasional fur-trapping mountain man,
no other Euro-Americans had set foot there. Meriwether Lewis
and William Clark explored and mapped the first land route from
Missouri to the Pacific, but didn't find a way through the Rockies
that could accommodate wagon traffic. In 1810, a second expedition—backed by John Jacob Astor, the richest man in America—
discovered South Pass, a wide and easy way across the Continental
Divide. But it wasn't until a mountain man named Jedediah Smith
rediscovered it and announced its existence that the idea of traveling west to settle became a reality. The trail was used by all sorts
of folks heading that way, including settlers, ranchers, farmers, and
miners; it took four to six months to cover the entire distance
from Missouri to the Pacific coast. Other trails followed the
Oregon Trail for part of its length, including the Mormon Trail
(Illinois to Utah) and the California Trail, which branched off in
Fort Bridger, Wyoming, or Fort Hall, Idaho, before heading for the
goldfields around Sacramento.

**Travelers:** The first large pioneer wagon train with nearly 1,000
people set off in 1843, starting the largest voluntary migration in
history. By the middle of the 1840s, the Oregon Trail was a well-
worn road. Records show that on one day, June 6, 1850, 550 wagons and 2,018 people stopped at Fort Laramie, Wyoming. That
same year on June 17, 6,034 people were counted on the trail. In
some places there were so many wagons that they spread out for
half a mile in width.

Most of the pioneers walked the trail; their wagons, usually
pulled by oxen, were for hauling goods. They would start from
Missouri in April or May and traveled an average of 15 miles a

---

**All lighthouses in the U.S. but one (in Boston) are now automated.**

day to reach Oregon before snow in the mountains made the route impassable. Although movies show fierce Indian attacks against Oregon Trail pioneers, in reality they accounted for only about 4 percent of the deaths on the trail. Disease, particularly cholera, was the biggest killer. In the worst years of cholera epidemics, some wagon trains lost two-thirds of their company. Accidents took more lives than Indian attacks. It's estimated that about 10 percent of those who journeyed on the Oregon Trail died along the way—about one grave for every 250 feet of the trail.

**Trail's End:** Between 1834 and 1867, the trail carried an estimated 80,000 emigrants to Oregon, 250,000 to California, and 70,000 to Utah. The transcontinental railroad, completed in 1869, was faster, safer, and cheaper. But some settlers were still using the trail in the 1890s. The states along the trail and the federal government have preserved landmarks along the route, including the wheel ruts formed by hundreds of pioneer wagons.

## 2. SANTA FE TRAIL

**Route:** Independence, Missouri, through Kansas, Oklahoma, and Colorado to Santa Fe, New Mexico

**Length:** About 900 miles

**Early History:** When Mexico gained its independence from Spain in 1821, it opened the borders of its territory (which then included Santa Fe) to trade from the United States. Just outside Dodge City, Kansas, travelers had to decide between two branches of the trail. Would it be the northern Mountain Branch (about 900 miles) or the shorter Cimarron Cutoff, which shaved 100 miles off the trek? Both routes had their dangers: the Mountain Branch featured a hair-raising trip through a pass so steep that, in order to make it through, a wagon's wheels had to be locked so it could be lowered by ropes. But travelers along the cutoff had a good chance of meeting up with some thoroughly unfriendly Comanches.

It took about eight weeks to cover the distance from Independence to Santa Fe, where the people eagerly awaited goods coming from the East and Europe and had the gold and silver to buy them.

**Travelers:** The people who used the trail were mostly traders, and business was good. In 1824, one trader carried $30,000 worth of merchandise from Missouri to Santa Fe and returned with a $150,000 profit. Hiram Young, a former slave in Independence,

Strongest earthquake: One that shook Chile in 1960 measured 9.5 on the Richter scale.

bought his freedom and became wealthy making trade wagons for the Santa Fe Trail. He became one of the area's largest employers.

Kit Carson grew up in Franklin, Missouri, the original starting point when the trail first opened. In 1826, still in his teens, he ran away from home and joined one of the caravans heading to Santa Fe, where he began his life as a guide, scout, trapper, and (after learning Spanish, French, and several Native American languages) interpreter. Carson died along the trail in 1868 at Fort Lyon, Colorado, after suffering an aneurysm.

**Trail's End:** Again, a well-traveled trail was done in by the railroad. By the 1880s, a spur line of the Atchison, Topeka, and Santa Fe Railroad had reached the city of Santa Fe and the trail gradually fell into disuse. Segments of the Santa Fe Trail are listed in the National Register of Historic Places. The longest identifiable section, a two-mile stretch outside Dodge City, Kansas, called "Santa Fe Remains" was declared a National Historic Landmark in 1963.

*More trails appear on page 333.*

\*　　\*　　\*

## HO CHI MINH TRAIL

The Vietnamese called it the "Truong Son Strategic Supply Route," but the Americans named it after Ho Chi Minh, North Vietnam's president from 1945 to 1969. It ran from Hanoi, the capital of North Vietnam, through Laos and Cambodia to Saigon (now Ho Chi Minh City), the capital of South Vietnam. During the Vietnam War, the Ho Chi Minh Trail was the route by which North Vietnam supplied the Vietcong in South Vietnam. The Ho Chi Minh Trail was more than just one trail, it was a network of paths through the jungles of Laos and Cambodia with so many byways and offshoots that the total length was more than 12,000 miles. First established in 1959, the trail was built and maintained by thousands of peasants. Supplies were moved on foot and by bicycle, although later in the war, trucks could navigate the trail. The swampy jungle route was ridden with disease: malaria and dysentery killed 10 percent of the supply haulers. The trail was essential to the Communist forces and was one of the main reasons why the war spilled over into Laos and Cambodia.

---

Motto on the first U.S. coins (copper cents, 1787): "Mind Your Business."

# GET FIT!

*Our list of six people who probably never
sat around reading a book like this one.*

If you like shopping at the health-food store or running on your treadmill—or even if you're a couch potato who clicks past all those exercise channels with your remote—take a moment to give some thanks to six fitness gurus who put their formidable energy into making us healthier. Darn them!

## 1. MEDICATION IN MOTION

**The Father of Modern Tai Chi: Yang Cheng-Fu (1883–1936).**
Tai chi is viewed mostly as an exercise favored by senior citizens in China, but it was once a secret and deadly martial art. It was said that Yang-style tai chi, developed by Yang Lu-Chan, was so formidable that Yang never lost a fight.

**The Slo-Mo Version.** Lu-Chan's grandson, Cheng-Fu, also taught the family's style of tai chi, but he slowed down the movements to make them gentler, more expansive, and with a continuous flow. In 1914, Cheng-Fu began to teach his brand of tai chi to the general public at the Beijing Sports Society. Fourteen years later, he opened a school in Shanghai. He wrote two books about his method and posed for photos illustrating the proper movements. His students and family carried on his traditions and today the tai chi routines that most people practice are the legacy of Cheng Fu. Its graceful routines have been called "meditation in motion" and "medication in motion," the latter because of tai chi's ability to improve a person's health and fitness.

## 2. PUMPING IRON

**The Father of Modern Bodybuilding: Eugen Sandow (1867–1925).**
The world's first bodybuilding celebrity was born Friederich Wilhelm Müller, but he changed his name to Eugen Sandow to keep the authorities off his trail after he'd dodged the draft back in Prussia, where he was born. Sandow began his career as a circus strongman. In a time when many strongmen relied on tricks, he

---

was the real thing: a bodybuilding perfectionist who even measured classical statues of gladiators and mythical heroes in order to sculpt his body to those exact proportions.

**Muscling His Way to the Top.** In 1893, showman Florenz Ziegfeld caught the strongman's act (in which three horses walked across a plank on Sandow's stomach), and made him a star. Sandow used his international celebrity to promote bodybuilding. He wrote books on physical training and launched a fitness magazine. He invented and sold home exercise equipment, as well as his own brand of health cocoa. In England, he opened the world's first fashionable health clubs and even became a fitness instructor to the king.

### 3. NAMASTE YOU SAY

**The Father of Modern Yoga: Tirumali Krishnamacharya (1888–1989).**

It's easy these days to find teachers of hatha yoga and its stretching poses, or *asanas*. But when Tirumali Krishnamacharya was born in a small village in India, Britain ruled the country, and India's 5,000-year tradition of hatha yoga had been nearly forgotten. But not in Krishnamacharya's family. His father had taught him asanas from the age of five; as a young man, he traveled to a remote cave in Tibet and stayed there for more than seven years as the disciple of a hatha yoga master. When asked to spread the knowledge of hatha yoga, Krishnamacharya started marketing yoga with "propaganda tours."

**Tricks of the Trade.** In addition to performing pretzel-like poses, Krishnamacharya could stop his pulse at will for up to two minutes and also stop cars with a push of his bare hands. By 1931, a maharajah was sponsoring Krishnamacharya's school in Mysore, India, where many of the best-known teachers of modern yoga schools would take their training. The school's first female student, Indra Devi, brought Krishnamacharya's asanas to Hollywood, where movie-star clients like Gloria Swanson and Jennifer Jones helped popularize yoga in the West. Krishnamacharya lived to be 100—long enough to see hatha yoga rediscovered in India, and practiced internationally.

## 4. A BODYWORKER TO THE CORE

### The inventor of Pilates: Joseph Hubertus Pilates (1880–1967)

The exercise system called Pilates was first developed in a prison camp during World War I. Born near Düsseldorf, Germany, Joseph "Joe" Pilates was a sickly boy who tried to heal his body with exercise, bodybuilding, wrestling, and gymnastics. In 1912, Joe arrived in Britain, where he worked as a boxer and circus gymnast until, in 1914, the British government started sending German nationals, including Joe, to an internment camp on the Isle of Man.

**Moving Right Along.** In the camp, Pilates invented ways to stay strong and fit—and he helped his fellow inmates do the same. He designed floor exercises that didn't need much space but kept the body flexible and strengthened the abdominal and back muscles to build what he called "core body strength." He used bedsprings to create exercise aids; they provided resistance so that even bedridden inmates could strengthen their pelvic, back, and shoulder muscles.

**The Man in Manhattan.** After the war, Joe Pilates went to New York to teach the techniques he'd developed. His bedspring inventions became the basis for Pilates equipment like the Reformer—an exercise platform that has built-in gears that create resistance. Dancers were the first to discover Pilates; they practiced it to rehabilitate their injuries and stay graceful and flexible. Pilates taught well into old age and was often seen around the city in the white swimsuit trunks and sneakers that he wore in the gym. But eccentric or not, admiration for his exercises spread; today, millions of people practice Pilates.

## 5. BEND AND STRETCH WITH PAIGE

### The First Lady of Fitness: Paige Palmer (c. 1906–2009)

Paige Palmer was a go-getter from the start. At 16, she was running her own dance studio in Akron, Ohio; two years later, she was the physical education director at a local high school. Palmer also had a flair for fashion and, after working in New York fashion for a time, got a textile company to sponsor her first TV show, *Fashion for Women*.

**Fitness First.** Back in Cleveland in 1948, she hosted the *Paige Palmer Show* for WEWS, Ohio's first TV station. The show fea-

---

In 1876, St. Louis's George W. Bradley threw baseball's first official no-hitter (against Hartford).

tured guest celebrities and fashion designers like Oleg Cassini. Guest chefs taught healthy cooking, and Palmer also reserved a segment for exercise routines. Always dressed to the nines, Palmer made exercise glamorous and feminine—even her workout clothes were fashion-forward. Originally optioned for a 13-week run, her show, the first TV show to teach exercise and fitness, lasted 25 years on the air.

## 6. THE GODFATHER OF FITNESS

### The First Man of Fitness: Jack LaLanne (1914– )

When young Jack LaLanne was sick and the doctors couldn't help him, his mother dragged him to a nutritionist who recommended cutting out junk food, white flour, and sugar—a pretty revolutionary concept in 1929. Jack followed the nutritionist's instructions and got well; he also got hooked on exercise, nutrition, and supplements. In 1936, he opened the Jack LaLanne Physical Culture Studio in Oakland, California. It was the world's first health club that was open to men and women of all ages, and it featured exercise machines of Jack's own invention that are still used today.

**Jack's Rx.** LaLanne launched the first national TV show devoted solely to exercise and health in 1951. At a time when many doctors contradicted LaLanne's advice—because weightlifting and "over-exercise" were considered unhealthy, and eating health food was considered a fad—Jack's viewers ignored the "experts." They did calisthenics with him, listened to his nutritional advice, bought his health-food products, took vitamin supplements he recommended, and made *The Jack LaLanne Show* the longest-running TV exercise show in history, keeping it on the air until 1985.

**Birthday Boy, Oh Boy!** LaLanne performed feats of strength and endurance on each of his birthdays. At age 42, in 1956, he set a world record of 1,033 push-ups in 23 minutes. At 60, he swam a mile and a half from Alcatraz Island to Fisherman's Wharf while handcuffed and shackled to a 1,000-pound boat that he towed behind him. He was honored with a star on the Hollywood Walk of Fame in 2002, at age 88.

---

Little, Brown & Co. published J. D. Salinger's *The Catcher in the Rye* in 1951.

# THE POKEY AWARDS

*Today, they're tourist sites, but at one time, these prisons were fearsome places. Each is the perfect representation of the social evils of its day, with its own very special techniques of housing criminals. Uncle John got to wondering: what were the most pleasant or unpleasant places to "do time" in history?*

## 1. MOST SNOBBY: THE TOWER OF LONDON

Construction on the Tower of London was begun in the 11th century; it was added to and remodeled by various English monarchs over the next few centuries. At first the building was a fortress and a palace with a few areas reserved for prisoners, but during the reign of the Tudors, it became more of a prison and less of a royal home. In the 16th century, fickle Henry VIII used the Tower to imprison former friends and lovers that he decided were traitors.

**Living in Luxury—And Not.** The Tower of London was a virtual revolving door for some of England's most famous royals. Even Queen Elizabeth I was held in the Tower for treason as a young princess. Some of the prisoners had spacious apartments there, ate sumptuously, and had servants to cater to their needs. Prisoner of war King John of France held banquets there, and Sir Walter Raleigh (who was imprisoned by Elizabeth for marrying without her permission) remodeled his prison digs to his liking, wrote a book during his stay, and grew his favorite smoking tobacco on the Tower Green. Even Anne Boleyn had her own retinue of servants until she lost her head in a private execution there.

Executed or not, some prisoners found living in the Tower most unpleasant—especially Catholics in the time of Protestant monarchs and vice versa. There was a torture room featuring a famous rack that stretched the body until joints were dislocated and even separated completely. From 1388 through 1747, the Tower saw more than 130 prisoners beheaded—a far more genteel way to go than being hung, drawn, and quartered like a common criminal.

## 2. MOST ROMANTIC: RED FORT'S MUSAMMAN BURJ

Thousands of tourists in Agra, India, visit the Musamman Burj, an octagonal marble tower decorated with tiles of intricate design and walls inlaid with precious stones. Looking like an illustration in a fairy tale, the multistoried tower rises gracefully above a 94-acre red sandstone fortress called the Red Fort, which was built in the 17th century as the residence of the royal family. The powerful Mughal emperor Shah Jahan added the tower for his favorite wife, Mumtaz Majal, as a symbol of his love. Their relationship became world-renowned when Mumtaz died and the grieving emperor built her a mausoleum of marble and jewels—the famous Taj Mahal.

**Talk About Sibling Rivalry.** The love between Shah Jahan and Mumtaz didn't trickle down to the next generation. In 1658, when the 74-year-old Shah Jahan became ill, his four sons fought among themselves to be his successor. The third son, Aurangzeb, captured the throne and imprisoned his father in the Musamman Burj. For the next eight years until his death, Shah Jahan, who'd once been the most powerful man in India, remained jailed and frustrated. It was said his only consolation was to stare out at the view that brought him closer to his love, Mumtaz—because the tower looked out on the Taj Mahal.

## 3. MOST RESENTED: THE BASTILLE

The Bastille was built in the 1300s to defend Paris during the Hundred Years' War. In the 1600s, King Louis XIII converted it to a prison for his aristocratic enemies, and by the 1700s common criminals were also housed there. Conditions in the Bastille for those of high birth were relatively comfy: they had visitors, servants, good furniture, and were served the four-star cuisine of the day.

The Bastille became a symbol of injustice because all it took to land in that particular clink was a *lettre de cachet*, or a warrant with the seal of the king. Prisoners didn't appear before a judge before they were locked away. Even Voltaire, France's most famous writer and thinker, cooled his heels in the Bastille for months because he'd offended some powerful nobles.

**Bastille Day #1.** By 1789, rumors began to circulate about atrocities against prisoners. That same year, the Marquis de Sade, who'd been imprisoned under a lettre de cachet obtained by his mother-in-law, added fuel to the fire. Yelling through his cell window, he declared (untruthfully) that prisoners were being massacred.

Finally on July 14, 1789, an angry mob broke in and liberated

**April 17, 1956: Willie Mosconi sank 150 consecutive balls during a billiards tournament.**

the prisoners. They found only seven convicts: four forgers, two mentally ill prisoners, and one misbehaving nobleman whose family had arranged for his imprisonment because of his deviant behavior (not de Sade, who'd been transferred to an insane asylum a few days previously).

Prisoners or no, the end of the Bastille marked the beginning of citizen rule, and from 1880 on, July 14 was France's Bastille Day, celebrating the overthrow of the French monarchy. The Bastille was demolished in 1791; its original outline is marked with paving stones along the streets and sidewalks where it once stood.

## 4. MOST SPACIOUS: THE CONTINENT OF AUSTRALIA

When Captain Cook discovered Australia, he also discovered a solution for Britain's overcrowded prisons. In the late 1700s, Britain was mainly divided between the rich and the desperately poor; although theft had long been a hanging offense, judges and juries were rethinking capital punishment for people who stole to eat. In 1788, the first batch of convicts—the first Europeans to settle Australia—arrived at Sydney, New South Wales.

Imprisoned for theft or for resisting English power in countries like Ireland and Scotland, the early convicts (20 percent of whom were women) faced high mortality rates because of the lack of food, medicine, and proper housing. But rather than try to escape into the wilderness, many prisoners were frightened of the unknown land they thought of as "the bottom of the world."

**Life at the Bottom.** The penal colonies spread across Australia; convict labor built public roads and buildings, and logged lumber for ships and furniture. Women made textiles in what were called "female factories." Work days for some lasted 14–18 hours and "problem prisoners" worked in leg irons on chain gangs.

When free settlers began to arrive in the 1820s, convicts were assigned to work for them. In 1830, a limit of 50 lashes was put on floggings. By the time the transport of convicts to Australia ended in 1867, many of those who'd served their time stayed on as ordinary citizens and became some of Australia's most notable architects, merchants, and educators.

## 5. MOST INFAMOUS: DEVIL'S ISLAND

The penitentiary system that came to be known as Devil's Island

---

The "Mediterranean triad" of ancient Greek cuisine: grain, grapes, and olives.

began with a seemingly idealistic idea based on the settling of Australia. France's convicts who were imprisoned in French Guiana would be granted land in the colony upon their release—giving them a chance for a fresh start. In 1852, prisoners began arriving on the small Caribbean islands of Ile Royale, Ile St. Joseph, and Ile Diable (Devil's Island), as well as on French Guiana's mainland. Shark-filled waters surrounded the islands; on the mainland there were impenetrable jungles and rivers filled with crocodiles. The prisons were considered nearly escape-proof.

**Devilish Conditions.** Far from any oversight or advocacy for the prisoners, the system on Devil's Island became brutal. Prisoners toiled as slave laborers in searing heat and torrential rains. Their labor was often meant to punish rather than accomplish anything—like work on a road that the convicts called Route Zero because it never got longer than 15 miles. Overworked, underfed, and plagued by clouds of mosquitoes that carried yellow fever, thousands of prisoners escaped Devil's Island—by dropping dead. Punishments for infractions included solitary confinement and/or leg shackles, not to mention execution by guillotine in front of fellow prisoners.

Inmates who somehow survived were given a piece of land, then forced to stay in French Guiana for the same number of years as their sentence. Few had the money or skill to make a home in the inhospitable jungle; most begged for menial jobs or returned to crime. In 1895, French army officer Alfred Dreyfus was sent to Devil's Island on false charges of treason. Interest in Dreyfus's plight exposed the horrors there, as did later autobiographies written by former convicts. Despite plenty of indignation and protests, the notorious prison wasn't closed until 1952.

## 6. MOST MIND-NUMBINGLY MONOTONOUS: ALCATRAZ

A small sandstone island only a mile and a half mile from San Francisco, Alcatraz is surrounded by fast-moving currents of icy water. It was believed that no one could swim from Alcatraz to the mainland, so the place seemed ideal for a prison. It was used to house Civil War prisoners as early as 1861; later, in 1909–1911, the military built a prison to hold about 300 convicts. In 1933, Alcatraz was handed over to the Federal Bureau of Prisons, which, with additional guard towers and armaments, made it a maximum-security facility for the country's toughest convicts. Popularly known as "the Rock," its grim harshness also gave it the nickname "Uncle Sam's Devils Island."

**The Baddest of the Bad.** The Rock took the worst troublemakers from other federal prisons and was supposed to "rehabilitate" them into rule-abiding prisoners. The first warden, James Johnston, devised a system for that rehabilitation: every prisoner had his own cell and relatively good food. Along with clothing and medical care, that was all a prisoner was entitled to. Anything else—including books from the library, music, correspondence, or even working—was a privilege to be earned by following a highly structured, boring daily routine (wake up, tidy up, line up for counting, etc.) designed to teach the men to follow rules. During the Rock's early years, prisoners conducted that monotonous routine in enforced silence—which is said to have driven some inmates insane.

**The Hole Thing.** Alcatraz's most infamous punishment was isolation in "the Hole." Cells in the prison's damp, cold "dungeons" held shivering prisoners who existed mainly on bread and water in total darkness with no human contact. But for many of the 1,576 prisoners on the Rock, the worst punishment was the view of San Francisco—totally out of reach but less than two miles away. By the time the deteriorating prison closed in 1963, 36 prisoners had made a break for liberty. Twenty-three were caught, six were shot, and two drowned in the bay. Five were "presumed" drowned, but rumors persist that some of them actually made it to freedom.

\* \* \*

## STRUCTURE OF LA COSA NOSTRA
Commission (heads of most powerful families)
Capo di tutti capi, or Boss (subservient only to above)
Underboss
Consigliere (counselor)
Capo (captain to underboss)
Soldier

---

In 1837, the earliest known comic book, Rudolphe Töpffer's...

# HOW THE WEST WAS WON

*America's great westward expansion took place between 1807 and 1912. Aside from the people and events that speeded the opening of new frontiers and the move west, the giddy-up-and-go along the road to the Pacific was made possible by six important factors.*

## 1. TRADING POSTS

The first explorers of the North American frontier were interested in one thing: making money by hunting the pelts of wild animals. Trading posts gave the fur hunters a market and supplied them with provisions. From the late 1600s to about 1850, posts were built along a vast arc of wilderness from Canada to the northern border of Mexico, mostly on waterways that linked them to the East Coast and the shipping lanes to Europe. Pockets of civilization grew around the posts, a melting pot of Native Americans, Spaniards, French, Dutch, and English, all bartering with each other.

**Significance:** Believe it or not, it was fashion. European high style at the time was all about fur—beaver in particular—and North America had a seemingly an inexhaustible supply.

**Story:** England's Hudson's Bay Company got exclusive trading rights to the watershed of Hudson Bay in Canada in 1670 and constructed the first trading posts on the Western frontier. The posts hired white frontiersmen to trap animals, since the Indians had little interest in doing it. The traders shipped the furs to Europe to rake in huge fortunes. By the late 1700s, rival companies set up trading posts deep in the interior of Canada and points south. By 1808, John Jacob Astor's American Fur Company—with its own frontier posts—dominated the West and made Astor the richest man in America. Many major North American cities began as trading posts, such as Detroit, Chicago, St. Louis, New Orleans, Edmonton, Quebec City, Winnipeg, and Montreal.

**Demise:** The demise of trading posts was due to a shortage of animal furs, caused by overkilling in North America and the introduction of silk as the new stuff of haute couture in Europe.

---

*...The Adventures of Obadiah Oldbuck,* was published in Switzerland.

## 2. CONESTOGA WAGONS

From the late 1700s to the early 20th century, these famous covered wagons were as common on trails heading west as today's tractor-trailers. The average 21-foot-long, 11-foot-high, 4-foot-wide wagon could carry two tons of cargo. Some freighter wagons with seven-foot-tall wheels were capable of carrying a massive eight tons. Designed like boats, with ends that were higher than the middle, once the wheels were removed the heavily caulked wagon body could be floated across Western streams. The ride wasn't as smooth on land: pulled by horses, mules, or oxen, the Conestoga moved over roads so rough and mountainous that most people preferred to walk alongside. But they slept inside at night for protection against inclement weather and wild animals.

**Significance:** At the time, the wagon was the only means of transporting heavy cargo to settlers in the remote West, far from any navigable rivers. Wagon handlers also brought the only news from the outside world, even if it was outdated by the time they got where they were going.

**Story:** James Logan invented the Conestoga in 1716. As William Penn's commercial representative in the colony of Pennsylvania, he established freight service between Philadelphia and the Conestoga Valley in Lancaster County 60 miles away and named the wagon after its valley destination. It's believed that Logan based the design on army supply trains then used in Europe. In the wagon's heyday, big factories like future carmaker Studebaker in South Bend, Indiana, could turn out a complete wagon in seven minutes. The Fort Smith Wagon Company in Fort Smith, Arkansas, built 10,000 in a single year.

Conestogas were also called "prairie schooners" because they appeared in the distance like sailing vessels with their weather-resistant canopies of white canvas stretched over wooden hoops and billowing in the wind as they moved across the Great Plains. The expectation was that each animal hitched to a wagon could pull a payload equal to its own weight, thus the modern expression "pull your own weight."

**Demise:** Railroads and motor vehicles ended the reign of the Conestoga wagon. The last one was manufactured in 1952 at the Springfield Wagon Company in Fayetteville, Arkansas.

In 1899, Jules Alciatore of Antoine's in New Orleans created the dish Oysters Rockefeller.

## 3. THE STEAMBOAT

Until the steamboat's arrival on the frontier in 1820, it took skilled oarsmen piloting flatboats downstream to get goods to market. Since it was too difficult to paddle back upstream, the flatboats were normally broken up for firewood and the return trip was made by horseback or on foot. The steamboat changed all that.

**Significance:** Their speed and ability to carry huge cargoes made them indispensable to the frontier economy at port cities along the inland waterways. By the mid-1800s, steamboats were seen everywhere on all the rivers to the frontier—the Cumberland, Tennessee, Ohio, Illinois, Missouri, and Mississippi. The month-long trip upriver 700 miles from New Orleans to Louisville in 1820 became a mere jaunt of four and a half days by 1854.

**Story:** On August 22, 1787, John Fitch demonstrated a steam-powered watercraft on the Delaware River before members of the Continental Convention in Philadelphia. He patented the idea and went into the steamship business, carrying passengers and freight in either direction on the Delaware at four times the speed of previous riverboats. But it was Robert Fulton, who usually gets the undeserved credit for the invention, who saw its commercial potential in settling the West. Fulton partnered with wealthy New York politician Robert L. Livingston and inventor Nicholas Roosevelt to begin building large steamboats in 1817 in Pittsburgh. The result was a ship that could make the round-trip to New Orleans on the Ohio and Mississippi rivers, setting a speed record of 10 mph downstream and 3 mph upstream.

For the first 40 years of their development, steamboats were an extremely dangerous way to travel: an estimated 500 vessels were lost, causing 4,000 deaths. Accidents were so frequent—due to fire, steam boiler explosions, and running aground—that the average life span of a steamboat was about five years.

**Demise:** Railroads began taking business away from steamboats in 1870. By 1880, steamships had given way to the 93,000 miles of rail lines that served all corners of the United States.

*The exciting conclusion of this story can be found on page 442.*

# KODAK MOMENTS

*We continue our look through the lens of a camera begun on page 381.*

## 1. FIRST PHOTOS OF BATTLEFIELD CARNAGE (1875)

Though John Fenton is credited with the first photos of a war, he did not have access to battlefields and thus could not show the horror of the Crimean War of 1853–56. It was Matthew B. Brady who brought to the public for the first time the bloodshed of combat during the Civil War of 1860–65. The 10,000 photographs he and his team of 20 photographers made included many horrific battlefield scenes and portraits of generals, officers, and enlisted men on both sides of the conflict. The grim reality of dead soldiers jarred a public used to the romanticism and heroism that had previously characterized war coverage. Commenting in the *Atlantic Monthly* after viewing Brady's works, Oliver Wendell Holmes put it bluntly: "Let him who wishes to know what war is look at this series of illustrations. These wrecks of manhood thrown together in careless heaps or ranged in ghastly rows for burial were alive but yesterday."

Brady spent $100,000 and was counting on the U.S. government to buy his photos after the war. When they didn't, he declared bankruptcy. He died penniless in 1896 in the charity ward of a New York hospital. But his legacy would live on. In 1856, he created the first ad in a newspaper where the headline fonts were distinctly different from news type, becoming the norm in publishing. His photographs of President Abraham Lincoln also became the model for the $5 bill and the one-cent Lincoln head penny.

## 2. FIRST HIGH-SPEED PHOTO SERIES (1878)

Those who followed horse racing in the 19th century hotly debated in turf clubs whether all four hooves of a 1,000-pound racehorse came off the ground at one time. Could a horse fly? Enter Eadweard Muybridge in 1877. The San Francisco photographer made a bet with good friend Leland Stanford, the Southern Pacific railroad tycoon and founder of Stanford University, that he could prove Stanford's stable of thoroughbreds became airborne while

---

In 1989, Ben & and Jerry's discontinued its Tennessee Mud ice cream...

running. Muybridge learned of an instrument called the zoetrope that could make a synchronized series of images that showed movement. Using the device, the photographer was the first to make serial photos of fast motion, that of Stanford's horses. One was filmed running, the other trotting. He set up cameras to shoot a synchronized series of stop-action photos. Trip wires set off the shutters as a jockey astride one of the horses darted past in June 1878. The images were developed immediately so no one could accuse Muybridge of doctoring the film. The photographer had Stanford view the photos in quick sequence. One clearly showed one of his horses with all four hooves off the ground.

Muybridge won the bet and his photos made history as the first high-speed photo series, giving inspiration to Thomas Edison 10 years later to develop a motion picture camera, the Kintograph.

## 3. FIRST MOTION PICTURE (1888)

There would be no time to enjoy even a handful of popcorn at a showing of the world's first motion picture. It lasted just two seconds. Still, those handful of recorded frames on a single-lens camera showed people walking, something never seen before on film. French inventor Louis Le Prince was the filmmaker. He recorded his masterpiece at the home of Joseph and Sarah Whitley in West Yorkshire, England.

A bizarre set of circumstances followed. Sarah Whitley, Le Prince's mother-in-law, who was in the film, died 10 days after the film was made. Two years later, after Le Prince was denied a patent in America for his single-lens motion picture camera, he vanished shortly before a public demonstration of his camera. He was last seen on a train between Dijon and Paris. Louis's son, Adolphe Le Prince, also in the film, had worked closely with his father in developing the single-lens motion picture camera. He was called to testify in 1898 for the American Mutoscope Company in New York in its attempt to nullify Thomas Edison's patent for the same kind of camera that Le Prince had designed. The trial went against Mutoscope, and Edison went on to make motion picture history.

## 4. FIRST REMOTE AERIAL PHOTO FROM A PIGEON (1903)

In the year the Wright brothers proved that man could fly, Julius

Neubronner, a druggist in Kronberg, Germany, had developed remotely controlled aerial photography using birds. He was in the habit of using carrier pigeons to relay prescriptions and medicines between him and a distant sanatorium. Sometimes the birds got lost, delaying their return. So Neubronner built miniature cameras weighing less than three ounces that could be strapped around the necks of the birds to film their flight paths. The cameras, fitted with self-timers, were a success. The first image—three pigeons sitting on a building ledge—made history.

The German military became aware of the druggist's experiments and employed pigeons with Neubronner's cameras to fly over enemy lines at the outset of World War I to bring back intelligence photos. That continued into World War II until France countered with similar camera-equipped pigeons with a twist: the French trained dogs to carry the pigeons behind enemy lines and then release them to fly back, snapping pictures the whole way.

## 5. FIRST PHOTO FROM SPACE (1946)

Germany developed the V-2 rocket to bomb England in World War II. The United States seized unused V-2s after the war and transported them to New Mexico. On October 24, 1946, scientists placed a 35-millimeter motion picture camera on the nose of one of the missiles and launched it vertically into space from the White Sands Missile Range. The camera clicked a new image every few seconds as the rocket climbed to an altitude of 65 miles.

Out of fuel, the rocket fell back to earth. Enlisted soldier Fred Rulli, 19, was on the recovery team that drove into the dessert and located the wreckage. Though the camera was destroyed, the film, in a steel cassette, survived unscathed. Range scientists "were jumping up and down like kids," said Rulli. Later he watched with them as the film was shown for the first time. "The scientists just went nuts," he recalled. It was incredible, noted Clyde Holliday, the engineer who developed the camera, since the images showed for the first time "how our Earth would look to visitors from another planet coming in on a space ship"

## 6. FIRST DIGITAL PHOTO (1957)

Russell Kirsch helped design the first digital computers at the National Institute of Standards and Technology in the United

In the 14th century, Europeans commonly ate their main meal at 9:00 a.m.

States. He conceived a process by which the image from a camera could be fed into a computer. To prove it, he took a photo of his three-month-old son, sent the image electronically into his computer, and out came the world's first digitally scanned photograph.

It took another 40 years for digital cameras to become commonplace. As for Kirsch, he went on to pioneer artificial intelligence, computer natural language processing and bio-medical computers, among other achievements.

\*     \*     \*

## PHOTOS FOR SALE

Polaroid was founded in 1937 by Edwin H. Land. The company fell victim to the digital revolution and tried to regroup in 2001, but finally went bankrupt in 2008. To pay off creditors, it was ordered to sell a portion of its collection of 400 photographs. These photos were part of the Artist Support Program started by Land. He provided some of the world's best photographers with equipment and film in return for some of their work.

In June 2010, Sotheby's conducted a sale that netted more than $7 million and brought a record price for an Ansel Adams picture. According to Sotheby's auction Web site, the top money-getters were as follows:

**1.** Ansel Adams, "Clearing Winter Storm" (flash-only), Yosemite, $722,500

**2.** Ansel Adams, "Moonrise," Hernandez, New Mexico, $518,500

**3.** Ansel Adams, "Aspens," New Mexico, $494,500

**4.** Ansel Adams, "Winter Sunrise," Sierra Nevada, $482,500

**5.** Ansel Adams, "The Tetons and Snake River," Grand Teton National Park, Wyoming, $350,500

**6.** Ansel Adams, similar/same as above, $326,500

**7.** Chuck Close, "9-part Self Portrait," $290,500

**8.** Andy Warhol, "Self Portrait" (eyes closed), $254,500

**9.** Harry Callahan, "Trees and Mist," Chicago, $254,500

**10.** Robert Rauschenberg, "Japanese Sky" (The Bleacher Series), $242,500

# THE RIGHT SHORT STUFF

*In the annals of famous short men, one tops them all—Gul Mohammed.*
*He was born in 1957 in India. By the time he stopped growing, he measured*
*22½ inches in height, short enough to fit in a violin case. Today he has the*
*distinction of being the shortest man in recorded history, according to*
*the* Guinness World Records. *He had a morbid fear of big dogs and*
*a dislike of children his entire life. He turned to heavy smoking—*
*and that did him in at age 40, according to his doctors.*

## GREATNESS IN SMALL PACKAGES

Mohammed's name appears on most of the world's "famous short men" lists. To qualify in today's tall world, there's an upper limit to being short: 5 feet 5 inches. Uncle John recently took a look at a magnificent seven on the list—from the shortest of the short to the tallest of the short.

### 1. THE GENERAL

Born Charles Sherwood Stratton in Connecticut in 1838, he was perfectly proportioned but stopped growing when he reached 25 inches tall and weighed 15 pounds. Circus pioneer P. T. Barnum convinced Stratton's parents to allow him to take their son under his wing at an early age. Barnum hoped to add Stratton to his New York City museum and circus, which already featured the tallest man. Fibbing that he brought him from Europe at great expense, the promoter gave Stratton a new name: "General Tom Thumb," taken from English folklore. Barnum then taught Stratton how to dance, sing, do imitations, and trade quips with Barnum, who played straight man in their stage acts.

The act was an instant hit and led to worldwide acclaim, including a command performance before Queen Victoria in Buckingham Palace. In his late teens, Stratton began to grow again and achieved a final height of 3 feet. In the 1860s, he married a small woman, Lavinia Warren, who was also in the employ of Barnum. The *New York Times* trumpeted the "Loving Liliputians" in an article about their elaborate wedding on Broadway. Tom Thumb and his bride visited the White House as President Abraham Lincoln's guests for a honeymoon party before

---

June 10, 2000: Governor George W. Bush officially proclaimed "Jesus Day" in Texas.

embarking on a worldwide tour. In 1883, the wealthy Tom Thumb died of a stroke at age 45. Lavinia remarried and lived until 1919.

## 2. THE ATHLETE

Eddie Gaedel, at 3 feet 7 inches and 65 pounds, is the smallest player to ever appear in a Major League Baseball game. A veteran stage performer, he jumped out of a cake during the intermission of a doubleheader between the St. Louis Browns and Detroit Tigers on August 19, 1951, in Sportsman's Park in St. Louis. Bill Veeck, the Browns' owner, hatched the idea to mark the 50th anniversary of the American League. Gaedel, who was paid $100, wore a Browns uniform with the number 1/8 and elf slippers turned up at the tips.

In the bottom of the first inning of the second game, Browns manager Zack Taylor sent Gaedel to pinch-hit against pitcher Bob Cain. Detroit skipper Red Rolfe protested the move, but Taylor showed the umpire a legitimate contract filed with the league. Cain didn't know what to do, faced with a 1½-inch strike zone. He walked Gaedel on four pitches; upon reaching first base, Gaedel was replaced by a pinch runner and left the game to a standing ovation. He never appeared in a game again.

Gaedel passed away in 1961 at age 36. At his funeral, Bob Cain showed up. "I never even met him, but I felt obligated to go," he later told a sportswriter. Recalling the famous at bat, Cain explained, "I didn't know whether to throw the ball underhanded or overhanded to Gaedel. I just wanted to be careful not to hit him. Dizzy Trout told me later that if he'd been the pitcher, he'd have thrown the ball right between his eyes."

## 3. THE SINGER

Thomas Quasthoff is only 4 feet tall, but he has a voice for the ages. He was born in 1959 with birth defects caused by the drug thalidomide, which his mother had taken to combat morning sickness. Despite his well-below-average height, Quasthoff studied law and became a celebrated bass-baritone, winning Grammy Awards for best classical vocal performances in 2000, 2004, and 2006.

By 2010, he was a full-time voice professor at the Hanns Eisler School of Music in Berlin. He is married to German TV journalist Claudia Schtelsick and has dabbled in jazz recordings since 2006.

---

North America has proportionately more wilderness area (38%) than Africa (28%).

## 4. THE PAINTER

Henri de Toulouse-Lautrec, a hair over 5 feet, needed no introduction in his time. Born in 1864, he was a famed illustrator and painter whose contemporaries in the Postimpressionist period of French painting included Cezanne, Van Gogh, and Gauguin. His physique was distinctive—a normal-sized torso and childlike legs, caused by a childhood illness. He devoted himself to the art world and his works revealed the Bohemian lifestyle of Paris in the late 1800s. Though successful as an artist, Toulouse-Lautrec was often mocked due to his physical appearance and turned to alcohol to drown his sorrows. That cost him his life at age 36.

Toulouse-Lautrec's fame endured far beyond his passing. Christie's auction house set a record in the sale of *La Blanchisseuse*, his painting of a Parisian laundress, when it sold for $22.4 million in 2005.

## 5. THE DICTATOR

Engelbert Dollfuss—all 4 feet 11 inches of him—became dictator of Austria in the 1930s. Born in 1892, he studied law and economics and rose to fame in Austria as a statesman. He was chancellor from 1932 to 1934, at the time of Adolf Hitler's ascension in Germany and Benito Mussolini's in Italy. Worried that Hitler would move against Austria, Dollfuss seized control of the country, established an authoritarian government, and aligned it closely with Roman Catholicism and Italian fascism in the hopes that Mussolini would protect Dollfuss's regime.

After escaping an assassination attempt by a Nazi sympathizer in 1933, Dollfuss wasn't so lucky a year later. His reign came to a quick end when he was shot to death by ten Nazi agents during an unsuccessful coup d'etat.

## 6. THE CHIEF JUSTICE

Melville W. Fuller, at 5 feet 3 inches, was the shortest chief justice to ever serve on the U.S. Supreme Court. The Maine native passed the bar exam after graduating from Bowdoin College. He moved to Illinois, where he managed the unsuccessful presidential campaign of Stephen Douglas against Abraham Lincoln in 1860, and later served in the Illinois House of Representatives. President Grover Cleveland appointed him chief justice in 1888. Fuller managed a court that was under constant attack by critics. It is from his opinion in the case of *Caldwell v. Texas* in 1891 that the phrase "equal justice under the law" came into vogue. Five years later, another phrase—"separate but equal"—gained currency out of the Fuller court's decision in *Plessy v. Ferguson*, which justified segregation in the South. In 1904, his court decreed that Puerto Ricans were neither aliens nor U.S. citizens. The effect was to allow Puerto Ricans to immigrate at will to the United States.

Fuller looked a lot like writer Mark Twain. The novelist recalled encountering an autograph seeker who mistook him for Fuller. Twain seized the moment, writing, "It is delicious to be full, but it is heavenly to be Fuller. I am cordially yours, Melville W. Fuller." During his tenure as chief justice, which lasted until 1910, Fuller administered the oath of office to Presidents Benjamin Harrison, Grover Cleveland, William McKinley, Theodore Roosevelt, and William Howard Taft.

## 7. THE WAR HERO

At 5 feet 5 inches, Audie Murphy achieved immortality in World War II. The son of an impoverished Texas sharecropper, he enlisted as a private in the U.S. Army and became the most decorated American combat soldier of the war. He is credited with killing over 240 enemy soldiers as well as wounding or capturing many others. He was wounded three times and saw action in nine major campaigns in Europe.

Following the war, actor James Cagney invited Murphy to Hollywood after seeing him on the cover of *Life* magazine. The first few years were lean, but eventually Murphy performed in 42 movies, mostly Westerns. In 1955 he starred in the film version of his own best-selling autobiography, *To Hell and Back,* which was Universal-International's highest-grossing film until *Jaws* in 1975.

In his private life, Murphy was a country songwriter, racehorse breeder, and consummate poker player who frittered away fortunes and won them back again. He suffered major bouts of insomnia and depression that were traced to his wartime experiences, and became an advocate for veterans' health causes. On a business trip in 1971, he died at age 46 when the plane he was in ran into a fog-draped mountainside outside Roanoke, Virginia. Murphy's grave at Arlington National Cemetery is the second most-visited next to that of President John F. Kennedy.

# TWO FIRES, ONE DAY

*The day Chicago—a.k.a. the Second City—took first place in the news. Two of the worst fires in American history happened on the exact same day, at almost the exact same time. One is the stuff of legends, the other has been virtually forgotten.*

## 1. THE GREAT CHICAGO FIRE

In 1871, Chicago was fast-growing city—the center of commerce in the Midwest. On October 8, a fire started that burned for more than a day; it did $200 million of property damage, killed 300 people, and left more than 90,000 homeless. But the Great Chicago Fire probably wouldn't have been all that great if the worst fire in Chicago's history to that point hadn't taken place the night before.

**Yesterday's News.** A drought had contributed to more than 700 small fires in Chicago already. On October 7, a fire that started in a lumber mill spread to four city blocks, and it took the entire Chicago fire department 17 hours to put it out, injuring many firefighters in the process. Less than 12 hours later, still exhausted, the firemen were called to the site of another fire. They were first told the wrong address, which wasted valuable time, and when they reached the actual fire, the second engine to arrive was out of fuel to run its water pump, and was therefore useless. By the time backup arrived, the blaze was too big to put out.

**Ready to Ignite.** Chicago had very lax building regulations at the time—there were miles and miles of small wooden houses along wooden streets and sidewalks, all of which was dry as tinder, given the months-long drought conditions in the city. It didn't take much for the fire to spread quickly through Conley's Patch, a notorious slum. The first big building to catch fire was the gasworks—it exploded and plunged the city into darkness.

**Getting Down to Business.** Now the fire turned toward the business district—an area filled with buildings certified as "fireproof." They were built of marble, brick, stone, and iron, but had wooden roofs. When the courthouse caught fire, the prisoners were freed from the jail and immediately looted a neighboring jewelry store. The post office went up, destroying mail and a million dollars'

---

Wilt Chamberlain won the NBA rebounding title a record 11 times in his career.

worth of stamps. All but two of Chicago's banks were destroyed. After the fire, rescue workers found a million dollars of gold bullion melted into a solid lump in the vault of the customshouse. So confident were people that the Historical Society building was fireproof that the original copy of the Emancipation Proclamation (handwritten by Abe Lincoln himself) had recently been brought there. A secretary tried to rescue it, but couldn't get at it, and had to flee for his life. From there, the fire jumped the river to the north side of the city.

**Pandemonium.** By this point, about 2:00 a.m., as many as 75,000 Chicagoans were fleeing in panic from residential areas. Amid massive looting, people with any kind of transport were charging passengers exorbitant fees to take them out of the city. The fire was so large it created its own wind, sucking in air to feed the flames and spreading it farther across the city. At 5:00 a.m., the waterworks burned down and all hope of fighting the fire was lost; the city's fire hoses lay empty and useless.

**The Blame Game.** The fire finally burned out in the early morning of October 10, extinguished by a drizzling rain. The insurance claims on the damaged buildings bankrupted many of the city's insurance companies and sent the stock market into a decline. Mrs. O'Leary and her cow have long been blamed for the start of the fire, fueled by rumors in newspapers, but an inquiry found that all the O'Learys were in bed that night. Others theorized that drunken partygoers had started the blaze, but it could as easily have been a careless match or cigarette in the tinderbox that was Chicago that October.

## 2. THE GREAT PESHTIGO FIRE

At the same time that flames were devouring Chicago, another fire was burning some 250 miles away in eastern Wisconsin, with far deadlier results. The drought was affecting the mill town of Peshtigo as well, where not a drop of rain had fallen since July 8, three months earlier. The area around Green Bay, where Peshtigo lay, was heavily forested and a center for lumber.

In the weeks before the great fire, it wasn't uncommon to see smoldering fires burning in the forest. A local minister recalled being surrounded by a circle of fire on a walk in the woods and having to beat a path through the flames so he could return home.

Smoke was often so thick that ships on Lake Michigan were in danger of running aground; many of them turned away from scheduled trips.

**Nice Try, People.** Peshtigo's residents reacted to the threat of a bigger fire by clearing their town of as many combustible materials as they could and filling barrels throughout the town with water. But no precaution could have saved them. On October 8, a windstorm moved in over the Midwest, and the winds turned the small forest fires plaguing the area into something else entirely.

**Red Sky at Night.** That evening, residents looked to the west and saw an enormous cloud of smoke and a red glow. As the glow advanced, there was a distant roar, like never-ending thunder. Some residents buried possessions to try to protect them from the fire; many fled, but they had nowhere to go—they were completely surrounded by fire. The town's one bridge was a mass of confusion, as the people on the east side fled to the west, and those on the west fled to the east, though there was no safety in either direction. The roar they'd heard was from a firestorm, hundreds of miles across, that would center over Peshtigo. Many tried to run, but it was impossible to outrun those flames. People huddled in basements, where they were later found dead. A number tried hiding in a well, but the fire was so enormous, it sucked up all the oxygen, suffocating them.

**How Hot Was It?** The few that survived hid in the Peshtigo River. There they stood, in water up to their necks, while a tornado of fire surrounded them. The fire was creating its own winds, up to 80 miles per hour, which sucked smoke away from the survivors, a sight that very few people have lived to talk about. Everywhere they looked was fire, filling even the sky. The air was so hot—between 500°F and 700°F—that if they stopped continually dousing their heads, their hair would catch fire. One woman asked the minister if this was the end of the world.

**Up in Smoke.** The fire abated after five and a half hours, when there was nothing left in Peshtigo to burn. But there was no immediate help for the survivors. The fire killed more than 2,000 people and burned more than 1.25 million acres of forest. Peshtigo and the nearby towns of Holland, Manistee, and Port Huron were wiped off the map.

**The Second Second City.** The destruction was so total, it took days for word of the fire to reach the nation. When news finally reached the capital city of Madison days later, all of Wisconsin's state officials were in Chicago, helping with relief efforts. The Great Chicago Fire so dominated newspaper headlines for weeks that the governor of Wisconsin had to issue a special proclamation to divert aid from the big city to the south to the Peshtigo area. Thousands of dollars of relief money soon poured in to Wisconsin's burned-out towns.

Peshtigo was eventually rebuilt, though it would never regain its status as a lumber town—all the trees were gone. The Great Peshtigo Fire remains the deadliest fire in American history, though it was doomed from its start to be forever overshadowed by the far more famous—though far less deadly—fire that started the same night.

\*     \*     \*

## DEATH AND TAXES

• **1887:** The American Association of public accountants was established with 31 members.

• **1913:** The 16th Amendment to the U.S. Constitution was signed into law. It allowed the federal government to collect income tax.

• **1913:** The 1040 tax form also made its debut.

• **1955:** H&R Block was launched in Kansas City, Missouri, by brothers Henry and Richard Bloch. They charged $5 for the preparation of an income tax return.

• **1986:** Tax payers were allowed to file electronically, as long as a professional prepared the form.

---

As late as 1720, many Americans believed that eating potatoes would shorten a person's life.

# NAME CALLING

*Have you ever wondered why golfer Jack Nicklaus is known as
"the Golden Bear," or why baseball fans refer to Larry Jones
as "Chipper"? Come along as we examine the origins
of ten of the most colorful nicknames in sports.*

### 1. MILDRED ELLA "BABE" DIDRIKSON ZAHARIAS

Regarded by many as the finest female athlete of the 20th century,
Mildred Ella Didrikson Zaharias was a celebrated track and field
star who captured a pair of gold medals at the 1932 Olympics
before picking up the sport of golf and going on to win 41 events
on the LPGA Tour. She was also a pretty fair baseball player who
once hit five home runs in a game as a child. That feat prompted
comparisons to legendary Yankees slugger Babe Ruth, and before
long everyone was referring to Mildred as "Babe."

### 2. KARL "THE MAILMAN" MALONE

The second-leading scorer in NBA history, Karl Malone earned his
nickname at Louisiana Tech University thanks to his tireless work
under the basket and his propensity for always "delivering."
Although Malone embraced his nickname, it came back to haunt
him during game one of the 1997 NBA Finals. With the contest
tied in the fourth quarter and Malone on the line, Chicago Bulls
forward Scottie Pippen causally approached the Utah Jazz star and
whispered into his ear, "Just remember, the Mailman doesn't deliver on Sundays." Malone missed both of his free throws and the
Bulls went on to win the game. Several days later, the Bulls
claimed the championship.

### 3. ANTHONY "SPUD" WEBB

A David in a world full of Goliaths, 5' 7" NBA player Anthony
Webb—most famous for winning the 1986 NBA Slam Dunk
Contest—was saddled with his nickname shortly after being born
on July 13, 1963, when a relative remarked that his oversized cranium reminded her of the Soviet satellite *Sputnik*. The name was
quickly shortened to "Spud," and it continues to be his calling
card to this day.

## 4. "SHOELESS" JOE JACKSON

One of the top hitters in Major League Baseball history, Joe Jackson earned his colorful nickname in 1908 during a semipro game in Anderson, South Carolina. According to legend, the slick-hitting outfielder was suffering from blisters due to an ill-fitting pair of spikes and intended to sit out the game. But his team was short of players, so Jackson doffed his footwear and played in his stocking feet. Despite having little traction, he managed to hit a triple in his first at bat, prompting one fan to yell, "You shoeless son of a gun, you!" The nickname stuck with Jackson for the rest of his life.

## 5. JACK "THE GOLDEN BEAR" NICKLAUS

Jack Nicklaus has never been petite, but he was especially pudgy early in his career, earning him the derisive nicknames "Fat Jack" and "Whale Boy." Fortunately, not everyone was so dismissive of his size. Australian journalist Don Lawrence helped change fans' perceptions of Nicklaus in the 1960s when he wrote that the Columbus, Ohio, native reminded him of a "cuddly golden bear." Nicklaus liked the moniker so much that he later adopted it as the name of his company, Golden Bear International.

## 6. ADAM "PACMAN" JONES

Adam Jones can thank his mother for his colorful nickname. According to the speedy cornerback, his mom began calling him "Pacman" while he was still an infant after observing how he would drink his milk nearly as fast as Pac-Man gobbled power pellets and ghosts in the classic video game.

## 7. DENNIS "OIL CAN" BOYD

Although he's best known for leading the Boston Red Sox to the 1986 World Series, Dennis Boyd earned his nickname for his antics away from the field. According to Boyd himself, his handle harkens back to his prodigious beer-drinking days in his hometown of Meridian, Mississippi, where beer is still occasionally referred to as "oil."

## 8. PAUL "BEAR" BRYANT

Long before he became one of the most successful coaches in

college football history, Paul Bryant was just a dirt-poor Arkansas farm boy who plowed his family's fields every morning before going to school. That's why he jumped at the opportunity to make a little cash one day in 1927 when a touring carnival operator offered to pay him $1 a minute to wrestle a trained bear. Sadly, the 13-year-old Bryant didn't last long, fleeing soon after the bear bit him in the ear, but he earned a nickname that stayed with him.

## 9. LARRY "CHIPPER" JONES

Baseball fans can be forgiven for assuming that Larry Jones's nickname relates to his upbeat demeanor and passion for baseball. The all-star third baseman actually received his moniker in his infancy thanks to a family member who noted he was a "chip off the old block" of his father, Larry Jones Sr.

## 10. RICHARD "DIGGER" PHELPS

One of the most respected voices in college basketball as an analyst for games televised by ESPN, Richard Phelps's nickname hints at his boyhood in Beacon, New York, where his father, Dick, owned and operated a funeral home. Phelps later embraced his morbid tag in his autobiography, *Undertaker's Son: Life Lessons from a Coach.*

\*     \*     \*

## BEST WINNING STREAK YOU NEVER HEARD OF

There's only one on this list. From January 30, 2003, to 2010, Esther Vergeer has won 386 consecutive singles tennis matches, surpassing the record of even Marina Navratilova. Few sports fans know of this historic winning streak because Vergeer plays in a wheelchair. When she was eight years old, an operation to correct a birth defect left her unable to walk; as part of her rehabilitation process she turned to sports, including wheelchair tennis. Born in Holland in 1981, Vergeer was still a teenager in 1999 when she became the world's top-ranked player. As of 2010, it's a title she's held consecutively for 11 years. Vergeer has won 15 Grand Slam singles titles since 2003, and is a five-time Paralympics tennis champion. She's won at doubles at Wimbledon but has yet to have one of her matches shown on a major network.

---

Female foresters in Britain's Women Timber Corps were called "Lumber Jills."

# NOW HEAR THIS!

*During America's wars, they were considered entertainers more than harbingers of fear to U.S. troops. But sometimes media stars like Tokyo Rose and Hanoi Hannah broadcast strategic information that there's no way the enemy should have known.*

As radio propagandists transmitting from enemy capitals, their job was to undermine the morale of opposing troops in World War II, the Korean War, and the Vietnam War. Uncle John examines the careers of seven infamous enemy broadcasters of the 20th century.

## 1. TOKYO ROSE

Iva Toguri was born in Los Angeles in 1916 and graduated from UCLA with a zoology degree; she was visiting Japan when war broke out in 1941. She was hardly a household name in World War II—until the name given her by Allied forces in the Pacific made her an international celebrity.

**Wartime Activities:** Tokyo Rose played American music and used American slang during her 20-minute daily newscast on Radio Tokyo's "The Zero Hour" while she predicted attacks, identified American ships and submarines, and even peppered her conversation with the names of prominent individuals. Listeners thought she was uncannily accurate, but she had little impact on the offensive juggernaut that first isolated and then defeated Japan.

**Postwar:** After the war, Toguri was arrested, convicted of treason, and imprisoned; she was released for good behavior in 1956 after serving six years. Upon moving to Chicago, where her family ran a store, she insisted she had always been a loyal American. She claimed that she was forced to make the broadcasts, and Allied POWs who worked with her confirmed her story years later, convincing President Gerald Ford to pardon her in 1977. In January 2006, she received the Edward J. Herlihy Citizenship Award from the World War II Veterans Committee; she died in September of that year.

Since 1954, the venomous box jellyfish has caused more than 5,500 deaths.

## 2. LORD HAW-HAW

The British gave the nickname "Lord Haw-Haw" to a collection of announcers on English-language propaganda broadcasts from Hamburg, Germany, during World War II, but it was William Joyce, who claimed to be a British citizen, who came to symbolize Lord Haw-Haw as the chief Nazi sympathizer. Born in the United States and raised in England and Ireland, Joyce was a member of the British Union of Fascists and was about to be arrested when he fled to Germany in 1939.

**Wartime Activities:** From 1939 to 1945, his radio broadcasts to England on the "Germany Calling" program were designed to undermine the morale of English, Canadian, Australian, and American troops, as well as the citizens of the British Isles. Joyce reported Allied ship losses and planes shot down, and bragged about Nazi secret weapons with the goal of demoralizing the Allies.

"Lord Haw-Haw" was originally the nickname of James Brudenell, the 19th-century British general who led the infamous Charge of the Light Brigade. A British radio critic borrowed the moniker and, whether or not he was referring specifically to Joyce, it stuck to him because he was the most popular announcer on "Germany Calling." The radio critic noted sarcastically, "He speaks English of the 'haw-haw, dammit-get-out-of-my-way' variety." The name stuck and his fame grew to the point that even the Germans introduced him on the air as "William Joyce, otherwise known as Lord Haw-Haw."

**Postwar:** Joyce was captured by British troops, who got the last "haw" when the war ended. He was tried and hanged for treason in early 1946.

## 3. LORD HEE-HAW

A native of Dubuque, Iowa, Frederick Wilhelm Kaltenbach was on a bicycle tour of Germany after his high school graduation in 1914 when he was detained due to the outbreak of World War I. He liked Germany well enough, but after his release a few months later, he returned home and went to college. He joined the U.S. Army in 1918 but stayed stateside for the duration of the war, after which he earned his master's degree in history from the University of Chicago. As a schoolteacher in Dubuque, he founded a Nazi-style club for boys in 1935 that was so controversial, the school board fired him. Kaltenbach promptly returned to Germany and went to work for Joseph Goebbels's propaganda ministry as a broadcaster.

**Wartime Activities:** Kaltenbach's thick Midwestern accent became familiar to British listeners, who dubbed him "Lord Hee-Haw" to differentiate him from "Lord Haw-Haw." Kaltenbach's reign on the air came to an end with the collapse of the Third Reich.

**Postwar:** He was under indictment in the United States for treason, but the Soviets got the last "hee." They arrested him in Berlin in 1945 and refused to release him to American forces. The broadcaster died within a year in a Soviet prison.

## 4. AXIS SALLY

British and American GIs on the march through Italy in the last months of World War II were familiar with the radio voice of "Axis Sally." Rita Luisa Zucca, born to a Manhattan restaurateur, called herself "Sally" while broadcasting propaganda first for Benito Mussolini's fascist government and then for Nazi Germany. She was a regular voice on the "Jerry's Front" program that aired from Rome. She'd come to Italy before the war to look after her family's estate and was forced to renounce her American citizenship to keep the property from being expropriated by Mussolini's government. She was 30 when she was hired as a radio announcer in February 1943.

**Wartime Activities:** Her theme song was "Between the Devil and the Deep Blue Sea" and her signature sign-on was "Hello, suckers!" She mixed pop music, news of Allied troop movements, and appeals to the British and American troops to surrender.

**Postwar:** Sally was captured by the U.S. Army in Milan on June 5, 1945, with her newborn baby. Tried in Italy for collaboration with the enemy, she was convicted and sentenced to four and a half years in prison. Released after nine months, she lived the rest of her life in obscurity in Italy.

---

...It was a meat pie made from a deer's "humbles"—intestines, liver, kidney, etc.

## 5. BERLIN BESSIE

Mildred Gillars, who was born in Maine, dreamed of being an actress but instead wound up as radio announcer "Berlin Bessie" for Radio Berlin in World War II. After dropping out of Ohio Wesleyan University, she left the United States in the 1930s for Dresden, Germany, to study music. She was working as an English teacher at the Berlitz School of Languages in Berlin when war broke out across Europe in 1939.

**Wartime Activities:** Radio Berlin hired her as an actress and announcer in 1940. The Allied soldiers called her a variety of names: "Berlin Bessie," "Olga," and "the Bitch of Berlin." Introducing herself on air as "Midge," she tried to convince listeners that their wives and sweethearts back home were being unfaithful. Between American tunes, she made anti-Semitic remarks and criticized President Franklin D. Roosevelt. She stayed on the air until Berlin fell in 1945.

**Postwar:** Gillars tried to blend in among the thousands of displaced Germans, but she was captured and flown to the United States in 1948 and charged with treason, convicted, and imprisoned until her release in 1961. She took up residence in an Ohio convent and later earned her degree from Ohio Wesleyan in 1973. She went on to teach French and German at a prep school, and died of natural causes in 1988 at age 87.

## 6. SEOUL CITY SUE

During the Korean War, a Methodist missionary from Lawrence County, Arkansas, became the North Korean radio announcer better known as "Seoul City Sue." Born in 1900, Anna Wallis Suh graduated from the Scarritt College for Christian Workers in Nashville, Tennessee, in 1930 and undertook a mission to Korea. After marrying Korean schoolteacher Suh Kyoon Chul, she dropped out of the missionary service of the Southern Methodist Conference and became interested in Korean politics.

**Wartime Activities:** When the Korean People's Army captured Seoul in 1950, Anna went to work as an announcer on Radio Seoul. Her programs featured names of American soldiers captured or killed, and threatened newly arrived soldiers and ships sitting off the coast. She also taunted African American soldiers for their

---

*Tyrannosaurus rex* fossils have been found in the U.S., Canada, and Mongolia.

lack of civil rights in the United States. She delivered all this in a monotone against a backdrop of soft music. American soldiers dubbed her "Seoul City Sue" after the 1946 pop tune "Sioux City Sue."

**Postwar:** A few days before U.S. forces retook Seoul from the North Koreans, the Suhs evacuated to the north. Anna lived there until her death in 1969.

### 7. HANOI HANNAH

Trinh Thi Ngo, born in Hanoi in 1931, was a Vietnamese radio personality who became the voice of anti-American propaganda during the Vietnam War in the 1960s and 1970s. She was the daughter of a prosperous factory owner and learned English because she loved American movies like *Gone With the Wind*. By age 25, she was an English-language news broadcaster on Vietnam's national radio in Hanoi.

**Wartime Activities:** Trinh made as many as three radio broadcasts daily in an attempt to demoralize the American troops who were defending South Vietnam from an insurgency from the north. To the GIs, she became "Hanoi Hannah" and "the Dragon Lady." She played antiwar songs popular in the United States, and read the names of soldiers who had recently been killed or imprisoned. U.S. forces were impressed by her military intelligence, which included details about where individual units were deployed.

**Postwar:** After the war, Trinh and others revealed that her wartime information came from the American military newspaper *Stars and Stripes*. Today, she lives in relative obscurity with her husband in Ho Chi Minh City (the former Saigon). In the United States, her voice can be heard on the computer game "Battlefield Vietnam."

\*　　\*　　\*

"The man who fights against his own country is never a hero."

—Victor Hugo

In 1848, John Curtis sold the first commercial chewing gum: Maine Pure Spruce Gum.

# ON THE ROAD AGAIN

*Part one, "Roads Most Traveled" on page 125 looked at ancient roads. Now we look at more modern highways.*

## 1. THE GERMAN AUTOBAHN

The German autobahn was the first high-speed, limited-access highway network in the world. Car enthusiasts love it because it has no speed limit for most of its length.

**Purpose:** When an autobahn was proposed in 1926 between Hamburg and Basel, the Nazis opposed it nevertheless; the first autobahn was completed in 1932, one year before Hitler came to power. But Hitler saw the propaganda value of taking credit for the concept, and by the time construction began on additional autobahn routes, the originators of the autobahn idea were warned by the Nazis to keep quiet: the autobahns were to be promoted as Hitler's roads. In fact, the construction of an autobahn system was the ideal government project for the Nazis, as it created jobs and was the kind of monumental work that would add glory to the Nazi cause.

**Construction:** The first autobahn ran between Cologne and Bonn. The planning that began in 1924 envisioned twice the total miles that exist today. From 1933 to 1938, 1,860 miles of roadway were added to the system before construction was stopped in 1941 by World War II. Today there are 6,800 miles of autobahn in Germany.

**Specs:** The autobahns are multilane freeways with a landscaped median that varies from 10 to 12 feet across. They route traffic around cities rather than through them. There are emergency telephones roughly every one and a half miles, and frequent rest stops.

**Factoids:**

• The German autobahn is the third-longest highway system in the world after the interstate highway system of the United States and the National Trunk Highway of China.

• During World War II, the autobahns couldn't be used by tanks because their weight and tracks tore up the pavement. In fact,

---

Publius Ostorius, a gladiator at Pompeii, is famous for surviving 51 fights.

most transport of troops and supplies was done by railroad. But late in World War II, the Luftwaffe used the autobahns as emergency runways.

• Three-quarters of the autobahn has no speed limit, although there is a general advisory speed limit of 130 kilometers per hour (80 miles per hour).

• During the energy crisis in November 1973, a national speed limit of 100 kilometers per hour (62 miles per hour) was enacted, then repealed less than four months later.

• The autobahns are monitored electronically so that a speed limit can be imposed depending on weather or traffic conditions.

• Despite the high speeds, fatality rates on German autobahns are lower than on U.S. interstate highways.

• It is illegal to run out of gas on the autobahn; drivers who do so are subject to a fine.

### 2. ROUTE 66
It lasted just 59 years, but Route 66 is legendary. Called the "Mother Road," it officially began at the corner of Jackson Boulevard and Michigan Avenue in Chicago and ended at the corner of Santa Monica Boulevard and Ocean Avenue overlooking the Pacific Ocean in Santa Monica, California. The road was famous as the route of the Dust Bowl migrants, for its fast-food stands, tepee-style motels, and as the inspiration for a pop song in the 1940s and a hit TV show in the 1960s.

**Purpose:** Route 66 was built to connect Chicago and Los Angeles and to give the small towns in between access to a major national road. As a result, it ran down the main streets of many rural towns.

**Construction:** Route 66 was commissioned in 1926. It ran through eight states and three time zones. But with the passage of the Interstate Highway Act in 1956, Route 66 was gradually swallowed up or bypassed by the interstates. The last section of Route 66, near Williams, Arizona, was superseded by a section of Interstate 40 in 1984, and it was officially removed from the U.S. highway system in 1985.

**Specs:** Route 66 was realigned many times over the course of its

---

In 1933, the first-known recipe for deep-fried onion rings appeared in the *New York Times*.

history, so its length varied, but it was between 2,200 and 2,450 miles. In 1926, the year it was commissioned, it had just 800 paved miles. The rest was gravel or graded dirt. In 1938, Route 66 became the first American highway to be fully paved.

**Factoids:**

• Route 66 was the route taken by migrants leaving the Dust Bowl of Oklahoma and other Great Plains states for what they hoped were better times in California. As memorialized in John Steinbeck's *The Grapes of Wrath*, families like the Joads packed up what they could from their farms and headed west to California on Route 66.

• Between 1935 and 1940, more than 250,000 poor migrants, most of them Oklahomans, traveled to California. But they weren't welcomed—the migrants were given the derogatory name "Okies" whether they came from Oklahoma or not. In 1936, the Los Angeles police established a "bum blockade" at the California border to keep out the "undesirables."

• One section of Route 66 near Oatman, Arizona, was so steep and had so many switchbacks that travelers hired locals to drive that stretch of highway for them.

• After World War II, travel along Route 66 boomed. The romance of a road trip to California was captured by Bobby Troup in his song "(Get Your Kicks On) Route 66." Troup wrote the song while driving Route 66 in 1946; he listed some of the towns along the route in the lyrics. The song was recorded by other musicians, from Nat King Cole to the Rolling Stones.

• Route 66 passed directly through the Petrified Forest in Arizona.

• The route was famous for its eye-catching motels and souvenir stands, and for the birth of fast food. The first drive-through restaurant was on Route 66 in Springfield, Missouri, and the first McDonald's sprang up in San Bernardino, California, also along the route.

• *Route 66* was the title of a TV series that ran on CBS from 1960 to 1964. The show featured two young guys driving around the United States in a Corvette, looking for (and finding) adventure along the way. Although the television show was filmed entirely on location, most of it was not shot on Route 66 because the

producers didn't think the scenery directly along the route was
attractive enough.

## 3. THE ALASKA HIGHWAY

The Alaska Highway runs from Dawson Creek, British Columbia,
to Delta Junction, Alaska, with an unofficial end farther north in
Fairbanks, Alaska, a distance of about 1,500 miles. A joint enterprise between the United States and Canada, the Alaska Highway
is considered to be one of the greatest engineering feats of the
20th century.

**Purpose:** The Alaska Highway was built in just eight months in
1942 by the Army Corps of Engineers to provide a land route for
war matériel during World War II. A Japanese invasion by way of
Alaska was feared, and when the Japanese did invade Alaska's
Aleutian Islands in June 1942, the building project became
urgent. In a bit of wishful thinking, a Japanese propaganda broadcast later thanked the highway workers for constructing a good
road that their troops could use.

**Construction:** The road was authorized in February 1942. Canada
supplied the right-of-way and construction materials, and the
United States mobilized 11,000 troops to build the road and paid
for the construction. Sixteen thousand civilians also worked on
the road, which cost $138 million to build. Construction began in
March 1942 and ended that October. The men worked seven days
a week, 16 hours a day in all conditions, often beset by mosquitoes
and blackflies or in below-freezing weather.

**Specs:** Crews worked south from Delta Junction, north and south
from Whitehorse, British Columbia, and north from Dawson
Creek. Like early explorers, the survey crews often relied on the
Native people to help them scout out the best route. Some sections followed existing trails, but where no trail existed, reconnais-
sance parties walked through waist-deep snow, across river valleys,
and up mountain passes to plan out the route. Permafrost (soil at
or below the freezing point for two or more years) was another
problem: constructing a road on top of it caused what's called
"thermal degradation"—the ground ice melted and the road would
sink into the ground in places. Sometimes weeks passed when the
field parties had no communications with the base camps. The

---

The *Empire Cloud*, a British cargo ship, was torpedoed on both her maiden and final voyages.

original route didn't follow the most direct path but linked existing airfields in Canada. Today, the highway is 35 miles shorter than it was in the 1940s due to reconstruction and rerouting, and it continues to get shorter as additional construction shaves off unnecessary miles.

**Factoids:**

• When it was a military-only road, it was called the Alcan Highway.

• The highway opened to the public in 1948.

• In 1996, the highway was named an International Historical Engineering Landmark.

• The actual current mileage of the Alaska Highway is vague. The last milepost in Canada is mile 1,187; the first milepost in Alaska reads 1,222. Historical mileposts have been left up along the entire route and are used as addresses for the businesses along the highway but no longer represent the actual miles driven, due to reroutings of the highway.

• The Alaska Highway is open all year-round—despite temperatures that can go as low as 50 degrees below zero.

• It can get so cold in Alaska that tires can freeze flat. They become round again after a few miles of driving.

• The road is entirely paved in Alaska. In Canada, it's either paved or packed gravel on tar.

• Today, about 100,000 travelers annually make the trip to Alaska using the Alaska Highway.

\*　　　\*　　　\*

"The guy who invented the first wheel was an idiot. The guy who invented the other three, *he* was the genius."

—**Sid Caesar**

# EPIC HISTORY
# MOVIES COUNTDOWN

*Calling all history buffs! You're going to want to check out these films.*

**10. The Great Escape (1963).** Based on a true story of the greatest Allied escape from a German POW camp in World War II, the movie details the escape of more than 70 prisoners and the massive search by the German Gestapo to find them.

**9. Der Untergang (2004).** The movie dramatizes the last days of Adolf Hitler and Eva Braun, trapped in Hitler's Berlin bunker.

**8. Schindler's List (1993).** Nazi businessman Oskar Schindler turns his factory into a refuge for Jews, 1,100 of whom he saves from death at the Auschwitz concentration camp.

**7. The Last Emperor (1987).** As the last of the emperor of China, Pu Yi was worshiped from a child by a half-billion people until the 1930s, when Japan invaded and exploited him. He died in obscurity as a peasant worker after the war.

**6. Das Boot (1981).** The movie examines the terrifying and fatalistic circumstances faced by a Nazi U-boat crew trying to stay loyal to their cause against impossible odds.

**5. Gandhi (1982).** The heart and soul of India's emergence as an Asian democracy is traced through the life of human-rights crusader Mahatma Gandhi, who leads and unprecedented nonviolent revolution.

**4. The Ten Commandments (1956).** The life and times of biblical prophet Moses are dramatized with special effects that were astounding for the times, including the parting of the Red Sea as Moses leads the Jews out of slavery in Egypt.

**3. Ivan the Terrible (Films I and II) (1944, 1958).** Both movies are brilliant portrayals of Ivan IV, who crowns himself tsar of Russia in the mid-1550s and proceeds to reclaim Russian territory in campaigns in the Baltic and Crimea.

**2. *Spartacus* (1960).** As a Thracian slave, Spartacus is one of Rome's greatest gladiators, and leads an ill-fated rebellion by Roman slaves against the state.

**1. *Ben-Hur* (1959).** Roman prince Judah Ben-Hur survives enslavement by the commander of the Roman garrison of Jerusalem, and seeks revenge and redemption for him, his mother, and his sister.

\* \* \*

## WORDS THAT HISTORY HAS CHANGED

**1.** Paper used to be called text, paper, or copy. "Hard copy" referred to printouts of microfilm. But when the primary source of information switched to online, we began to use the term "hard copy" to refer to printed paper documents.

**2.** TV was TV until it had to become broadcast TV—transmission over airwaves—to differentiate it from other delivery options—cable and satellite.

**3.** A telephone technically was always called a landline, but the latter term was rarely used. A landline meant the cable went over land as opposed to underwater. But cell phones necessitated referring to old telephone handsets that plug into the wall as landlines.

**4.** The original term for films was "silent movie." It was not until the 1920s and the arrival of the "talkie"—movies with built-in soundtracks—that the term changed from silent movies to talkies, and finally, when talkies became commonplace, the term was changed to just plain old movies.

**5.** Mail became "snail mail" when the 175 billion hard-copy letters sent each year needed to be distinguished from the trillions of e-mails, texts, and social messaging transmissions sent each year.

**6.** Hardcover books used to be the norm. But during the Great Depression, there was a demand for inexpensive literature and book publisher Penguin obliged by creating mass-market books. The term "paperbacks" emerged around 1949.

In 1991, a goat named Snowball killed his abusive owner by butting him twice in the stomach.

# FIRST MILITARY AWARDS

*Wars have been waged for thousands of years, but awards for valor and service during war are a fairly recent invention.*

## 1. THE PURPLE HEART

The Purple Heart dates back to the American Revolution. General George Washington established the honor in 1782—making it the oldest military decoration still awarded. Washington believed that ordinary soldiers deserved recognition for their bravery in action, but the Continental Congress didn't want to give out monetary awards. So Washington designed the "Badge of Military Merit," the first award granted to the common soldier. He personally selected the heart shape and the color purple. Originally the heart-shaped fabric badge edged in silver braid was sewn on the soldier's coat. Washington gave the award to three soldiers who had fought in the Revolutionary War: Sergeants Elijah Churchill, William Brown, and Daniel Bissell Jr.

The award fell out of use after the Revolution, but in 1932, on the bicentennial of Washington's birth, it was revived and reinvented. The U.S. War Department commissioned Elizabeth Will to redesign it. She kept the heart shape and the purple color, but suggested that the badge should be an actual medal. Today's Purple Heart is made of purple enamel and has a brass relief of George Washington in profile wearing his general's uniform of the Continental army. The reverse side is inscribed with "For Military Merit," with the recipient's name below.

The award is now bestowed to American soldiers who were wounded or killed in the line of duty. And it can be awarded retroactively to any soldier back to the Civil War. Since it can be handed out on the battlefield and in hospitals, in addition to retroactive awards, no one's sure how many soldiers have received it, but the number is probably close to a million.

## 2. THE CROIX DE GUERRE ("CROSS OF WAR")

France began awarding this medal in April 1915—in the middle of World War I. The government wanted to recognize acts of bravery that were mentioned in dispatches from the trenches and battle lines. The medal was discontinued after the Great War ended…then reinstated in 1939, at the onset of World War II. Separate medals were issued for World Wars I and II, as well as for conflicts in the colonies. To add to the confusion, both Belgium and France issued their own versions of the medals, and so did the Vichy and Free French during World War II. However, most of the medal designs are similar, with to a large Maltese bronze cross with crossed words and the head of the French republic in the center suspended from a green-and-red-striped ribbon.

Many U.S. and British soldiers were recipients, including Alvin York, Eddie Rickenbacker, James Doolittle, and James Stewart. It is even said that a homing pigeon named Che Ami was a recipient for flying a message across enemy lines in the heat of battle.

### 3. THE VICTORIA CROSS

The Victoria Cross is Great Britian's highest award, and it is for members the Commonwealth armed forces and civilians under military command. Britain first awarded the Victoria Cross in June 1857, to honor exceptional valor during the Crimean War—111 participants in that conflict received it.

The medal is a cross pattee (similar to a Maltese cross) with a crown surmounted by a lion in the center and the words "For Valour." On the back is engraved the name, rank, serial number, and the date of the action for which it was awarded.

Another medal, the George Cross, was created in 1940 for courage in action but not while under direct fire.

### 4. THE CONGRESSIONAL MEDAL OF HONOR

Usually just called the "Medal of Honor," this is the United States' highest military award, and it's given for risking one's life in service above and beyond the call of duty. Iowa senator James Grimes proposed a medal for individual gallantry at the beginning of the Civil War, but the top Union army commander, General Winfield Scott, squelched the idea—he felt that medals were too bourgeois and European. But the U.S. Navy had no such objections, so President Abraham Lincoln approved the medal for them in December 1861. The army eventually caught on and got their Medal of Honor approved seven months later.

First movie censorship: nude scenes were removed from *Tarzan and His Mate* (1934).

The earliest act of valor to earn the Medal of Honor did not occur in the Civil War, however. On February 13, 1861, army assistant surgeon Bernard Irwin rescued 60 soldiers who'd been captured by Apache Indians in Arizona. He was awarded the medal decades later.

## 5. THE IRON CROSS

Prussia, which later became part of Germany, instituted the Iron Cross for distinguished service in 1813 during the Napoleonic Wars. The design is a simple Maltese cross of cast iron edged in silver. About six weeks after King Frederick William III established the medal, the first man to receive it was named: Commander Karl Auguste Ferdinand von Borcke. Back then, the Iron Crosses were made by hand, and even though the war against Napoléon ended in 1815, manufacturing continued for years so that all the soldiers who earned the medal from that war actually got one.

The medal was revived several times—in 1870 for the Franco-Prussian War, in 1914 for World War I, and lastly by Hitler on the day German forces invaded Poland, September 1, 1939. Hitler also allowed the bestowal of the award for exceptional bravery by ordinary citizens and allies.

## 6. THE LEGION OF HONOR

Napoléon Bonaparte set up this award in 1802 to replace all the aristocratic honors wiped out by the French Revolution. The Legion was open to all who upheld liberty and equality regardless of rank, birth, or religion. Admission into the Legion for military service carries an automatic award of the Croix de Guerre.

The design of the award has changed along with the French rulers but finally was solidified with the depiction of the female head of the republic and the inscription "Republique Francaise"; on the reverse is a set of crossed tricolors and the motto "Honneur et Patrie" ("Honor and Fatherland").

Some well-known non–French civilian recipients include Barbra Streisand, Walt Disney, Prince Charles of Wales, and Julia Child.

# HOW THE WEST WAS WON

*It took a lot of people with a lot of gumption to tame the Old West, but those adventuresome types wouldn't have stood a chance without some important enterprises and contraptions.*

## 1. THE TELEGRAPH

The telegraph was an important form of long-distance form of communication in the Old West. Its birth meant that news from the outside world no longer arrived by horse or riverboats after weeks and months of travel; over telegraph wires strung from wooden posts, communication became almost instantaneous.

**Significance:** The telegraph was vital to both sides in the Civil War and was used effectively by law enforcement to hunt down desperados in the Old West. By closing the gap between east and west, it also helped unify the nation well into the 20th century.

**Story:** In 1831, Robert Morse invented a way of sending messages over a copper wire based on a series of dashes and dots that could be decoded by the receiver. Yet it wasn't until 1844 that he sent the first message over a telegraph line: "What hath God wrought!" Within six years, a group of businessmen in New York organized the New York & Mississippi Valley Printing Telegraph Company. Meanwhile, Ezra Cornell, who would go on to found Cornell University, organized a competing system, the New York & Western Union Telegraph Company. The two companies merged as the Western Union Telegraph Company in 1856 and the first transcontinental telegraph line came together on October 24, 1861, in Salt Lake City, Utah.

The first transcontinental message was sent by Stephen J. Field, chief justice of California, to Abraham Lincoln in Washington, assuring the president that the western states would remain loyal to the Union during the Civil War.

**Demise:** The telegraph died by inches as telephones steadily gained a foothold in the 20th century. On January 27, 2006, Western Union sent its last telegram.

---

In the Bahamas, a "banana wind" is strong enough to blow fruit off trees...

## 2. THE RAILROAD

Railroads were the primary mode of long-distance transportation from the 1830s to the mid-20th century. As far back as 1836, the idea of a nation-spanning rail line began to catch on—one that would shrink the travel time from Washington, D.C., to San Francisco from months of arduous journey by sea or wagon train to a mere eight days in passenger cars pulled by steam-powered locomotives. But the steep and rocky terrain, especially through the high sierras, seemed insurmountable.

**Significance:** The speed and safety of trains and their ability to carry huge quantities of cargo at low cost, made them preferable to riverboats and wagons. Whereas a Conestoga might make 25 miles in a day, an "iron horse" could pull a train that same distance in less than an hour.

**Story:** In 1826, John Steven, the "father of American railroads," demonstrated that steam locomotives were feasible by running one on a circular track built at his estate in Hoboken, New Jersey. Small steam railroads sprang up in the East to displace canal boats, but the people who dreamed of a transcontinental railroad would have to wait until the 1860s. President Abraham Lincoln saw the military advantages of such a railroad and as a means to bond the Pacific coast to the Union; he supported California railroad engineer Theodore D. Judah, who convinced some wealthy partners to back a transcontinental railroad as a means of exploiting gold and silver mines in the West. Judah hired 13,000 immigrant workers from China to drive construction of the Central Pacific Railroad over the 10,000-foot-high Sierra Nevadas and across the boiling deserts of Nevada and Utah. At Promontory, Utah, on May 10, 1869, the Central Pacific linked up with the Union Pacific line heading west. The driving of a ceremonial "golden spike" memorialized the moment: the creation of the first transcontinental line in North America.

Showman William George Crush lured a reported 40,000 spectators to a temporary town called Crush in western Texas, to see a publicity stunt: the crash of two trains. On September 15, 1896, Crush sent two six-car trains pulled by steam locomotives racing toward each other from a mile away. The engines collided head-on, causing their boilers to explode and sending shrapnel high into the air. At least three spectators were killed and many were injured.

---

...but it's not as powerful or dangerous as a hurricane.

**Demise:** Though far from dead, passenger travel was dealt near-fatal blows by the emergence of air travel and the interstate high-way system developed in the 1950s. Freight is still carried by rail, but trucking has become the main way to transport cargo.

## 3. THE GUN

The liveliest debate over what won the West is about firearms. Did the Colt six-shooter or the Winchester rifle tame the wilder-ness? Law-enforcement officers and peace-loving settlers in the Old West typically owned both—something like the army-issue .45-caliber Colt single-action revolver and the .44-caliber Winchester lever-action rifle. Revolver handguns were standard fare for close-range self-defense, but most experts agree that the Winchester rifle ruled because of its long-range accuracy and firepower.

**Significance:** To survive in the Old West, especially from 1800 to 1892, you needed a gun. Firearms were necessary for hunting and self-defense, especially in lawless areas—and it was a rite of passage to manhood to become skilled at shooting a gun.

**Story:** Two men gave their names to guns that ruled the West: Samuel Colt and Oliver Winchester. Colt, the son of a textile factory owner, patented his idea in 1836 and established a factory in Paterson, New Jersey. The Colt handgun became popular after soldiers reported success with it in the war with Mexico in 1846. It was standard fare during the Civil War and quickly took hold in the West, particularly the Colt .45 pistol.

Oliver Winchester improved on someone else's design. In 1848, Walter Hunt patented a "Volition Repeating Rifle"—the forerunner of the rifle made famous as a Union army firearm during the Civil War. One Confederate soldier called it "that damned Yankee rifle that they load on Sunday and shoot all week!"

As a safety measure, people who carried six-shooters loaded five rounds into the cylinder and left the hammer down on the empty chamber. There was no way to fire the gun without first cocking the hammer to advance to the loaded chamber. Gun-slingers in the Old West customarily stuffed a rolled-up $5 bill in the empty chamber to pay for their burial if they lost a showdown.

**Demise:** Law enforcement and time tamped down gun violence in the West, but today there are more guns in more hands than ever.

---

Idaho and Washington produce more than half of all U.S. spuds.

# THE *SUMERIAN TIMES* BEST-SELLER LIST

*Wonder what people were reading way back when? So did we.*

## 1. IN THE BEGINNING WAS THE (WRITTEN) WORD

Since you can't have literature without written words, kudos to the ancient Sumerians of Mesopotamia (now Iraq), who invented cuneiform script, the first known writing. Rather than an alphabet with letters, cuneiform script consisted of pictographs, simple pictures that represented words. Back in 3000 BC, there were no pencils, pens, or even quills dipped in ink, so Sumerian "books" were made of soft clay tablets. Scribes scratched the cuneiform script into the clay with a sharpened reed called a stylus.

Over the 3,000 years that cuneiform was used, the pictographs became stylized and abbreviated so that the process of scratching words on tablets could be shortened. Though the system began with 1,500 different representations for words or syllables, the number of pictographs shrank to about 600 so scribes could write more quickly.

Written language continued to be developed by others around the world, including the Egyptians, whose hieroglyphs were likely influenced by the Sumerians' cuneiform. The Egyptians went on to create the world's oldest known alphabet in 2000 BC. This meant that fewer symbols were needed to tell a story—which led to much less scratching.

## 2. FIRST NAMED AUTHOR

The first author known by name is believed to be a poet who lived 4,300 years ago. Enheduanna (2285–2250 BC) was the daughter of a Sumerian ruler who kept his power in the family by making her the high priestess of the moon god Nanna. Hers was an important position because Nanna was also the patron saint for the city of Ur, the center of power in the kingdom. As his high priestess, Enheduanna shared in Nanna's glory and managed his property.

Though it was Enheduanna's day job to serve a god, her claim to eternal fame came from the poems she wrote for a goddess

---

**Llanito**, a mix of Spanish and British English, is spoken on Gibraltar.

named Inanna. Hymns to Inanna praise this goddess of love, fertility, and war. Enheduanna tells of what it was like when the goddess made her suffer by sending a rebel who took over Sumeria, took away her high priestess status, and even tried to get her in his bed. She then praises the power of Inanna, who overthrew the rebel and made her priestess once again.

Some historians claim that the hymns are political. By praising an all-powerful goddess, Enheduanna could help her father wrest authority away from lesser local rulers and unite his kingdom. Others claim that Enheduanna was an early feminist who was passionately celebrating the goddess's power. Whatever her motives, she's been recognized for the poetic power of her hymns of praise and as the first author to explore a personal relationship with a spiritual higher power—not to mention the first to record a case of sexual harassment.

## 3. FIRST SUPERHERO

Thousands of years before the Hulk, there was King Gilgamesh, who ruled the city-state of Urak in Sumeria around 2700 BC. The world's oldest adventure story comes from an epic poem based on legends of the king. It was inscribed on clay tablets that date back as far as 2000 BC, and is known as *The Epic of Gilgamesh*.

Gilgamesh is one-third man and two-thirds god, with superhuman strength and intelligence. On the down side, he uses his powers to enslave his subjects. In despair, people pray to the gods, who send Gilgamesh an enemy almost as powerful as he is—with the idea that the two will keep busy fighting each other and the poor souls of Urak will finally have some peace and quiet. Naturally, the gods make more trouble than they intended to and Gilgamesh must use all his special powers to cope.

*The Epic of Gilgamesh* was a long narrative poem of high adventure with important cultural significance. Written over 4,000 years ago, it was the forerunner to ancient works like Homer's *Iliad* and the Anglo-Saxon epic *Beowulf*, both of which became 21st-century films.

## 4. FIRST PSYCHOLOGICAL NOVEL

Murasaki Shikibu wrote it sometime around AD 1002, but literary historians still argue about *The Tale of Genji*. Some claim it's the world's first novel, others that it's the first modern psychological novel, and still others say it's the first classical novel.

Murasaki Shikibu was a widow with one child. She was also an aristocratic member of the emperor's royal entourage, and her novel is a drama of the court life of Hikaru Genji and his family. Genji is the beloved son of Japan's emperor and the emperor's favorite (though lowly) concubine. Court intrigue leads to the death of Genji's mother, and her death and status keep him from inheriting his father's throne. Nevertheless, Genji manages to have an influential and highly romantic life at court, and he ultimately becomes the secret father of the heir to the emperor's throne.

*The Tale of Genji*'s status as the first novel rested on the fact that earlier literary works were mainly collections of fables, legends, or poems. *The Tale of Genji* wasn't the first work written as a narrative in prose, but it was the first to explore the inner lives of very human characters. Rather than following a series of adventures, it followed one small group of courtiers through time, and the emphasis was on how they interacted and changed as they grew older. *The Tale of Genji* is a Japanese classic that still influences modern writers. When he accepted the 1968 Nobel Prize for Literature, novelist Yasunari Kawabata described *The Tale of Genji* as "the highest pinnacle of Japanese literature."

## 5. FIRST, FIRST EDITIONS

Before the invention of printing, each copy of a bound paper book was laboriously written out. In Europe, it could take 20 years for a monk to handwrite a single copy of the Bible. With movable type, a printer can reuse characters or letters, set them up in lines or pages, and print material much faster. In the 13th century, Koreans invented movable type made of durable metal. The oldest existing book made from movable metal type is the Jikji, a collection of Buddhist teachings, hymns, eulogies, and poetry. The Jikji was compiled by a Korean monk named Baegun and printed in 1377.

Around 1440, a German goldsmith named Johannes Gutenberg invented his own printing system using metal movable type. He also set up a mechanical printing press for mass production. Gutenberg's press produced the first of about 180 printed copies of the Bible. Known as the Gutenberg Bible, or the 42-line Bible, it was the world's first mass-produced book.

Plymouth colonists John Alden and Priscilla Mullins had ten children.

The printing run for the Gutenberg Bible was finished around 1455. Each Bible contained 1,272 pages and was printed in a typeface designed to resemble handwriting. In most copies, the headings before each book of the Bible were blank spaces, which allowed the owner to add headings decorated by hand. All 180 copies were sold, and fans like Pope Pius II marveled at how easy they were to read—even without glasses! Today, 21 complete Gutenberg Bibles are known to exist.

## 6. FIRST CREEPY CASTLE

If you're a fan of novels and movies where the nights are stormy, moonlight gleams on spooky castle turrets, heavy door hinges creak, and desperate heroines run along gloomy passages to escape powerful, aristocratic villains, then you owe thanks to Horace Walpole, the inventor of the Gothic novel.

In 1764, Walpole published *The Castle of Otranto, A Story Translated by William Marshal, Gent. From the Original Italian of Onuphrio Muralto, Canon of the Church of St. Nicholas at Otranto.* That not-so-succinct title was Walpole's attempt to give added romance by pretending the book was from a 1529 Italian manuscript. This proved to be good marketing. Critics and the public alike loved *The Castle of Otranto.*

When the truth came out, critics were infuriated, but the popularity of Walpole's style of bloodcurdling romance endured. His influence led, for example, to Bram Stoker's *Dracula* (1897) and Daphne Du Maurier's *Rebecca* (1938), and laid the foundation for the long careers of horror actors such as Vincent Price and Bela Lugosi.

## 7. FIRST BRILLIANT DETECTIVE

In 1841, the world of literature changed forever when Edgar Allan Poe's short story "The Murders in the Rue Morgue" was published in *Graham's Magazine.* The story told of a puzzling murder mystery solved by a Parisian detective, C. Auguste Dupin.

"The Murders in the Rue Morgue" wasn't the earliest murder mystery, though. "Three Apples" is a story from the *Arabian Nights* that dates back to the 10th century. However, in "Three Apples," the detective does no investigation and the crime is solved only through luck and coincidence. Auguste Dupin—who was based on the 19th century's most famous sleuth, Eugene François Vidocq—is an active detective who uses his powers of observation and deduction to solve baffling crimes.

Readers were taken with the character of Dupin, and he appeared twice more: in "The Mystery of Marie Rogêt" (1842) and "The Purloined Letter" (1844). But authors were even more impressed. "The Murders in the Rue Morgue" launched an entire genre of detective fiction. Dupin became the forerunner of other brilliant fictional investigators, including Sherlock Holmes and Hercule Poirot.

## 8. FIRST BOOK PUBLISHED FROM A TYPEWRITTEN MANUSCRIPT (SORT OF)

In 1905, Samuel Clemens, better known as Mark Twain, announced that he was the first "to apply the typemachine to literature." Twain bought one of the earliest typewriters invented, a Remington No. 1, in 1874, and used it to pound out the first typed manuscript. Twain published *The Adventures of Tom Sawyer* in 1876, first in Britain and then in the United States.

With all the controversy surrounding most literary firsts, it's refreshing to have a written claim of being "first" from the author himself. Unfortunately, Twain had written earlier that he stopped using his typewriter in 1875 because whenever he typed a letter, all anyone cared about was his newfangled machine. Twain had even given "the little joker" away twice, only to have it returned to him.

Typewriting historian Darryl Rehr found that Twain's first typewritten submission (typed by Twain's secretary) was actually *Life on the Mississippi*, a novel based on his experiences as a riverboat captain; it was not published until 1882. Literary historians did their own checking and backed up Rehr's research. But was *Life on the Mississippi* the first-ever typewritten submission to be published? Actually, publishers, not authors, knew which typed manuscript was the first they'd ever published, and no publisher ever recorded that information. Still, despite his grumbling, Twain was a typing pioneer and many believe he did, indeed, produce the first typewritten manuscript.

# LUCKY FINDS

*Just the artifacts, ma'am.*

Some of the best finds in history have been the result of happy accidents. Here's our list of what we consider the most fabulous and fortuitous finds of all time.

## 1. THE TERRA-COTTA WARRIORS

**The Find:** While digging a well near Xian, China, in March 1974, a group of farmers struck what they thought was an oddly shaped rock. The rock turned out to be a life-size clay statue of a man's head with his hair in a topknot.

**What's the Big Deal?** The farmers had accidentally unearthed the first of an estimated 8,000 life-size armed warriors, chariots, charioteers, horses, and a cache of swords and spears buried and forgotten for more than 2,200 years. The find was the terra-cotta army of China's first emperor, Qin Shi Huang, who died in 210 BC. It's believed that the army was built to guard the mausoleum, one mile away. In the practice of the day, the emperor's childless concubines and all of the artisans who'd constructed the mausoleum were killed and buried with him. Although the tomb was mentioned in the works of a Chinese historian writing 100 years after the emperor's death, the army of figures was not.

**Where to See for Yourself:** Three excavations have been enclosed as museums where visitors can walk around and above the already-excavated pits and even watch the white-coated museum staff at work restoring the figures. The emperor's tomb is still to be excavated.

## 2. THE ROSETTA STONE

**The Find:** One of the most important finds in archaeology was discovered in August 1799 by soldiers in Napoléon Bonaparte's army in Egypt. The soldiers were either demolishing an old wall to extend a fort or digging a trench (the stories vary) near the town of Rosetta when they uncovered a smooth, black lump of basalt. Fortunately, Napoléon's army included a team of traveling scholars who recognized that the inscriptions on the stone were in three different languages—Greek, hieroglyphics, and demotic script (a writing system derived from hieroglyphics).

**What's the Big Deal?** In 1802, the Greek was translated as a decree by priests praising the pharaoh Ptolemy V, who reigned from 205 BC to 180 BC, but the other markings on the stone were a mystery. Hieroglyphics hadn't been used since the fourth century AD, and no one knew how to read them until they were deciphered by French linguist Jean-François Champollion, who worked on the task for 20 years. Working independently, Thomas Young, an English physicist, determined that the names of pharaohs were circled, and he was able to translate the name "Ptolemy" phonetically. Later, Champollion solved the rest of the stone, determining that some signs were alphabetic, some phonetic, and some symbols were translated as whole ideas. Without the Rosetta stone, the translation of ancient Egyptian hieroglyphics would have remained a mystery and much of what we now know about ancient Egypt's history and culture would have remained a mystery.

**Where to See for Yourself:** The Rosetta stone passed into British hands after the French surrender of Egypt in 1801. It now resides in the British Museum in London.

## 3. THE LASCAUX CAVES

**The Find:** There was a legend in the Dordogne region of France about a tunnel deep in the woods leading to a hidden treasure. In September 1940, four young boys and their dog, Robot, set out to find it. Robot ran ahead and began to sniff at a deep hole hidden in the undergrowth. Thinking this was the tunnel to the treasure, the boys lowered themselves down. What they found was a treasure of a different kind. The tunnel was an entrance to a cave complex, the upper walls and ceiling of which was covered with huge bulls painted in brilliant tones of red, black, and brown. Other rooms were painted with prehistoric horses, cats, and even rhinos.

**What's the Big Deal?** The boys had discovered the best prehistoric cave paintings ever found before or since: images of animals that lived 15,000 years ago. The Lascaux caves came to be known as the Sistine Chapel of prehistoric art. Scientists believe that the

---

In 1931, Jane Addams became the first American woman to win the Nobel Prize for Peace.

paintings were done to pass on information rather than for decoration, as there is no evidence that humans ever lived in the caves.

**Where to See for Yourself:** The boys had begun giving tours in 1940, but it wasn't until 1948 that the caves were officially opened to the public. By 1963, the caves were closed again because of the damage caused by light, algae, bacteria, and tourists. A replica, painted by a local artist and called "Lascaux II," was opened to the public in 1983. One of the boys who found the caves was so devoted to the cave complex and its paintings that he guarded the entrance to the caves day and night and eventually became the chief guide to the caves until his death in 1989.

## 4. THE TOMB OF QUEEN HETEPHERES

**The Find:** In 1925, a photographer traveling with an American Egyptologist was setting up his tripod in Giza, Egypt, near the Great Pyramid of Khufu when the legs of the tripod sank into a hidden shaft. The shaft was the entrance to an underground staircase that led to another, vertical shaft that had been filled with limestone to protect the tomb beneath it from grave robbers. It took archaeologists 10 years to excavate the shaft.

**What's the Big Deal?** When they entered the tomb, they found it filled with beautiful gilded wooden furniture and 20 silver bracelets inlaid with turquoise, lapis lazuli, and carnelian—some of the finest examples of ancient Egyptian jewelry and furniture ever found. Inscriptions showed that the tomb was for Queen Hetepheres, mother of the pharaoh Khufu, and while filled with treasure, the sarcophagus was empty, a mystery that archaeologists have never been able to explain. King Khufu's mummy's mummy was gone.

**Where to See for Yourself:** The precious artifacts were divvied up between Cairo's Egyptian Museum and Boston's Museum of Fine Arts.

## 5. THE DEAD SEA SCROLLS

**The Find:** The western shore of the Dead Sea is desolate and remote, just the sort of area a goat smuggler needed to avoid customs officers. In 1947, a Bedouin boy herding contraband goats lost one and scrambled up a cliff to search for it. Instead, he discovered a long-lost cave.

**What's the Big Deal?** Hidden in the cave in ancient pottery jars were texts written on papyrus and animal hides that experts determined dated back to between 200 BC and AD 100. More explorations were done and eventually over 800 scrolls were found in 11 caves in the area of Qumran, now part of Palestine's West Bank. They contained nearly all the books of the Bible, the only known surviving biblical documents written before AD 100. The find confirmed the accuracy of the transmission of the biblical texts over thousands of years. The caves had once been a base for Jewish resistance against the Romans, and the Dead Sea Scrolls, preserved by the extremely dry conditions, had remained hidden there for around 2,000 years.

**Where to See for Yourself:** Most of the fragments of the Dead Sea Scrolls are preserved in the Shrine of the Book, a wing of the Israel Museum in Jerusalem.

\*      \*      \*

## WEIRD NAMES FOR UNDERWEAR

**1. Singlet:** British term for sleeveless underwear; the word refers to the fact that the item is made of only one thickness of cloth. ("Doublet" refers to a lined jacket—or two thicknesses of cloth.)

**2. Union Suit:** Comes from the fact that the upper shirt and lower drawers were "united" in one garment.

**3. Knickers:** British term for underwear. It comes from "knickerbockers"—short knee britches worn by New York's early Dutch settlers. The Dutch came to be known as Knickerbockers, and eventually that became shorthand for New Yorkers. (Later, it would be shortened to Knicks for the city's basketball team.)

**4. Cutty Sark:** "Cutty" used to mean "short"; a "sark" was a shirt—hence a short shirt became a skimpy nightgown.

**5. Pretties:** This term used for dainty lingerie dates back to the 1700s.

**6. Tap Pants:** Named after the loose, boxerlike pants worn by tap dancers.

**7. Merry Widow:** Inspired by a strapless corset worn by actress Lana Turner in the 1952 musical of the same name.

---

*...But then came World War II.*

# WITHOUT A TRACE

*How does someone vanish into thin*
*air, never to be heard from again?*

Here we present five of our favorite stories of people who disappeared without a trace, and the endless speculation and countless theories that attempt to answer the question of "What the heck happened?"

## 1. AMBROSE BIERCE (1842–?)

Newspaper columnist and author Ambrose Bierce was a cynic and a curmudgeon, not someone who made friends easily. After fighting for the Union in the Civil War, Bierce headed west and wound up in California, where he took a job at the U.S. Mint in San Francisco. Although he traveled widely—including an extended stay in England, where he made a living as a writer— he was always most closely associated with San Francisco, especially when he went to work for William Randolph Hearst's newspaper, the *San Francisco Examiner*. It was on the pages of the *Examiner* that Bierce's famous short story "An Occurrence at Owl Creek Bridge" was published in 1890; Kurt Vonnegut later called it the greatest American short story ever written.

**A Popular Unpopular Guy.** Hearst actively courted Bierce for the job at the newspaper, and gave him editorial control of his articles: Bierce wrote what he wanted, the way he wanted to write. He skewered politicians, the social elite, and other writers, and generally proved to be a thorn in everyone's side. His writing also gained him a legion of admirers who were distressed—but perhaps not surprised—when he disappeared in 1914.

**A Few Clues.** Bierce had left for Mexico in 1913 hoping to meet with Pancho Villa, leader of the rebel forces during the Mexican Revolution. One tribute to Bierce in the *New York Times* following his disappearance said that he went to Mexico with the intention of fighting in the war. But he would have been 71 years old at the time; presumably his fighting days were behind him. Certainly, he would have sent letters to his family and his secretary—he was a devoted correspondent—and he would have cashed the royalty checks his publisher sent while he traveled. So when no one had heard from him for nine months after his last letter, Ambrose Bierce was said to be missing and presumed dead.

**Not-So-Famous Last Words.** "I leave here tomorrow for an unknown destination" is the much-quoted last line of Bierce's last letter to a friend, mailed on December 26, 1913. But his letter to his niece Lora on October 1 of that year might be more revealing: "Good-bye—if you hear of my being stood up against a Mexican stone wall and shot to rags, please know that I think that a pretty good way to depart this life. It beats old age, disease, or falling down the cellar stairs."

## 2. RAOUL WALLENBERG (1912–?)

A Swedish diplomat who was directly responsible for saving the lives of tens of thousands of Jews during World War II, Raoul Wallenberg disappeared without a trace in 1945. His abduction and death were among the great tragedies of the war and its aftermath, and despite continuing attempts to discover the truth, the question surrounding his last days has never been resolved.

**Doing Good Works.** Working on behalf of the War Refugee Board, which was created by U.S. president Franklin D. Roosevelt and implemented with the help of the Swedish government, Wallenberg went to Hungary in 1944. By then, more than two-thirds of Hungary's Jews had been deported or killed by the Nazis, but there was still time to protect those living in the capital of Budapest, and that's what Wallenberg managed to do. He set up shelters for displaced people and orphaned children; arranged for identity papers and passports that protected people from harassment by the Nazis or allowed them to flee to safety; and kept the Nazis at bay thanks to his status as a Swedish government official.

**A Diplomat Without Immunity.** In January 1945, when it became clear that a German surrender was imminent and that the Soviet Union would enter Hungary to "liberate" it, Wallenberg approached Soviet officials to negotiate for the protection of the Hungarian Jews he had saved. He was last seen in the company of Soviet soldiers on January 17—the Soviet government would later contend that they were protecting Wallenberg, until it became clear that they had in fact arrested him on suspicion of being an

American spy and transported him to Lubyanka, the KGB's prison in Moscow.

**A Mess of Contradictions.** Halfhearted negotiations began for Wallenberg's release and continued until 1957, at which point the Soviet Union claimed that Wallenberg had died of a heart attack in prison 10 years earlier. The report was accepted at face value and official inquiries ended, even though Sweden was still very suspicious. Later, the Soviets said that Wallenberg had been shot in prison. In 2000, when Russia opened its KGB files, Swedish and Russian researchers tried to find out what really happened. Their findings were inconclusive, but there was reason to suspect that Wallenberg might have been alive as late as 1989.

### 3. KING EDWARD V OF ENGLAND (1470–?) AND RICHARD, DUKE OF YORK (1473–?)

King Richard III ruled England for just two years—from 1483 until his death in 1485 at the Battle of Bosworth Field. He'd succeeded to the throne on the death of his brother King Edward IV, but Richard wasn't supposed to become king of England; he was supposed to serve as lord protector for the true successor to the throne, Edward IV's son (and Richard's nephew) Prince Edward, who was just 12 when his father died.

**Coronation Canceled.** Young Prince Edward was on his way from Wales to London, where he was to be crowned king. Along the way he was met by representatives of his uncle, who took him to the Tower of London. The young prince assumed he was to await his coronation there. Not long after, his brother Richard was sent to join him in the Tower. The two princes were never released, and what happened to them remains a mystery that has puzzled scholars for centuries.

**The Kids Are Not All Right.** It's generally agreed that both princes were murdered in the Tower of London, but who actually committed the crime—or gave the order to do so—is still up for debate. Richard III is the likeliest suspect, but there are others. How and when the princes were killed is also in question. In 1674, two partial skeletons that were discovered in the tower were assumed to be the bones of the princes, but experts have never been able to positively identify them.

---

**August 6, 1991: The first Web site, built at CERN in Switzerland, went online.**

## 4. EVERETT RUESS (1914–?)

Everett Ruess was just a teenager when he left his family home in California and began wandering around the southwestern United States. He wrote, sketched, took photographs, and just generally absorbed the unspoiled landscape around him. Occasionally he'd return home and use his sketches and photos as the basis for linoleum block prints that he'd sell to finance his next journey. He was young and optimistic, and his letters to his parents and brother made it sound as if nothing made him happier than wandering through the desert. Then in 1934, Ruess disappeared in Utah and was never heard from again.

**Skeleton #1.** To this day, no one is sure what happened to him, but the mystery has made the vibrant, talented Everett Ruess a folk hero. In 2008, when an elderly Navajo man admitted he'd witnessed a young man being murdered in the desert back in 1934 and that he'd buried the body, historians, archaeologists, forensic scientists, and mystery lovers thought they'd finally found the secret of Everett Ruess's disappearance. They uncovered a skeleton that matched Ruess's age, height, and body type at the time of his disappearance, but DNA tests proved that the skeleton wasn't Ruess after all.

**Skeleton #2.** Ruess's whereabouts remain a mystery, but his story continues to inspire: paleontologists working in the Utah desert in 2010 unearthed the skeleton of a new species of dinosaur. They christened it *Seitaad ruessi* for the Navajo Seit'aad (a legendary desert monster) and for the man who wandered off into the desert decades ago.

## 5. HAROLD HOLT (1908–?)

Thousands of people swim in the rampant surf on Australia's beaches, and dozens of them drown every year. But when one of the suspected drowning victims is the Australian prime minister and his body is never recovered, it makes headlines. Such was the case of Harold Holt, who had served as prime minister for less than two years when he waded into the rough surf at Cheviot Beach near Melbourne and was never seen again.

**Wet and Wild.** Holt was an experienced snorkeler but not a par-

---

In 1868, Alvin J. Fellows patented the modern spring-type tape measure.

ticularly powerful swimmer and suffered from a shoulder injury. Nevertheless, his disappearance on December 17, 1967, was surprising. A dashing, athletic man, Holt loved the outdoor life and the ladies (among those accompanying him that fateful weekend was a woman who later admitted she was his mistress). Almost immediately, theories began to spread. Some believed Holt faked his death so he could run away with his mistress, but there was no evidence that Holt had any intention of leaving his wife, family, and career.

**Theories Abound.** One explanation was that Holt had committed suicide, although why he would have done so was up for debate. Another theory held that Holt was murdered by the CIA because he'd threatened to withdraw Australian troops from Vietnam. But Holt had actually increased Australia's participation in the war. Even less plausible was the one that conspiracy theorists still cling to: that Holt was leading a double life as a communist spy and made his way out to sea, where he was picked up by a Chinese submarine and taken away to Beijing. And we hesitate to mention the UFO abduction theory. (Yes, there was one.)

**Case Closed.** Various theories persist, but a coroner's report in 2005 officially closed the case, declaring that Harold Holt's death was the result of accidental drowning. Holt has been memorialized in many ways, but none quite so ironic as the Harold Holt Memorial Swim Centre near Melbourne, which was under construction when he disappeared.

\*     \*     \*

## ONE MYSTERY SOLVED

Lisa Lindahl, a student at the University of Vermont, liked to jog—up to 30 miles a week. But she had a problem—her bra was not holding up. She and some friends came up with the idea of sewing two jockstraps together. Eureka! The sports bra was born and a year later Lindsay and her friends founded Jogbra in 1977.

---

Multiple birth is a regular phenomenon in Kodinija, India...

# WHAT A WAY TO GO

*Not everybody goes out in a blaze
of glory. Some people die for
the most pointless reasons.*

As anyone who's ever made a list will tell you, when your number's up, your number's up. No matter how famous or powerful you are.

## 1. DOES THIS FISH TASTE FUNNY?
## KING HENRY I OF ENGLAND (D. 1135)

England's King Henry I was crowned in 1100. He was popular with the people, especially the ladies, fathering at least 20 illegitimate children through his many mistresses. He found food hard to resist, too: even though his doctors had warned him not to consume one of his favorite foods, sea lampreys, which can be toxic, the king threw caution to the wind and wolfed down a large meal of the fatty fish one evening. He consequently suffered food poisoning, became feverish, and never recovered.

## 2. JUST ONE MORE TWINKIE:
## KING ADOLF FREDERICK OF SWEDEN (D. 1771)

By the time Adolf Frederick became king of Sweden in 1751, much of the government's power lay in the hands of the parliament. Despite being little more than a figurehead, Adolf Frederick was considered a kind and caring man. And like most kings, he liked his sumptuous meals—and who was going to say, "Hold on there, King" to a king, anyway? So one night, the king sat down to a rich meal of lobster, caviar, sauerkraut, herring, and champagne. Still not satisfied, he polished it all off with 14 cream-filled pastries for dessert. Maybe he should have stopped at 13—who knows?—but all that food gave him such severe indigestion that he died soon after. In Sweden, he's remembered as "the king who ate himself to death."

---

**...The village is home to more than 204 pairs of twins.**

### 3. "OW, MY @#$%^&* TOE!"
### JACK DANIEL (D. 1911)

Jack Daniel was just a teenager when he bought a distillery from Reverend Dan Call in 1863 after the reverend's wife persuaded the preacher to give up the evils of alcohol. Daniel went on to perfect his sour-mash process from there. In 1905, the 60-year old master distiller was in his office trying to open his safe, but couldn't remember the combination. Out of frustration, he kicked the safe, crushing his big toe. The toe became gangrenous, which brought on a slow accumulation of blood poisoning. The infection caused Daniel's health to slowly decline over the next six years until it eventually killed him. His last words were reportedly, "One last drink, please."

### 4. NO ESCAPE:
### HARRY HOUDINI (D. 1926)

The 52-year-old escape artist was resting after a show in Montreal when he was approached by a local university student who asked if it was true that he could absorb any blow to his body above the waist. Houdini said yes, but before he could tighten his stomach, the student delivered a series of punches that left the performer writhing on the floor. Houdini had been suffering from appendicitis for a few days, but had refused treatment. The punches ruptured Houdini's appendix, which caused peritonitis (stomach inflammation). In Detroit a week later, Houdini's temperature reached 104°F and he passed out while onstage; he was revived, finished the show, and was then rushed to the hospital, where he died.

### 5. DEATH BY MARTINI:
### SHERWOOD ANDERSON (D. 1941)

The author of the classic *Winesburg, Ohio*, had a brief but influential literary career. After publishing his first novel in 1916 at age 40, he wrote more than two dozen novels, memoirs, and short-story collections. Only one of his books, *Dark Laughter* (1926), was a best seller, but other writers like John Steinbeck and William Faulkner considered Anderson an important influence. The 64-year-old Anderson was on a cruise to Panama when he died: an autopsy revealed that a three-inch toothpick—which had been in the olive of a martini and which he'd swallowed by accident several days earlier—had penetrated his abdominal cavity by way of his colon, resulting in a fatal case of peritonitis (see Houdini).

## 6. THAT'S JUST SWELL: BRUCE LEE (D. 1973)

Martial artist and world-famous actor Bruce Lee was renowned for his dedication to physical fitness. But nothing could have prepared him for what happened in Hong Kong in 1973. While working on the movie *Enter the Dragon*, he experienced seizures and headaches due to a cerebral edema, or swelling of the brain. Doctors managed to reduce the swelling, but two months later Lee experienced further headaches and was given Equagesic, a powerful aspirin and muscle relaxant, by a coworker. He fell into a coma that night and never woke up. Doctors determined that he had died of a second cerebral edema, caused by an allergic reaction to the aspirin.

\*　　\*　　\*

## JUST THE FACTS

• In the Middle Ages belts were a status symbol—the quality of the jewels and the type of metal used to make them were indicative of the wearer's wealth.

• Abercrombie and Fitch was founded in 1892 as a camping supply store. Back in the day it outfitted Theodore Roosevelt for an African safari and Charles Lindbergh for his historic flight across the Atlantic Ocean.

• A chef's toque has more than 100 folds on it. These are said to represent the number of ways a skilled chef should know how to prepare an egg.

• The original Burberry trench coat was made of gabardine and appeared in World War I.

# HISTORY MNEMONICS

*Most people have heard the following ditty to remember when
Columbus arrived in North America: "In fourteen hundred
and ninety-two, Columbus sailed the ocean blue." Here
are some more history mnemonics to help you out.*

Before humans had printing presses or even a written language
and an alphabet, they needed to be able to record history
and conduct business. So people relied on passing down
their histories via stories and legends. Another device they used
was *mnemonics*—catchy rhymes used to store a lot of data in their
heads for easy recall. Here are some fun ones:

### 1. ALASKA AND HAWAII GAIN STATEHOOD
*"Fifty-nine was the date,
when Alaska and Hawaii became new states."*

### 2. THE FIRST 14 U.S. PRESIDENTS
*"When a joke made me a joker,
Van had to poke the fiery poker."*

(For: Washington, Adams, Jefferson, Madison, Monroe,
[Quincy] Adams, Jackson, Van Buren, Harrison, Tyler, Polk,
Taylor, Filmore, Pierce)

### 3. IMPORTANT DATES DURING THE CIVIL WAR
*In 1861, the war begun.
In 1862, the bullets flew.
In 1863, Lincoln set slaves free.
In 1864, there still was a war.
In 1865, hardly a manwais still alive.*

### 4. THE FIRST SUCCESSFUL FLIGHT OF THE WRIGHT BROTHERS
*"In 1903, the Wright brothers flew free."*

---

**In the ninth century, Baghdad's streets were paved with tar.**

# GREAT LOVE AFFAIRS

*Romeo and Juliet. Tristan and Isolde. Paris and Helen. Odysseus and Penelope. When you think of great love stories, these couplings represent literary masterpieces. But true life isn't far off. And when love is in the air, life often imitates art.*

We at the BRI allowed ourselves to become a little misty-eyed trolling through the history books to rank what we believe are a few of the best true love stories of all time. Drum roll, please...

## UNCLE CUPID'S NUMBER 1

**Anthony & Cleopatra.** He was the ruler of the Roman Empire in 41 BC. She was the Queen of Egypt. He was handsome, virile, and ambitious. She wasn't particularly attractive but intelligent, witty, and ambitious. The two met in Turkey to firm up a political alliance to assert control over the Mediterranean and Rome. He fell in love and followed her back to Egypt. Cleopatra, former mistress of Julius Caesar until his assassination in Rome three years earlier, and Mark Anthony made a power couple that posed a threat to Gaius Octavian, Caesar's grand-nephew, who wanted to be supreme ruler of the empire. He was angry also that Anthony had left his wife, Octavian's sister Octavia, for the devious Egyptian temptress. So he declared war on both.

Octavian's naval fleet defeated the combined fleet of Anthony and Cleopatra in the Battle of Actium off western Greece in 31 BC, then chased the couple back to Egypt. Anthony, on receiving a false report that Cleo had committed suicide rather than be taken prisoner, was grief-stricken and stabbed himself with a sword. His men carried him to the queen, where he died in her arms. Taken prisoner, she smuggled a poisonous snake into her cell, where it delivered the fatal strike. Cleopatra and Anthony were buried together as Octavian consolidated control of the empire.

## UNCLE CUPID'S NUMBER 2

**Prince Edward & Wallis Simpson.** He was the Prince of Wales,

---

In 1902, Barnum Brown found the first *Tyrannosaurus rex* fossil in Hell Creek, Montana.

handsome, debonaire, and—most important—heir to the British throne in the early 1930s. She was a married American socialite. It was a love that grew over time, as both traveled in the same social circles. Slowly, she charmed the prince and finally separated from her husband in 1934. When the king died in 1936, the subject of Edward's ascendancy to the throne created a media frenzy because of his liaison with Wallis. The fact that she was American made such a union impossible if Edward were to be king. Subsequently, he abdicated the throne in a radio broadcast while confessing his inability to be king "without the woman I love."

Edward's younger brother became King George VI. Edward was forced to relinquish his title of Prince of Wales and step down to Duke of Windsor. However, the new King George made sure his brother forever would be addressed as "His Royal Highness" in the presence of others. As for Edward and Wallis, she divorced her husband in 1937 and married Edward in a modest ceremony. The two resided the rest of their lives in France.

## UNCLE CUPID'S NUMBER 3

**Charles Lindbergh & Anne Spencer Morrow.** In 1927, young and handsome Charles Lindbergh became the most famous aviator in history by making the first solo, nonstop flight across the Atlantic Ocean. At the time, Anne Spencer was an extremely shy, self-conscious daughter of the U.S. ambassador to Mexico. On a goodwill tour of Latin America after his historic flight, Charles met Anne and began seeing her, the beginning of a storybook romance. Their courtship made headlines wherever they went.

Married in 1929, they became the most engaging couple in America. Not only did they love each other, the couple loved to fly. Under Charles's tutelage, Anne became the first licensed female glider pilot in the United States. The two stormed the country, charting air routes for future commercial airlines. They also set an air speed record by flying cross-country from Los Angles to New York in 1930—when Anne was seven months pregnant. Later, Charles encouraged Anne to write memoirs of their life together, turning that talent into 13 books that became best sellers. Though both had short-lived affairs with others and endured the kidnapping and murder of their son in 1932, they remained largely devoted to one another throughout their lives.

---

**What are those stars on the Hollywood Walk of Fame made of? Terrazzo and brass.**

## UNCLE CUPID'S NUMBER 4

**Napoléon and Josephine.** At the end of the 16th century, Napoléon Bonaparte was a rising young officer in the French military when he met and was smitten by beautiful Parisian socialite Josephine de Beauharnais. However, the 32-year-old widowed mother of two remained aloof from Napoléon's approaches. Who could blame her? Napoléon was short, unkempt, and rather homely, hardly Europe's babe magnet. Yet his genius for military strategy and his quick ascent in the military had its attractions. By 1796, Josephine had come around and married the hard-charging amour who would leave Paris shortly after their honeymoon for a series of military campaigns.

It was during this time that Josephine entered a series of adulterous affairs. Napoléon was alerted to what was happening back home and confronted his wife, demanding a divorce. She, however, begged forgiveness and he relented. Crowned emperor of France in 1804, Napoléon desired a son. When Josephine was unable to do so, he divorced her in 1809 to marry Austria's Marie Louise, 18, who bore him a son. A series of stinging military defeats afterward weakened Napoléon, who fell from grace and was exiled to the island of Elba in 1814. Josephine, saddened by her failed marriage and his exile, begged to join him. Napoléon replied that it was impossible but the letter didn't arrive in time. Josephine had died. Escaping Elba in 1815, Napoléon returned to Paris and sought out Josephine's physicians, who told him she had died of a broken heart. Aggrieved, the ex-emperor went to Josephine's garden, where he picked violets that he wore in a locket until his death in 1821.

## UNCLE CUPID'S NUMBER 5

**Catherine the Great & Grigory Potemkin.** In 1762, she was the wife of Russian czar Peter III. He was an imperial soldier whose duty was to guard the czarina. By all accounts, Catherine the Great was intelligent, attractive, ruthless, and sexually insatiable with many lovers, even during her marriage to Peter. One of her amours was Grigory Potemkin, who was tall with a handsome face but also obese, vain, and missing an eye. Nevertheless, the stars aligned for the couple. The czar was overthrown by a coup led by Potemkin and army loyalists. Though Peter III abdicated, he was assassinated eight days later on orders believed to hve been issued by his wife. Moving quickly, Catherine declared herself empress and bound herself closely to Potemkin.

Catherine's love for Grigory deepened as their affair continued for 14 years. During that time, she made him an official Russian statesman, a count, and the commander of her armies. Meanwhile, she helped Westernize Russia by establishing warm relations with Prussia, France, and Austria. When Potemkin died at age 52 in 1791, Catherine the Great went into deep mourning at the separation from her one true love. She continued to be lovesick the rest of her life, which ended in 1796.

\*     \*     \*

## PLASTIC SURGERY THE EARLY YEARS

Medieval people lost body parts and limbs to syphilis, battle, and everyday accidents. Italian physician Gaspare Tagliacozzi was taken with the idea that syphilitics, who commonly lost noses to the disease, might overcome the disfigurement through surgery. Tagliacozzi experimented unsuccessfully with moving skin to the face from other parts of his patients' bodies. Finally he hit on the idea of moving the skin slowly by attaching the arm to the face until the new blood supply was established. Although patients had to endure the indignity of having their arms strapped to their faces for two to three weeks, it worked. Tagliacozzi wrote a book on repairing facial features and he was a hero…for a time. After his death in 1599, the Italian Church accused him of practicing magic, but he was acquitted.

It's surprising that later physicians didn't heed the advice and work of Tagliacozzi in their zeal to enhance the appearance of their patients. Instead of adapting and perfecting his work, doctors used ivory, tree sap, celluloid, metal, animal skin, cartilage, and paraffin to repair human bodies, all to no avail and sometimes to the detriment and death of their patients. During World War I, physicians returned to Tagliacozzi's methods to repair devastating war wounds. Because of the skin-grafting skills and knowledge that doctors gained during this time, it was a short step from repairing wartime wounds to ridding people of their wrinkles.

# ART HISTORY 101

*Uncle John continues his review of historic works
of art that you should be familiar with.*

## 1. FOLLOW THE DOTS

### *A Sunday Afternoon on the Island of La Grande Jatte*

**Artist:** Georges Seurat

**Where:** The Art Institute, Chicago, Illinois

**Medium:** Oil on canvas

**Appearance:** Painted in Seurat's signature pointillist style (the technique of using dots of color instead of brushstrokes), a crowd of Parisians in their Sunday best—ladies in long dresses with bustles and carrying parasols, men in top hats—enjoy a sunny day in the park. It's a biggie: 6 feet 10 inches tall by 10 feet 1 inch wide, which is probably why it took Seurat from 1884 to 1886 to finish it. All those dots! (Estimated at more than three million.)

**Details of Interest:**

• Stephen Sondheim wrote a musical based on the painting called *Sunday in the Park with George.*

• Another of those easily parodied artworks, versions of it have appeared in *Die Hard with a Vengeance, Ferris Bueller's Day Off*, and a Bugs Bunny cartoon in which Elmer Fudd chases Bugs and Daffy Duck into the painting and emerges as a pointillist version of himself. Bugs, of course, takes out a fan and blows Elmer Fudd away.

## 2. SOME ENCHANTED EVENING

### *The Starry Night*

**Artist:** Vincent van Gogh

**Where:** Not the Van Gogh Museum in Amsterdam, but New York's Museum of Modern Art, which acquired it through a bequest in 1941.

**Medium:** Oil on canvas

**Appearance:** The night sky over a little village is filled with swirls of blue and white-yellow clouds, blazing stars, and a bright crescent moon. In the left foreground is a dark green cypress tree

---

Tally's Electric Theater in Los Angeles became the first permanent movie house in 1902.

like a flame. The canvas is smallish (29 inches high by 36 inches wide), but van Gogh packed a lot of emotion (okay, lunacy) into the space.

**Details of Interest:**

• Painted during the artist's official crazy period, *The Starry Night* is among the 142 paintings van Gogh worked on while staying in an insane asylum in Saint-Rémy-de-Provence in 1889–90. The artist voluntarily committed himself there just after the ear-cutting incident in Arles. He stayed for one year and, during his lucid moments, produced some of his best work.

• The painting inspired Don McLean to write the song "Vincent" in 1970.

### 3. I'M OK, YOU'RE OK, BUT HE'S NOT

*The Scream*

**Artist:** Edvard Munch

**Where:** The National Gallery, Oslo, Norway

**Medium:** Oil, tempera, and pastel on cardboard

**Appearance:** A strange-looking sexless figure stands, mouth open in an agonized scream, next to a wavy blue bay with a wavy red sky overhead. Munch fooled around with a few other versions in various sizes and mediums; this one—painted in 1893—is 36 inches high by 29 inches wide.

**Details of Interest:**

• Munch wrote that the image was inspired by a real event: while walking with some friends at sunset, he observed a red sky and was overcome with anxiety. Which kind of makes it a self-portrait, although some art scholars think that the screamer was inspired by mummies that Munch could have seen in Paris or Florence.

• The painting was stolen from Oslo's National Gallery in February 1994, when everyone's attention was focused some 100 miles away in Lillehammer on the opening day of the Winter Olympics. The four thieves left a note that read, "Thanks for the poor security." The painting was recovered the following May.

• The killer in Wes Craven's fright flick *Scream* wears a mask based on *The Scream*.

# THE FIGHT CLUB

*Uncle John looks at five ancient fight
clubs to determine the winning
warrior in a mythical contest.*

I f you pitted a Spartan, a gladiator, a samurai, a ninja, and a
knight against each other, who would win? In our showdown,
we've resurrected five famous battlefield heroes to help us figure
out who among them would be the fight club champ of all time.

## 1. THE SPARTAN: KING LEONIDAS

**Origin:** King Lycurgus transformed the city of Sparta in the seventh century BC from an aristocracy into an oligarchy (government by the few) totally committed to war. The city's one governing principle was that all males would be bred from infancy to fight and die for Sparta. Sickly male babies were left to die; the rest were nurtured until age seven, when they were taken from their mothers to begin military training.

By 500 BC, Sparta had overrun all of its neighbors and secured control of southwest Greece to create an city-state of 25,000 citizens. The warrior-king Leonidas was just the kind of combatant that Lycurgus had envisioned when he founded Sparta.

**Training:** Leonidas grew up under a code of tough discipline, deprivation, and obedience. As children, Spartan males wore no clothes and were starved to encourage them to steal food. Punishment was doled out to those found stealing—not for the act of doing so, but for being caught.

Their training included swimming, running, jumping, wrestling, boxing, and dancing—the latter emphasizing rhythmical movement needed in Sparta's specialized warfare. Every Spartan warrior-in-training was also expected to memorize patriotic ballads to improve his memory. Leonidas became a soldier at age 20, a citizen by 30, and—if he'd survived—would have continued to serve as a warrior until the age of 60. Married or not, all Spartan soldiers were required to live in austere barracks until at least age 30 to create a permanent bond between the men as a fighting unit, and to make them selfless and devoted to defending Sparta to the death.

---

The warriors dined together on a high-protein diet to build strength—often a soup of boiled pig's blood, pork, and vinegar.

**Weapons:** Leonidas's offensive arsenal included a long spear known as a dory, unwieldy except in the hands of the well-trained Spartan. He also carried a short sword for stabbing opponents who got up close and personal. For defense, he wore a leather chest plate covered by a wraparound bronze piece of armor to protect his torso from his neck to his waist, more armor to protect his legs, and a helmet with a crest. He also carried a shield called an aspis that weighed 15 pounds—big enough to carry a wounded comrade off the battlefield and emblazoned with a large "L," the symbol for Laconia, the area of southern Greece that Sparta had conquered.

**Combat Style:** Leonidas was indoctrinated in the unique Spartan technique of mobilizing all warriors in a rectangular mass formation known as a phalanx—tightly bound lines of soldiers protected by their impenetrable shields. The warriors moved forward, smashing enemy lines while thrusting their long spears between the shields to slay the enemy.

**The Fight Stuff:** King Leonidas was famous for his defense against an army of 200,000 Persians led by Emperor Xerxes in 480 BC. Leonidas and 300 Spartans fought to the death at the Battle of Thermopylae. Persians fell in staggering numbers, as their wicker shields and short javelins were no match for Leonidas's Spartan phalanx. However, the king and his 300 Spartans eventually died fighting. Their valiant stand inspired the Greeks, who, at the subsequent Battle of Plataea in 479 BC, avenged the massacre at Thermopylae and drove Xerxes back to Persia permanently.

**Fight Club Advantage:** Leonidas is totally committed to defeating his opponent. There will be no retreat without death. He is well armed, both defensively and offensively, strong and gifted at battlefield tactics. But this time he'll have to do it alone; Spartans believe power came from the group, not the individual.

## 2. THE ROMAN GLADIATOR: FLAMMA THE SYRIAN

**Origin:** Lasting for 700 years, from about 310 BC to the mid-fifth century, the bloody gladiatorial sport began with retribution: slaves, captured soldiers, rebellious leaders from a conquered territory, or criminals faced public execution by being pitted against one another in an arena. As the spectacle increased in popularity, it transformed into a sports enterprise that included public wagers on the outcome. At stake were large bonus purses as well as fame to the victors. A few emperors and even female gladiators fought in the arena for personal glory.

Adored by the public, gladiators shared a brotherhood and worshipped the Roman god Hercules, known for his superhuman strength. Flamma, a captured Syrian, typified the glory that a Roman gladiator could achieve in his lifetime.

**Training:** Flamma was well cared for at state-owned gladiator clubs. He ate three high-protein, high-fat meals a day, and received above-average medical care. Training involved not only how to attack and defend against humans, but also against wild animals that were often brought into the arena by the hundreds in a single day. The regimen included daily practice with all the gladiatorial weapons.

Flamma learned how deal a fatal blow to an opponent—and how to offer himself up for a quick death if defeated. He fought just a few matches a year, each highly publicized beforehand. Gladiators like Flamma got rich by winning, and if they survived three to five years, they could also earn their freedom. They couldn't become citizens of Rome, but their offspring were citizens at birth.

**Weapons:** Flamma had an array of weapons: tridents, javelins, short and long spears and swords, daggers, casting nets, and bows and arrows. He carried a small shield for defense and typically wore the armor of a Syrian soldier to distinguish him as non-Roman and as one of Rome's enemies. As a Syrian, Flamma's weapon of choice was the bow and arrow, along with spears and other weapons to throw at the enemy.

**Combat Style:** An expert at hand-to-hand combat, Flamma fought as a "secutor," or "chaser," a class of gladiator who wore a helmet with two small eyeholes, and was trained to fight a *retiarius*, who was armed with a trident and a net.

**The Fight Stuff:** Flamma was adored by the Roman populace and lived to age 30, old by Roman standards. He fought 34 times, scoring 21 victories, 9 draws, and 4 losses. He earned his right to be a free man four times yet chose to remain a gladiator. His record is engraved on his tombstone in Sicily.

**Fight Club Advantage:** Flamma is trained to use all sorts of weapons, and his career is devoted to performing with cunning and lightning reflexes in a public arena.

## 3. THE SAMURAI: MIYAMOTO MUSAHI

**Origin:** The samurai style of warfare and chivalry rose to prominence around AD 800 but was abolished when Japan became united 1,000 years later. The warriors emerged as the result of nearly continuous land battles between the three main clans of Japan. Samurai were required to fight whenever property rights were at issue between feuding lords. During periods of tranquility, samurai worked on farms and studied military strategy, art, calligraphy, and poetry. By the 1600s, the samurai were at the top of Japan's caste system. Miyamoto Musahi is Japan's most famous samurai.

**Training:** Musahi lived by a code of conduct called *bushido*—the "Way of the Warrior," which emphasized fierce loyalty to a feudal lord (the *daimyo*), rigid self-discipline, ethical behavior, and a philosophy of duty and freedom from fear. Musahi practiced fighting from horseback and on foot, sometimes armed and sometimes not, but preferred fighting on foot so he could wield his swords in one-on-one battles that ended with the beheading of his enemy. To be defeated was unforgivable and required *seppuku*—a ritual suicide performed by slicing the abdomen with a sword.

**Weapons:** Musahi used bows, arrows, spears, and curved-blade swords; his swordsmanship was especially first-rate because of his martial-arts training. He wore two swords called *daisho*, one longer than two feet and the other short. The swords were given names to honor the "souls" within them, made by craftsmen who tested their sharpness and strength by cutting through the bodies of corpses or condemned criminals. Musahi's armor included a helmet to protect his head and neck, a belly wrap, plus chest, arm, and shoulder protectors.

**Combat Style:** Musahi wore brightly colored armor to denote his clan and was trained to announce himself to his enemy before attacking. He preferred to fight on foot, abandoning his horse in favor of close-in battle. He would challenge a single opponent, announce his intention, list his family pedigree, and then attack.

**The Fight Stuff:** Miyamoto Musashi fought and won more than

60 sword fights before he turned 30. He founded the Individual School of Two Skies and taught the samurai code for many years. At 60, he wrote *Gorin No Sho* (The Book of Five Spheres), about the Japanese art of sword fighting.

**Fight Club Advantage:** Musahi's whirling windmill of sword action is second to none.

## 4. THE NINJA: SASUKE SARUTOBI

**Origin:** The ninja was trained as a professional spy in Japan and came to prominence in the 14th century, but most believe the ninja's art of stealth was developed around AD 600–900 by Chinese warrior-monks to oppose the samurai. Japanese clans sent ninjas into enemy territory to gather intelligence and attack at night, stealing enemy stores of food and weapons. Ninjas also served as well-paid assassins. Their power bases at Iga and Koga were destroyed in 1582, and the ninja way of life came to an end in 1603 when peace came to Japan.

Sasuke Sarutobi, also known as "Monkey Jump," was famous for his acrobatic skills as a ninja. Admirers say he lived in trees with monkeys, which made him incredibly fast at dodging, ducking, and jumping out of danger.

**Training:** Under *ninjutsu*, the opposite code to bushido, Sarutobi was schooled to use any means to reach his objective: sneak attacks, poison, even seduction—all were fair game. Female ninjas were just as apt to infiltrate the enemy by posing as concubines, dancers, or servants. Sarutobi was taught by a *jonin*, a disgraced samurai who fled battle rather than commit seppuku. This new form of guerrilla warfare included training in physical fitness, karate, spear fighting, blade throwing, strategy, and concealment.

**Weapons:** Sarutobi's arsenal included medium-length swords, blow darts, and a lance. He also carried *shukos*, iron crampons used for climbing castle walls; and tessens, sharpened, fanlike metal blades thrown with deadly force. Sarutobi was highly trained in martial arts. He was also an expert in the use of poison—either sneaked into an enemy's food or put on the tips of his tessen blades.

**Combat Style:** Like other ninjas, Sarutobi was an acrobat who could jump high, scale walls, dart through forests without being seen, and slither unseen into an enemy camp. His razor-sharp weapons came at his quarry without warning. He wore dark navy blue clothing at night or the same clothing style of his targets if moving among them in daylight.

**The Fight Stuff:** Sasuke Sarutobi was famed for making a successful entry into a well-fortified shogun's castle, where he overheard a plot to attack the lord who had sent him. On trying to leave the castle, he was spotted by guards, who set after him as he fled to the castle wall. There he used a springboard to leap high up on the wall to escape.

**Fight Club Advantage:** Stealth is Sarutobi's greatest asset. He moves like a shadow, the harbinger of death to his enemies.

## 5. THE KNIGHT: GODFREY DE BOUILLON

**Origin:** The word "knight" is derived from *cniht*, the Anglo-Saxon term for "boy." The original knights were hired boys who entered military service in loyalty to a nobleman or warlord who promised cash or booty from their conquests. With the collapse of the Roman Empire in western Europe, there was a disintegration of society. Local lords gathered fighting-age men to protect them and extend their holdings. To reward them, the barons deeded land grants to young knights like de Bouillon with hereditary rights that ushered in the era of the medieval knight.

Godfrey de Bouillon was born in 1058 in France and, as a Templar knight, led the First Crusade to establish Christian control of Jerusalem.

**Training:** In Godfrey's day, only boys born of noble birth could become knights. Training began at age seven, when Godfrey was sent to live in the castle of a local lord. As a knight-in-training, he spent years as a page, running errands for the household, learning good manners, becoming a devout Christian, studying, performing the arts, and learning to ride a horse and use a sword. At age 13, Godfrey became a squire, or apprentice, to a knight who taught him swordsmanship and how to use a lance and a shield in combat. He engaged in mock battles with other squires or against dummies; his effectiveness depended on his ability to stay on his horse during a fight. As Godfrey grew older, his duty was to follow his knight into battle and protect him if he fell or was wounded. Godfrey was knighted by his lord in an elaborate ceremony when he returned home in his early 20s. Chivalry, courage, and honor are at the heart of Godfrey's creed. The code of chivalry called on every knight to uphold the honor of women and protect the weak.

**Weapons:** Godfrey wielded a long lance while making a horseback charge on an opponent; his other weapons included various daggers and a double-edged slashing sword. Colorful designs on his armor identified him on the battlefield so his fellow knights didn't attack.

**Combat Style:** Everything depends on Godfrey's ability while in full armor to charge his opponent on horseback and deliver a knockout blow with his lance.

**The Fight Stuff:** One of the most famous knights in history, Godfrey de Bouillon was the Duke of Lower Lorraine and fought for King Henry IV against Pope Gregory VII but later left for the holy land in 1096 with other French knights and thousands of foot soldiers in response to Pope Urban II's call for the First Crusade. Godfrey reached Constantinople, got the support of Byzantine emperor Alexius I Comnenus, and in 1099 set siege to Jerusalem. The knights breached the walls of the city, captured it, then massacred its Jewish and Muslim inhabitants. Godfrey was chosen by the crusaders to rule the holy city, but he took ill from the plague and died in Jerusalem in July 1100.

**Fight Club Advantage:** The speed and power of Sir Godfrey in full charge on his horse, fully armored, could overwhelm any adversary.

## AND THE WINNER IS...?

Here's our decision: Flamma the gladiator and King Leonidas the Spartan are better trained in hand-to-hand combat, but they lack the full armor of the knight and the samurai, so they would suffer more wounds. sir Godfrey de Bouillon and Miyamoto Musahi the samurai use horses and are well-armored, but Miyamoto one-ups Godfrey because he's just as well trained as a foot warrior. Enter Sasuke Sarutobi the ninja. He attacks the knight without warning and takes him completely by surprise. But the samurai, of course, knows all too well about the ninja and is waiting and ready for his attack. So Uncle John's winner is the samurai, Miyamoto Musahi.

# FINE AND DANDY!

*Most people think that "dandy" describes a buffoonish man in elaborate
and outrageous clothing. Though style of dress is certainly a part of it,
Dandyism is an entire lifestyle—an attitude and a way of viewing the world.*

## STRIKE A POSE

Dandyism as a movement, first appeared toward the end of
the 18th century and lasted well into the 19th. The late
1700s marked a time of political and social upheaval. In Europe,
the French Revolution was at the forefront of change, with a growing egalitarian movement. Dandyism is thought to have arisen as a
reaction to the blurring of the lines between social classes—an attempt to return to an earlier time when the upper classes, and especially gentlemen of leisure, held sway.

Not only did the dandy invest huge amounts of time and money
in his appearance, but he must also be a man of wit, charm, and elegance. Preferably, he should not have anything so common as a job.
If he must stoop to earn a living, he should do it in the rarified
fields of art or literature. The most desired pose is one of boredom
and world weariness. And so, without further ado, here's our list of
history's most notable dandies.

## 1. BEAU BRUMMELL (1778–1840)

It is generally accepted that George Bryan Brummell was the first
dandy, and that he set the bar for others to follow. As modesty was
not part of a dandy's character, he enjoyed being called Beau.

Although the London-born Brummell was of humble birth,
from an early age he hobnobbed with aristocrats. His grandfather
was a shopkeeper who supplemented his income by renting rooms
to upper-class gentlemen. His father was private secretary to a
lord. Upon his father's death, Brummell inherited a substantial
sum of money, which should have kept him solvent for life.

**Trail Blazer.** As a young man, he forged his own distinctive style
of dress, which was at odds with prevailing fashions of the time.
Brummel bathed regularly, which was not the norm. As a result,

he didn't stink, so had no need for perfume or powder. He wore his hair cut short in the classical Roman style and refused to wear a wig. When the British government imposed a tax on hair powder in 1795 to finance the war in France, Brummell's hairstyle began to make a lot of sense.

Brummell's style was one of understated yet meticulous elegance. He wore a simple dark blue coat with brass buttons (a forerunner of today's classic blue blazer), a simple tailored shirt, and an intricately knotted tie of muslin, never silk. He was one of the first men to abandon knee britches in favor of long pants called pantaloons. Because everything had to fit perfectly, his tailoring bills were astronomical, as were his liquor bills; he was known for polishing his boots with champagne.

**Not in the Pink.** Brummell spent hours each day at his toilette. Once dressed, he had nothing to do for the rest of the day but hang around with the nobility, make witty remarks, and gamble huge sums of money. He became friends with the Prince of Wales, or Prince Regent—the future King George IV of England. Prinny, as some people called him, was something of a fashion victim before he met Brummell. For his first public speech at the House of Lords, the prince wore pink high heels that matched the pink satin lining of his black velvet outfit with gold and pink embroidery.

Eventually, things began to go downhill for Brummell. Mounting debts consumed his inheritance. Then he lost favor with Prince George. When the prince snubbed him at a party, Brummell famously turned to the prince's companion and loudly asked, "Who is your fat friend?" Unsurprisingly, Brummell's popularity plummeted. With creditors nipping at his heels, Brummell fled to France. He let his appearance and personal hygiene deteriorat and, sadly, died in a French insane asylum for paupers.

## 2. LORD BYRON (1778–1824)

Brummell's biggest fan was the English poet Lord Byron, who once said, "'There are three great men of our age: myself, Napoléon, and Brummell. But of we three, the greatest of all is Brummell."

George Gordon Byron became the sixth Baron of Byron when his great-uncle—"Wicked Lord Byron"—died and left him the title and estate. George was 10 years old. Byron's beginnings were unpromising. His father married George's mother for her money, which he quickly squandered before his death when George was three years old. George was born with a club foot, which caused him continual pain and embarrassment. His mother was mentally unbalanced and their relationship was strained.

**Poet and Philanderer.** Like a true dandy, Byron had a rebellious streak a mile wide. He kept a pet bear at Cambridge in protest of the school's rule forbidding pet dogs. After college he traveled and wrote prolifically. His most acclaimed works include *Don Juan* and *Childe Harold's Pilgrimage*. His works include what has come to be known as the Byronic hero--a passionate, idealistic, and talented but flawed and self-destructive individual. Save for his malformed foot, he was considered extraordinarily handsome. His individualism carried over to his style of clothes. He was the first to wear shirts with ruffled necks and cuffs, which became known as the "poet shirt." When he had his portrait painted in 1813, Byron inexplicably chose to pose in full Albanian military costume.

In his day, Byron was sometimes better known for his sexual exploits than for his poetry, which often met with critical derision. His many lovers of both sexes were scattered throughout society. He had a muc-publicized affair with married lady Carolyn lamb, who famously described him as "mad, bad, and dangerous to know." He was rumored to have indulged in an incestuous relationship with his half-sister, Augusta Leigh. Public outcry over his outlandish amatory behavior, along with his massive debts, forced him to flee England. He left in 1816, never to return. He died of an infection while fighting for independence in Greece in 1824.

### 3. CHARLES BAUDELAIRE (1821–67)

The French poet and social critic Charles Baudelaire seems to have spent more time examining dandyism and its implications than anyone else. Many of his essays sought to define just what dandyism was. It was "a cult of self," he wrote, "a new kind of aristocracy."

> "Dandies have no profession other than elegance...no other status but that of cultivating the idea of beauty in their own persons...The dandy must aspire to be sublime without inter ruption; he must live and sleep before a mirror."

---

The tallest standing *moai* (monolithic statue) at Easter Island was called Paru...

Baudelaire's approach involved dressing entirely in black. "The perfection of [the dandy's] toilet [dress] will consist in absolute simplicity," he said.

Baudelaire is famous primarily for his single volume of poems, *Les fleurs du mal* (*The Flowers of Evil*). The images he evoked were so dark and filled with lust that he was convicted of blasphemy and obscenity. The French Ministry of the Interior called it an "outrage to public decency" and banned the book. Only after he deleted some of the more offensive poems was he allowed to publish the book.

Dandyism, Baudelaire believed, was "the last spark of heroism amid decadence." His own life was undeniably decadent. Baudelaire lived on an inheritance and racked up gigantic debts. He enjoyed partaking of hashish and opium, and had many mistresses. He was penniless when he died of syphilis in his mother's arms.

## 4. OSCAR WILDE (1854–1900)

Oscar Wilde is one of the most frequently quoted figures in the English language. Chances are you have heard, or even quoted, some of his more memorable pithy sayings and aphorisms without knowing who coined them. It was Wilde who said:

• "There is only one thing in the world worse than being talked about, and that is not being talked about."

• "I can resist everything except temptation."

• "Moderation is a fatal thing...nothing succeeds like excess."

• "Some cause happiness wherever they go; others whenever they go."

• "[He is] a man who knows the price of everything and the value of nothing."

Oscar Wilde was born in Ireland to two accomplished and literary parents—his mother was a poet and feminist, and his father was a specialist in diseases of the eyes and ears, as well as a writer. Oscar was their second son, and it has been suggested that his mother, disappointed that he wasn't the daughter she had hoped for, dressed him in girl's clothing. (Wilde did eventually have a younger sister, but she died of meningitis at the age of eight. He carried a lock of her hair for the rest of his life.)

---

...It stood 33 feet high and weighed 75 tons (about 165,000 pounds).

Wilde is known for just one novel, *The Portrait of Dorian Gray*, the story of a beautiful young man who sells his soul in return for eternal youth and good looks. Released to mixed critical reviews, the book created a stir for some of its homoerotic implications. However, Wilde achieved his greatest success as a playwright. His satirical comedies, most notably *The Importance of Being Earnest*, are still performed today.

**Coming Undone.** A true dandy, the young Wilde seemed to want to turn the fashion clock back to pre-Brummell times. He wore knee britches—long out of style—with long silk stockings and patent leather pumps with moiré bows. His hair was long and flowing. He also wore a green carnation in his lapel, which later generations of gay culture adopted as a symbol.

Wilde seems to have been heterosexual for much of his early life. He married Constance Lloyd in 1884, and they had two sons: Cyril in 1885; Vyvyan in 1886. The marriage ended in 1893. Two years before his marriage ended, Wilde had fallen in love with Lord Alfred Douglas, nicknamed "Bosie"—who is widely described as the love of his life, as well as his downfall. Bosie's father, the Marquis of Queensberry, publicly accused Wilde of homosexuality, and Wilde countersued for libel. He lost both cases and was arrested and convicted of "gross indecency," as homosexuality was illegal in England at the time. Wilde spent two years in prison, which inspired one of his most famous poems, "The Ballad of Reading Gaol."

Upon his release, Wilde fled to France, where many of his fellow dandies also gathered. He died penniless—a common dandy fate—in a Paris hotel. His final words are reputed to have been "Either that wallpaper goes, or I do."

\*   \*   \*

"Pleasures a sin, and sometimes sin's a pleasure.
—Lord Byron, *Don Juan*

# DISASTERPIECE THEATER

*These natural disasters did more than just leave behind huge death tolls.*
*They also had historic consequences that changed the world.*

## 1. BHOLA CYCLONE AND CIVIL WAR

**Disaster:** In 1970, Pakistan was divided into two regions, East and West Pakistan. East Pakistan (now Bangladesh) lay along the Bay of Bengal and had islands and peninsulas that were barely 20 feet above sea level. East Pakistan was densely populated and desperately poor—people there faced shortages of electricity, clean running water, sturdy homes, good roads, and hospitals.

Just before midnight on November 12, 1970, the Bhola Cyclone blew into the region. Its winds of up to 100 mph combined with high tides to whip up a tidal surge and a wave more than 20 feet high. The onrushing water caught East and West Pakistan by surprise, and thousands of people suddenly awakened to a roar of water. Many were instantly swept into the flood. Crops, livestock, fishing boats, bridges, telephone lines, and roads in the area—nearly all were destroyed or swept away. In the weeks that followed, the flood took more lives through starvation, typhus, and cholera. The death and damage was so severe that exact records of mortality were impossible. The number of estimated deaths varied from 200,000 to one million. However, all estimates agreed that it was the deadliest cyclone on record.

**Consequences:** East Pakistanis already held resentments against their government when the cyclone hit. That region had the highest population and paid the most taxes, but the central government operated primarily out of West Pakistan. Easterners felt short-changed on services and resented their lack of power. Pakistan's government was blamed both for failing to alert people to the dangers of the coming storm and for a slow and inefficient reaction that compounded the misery and death toll. The growing anger against the government triggered East Pakistan's secession from Pakistan, the subsequent Bangladesh Liberation War, and finally the establishment of East Pakistan as the independent nation of Bangladesh.

---

Jimmy Hoffa's middle name was Riddle.

## 2. THE GREAT HURRICANE AND AMERICAN INDEPENDENCE

**Disaster:** From October 10 to October 16, 1780, the storm known as the "Great Hurricane" pounded the West Indies, including the islands of Barbados, Martinique, Saint Eustatius, Saint Lucia, Martinique, Puerto Rico, and what is now the Dominican Republic. By the time it blew through the Caribbean, more than 22,000 people had been killed in the deadliest Atlantic hurricane in recorded history.

On October 10th, the hurricane first struck Barbados with winds estimated at 200 mph, upending nearly all the houses, even those made of stone. British forts were demolished and not a tree remained standing. As the hurricane rampaged on—leaving thousands dead on St. Eustatius and Martinique—it also struck ships offshore. The British fleet in harbor at St. Lucia lost eight of its twelve ships and hundreds of sailors. (One British warship was dumped down on top of a hospital.) a French fleet of 40 ships sank near Martinique.

**Change:** In 1780, the Revolutionary War was still dragging on, and though America's allies (the French) had heavy losses, the British were in a tighter spot. England's war plans relied heavily on its mighty navy, which had suffered a heavy blow, and the country had only a small land army. Historians believe that ship losses in the Great Hurricane helped lead to Britain's naval defeat at the Battle of the Chesapeake—a defeat that finally allowed George Washington to force the British Army's surrender.

The Great Hurricane's costly damage to British colonies like Barbados also bolstered the power of London's pro-peace faction, which had long been in favor of quitting the protracted and expensive Revolutionary War. They helped to persuade Parliament to concentrate on Britain's more profitable colonial ventures and just grant those pesky Americans their independence.

## 3. PORT ROYAL'S EARTHQUAKE PUNISHES THE PIRATES

**Disaster:** In 1692, Port Royal was the unofficial capital of Jamaica and one of the richest cities in the New World. Located in the center of the Caribbean, the bustling port was home to great merchant fleets, but also had a darker side as the center for the slave trade and stolen goods, and as a haven for pirates like Henry Morgan and Jack Rackham. Hanging out in "grog shops," brothels, and gambling dens, the pirates of the Caribbean helped give Port Royal her nickname, "the wickedest city in the world."

On June 7, 1692, a little before noon, an earthquake hit that was measured approximately 7.5 on today's Richter scale. Port Royal was built on a base of sand, and as the shaking began, the sand liquefied. Within minutes, 33 acres of the 50-acre city simply sank into the ocean. Wharves and brick buildings disappeared. People were pulled into newly formed fissures that seized up again and crushed them. Offshore, ships capsized and a huge wave carried one British frigate, *The Swan*, over the tops of buildings to rest in the middle of town. In the first shock of the quake, 1,500 to 2,000 people were killed—the next day, 3,000 more died from their injuries.

**Consequences:** The 17th century was a time when scientists were arguing that the world worked on natural laws rather than under the direction of a supreme being. As news of the Port Royal disaster spread, many people believed that a higher authority had aimed a direct punishment at the pirates in "sin city." And when word got out that survivors in Port Royal were busy looting buildings and robbing the dead during the aftershocks, some observers thought that the punishment hadn't gone far enough.

As a result, the once bustling city of Port Royal became a small scattering of houses—practically a ghost town. All attempts to rebuild it to its former glory failed. Commerce and wealth moved across the harbor to Kingston, which became Jamaica's capital. And without their haven, the heyday of the Caribbean pirates came to an end.

## 4. THERA'S ERUPTION DESTROYS CIVILIZATION

**Disaster:** The islands of Crete and Thera were once home to the Minoans, one of the world's first great civilizations. During the Bronze Age, the Minoans were the first Europeans to have paved roads, running water, and even flush toilets. These wealthy, seafaring people had a peaceful, artistic culture that was the envy of the ancient world.

---

First person known to encode communications: Julius Caesar.

In 1450 BC, the Thera volcano exploded. What once had been a mountain collapsed into the Aegean Sea. The explosion sent pillars of fire, smoke, ash, and poisonous sulfur clouds into the stratosphere—rocks from the explosion were found as far away as Israel and the Black Sea. The worst volcanic disaster in the ancient world left a 92-mile area covered with pumice stone and hot ash. It also produced shock waves that triggered a tsunami with waves a hundred feet high.

As Minoan cities on Thera and on parts of Crete were buried in the volcanic debris, a tsunami destroyed the Minoans coastal cities and their great fleet of ships. Sulfuric gases from the volcano caused a cooling in the atmosphere known as a "volcanic winter," which brought abnormally cold summers and deluges of rainfall that lasted several years. Crops failed. And with their great navy was gone, the Mionan people suffered from famine and chaos.

**Consequences:** Some Minoans left Crete for Greece, where they helped create Greece's golden age. The Minoans who remained on the battered island were easy prey for conquerors, and within a generation, the Minoan Civilization disappeared. Although maybe they still exist in legend—some historians believe that Plato's famous tale of Atlantis, a glorious civilization that sank into the ocean, is actually about the Minoan Empire.

\*　　\*　　\*

"In Italy for thirty years under the Borgias, they had warfare, terror, murder, and bloodshed, but they produced Michelangelo, Leonardo da Vinci, and the Renaissance. In Switzerland, they had brotherly love, they have five hundred years of democracy and peace—and what did they produce? The cuckoo clock."
**—From the movie, *The Third Man*, 1949**

# PARTING REMARKS

*Here's what some pundits have to say about history.*

"Historical reminder: always put Horace before Descartes."
—**Donald O. Rickter**

"History is the short trudge from Adam to atom."
—**Leonard L. Levinson**

"Very few things happen at the right time and the rest do not happen at all. The conscientious historian will correct these defects."
—**Herodotus**

"History will be kind to me for I intend to write it."
—**Winston Churchill**

"Without question, the greatest invention in the history of mankind is beer. Oh, I grant you that the wheel was also a fine invention, but the wheel does not go nearly as well with pizza."
—**Dave Barry**

"I think a secure profession for young people is history teacher because in the future, there will be so much more of it to teach"
—**Bill Muse**

"That men do not learn very much from the lessons of history is the most important of all the lessons that history has to teach"
—**Aldous Huxley**

"The only thing new in this world is the history that you don't know."
—**Harry S Truman**

"History, although sometimes made up of the few acts of the great, is more often shaped by the many acts of the small."
—**Mark Yost**

---

**...he was a talent agent who worked with acts like Simon & Garfunkel and the Supremes.**

# INDEX

# MORE BATHROOM READER TITLES FOR HISTORY LOVERS!

Find these and other great *Uncle John's Bathroom Reader* titles online at **www.bathroomreader.com**. Or contact us:

Bathroom Readers' Institute
P.O. Box 1117
Ashland, OR 97520

# THE LAST PAGE

**F**ELLOW BATHROOM READERS:
The fight for good bathroom reading should never be taken loosely—we must do our duty and sit firmly for what we believe in, even while the rest of the world is taking potshots at us.

We'll be brief. Now that we've proven we're not simply a flush-in-the-pan, we invite you to take the plunge: Sit Down and Be Counted! Log on to *www.bathroomreader.com* and earn a permanent spot on the BRI honor roll!

---

If you like reading our books...
VISIT THE BRI'S WEB SITE!
*www.bathroomreader.com*

• Visit "The Throne Room"—a great place to read!
• Receive our irregular newsletters via e-mail.
• Order additional *Bathroom Readers*.
• Read our blog.

*Go with the Flow...*

---

Well, we're out of space, and when you've gotta go, you've gotta go. Tanks for all your support. Hope to hear from you soon. Meanwhile remember...

*Keep on flushin'!*